United Kingdom Balance of Payments

The Pink Book 2003

Editor:

Simon Linden

London: TSO

© Crown copyright 2003

Published with the permission of the Controller of Her Majesty's Stationery Office (HMSO).

ISBN 0 11 621646 8

ISSN 0950-7558

Applications for reproduction should be submitted to HMSO under HMSO's Class Licence:

www.clickanduse.hmso.gov.uk

Alternatively applications can be made in writing to
HMSO
Licensing Division
St. Clement's House
2–16 Colegate
Norwich
NR3 1BQ

Contact points

For enquiries about this publication, contact the Editor, Simon Linden

Tel: 020 7533 6078

E-mail: simon.linden@ons.gov.uk

To order this publication, call The Stationery Office on 0870 600 5522. See also back cover.

For general enquiries, contact the National Statistics Customer Contact Centre on 0845 601 3034

(minicom: 01633 812399)

E-mail: info@statistics.gov.uk

Fax: 01633 652747

Letters: Room D115, Government Buildings, Cardiff Road, Newport NP10 8XG

You can also find National Statistics on the Internet – go to www.statistics.gov.uk

A National Statistics publication

Official statistics bearing the National Statistics logo are produced to high professional standards set out in the National Statistics Code of Practice. They undergo regular quality assurance reviews to ensure that they meet customer needs. They are produced free from any political interference.

About the Office for National Statistics

The Office for National Statistics (ONS) is the government agency responsible for compiling, analysing and disseminating many of the United Kingdom's economic, social and demographic statistics, including the retail prices index, trade figures and labour market data, as well as the periodic census of the population and health statistics. The Director of ONS is also the National Statistician and the Registrar General for England and Wales, and the agency administers the statutory registration of births, marriages and deaths there.

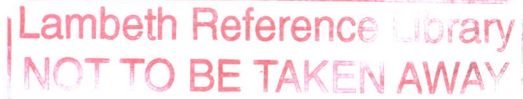

Contents

		Page
Introduction		1

Part 1: Current account

1	Summary of balance of payments	16
2	Trade in goods	26
3	Trade in services	36
4	Income	52
5	Current transfers	68

Part 2: Capital account, financial account & international investment position

6	Capital account	74
7	Financial account	76
8	International investment position	94

Part 3: Geographical breakdown

9	Geographical breakdown of current account	114

Supplementary information

Balance of payments and the relationship to national accounts	149
Methodological notes	152
Glossary of terms	183
Index	191

List of Contributors

Authors: Stuart Brown

Simon Humphries

Sharon Nevill

David Ruffles

Production Team: Shain Bali

Tristan Broderick

Tony Castro

Julian Collins

Alistair Dent

Deborah Kennion

John Lowes

Preface

The annual National Statistics *Pink Book* contains estimates of the balance of payments of the United Kingdom. The presentation of the accounts is based on the *IMF Balance of Payments Manual 5th edition (BPM5)*.

Pink Book data in computer-readable form

Free access to National Statistics data is available online at www.statistics.gov.uk

Access around 40,000 time series, of primarily macro-economic data, drawn from the main tables in a range of our major economic and labour market publications. Download complete releases, or view and download your own customised selection of individual time series.

Also access cross sectional data and metadata from across the Government Statistical Service (GSS), organised by theme and subject. Download many datasets, in whole or in part, or consult catalogue information for all GSS statistical resources, including censuses, surveys, periodicals and enquiry services. Information is posted as PDF electronic documents, or in XLS and CSV formats, compatible with most spreadsheet packages

Complete copies of this publication are available to download free of charge on the following web page: **www.statistics.gov.uk/products/p1140.asp**

Quarterly estimates

Quarterly estimates of the main components of the balance of payments for the last two years are published in a quarterly National Statistics First Release and in more detail in *UK Economic Accounts*.

Long run quarterly and annual estimates consistent with the *Pink Book* are published in the *Economic Trends* Annual Supplement. The latest estimates are also given in summary form in the *Monthly Digest of Statistics* and in *Financial Statistics*.

Comments and enquiries

The Office for National Statistics (ONS) is keen to receive comments on this publication and suggestions for improvements, which can be considered for future editions of the *Pink Book*. Comments can be sent in writing to:

Simon Linden
Pink Book Editor
Balance of Payments & Financial Sector Division
Office for National Statistics
Room D3/20
1 Drummond Gate
London SW1V 2QQ
Tel: **020 7533 6078,** Fax: 020 7533 6061
E-mail: **simon.linden@ons.gov.uk**

Enquiries regarding balance of payments estimates should be directed to the following:

Trade in goods:
David Ruffles 020 7533 6070
(david.ruffles@ons.gov.uk)

Trade in services, current transfers and capital account:
Tom Orford 020 7533 6095
(tom.orford@ons.gov.uk)

Income, financial account and international investment position:
Simon Humphries 020 7533 6075
(simon.humphries@ons.gov.uk)

An introduction to the United Kingdom balance of payments

Introduction

The balance of payments is one of the UK's key economic statistical series. It measures the economic transactions between United Kingdom residents and the rest of the world. It also draws a series of balances between inward and outward transactions, provides an net flow of transactions between UK residents and the rest of the world and reports how that flow is funded. Economic transactions include:

(i) exports and imports of goods, such as oil, agricultural products, other raw materials, machinery and transport equipment, computers, white goods and clothing;

(ii) exports and imports of services such as international transport, travel, financial and business services;

(iii) income flows, such as dividends and interest earned by foreigners on investments in the UK and by the UK investing abroad;

(iv) financial flows, such as direct investment, investment in shares, debt securities, loans and deposits; and

(v) transfers, which are offsetting entries to any one-sided transactions listed above, such as foreign aid and funds brought by migrants to the UK.

The international investment position measures the levels of financial investment with the rest of the world, inward and outward.

International statistical standards

The ONS follows the international standards relating to balance of payments and international investment position statistics. There are several reasons for this. First, domestic and foreign analysts will be assured that the UK's official balance of payments and international investment position statistics comply with objective, coherent international standards that reflect current, global analytic needs. Second, the UK is a member of the international community and international users need comparable data for comparison between countries. Third, the UK, as a member of the European Union, as well as organisations such as the IMF and OECD, needs to compile its various economic statistics in conformity with standards set by those organisations. Fourth, the UK can compare and reconcile its data with those of other countries. Statistics need to be as comparable as possible in order to carry out this validation.

To facilitate such consistency and to provide guidelines for its members, the IMF issued the *Balance of Payments Manual*. The first edition appeared in 1948 and the most recent (fifth) edition in 1993. The conceptual framework of the UK balance of payments corresponds to that underlying the fifth edition of the IMF Manual, referred to as *BPM5*. *BPM5* was implemented in the UK's balance of payments accounts and international investment position statistics in September 1998.

A process of reviewing the existing international standards started in the mid 1980s with the specific objective of harmonising, to the maximum extent possible, the statistical concepts, definitions, statistical units, classifications and terminology. Release of the revised standards started in 1993 with *BPM5* and the third edition of the *System of National Accounts (SNA93)*. *BPM5* was prepared by the IMF in close co-operation with national compilers and with the Statistical Office of the European Communities, the OECD, the United Nations and the World Bank. Those five organisations jointly published *SNA93*. In 1995 the EU produced its own version of *SNA93*, the *European System of Accounts (ESA95)* upon which the UK's national accounts are based and which is consistent with *BPM5*. Both *SNA93* and *BPM5* were amended in 2000 to give more consistent guidance on the treatment of financial derivatives.

Conceptual framework definitions

Balance of payments

Broadly speaking, the UK balance of payments is a statistical statement designed to provide a systematic record of the UK's economic transactions with the rest of the world. It may be described as a system of consolidated accounts in which the accounting entity is the UK economy and the entries refer to economic transactions between residents of the UK and residents of the rest of the world (non-residents).

The balance of payments accounts are concerned not only with payments made but also any economic transactions during a period that give rise to a payment in an earlier or later period, e.g. goods may change ownership in one period, though payment may be made in an earlier period (pre-payment) or in a later period (trade credit). They also include transactions for which there may never be a payment, e.g. goods shipped under foreign aid or goods shipped between related enterprises. There is also more than one 'balance': the balance of payments is a system of accounts in which many balances can be derived, such as the balance of goods and services, the balance on current account, and the balance on capital and financial account.

Balance of payments statements cover a wide range of economic transactions which include:

(i) goods, services, income and current transfers; and

(ii) capital transactions, such as capital transfers; and

(iii) financial transactions involving the UK claims on, and liabilities to, non-residents.

Category (i) is shown in the current account, category (ii) in the capital account and category (iii) in the financial account.

International investment position

The UK's international investment position is a closely related set of statistics. It can be viewed as the balance sheet recording the UK's stock (or level) of foreign financial assets and liabilities at a particular date. The net international investment position is the difference between the stock of foreign financial assets and foreign liabilities at a particular date.

Viewed more broadly, the international investment position can be shown as a reconciliation statement of the stock of investment at two different points in time by showing financial transactions and other changes (non-transaction changes) such as price changes, exchange rate variations and other adjustments that occurred during the period. Financial transactions which are included in the reconciliation statement are equivalent to the transactions measured in the financial account of the balance of payments. The ONS does not currently compile a full reconciliation of the international investment position showing price, exchange rate and other changes.

Classifications such as assets and liabilities, type of investment (direct, portfolio and other investment and reserve assets), and instrument of investment, are used consistently in both the balance of payments and the international investment position.

Concepts of territory and residence

In compiling the UK balance of payments and international investment position, the UK economy is conceived as comprising the economic entities that have a closer association with the territory of the UK than with any other territory. Each such economic entity is described as a resident of the UK. Any economic entity which is not regarded as a resident of the UK is described as a non-resident. The concept of residency is not based on nationality.

The UK's economic territory is defined to include the territories lying within its political frontiers and territorial seas, and in the international waters over which it has exclusive jurisdiction. It also includes its territorial enclaves abroad holding embassies, consulates, military bases, scientific stations, information or immigration offices, aid agencies etc., whether owned or rented by the UK governments with the formal agreement of the countries where they are located.

The UK offshore islands – Jersey, Guernsey and Isle of Man – are classified as non-resident to the UK. Thus transactions between UK residents and the islands are in the balance of payments, but transactions between islanders are not counted in the UK balance of payments. The islands are not part of the EU, so statistics relating to them are not required under *ESA95* and they have to be excluded from the UK's economic territory to ensure full UK consistency with *ESA95*. This treatment is also technically consistent with *BPM5* recommendations which states that 'In a maritime country, economic territory includes islands that belong to the country and are subject to the same fiscal and monetary authorities as the mainland; goods and persons move freely to and from the mainland and islands...'. The offshore islands are subject to their own fiscal authorities and have their own tax systems. Furthermore, there are impediments to taking up residency on the Channel Islands.

Prior to the adoption of *BPM5* and *ESA95*, the UK offshore islands were treated as part of the UK and the Islands' transactions with the rest of the world were included in the balance of payments. Adoption of *BPM5* and *ESA95* meant that UK transactions with the Islands became part of the balance of payments and the Islands' transactions with the rest of the world had to be excluded. To comply with this change in definition, adjustments were made to the data to include UK transactions with the islands and to exclude the islands' transactions with the rest of the world. These adjustments mostly notably affected the investment account as the Islands are a major financial centre.

For balance of payments purposes, residents of an economy are generally deemed to have a centre of economic interest in the economy and to be resident for at least one year. The residents of the UK comprise:

(i) Resident general government institutions including the Scottish Parliament, Welsh Assembly, Northern Ireland Assembly and local government authorities and statutory bodies. The UK embassies, consulates, military establishments, etc. physically located abroad are included in the UK's economic territory and are therefore residents; similar entities of other countries physically located within the UK are outside the UK's economic territory and are therefore non-residents.

(ii) Resident financial and trading enterprises which include all enterprises engaged in the production of goods and services on a commercial or equivalent basis within the territory of the UK. Enterprises may be incorporated or unincorporated; privately or government owned and/or controlled; and locally or foreign owned and/or controlled. The definition of an enterprise in terms of the territory in which it is located often makes it necessary to divide a single legal entity into a head office operating in one economy and a branch operating in another economy. Resident enterprises include UK branches of foreign companies and exclude foreign branches of UK companies.

(iii) Resident non-profit bodies are those in which individuals and/or enterprises combine, as owners, to produce goods and services within the territory of the UK for purposes other than to provide a financial return for themselves. Examples are churches, charitable organisations and representative business organisations such as Chambers of Commerce.

(iv) Resident households and individuals which broadly encompass all persons residing in the territory of the UK for one year or more, whose general centre of economic interest is considered to be the UK. The UK's official diplomatic and consular representatives, the UK's armed forces, other UK government personnel stationed abroad and their dependants, and UK students studying abroad are also included even though they may all be abroad for one year or more. They are treated as UK residents since their centre of interest is considered to be the UK. Generally, the centre of economic interest of persons visiting the UK for less than one year is considered to be outside the UK and they are therefore regarded as non-residents, but if they stay for one year or more they are considered to be residents for balance of payments purposes. Irrespective of their length of stay, non-residents also include foreign diplomatic, consular, military and other government personnel, their dependants, and foreign students studying in the UK.

Double-entry system

Rules for the UK double entry system

Credit entries, changes in all economic resources resources provided by the UK to non-residents, including:	**Debit entries,** changes in all economic received by the UK from non-residents, including:
Exports of goods and services	Imports of goods and services
Income accruing on the resources to UK from residents	Income accruing on the resources to non-residents from UK
Financial liabilities of the UK to non-residents	Financial claims of UK on non-residents
Transfers which are offsets to debit entries	Transfers which are offsets to credit entries

---

Examples of UK double entry recording — Credits / Debits

1. Sales of goods (value 100) to non-residents for foreign exchange (i.e. goods provided and bank payment (a bank deposit) received in an account held abroad)
   - Goods — 100
   - Bank deposits, foreign currency assets — 100

2. Purchase of goods (value 120) from a non-resident using trade Credit (i.e. goods received and a claim on a resident (trade credit liability) provided)
   - Goods — 120
   - Trade credit liabilities — 120

3. Food aid (value 5) provided to non-residents (i.e. goods provided and transfer imputed)
   - Goods — 5
   - Current transfers — 5

4. payment of a loan (value 25) by a resident company to a non-resident lender (i.e. liability to a non-resident reduced and a reduction in bank deposits held abroad)
   - Loan repayment — -25
   - Bank deposits, foreign currency, assets — -25

Conceptually, an economic transaction has two sides: something of economic value is provided and something of equal value is received. The balance of payments reflect this in a double-entry recording system of credits and debits. When an economic value is provided (e.g. UK exports a car) a credit entry is made, and when the corresponding economic value is received (e.g. a payment for the car) a debit entry is made. For example, when an exporter sells (provides) goods to a non-resident, the exporter may receive cash (a financial asset) or another type of financial asset (e.g. a trade credit claim) in return. The export is represented by a credit entry and the financial asset acquired is represented by an offset debit entry. Similar entries are made when an importer buys a car (debit) and pays for it (credit). So a credit entry represents a change in rest of world ownership of any sort of UK asset (real or financial); a debit entry represents a change in UK ownership of rest of world assets.

An understanding of the double-entry recording system is necessary for a complete understanding of balance of payments statistics.

Under the double-entry system, by definition credit entries must equal debit entries. Credit entries are required for exports of goods and services, income receivable, and changes in financial liabilities. Likewise, debit entries are required for imports of goods and services, income payable, and changes in financial assets. Where something of economic value is provided without something of economic value in exchange (i.e. without a *quid pro quo*) the double-entry system requires an offset to be imputed (a transfer entry) of equivalent value. For example, food exported as aid requires a credit entry for the goods provided and a debit transfer as the aid offset.

Sign convention in the UK balance of payments statistics

The sign convention used in presenting the UK balance of payments statistics is to give a positive sign to an increase in either credit or debit entries and a negative sign to a decrease in credit or debit entries. Balances (calculated as credits less debits) or items which are net credits have no sign, while balances which are net debits have a negative sign.

When considering making international comparisons it should be borne in mind that there is no unique or correct sign convention and other countries/institutions use variations. In particular the convention used by the IMF in their publications gives no sign to credit entries and a minus sign to all debit entries (e.g. imports and acquisitions of assets).

Errors and omissions

It follows that, in principle, under a double-entry accounting system, the difference between the sum of credit and debit entries must be zero. In practice, some transactions are not measured accurately (i.e. errors) and some are not measured at all (i.e. omissions). Data sources used to compile the accounts often measure the credit and debit sides from different data sources and may not always do so consistently. There could be many reasons why these sources may not measure the acquisition side of the transaction and the corresponding payments, either in the same accounting period or at the same value. To restore the equality of credit and debit entries, a net errors and omissions item is included in the balance of payments accounts. The item indicates whether credit or debit transactions would be needed to balance the accounts, but does not show where the discrepancy lies. Usually the financial account is considered to be the most likely source.

Valuation

It is important that the balance of payments and international investment position statistics carry values that have economic meaning to enable useful analysis, and to provide meaningful indicators of cross-border economic activity. It is also important for the double-entry accounting system that a uniform valuation is adopted. This means that the credit and debit entries of each transaction – which in practice may be derived from independent sources – should be valued at the same price. In addition, a uniform valuation is essential to sum different types of transactions on a consistent and comparable basis. The use of a uniform valuation principle aids understanding by users. Moreover, statistics for different countries will not be comparable unless both parties to a transaction adopt the same valuation principle. It is also important to use a principle which is consistent with national accounting principles. For all these reasons, market price is used in UK economic statistics for valuing transactions.

Market price is the amount of money that a willing buyer pays to acquire something from a willing seller, when such an exchange is between independent parties and involves only commercial considerations. In practice, one or more of the conditions needed to establish a market price may be absent and other valuations may be used.

For the most part, the price at which a transaction is recorded in the accounts of the transactors or in the administrative records used as data sources will be the market price or a very close approximation of it. This valuation is known as the transactions price and is the practical valuation basis used in the balance of payments, both because it aids consistent recording of credits and debits and because of its usual proximity to the ideal market valuation. The following paragraph discusses a special case of transactions where market prices may not apply, namely transfer pricing between affiliated enterprises in different countries.

Transfer pricing

Where transactions are between affiliated enterprises in different countries, the prices adopted in their books for recording transactions in goods and services and any associated indebtedness and interest – referred to as transfer prices – may not correspond to prices that would be charged to independent parties. There will be some departure from the market price principle if transfer prices are different from those charged to enterprises outside the group. However there are practical difficulties in identifying and suitably adjusting individual cases. Transfer pricing to avoid tax is illegal in the UK so the distortions in the international accounts caused by transfer pricing are not considered widespread. For both reasons, adjustments to account for transfer pricing are rarely made in practice.

Assets and liabilities

As with all international investment position statistics, foreign financial assets and liabilities should, in principle, be valued at their current market price at the reference date. In practice this is not always possible and valuation guidelines are adopted in order to approximate market valuation, particularly for those financial assets and liabilities that are only rarely transacted. For example, in measuring the value of direct investment in equity capital, much of which is never traded or is traded infrequently, market value is approximated by one of the following methods: a recent transaction price; directors' value; or net asset value. Over time, this is likely to underestimate the true market value of Foreign Direct Investment.

Unit of account and conversion

Transactions and stock positions originally denominated in foreign currencies need to be converted to pounds sterling using market rates of exchange prevailing at the time of the transaction (balance of payments) or at the reference date (international investment position). Transactions should be converted at the mid-point of the buying and selling exchange rates applying at the time of transaction. Stocks should be converted at the mid-point of the buying and selling exchange rates applying at the beginning or end of the period. In practice, the actual rate used varies according to the source of the transaction or stock data.

Time of recording

Transactions

The time of recording of transactions in balance of payments and international investment position statistics is, in principle, the time of change of ownership (either actual or imputed). Under the double-entry system, both sides of a transaction should be recorded in the same period. This is consistent with the principle of accrual accounting, which requires that transactions be recorded when economic value is created, transformed, exchanged, transferred or extinguished.

Change of ownership is considered to occur when legal ownership of goods changes, when services are rendered and when income accrues. In the case of transfers, those which are imposed by one party on another, such as taxes and fines, should ideally be recorded at the moment at which the underlying transactions or other flows occur which give rise to the liability to pay; other transfers should be recorded when the goods, services etc. change ownership.

For financial transactions, the time of change of ownership is taken to be the time when transactions are entered in the books of the transactors. That is taken to be the time when a foreign financial asset or liability is acquired, relinquished by agreement, sold or repaid. The commitment or pledging of an asset does not constitute an economic transaction, and no entry should be shown unless a change of ownership actually occurs in the period covered. Likewise, the entries for loan drawings should be based on actual disbursements and not on commitments or authorisations. Entries for loan repayments should be recorded at the time they are due rather than on the actual payment date.

Both sides of a transaction should be recorded in the same period. In practice the time of recording of transactions in the balance of payments and international investment position statistics will reflect the practices in data sources, and may diverge from the principle of time of change of ownership. For the UK, transactions in goods credits (exported goods) are mainly recorded at the time when goods are shipped as this is assessed to be a generally good practical approximation of the time when ownership changes. Goods debits (imported goods) are recorded when customs records relating to the movement of the goods across the frontier are processed, again in the expectation that this is the best practical approximation to change of ownership that can be generally achieved. For the remainder of the current account, the time of the recording of transactions generally complies with the time of change of ownership. Exceptions occur mainly because the record-keeping practices of some data providers may not be on this basis. Financial account transactions usually are recorded appropriately, that is, when the parties record transactions in their books. However, some transactions may be derived from information supplied by intermediaries that are not party to the transactions and may not be aware of the time of change of ownership. Also, some enterprises may adopt accounting practices that lead to inconsistent time of recording; a simple example is that different enterprises may close off their accounts at different times of day.

Stock
The time of recognising the stock of a foreign financial asset or liability follows naturally from the time of recording of a transaction in that asset or liability. For example, if a transaction is undertaken to acquire a foreign financial asset, there will also be a consequential increase in the stock of foreign financial assets at the end of that period. Of course, if the asset is disposed of before the end of the period, it will not contribute to the stocks statistics to be recorded for the period, but the disposal will have given rise to another transaction to be recorded for the period.

Types of transactions in the balance of payments

An economic transaction occurs when something of economic value is provided by one party to another. Transactions that are considered to have economic value comprise those in goods, services, income and financial assets and liabilities. The transactions recorded in a balance of payments statement stem from dealings between two parties, one being a resident and the other a non-resident. The types of transactions included in the balance of payments are exchanges, one-sided transactions and imputed transactions.

Exchanges
Exchanges are the most important and numerous type of transaction. They include transactions in which one transactor provides something of economic value to another transactor and receives in return something of equal value.

Special cases of imputation/estimation

Migrants' transfers

A special statistical treatment is required when a person migrates, that is when the person's status changes from non-resident to resident (or vice versa). When this change occurs, the property owned by the migrant becomes the property of a resident instead of that of a non-resident (or vice versa). This change of ownership of net worth between economies is included in the balance of payments. For example, any financial assets held abroad by the migrant become claims by the UK on the rest of the world.

Offset entries are made corresponding to the transfer of net worth and, by their nature, these are included as transfers in the capital account. This treatment amounts to envisaging a transfer of property from the person in their capacity as a non-resident to the person in their capacity as a resident (or vice versa). In principle, this transaction embraces all the migrant's property, whether or not it accompanies the migrant.

Reinvested earnings

A number of special cases of imputed transactions feature in balance of payments compilation. One case involves the reinvestment of earnings in resident enterprises by their non-resident direct investors. These *reinvested earnings* are regarded as being paid out as investment income and then reinvested in the enterprises from which they originated. They are therefore recorded both as a component of investment income in the current account and as a component of direct investment in the financial account. It is considered analytically useful to identify these transactions separately in economic statistics because of the substantial contribution they make to the stock of direct investment finance in a country.

Financial services

A further case relates to estimation for the implicit fees (financial services) associated with foreign exchange trading. Estimates of the implicit service fees being earned on foreign exchange trading with non-resident counterparties are made by splitting the total service fees reported by exchange traders into resident/non-resident shares using a number of assumptions and other published information.

Exceptions to change of ownership
In economic statistics, transactions are considered to occur when the goods and financial assets change ownership between transactors, when services are provided by one transactor to another, or when income is earned by one transactor from

another. However, there are certain situations in which no change of ownership legally occurs, but where transactions are nonetheless considered to have occurred for balance of payments purposes. The situations include financial leases, goods imported into or exported from the UK for processing and return, and transactions between a head office in one country and a branch in another.

Financial leases

A financial lease is regarded as a method of obtaining all the rights, risks and rewards of ownership of real resources without holding legal ownership. Although legal ownership remains with the lessor during the term of the lease, all the risks and responsibilities apply to the lessee. In these cases, the basic nature of the transaction is given precedence over its legal form, by imputing a change of ownership of the resource to the lessee. As a result of this imputation, a financial liability is recognised and lease payments are classified as partly loan repayments in the financial account and partly interest in the current account, rather than as services in the current account.

Goods for processing

In economic statistics, the value of goods entering or leaving the UK for processing and returning to the country of origin after processing, should be recorded on a gross basis, i.e. recording the goods both when they enter (as imports) and when they leave (as exports), even though there is no legal change of ownership of those goods. Thus a good entering the UK to be processed and returned to the country of origin, is recorded as an import at the appropriate value and subsequently as an export – recorded by the customs system at the original value plus the added value of the processing. A symmetrical treatment should be applied to UK goods exported for processing and return. The basis for this treatment is that such goods lose their identity during processing by being transformed or incorporated into different goods. On the other hand, for goods undergoing repairs only the value of the repair, not the gross value of the goods, is included in the goods credits or debits.

Branches

In economic statistics, it is usually necessary to split the activities of a legal entity and recognise two units, a head office in one country and a branch in another. Flows of goods, services, income and finance between the branch and its head office are therefore treated as transactions, even though they are legally part of the same unit. For example, goods and services sent from the head office to its branch are to be treated as exports of goods and services by the head office.

There are two cases where such splitting becomes necessary. The first occurs when production of goods and services is undertaken by the personnel, plant and equipment of the legal entity in an economic territory outside the economic territory of the head office, provided certain conditions apply. These conditions include: the intention to operate in the separate economy indefinitely or over a long period (12 months is used as a rule of thumb); keeping a set of accounts of the branch's activity (i.e. income statement, balance sheet, transactions with the parent entity); eligibility to pay income tax in the host country; having a substantial physical presence; and receiving funds for the branch's work which are paid into its own bank account.

The second case occurs when a person or legal entity resident in one economy owns land and buildings located in another economy. Ownership of immovable assets is always attributed in balance of payments and international investment position statistics to residents of the economy in which the assets are located. Thus land in the domestic territory, which is in fact owned by a non-resident, is treated as being owned by a notional resident entity, which in turn has a foreign direct investment liability to the real owner. It should also be recalled that the territorial enclaves associated with embassies, military bases etc. are regarded as part of the economic territory of the economy they represent. When these institutions buy and sell the land in these enclaves they are effectively adding to and subtracting from the economic territory of their government. Such transactions in land owned by foreign embassies are recorded in the capital account as the acquisition/disposal of non-produced, non-financial assets.

Other changes in the international investment position

In addition to the financial transactions included in the balance of payments, the international investment position reconciliation statement includes the other changes which contribute to differences between opening and closing positions for a period.

Other changes in position may occur through price changes, exchange rate changes and other adjustments. Price changes are valuation changes that occur because of changes in the market price of a financial instrument, such as a change in the price of a share or debt security, or through revaluing a company's net worth.

Exchange rate changes are due to fluctuations in the value of the pound, in which the accounts are compiled, relative to the currencies in which foreign assets and liabilities are denominated.

Other adjustments can arise from a number of causes such as write-off of bad debts, classification changes, monetisation/ demonetisation of gold, and the allocation/ cancellation of Special Drawing Rights. A reclassification would occur where a foreign investor's equity investment in an enterprise increased during the reporting period and the increase was sufficient to change the classification of the investor's total equity holding at the end of the period from portfolio investment to direct investment. Monetisation of gold occurs when the Bank of England monetises commodity stocks of gold and adds these to its monetary gold holdings as part of the UK's official reserve assets. Special Drawing Rights in the IMF are also included in the UK's official reserve assets. Allocations and cancellations of these instruments are included as other adjustments.

Gross and net recording

Entries for current and capital account items are generally treated so that credits for each component are recorded separately from debits. Current and capital account transactions, in this context, are described as being recorded gross.

Gross recording contrasts to the recording of transactions in the financial account, which is mainly on a net basis, although for long-term trade credits and loans, gross drawings and repayments are included in the financial account. The net recording of other financial account items means that, for each item, credit transactions are combined with debit transactions to arrive at a single result – either a net credit or net debit – reflecting the net effect of all increases and decreases in holdings of that type of asset or liability during the recording period. There are several types of netting in the financial account, e.g. the netting of purchases and sales within an instrument in an asset position, and netting of assets and liabilities as in the case of direct investment.

Standard balance of payments classification

Balance of payments and international investment position statistics need to be arranged in a coherent structure to facilitate their use and adaptation for purposes such as policy formulation, analytical studies, projections, bilateral comparisons, and regional and global aggregations. *BPM5* contains a *standard classification* and list of *standard components* of the balance of payments and international investment position. These standards were developed taking into account the views of national compilers and analysts, and the requirement to harmonise concepts and definitions with related international statistical standards and classifications. The classification also reflects the separation of categories that may exhibit different economic behaviour, may be important in a number of countries, are readily collectable, and are needed for harmonising with other bodies of statistics.

The standard balance of payments classification comprises two main groups of accounts – the *current account* and the *capital and financial account*. Transactions classified to the *current account* include goods and services, income and current transfers. Within the *capital and financial account,* the *capital account* includes capital transfers and the net acquisition or disposal of non-produced, non-financial assets. The *financial account* includes transactions in financial assets and liabilities.

Transactions in *current account* and *capital account* items are generally shown on a gross basis (gross debits and credits separately). Transactions in *financial account* items are mainly recorded on a net basis.

A Summary of balance of payments in 2002

£ million

	Credits	Debits
1. Current account		
A. Goods and services	272 727	304 016
1. Goods	186 257	232 712
2. Services	86 470	71 304
2.1. Transportation	12 019	16 739
2.2. Travel	13 995	27 847
2.3. Communications	1 943	2 025
2.4. Construction	176	111
2.5. Insurance	6 922	756
2.6. Financial	13 585	3 086
2.7. Computer and information	2 978	1 110
2.8. Royalties and licence fees	5 776	4 440
2.9. Other business	25 904	12 493
2.10. Personal, cultural and recreational	1 594	800
2.11. Government	1 578	1 897
B. Income	123 075	101 956
1. Compensation of employees	1 121	1 054
2. Investment income	121 954	100 902
2.1 Direct investment	49 881	19 892
2.2 Portfolio investment	31 949	31 420
2.3 Other investment (including earnings on reserve assets)	40 124	49 590
C. Current transfers	11 703	20 498
1. Central government	3 544	9 296
2. Other sectors	8 159	11 202
Total current account	**407 505**	**426 470**
2. Capital and financial accounts		
A. Capital account	2 311	1 266
1. Capital transfers	2 130	968
2. Acquisition/disposal of non-produced, non-financial assets	181	298
B. Financial account	128 620	125 084
1. Direct investment	18 474	27 812
Abroad		27 812
1.1. Equity capital		17 868
1.2. Reinvested earnings		28 561
1.3. Other capital[1]		−18 617
In United Kingdom	18 474	
1.1. Equity capital	11 812	
1.2. Reinvested earnings	8 583	
1.3. Other capital[2]	−1 921	
2. Portfolio investment	50 817	609
Assets		609
2.1. Equity securities		−2 451
2.2. Debt securities		3 060
Liabilities	50 817	
2.1. Equity securities	1 931	
2.2. Debt securities	48 886	
3. Financial derivatives (net)		−1 001
4. Other investment	59 329	98 123
Assets		98 123
4.1 Trade credits		559
4.2 Loans		15 976
4.3 Currency and deposits		81 336
4.4 Other assets		252
Liabilities	59 329	
4.1. Trade credits	–	
4.2. Loans	−30 047	
4.3. Currency and deposits	89 674	
4.4. Other liabilities	−298	
5. Reserve assets		−459
5.1. Monetary gold		−266
5.2. Special drawing rights		26
5.3. Reserve position in the IMF		469
5.4. Foreign exchange		−530
Total capital and financial accounts	**130 931**	**126 350**
Total current, capital and financial accounts	**538 436**	**552 820**
Net errors and omissions	14 384	

1 Other capital transaction on direct investment abroad represents claims on affiliated enterprises less liabilities to affiliated enterprises
2 Other capital transactions on direct investment in the United Kingdom represents liabilities to direct investors less claims on direct investors

Current account

Table A (opposite) shows the standard classification of the *current account*. Each of the broad categories is described briefly below, while individual component items are described in detail in subsequent chapters.

Goods and services are divided into separate accounts for *goods and services*. *Goods* comprise most movable goods that change ownership between UK residents and non-residents.

Services comprise services provided between UK residents and non-residents, together with some transactions in goods where, by international agreement, it is not practical to separate the goods and services components (e.g. goods purchased by travellers are classified to services).

Income refers to income earned by UK residents from non-residents and vice versa. Income covers compensation of employees and investment income. *Compensation of employees* comprises wages, salaries and other benefits earned by individuals from economies other than those in which they are residents, as well as earnings from extraterritorial bodies such as foreign embassies, which often employ staff from the economy in which they are located. *Investment income* comprises income earned from the provision of financial capital and is classified by direct, portfolio and other investment income and income earned on the UK's reserve assets.

Transfers represent offsets to the provision of resources between residents and non-residents with no quid pro quo in economic value (for example, the provision of food aid). *Current transfers* are distinguished from *capital transfers*, which are included in the *capital account*. *Current transfers* represent the offset to the provision of resources that are normally consumed within a short period (less than twelve months) after the transfer is made. In the example of food aid, the food is presumed to be consumed within twelve months of it being received. The classification of current transfers is by general government and other sectors.

Capital account

The *capital account* comprises both capital transfers and the acquisition and disposal of non-produced, non-financial assets (such as copyrights). The latter includes land purchases and sales associated with embassies and other extraterritorial bodies. Capital transfers entries are required where there is no quid pro quo to offset the transfer of ownership of fixed assets, or the transfer of funds linked to fixed assets (e.g. aid to finance capital works), or the forgiveness of debt. It also includes the counterpart to the transfer of net wealth by migrants, referred to as migrants' transfers.

Financial account

The *financial account* comprises transactions associated with changes of ownership of the UK's foreign financial assets and liabilities. The main classifications used in the financial account are discussed in conjunction with the international investment position classification below.

The *international investment position* measures the UK's stock of external financial assets and liabilities, whereas the *balance of payments financial account* measures transactions in these assets and liabilities. Hence the classifications used in the *financial account* and *international investment position* need to be essentially the same.

Major classifications of the financial account and international investment position

Items in the financial account and international investment position statement are classified on a number of bases. The main ones are *type of investment, assets and liabilities, instrument of investment, sector,* and *original contractual maturity of financial instruments*.

A comparison of the international investment position statement and the balance of payments financial account shows one minor difference. In the category of direct investment in the financial account, reinvested earnings are shown separately whereas, in the international investment position statement, where no separate market price valuation of reinvested earnings can exist, the reinvested earnings are grouped into a composite category for equity and reinvested earnings.

Type of investment

The type of investment used in the UK's balance of payments and international investment position consists of five broad categories:

(i) *Direct investment capital* refers to capital provided to or received from an enterprise, by an investor in another country (i.e. an individual, enterprise or group of related individuals or enterprises), who is in a direct investment relationship with that enterprise. A *direct investment* relationship exists if the investor has an equity interest in an enterprise, resident in another country, of 10 per cent or more of the ordinary shares or voting stock. The *direct investment* relationship extends to branches, subsidiaries and to other businesses where the enterprise has significant shareholding.

(ii) *Portfolio investment* refers to transactions in equity and debt securities (apart from those included in direct investment and reserve assets). Debt securities comprise bonds and notes and money market instruments. In comparison with direct investment, it indicates investment where the investor is not assumed to have any appreciable say in the operation of the enterprise (e.g. less than 10 per cent of the ordinary share or voting stock).

(iii) *Financial derivatives* covers any financial instrument the price of which is based upon the value of an underlying asset (typically another financial asset). Financial derivatives include options (on currencies, interest rates, commodities, indices, etc.), traded financial futures, warrants and currency and interest swaps. Under *BPM5*, transactions in derivatives are treated as separate transactions, rather than being included as integral parts of underlying transactions to which they may be linked as hedges. Only estimates for the settlement receipts/payments on UK banks' interest rate swaps and forward rate agreements are included in financial derivatives.

(iv) *Other investment* is a residual category that captures transactions not classified to direct investment, portfolio investment, financial derivatives or reserve assets of the compiling economy. *Other investment* covers trade credits, loans (including financial leases), currency and deposits, and a residual category for any other assets and liabilities.

(v) *Reserve assets* refer to those foreign financial assets that are available to, and controlled by, the monetary authorities such as the Bank of England for financing or regulating payments imbalances. Reserve assets comprise: monetary gold, Special Drawing Rights, reserve position in the IMF, and foreign exchange held by the Bank.

Assets and liabilities

A financial *asset* is generally in the form of a financial claim on the rest of the world that is either represented by a contractual obligation (such as a loan) or is evidenced by a security (such as a share certificate). Two financial assets – monetary gold and Special Drawing Rights in the IMF – are not claims on the rest of the world. They are, however, included in international investment assets because they are readily available for payment of international obligations. A financial *liability* represents a financial claim of the rest of the world on the UK. Assets and liabilities in the international investment position statement are components of the balance sheet of an economy with the rest of the world. In the financial account the asset and liability classifications in essence reflect, respectively, transactions in claims on non-residents (assets) and in claims by non-residents (liabilities).

In the international investment position, the difference between assets and liabilities is the *net international investment position,* also referred to as the *net liability position/net asset position,* depending on the balance.

For *direct investment,* in both the financial account and international investment position, the main classification is by direction of investment, i.e. *direct investment abroad* and *direct investment in the UK. Direct investment abroad* is derived by netting liabilities of the UK *direct investors* to their *direct investment enterprises* against claims on their direct investment enterprises abroad. Similarly, *direct investment in the UK* is derived after netting claims of the UK direct investment enterprises against their liabilities to those direct investors abroad.

Instrument of investment

Several instruments of investment are also identified. Some of these are only applicable to one type of capital, i.e. the instrument *reinvested earnings* is only applicable to direct investment, while *monetary gold* and *Special Drawing Rights* are only used for reserve assets.

The major instruments and grouping of instruments identified in balance of payments and international investment statistics include:

(i) monetary gold;

(ii) Special Drawing Rights;

(iii) foreign exchange;

(iv) reserve position in IMF;

(v) equity;

(vi) reinvested earnings;

(vii) debt securities;

(viii) financial derivatives;

(ix) trade credit;

(x) loans;

(xi) currency and deposits; and

(xii) other assets/liabilities.

Financial derivatives data are presented as an annex to the international investment chapter.

Similar instruments may be combined into groups or combined with certain types of investment to make statistical presentations less cluttered.

For example:

(i) trade credit, loans, deposits, and other forms of finance including all debt securities, but excluding equity capital and reinvested earnings, between non-financial enterprises in a direct investment relationship, are combined and shown only as *other direct capital*. Similar aggregation applies to finance between a financial enterprise and a non-financial enterprise and between financial enterprises only in case of permanent debt;

(ii) bonds, bills, notes and money market instruments within portfolio investment are shown separately but under a heading of *debt securities;* and

(iii) a number of financial assets, held as part of the UK's reserves assets (currency and deposits, bills, bonds, notes and money market instruments), are grouped under the category *foreign exchange* within the reserve assets category.

Foreign equity and debt

At a broader level, instruments may be combined to show foreign equity and foreign debt. Foreign equity includes equity capital, reinvested earnings and equity securities. Foreign debt is a residual item containing all other instruments. They may be compiled on a gross basis (e.g. foreign debt/ assets and liabilities) or on a net basis (e.g. net foreign debt).

Sectorisation

Transactor units within an economy may be grouped together into *institutional sectors*. Units within the same *institutional sector* may be expected to behave similarly in their financial and other dealings and in response to differing economic and political stimuli. The principle of classification by sector, or sectorisation, in the financial account and international investment position is to identify the sector of the domestic creditor for assets and the sector of the domestic debtor for liabilities.

Four sectors are generally distinguished in the standard components of the ONS balance of payments and international investment statistics: *monetary financial institutions; central government; public corporations;* and *other*.

Within the current and capital accounts, sectorisation is also applied to current and capital transfers, where a split between *general government* and *other* is used.

Original contractual maturity

The fifth edition of the balance of payments manual looks to distinguish between long-term or short-term investment. Investment longer than one year is deemed to be long-term and investment less than one year is deemed to be short-term.

Other financial classifications

Other classifications in the financial account and international investment position include the domicile of liabilities issued by residents, drawings and repayments for long-term liabilities in the form of both trade credits and loans and the currency of assets and liabilities.

Country classification

The general principles applying to the compilation of a global balance of payments statement for the UK can be applied to the preparation of a statement for the UK's transactions with an individual country or a group of countries.

Reliability of estimates

All the value estimates are calculated as accurately as possible, however they cannot always be regarded as being absolutely precise to the last digit shown. Similarly, the index numbers are not necessarily absolutely precise to the last digit shown. Some figures are provisional and may be revised later; this applies particularly to many of the detailed figures for 2001 and 2002.

Revisions since ONS Pink Book 2002

Data is revised from 1996 onwards.

Goods – the data is revised from 1999 to incorporate estimates of VAT missing trader intra-Community (MTIC) fraud, first published 9 July in the May 2003 UK trade first release.

Services – the data for the years 1996–2001 is revised due to the expansion of the annual ITIS inquiry.

Income – the revisions mainly indicate the inclusion of later inquiry results, particularly the latest Foreign Direct Investment annual inquiry.

Current Transfers – revisions to 2000 and 2001 are mainly due to the usual annual review of net non-life insurance estimates in accordance with the receipt of new benchmarked data. There are further revisions back to 1996 which indicate a reassessment of accruals adjustments to EU subsidies.

Financial account and IIP – FDI revisions in 2000 and 2001 reflect the latest annual inquiry results. Revisions to equity assets within portfolio investment reflect later inquiry results from insurance companies, pension funds and securities dealers, whilst equity liabilities are revised in line with later Share Ownership Survey results.

Symbols and conventions used in the tables

Rounding
As figures have been rounded to the nearest final digit, there may be slight discrepancies between the sums of the constituent items and the totals as shown.

Symbols
The following symbols are used throughout:

.. = not available

- = nil or less than a million

References

The internationally agreed framework for the presentation of the Balance of Payments and the National Accounts are described in the following publications.

Balance of Payments Manual (5th edition 1993), International Monetary Fund
(ISBN 1-55775-339-3).

Balance of Payments Textbook (1996), International Monetary Fund
(ISBN 1-55775-570-1).

Balance of Payments and International Investment Position, Australia: Concepts, Sources and Methods (1998) Australian Bureau of Statistics
(ISBN 0-642-25670-5).

European System of Accounts (ESA 1995), Office for Official Publications of the European Communities
(ISBN 92-827-7954-8).

System of National Accounts (1993),
(ISBN 92-1-161352-3).

Articles describing balance of payments statistics, published in *Economic Trends,* include:

"Overseas trade in services: publication of monthly estimates", September 1997;

"Geographical breakdown of exports and imports of UK trade in services by component", January 1998;

"Geographical breakdown of income in the balance of payments", November 1999 and December 2000;

"IMF Co-ordinated Portfolio Investment Survey", May 2003;

"Geographical breakdown of the UK International Investment Position", July 2003.

Part 1
Current account

Chapter 1

Summary of balance of payments

Current account

The UK has recorded a current account deficit in every year since 1984. Prior to 1984, the current account recorded a surplus in 1980 to 1983. Since the last surplus was recorded in 1983, there have been three main phases in the development of the current account. In the first phase, from 1984 to 1989, the current account deficit increased steadily to the record deficit of £26.3 billion recorded in 1989; during the second phase, from 1990 until 1997, the current account deficit declined to a low of £0.9 billion in 1997; in the third phase, since 1998, the current account deficit has widened again, to £19.0 billion in 2002.

The profile for the current account has historically followed that of trade in goods, its biggest and most cyclical component. The last trade in goods surplus, recorded in 1982, was the main driver of a current account surplus. From 1982, the goods deficit increased to a peak of £24.7 billion in 1989, while the current balance deteriorated to a record deficit of £26.3 billion. From 1989, both the trade in goods and current account deficits fell until the mid-1990s. The increasing current account deficit since then has been due to the increase in the goods deficit, from £12.0 billion in 1995 to a record £46.5 billion in 2002, although this has partly been offset by rising trade in services and investment income surpluses.

Trade in goods and services

The trade in goods account recorded a net surplus in the years 1980, 1981 and 1982, largely as a result of exports of North Sea oil. Since then, however, the trade in goods account has remained in deficit. The deficit grew significantly in the late 1980s to reach a peak of £24.7 billion in 1989, before improving in the 1990s to a level of around £12 billion. In 1998 the deficit jumped by about £10 billion, and it has continued to rise since, reaching a record £46.5 billion in 2002.

The trade in services account has shown a surplus for every year since 1966. The surplus on services increased fairly steadily until 1987 during which time it broadly offset the deficit on trade in goods. From 1988 to 1994 the surplus was around £5 billion annually. From 1995 to 1997 the services surplus increased significantly, to around £13 billion. It remained at this level until 2002, when it reached a record £15.2 billion.

Figure 1.1
Current account balance

£ billion

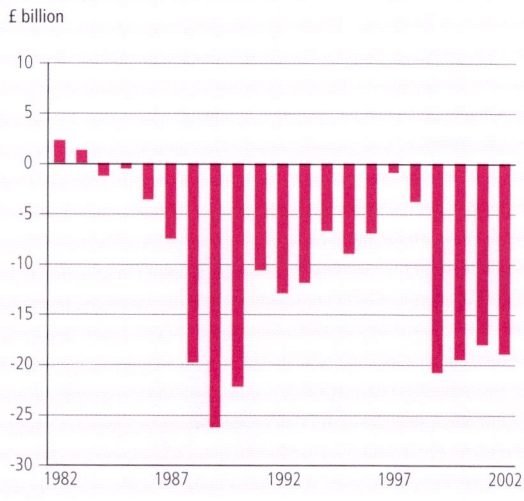

Figure 1.2
Trade in goods and services

Credits less debits

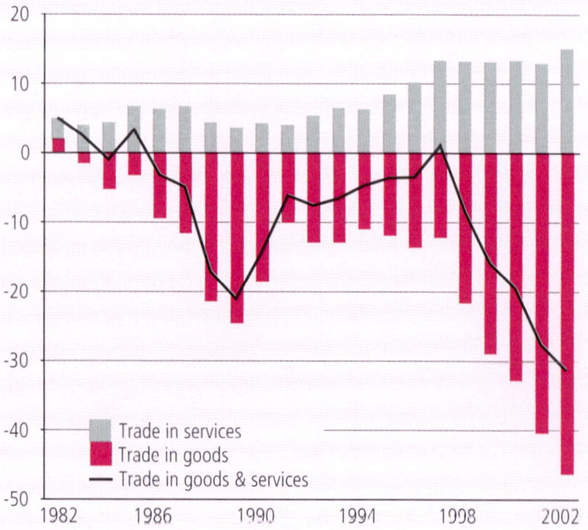

£ billion

Figure 1.3

Investment income

Credits less debits

£ billion

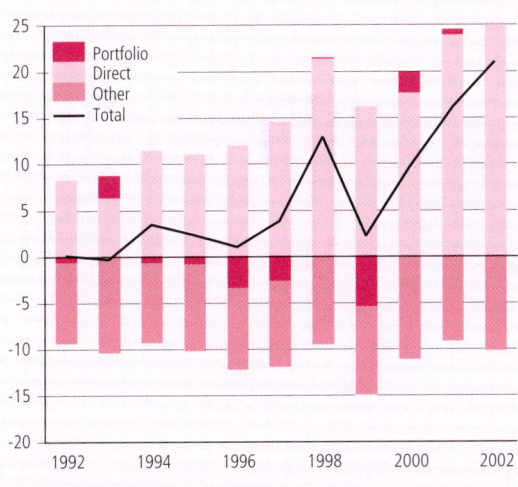

Income

The income account consists of compensation of employees and investment income, the latter dominating the account. Historically the balance on compensation of employees has generally been in deficit, but it moved into surplus in the late 1990s.

The investment income balance has generally shown a surplus (since records began in 1946 there have only been nine years which have shown a deficit) although it was not until 1994 that the surplus exceeded £3 billion annually. Surpluses on direct investment income have been partly offset by deficits on other investment – principally banks' net payments on loans and deposits. There has been a substantial improvement in the investment income balance since 1994, largely due to a steady increase in the surplus on direct investment. By sector, the improvement in the investment income balance has been driven by monetary financial institutions, moving from a deficit of £6.1 billion in 1993 to a record surplus of £14.2 billion in 2002.

Figure 1.4

Current transfers

Credits less debits

£ billion

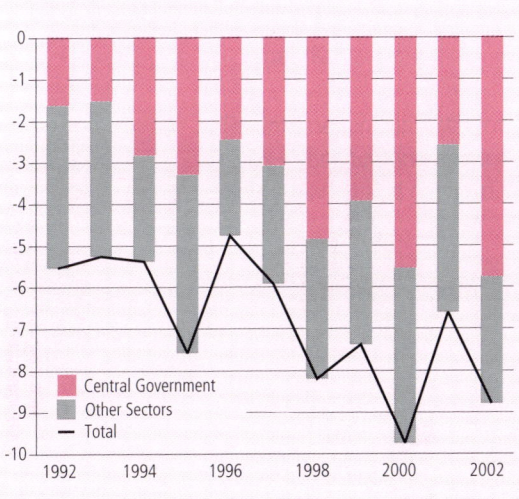

Current transfers

The transfers account has shown a deficit in every year since 1960. The deficit increased steadily to reach £4.9 billion in 1990. In 1991, the deficit reduced to £1.2 billion, reflecting £2.1 billion receipts from other countries towards the UK's cost of the Gulf conflict. The deficit has since increased, to reach a record £9.8 billion in 2000. Separate data for central government and other sectors are available from 1986 and show that surpluses on central government current transfers have been consistently outweighed by deficits with other sectors. The majority of payments to and receipts from EU institutions are recorded as other sector transactions as they relate to the original payee or ultimate recipient of the payment/receipt. The volatility in this account is driven by fluctuating net contributions to EU Institutions.

Revisions

Revisions in this year's *Pink Book* have generally been taken back to 1996 and reflect a number of changes to data sources and some methodological improvements. The main change has been to trade in goods and services. Substantial revisions have been made to imports from the EU from 1999 onwards to take account of VAT missing trader intra-Community (MTIC) fraud. The revisions involve upward adjustments to imports of £1.7billion in 1999, £2.8 billion in 2000, £7.1 billion in 2001 and £11.1 billion in 2002. Partly offsetting these changes, introduction of the new expanded sample for the International Trade in Services inquiry has resulted in a higher trade in services surplus in all years back to 1996. The overall impact of the changes has been to increase the current balance by around £1 billion in 1996 to 1998, but to reduce it thereafter. The largest change is to 2002, where the current balance has been revised down by £9.3 billion compared with data published in June.

Figure 1.5
Revisions since Pink Book 2002

Credits less debits

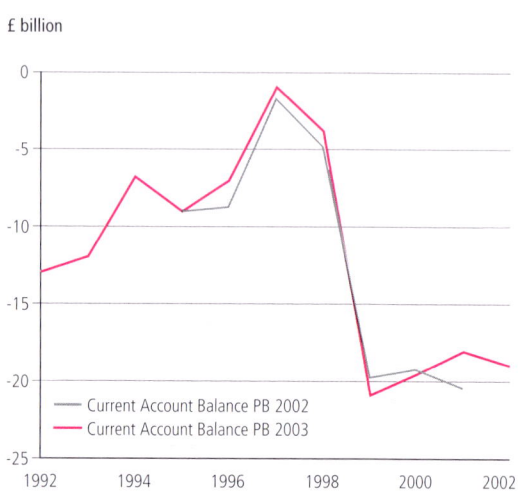

Investment flows, levels and income

One important set of relationships within the balance of payments is the link between the financial account (investment flows), the international investment position (levels or balance sheets), and the income deriving from the balance sheets. This is explained in more detail in the Introduction. Although a reconciliation between opening and closing levels and flows is not officially compiled in the UK, table 1.3 shows the rudiments of this relationship over the years for which consistent detailed data are available. Within the three main categories of investment (direct, portfolio and other), as well as reserve assets, it can be seen that the difference in the values of the balance sheet at the end of one year and the previous year is approximately equal to the value of financial transactions in that year. The difference between the two amounts is explained by valuation, exchange rate and other effects.

Figure 1.6
International investment position and income

Credits less debits

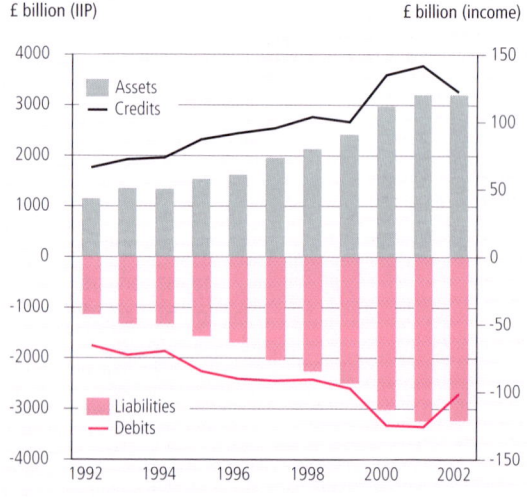

Figure 1.7

Implied rates of return on assets

Per cent

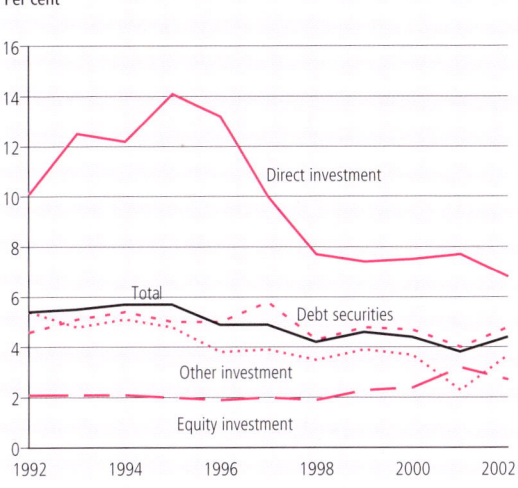

The value of both external assets and liabilities in the international investment position has been rising steadily since 1980, reflecting both the increased global investment and the increasing prices of external assets and liabilities. The UK's external assets exceeded external liabilities in every year until 1990. From 1995 to 1998, the level of UK's external liabilities grew more strongly that the level of external assets, so that the net international investment position moved from a net asset to a net liability position of £133.2 billion in 1998. Since 1998, the level of external assets has grown more strongly than liabilities, with the net liability position falling to £9.2 billion in 2002.

Another important relationship is that which exists between investment income and the international investment position. This can be considered most easily by looking at the implied 'rates of return' for both assets and liabilities. In total the implied rate of return on liabilities was higher than assets until around 1993 to 1994 since when, although the return on assets has been higher, both have been at relatively low levels. Since other investment constitutes around half of the value of the balance sheets it is not surprising therefore that the rates of return have reflected the movements in interest rates on loans and deposits such as LIBOR. The rates of return for direct investment are significantly higher than for other forms of investment. This is probably a consequence in part of comparatively lower valuations since direct investment levels are at book value rather than market value used elsewhere, but may also reflect the higher return required to make the longer term investment worthwhile. Within portfolio investment, debt securities, which are often used as a form of short term financing, have similar rates of return as other investment, whilst equity securities have the lowest returns, perhaps reflecting the comparatively lower risk on these instruments.

Figure 1.8

Implied rates of return on liabilities

Per cent

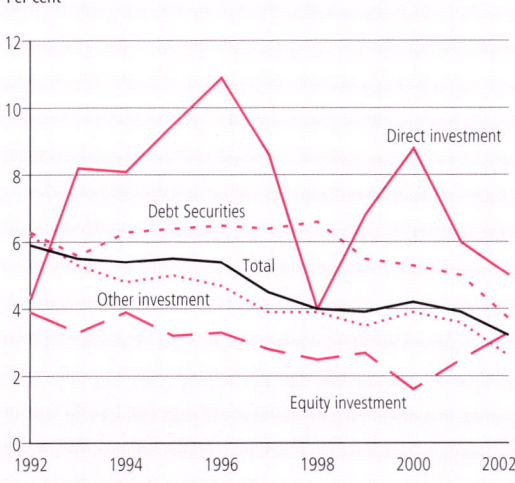

1.1 Summary of balance of payments
Balances (credits less debits)

£ million

				Current account							
	Trade in goods	Trade in services	Total goods and services	Compensation of employees	Investment income	Total income	Current transfers	Current balance	Capital account	Financial account	Net errors & omissions
	LQCT	KTMS	KTMY	KTMP	HMBM	HMBP	KTNF	HBOG	FKMJ	HBNT	HHDH
1946	−101	−274	−375	−20	76	56	166	−153	−21	181	−7
1947	−358	−197	−555	−19	140	121	123	−311	−21	552	−220
1948	−152	−64	−216	−20	223	203	96	83	−17	−58	−8
1949	−137	−43	−180	−20	206	186	29	35	−12	−103	80
1950	−54	−4	−58	−21	378	357	39	338	−10	−447	119
1951	−692	32	−660	−21	322	301	29	−330	−15	426	−81
1952	−272	123	−149	−22	231	209	169	229	−15	−229	15
1953	−244	123	−121	−25	207	182	143	204	−13	−177	−14
1954	−210	115	−95	−27	227	200	55	160	−13	−174	27
1955	−315	42	−273	−27	149	122	43	−108	−15	34	89
1956	50	26	76	−30	203	173	2	251	−13	−250	12
1957	−29	121	92	−32	223	191	−5	278	−13	−313	48
1958	34	119	153	−34	261	227	4	384	−10	−411	37
1959	−116	118	2	−37	233	196	–	198	−5	−68	−125
1960	−404	39	−365	−35	201	166	−6	−205	−6	−7	218
1961	−144	51	−93	−35	223	188	−9	86	−12	23	−97
1962	−104	50	−54	−37	301	264	−14	196	−12	−195	11
1963	−123	4	−119	−38	364	326	−37	170	−16	−30	−124
1964	−551	−34	−585	−33	365	332	−74	−327	−17	392	−48
1965	−263	−66	−329	−34	405	371	−75	−33	−18	49	2
1966	−111	44	−67	−39	358	319	−91	161	−19	22	−164
1967	−601	157	−444	−39	354	315	−118	−247	−25	179	93
1968	−708	341	−367	−48	303	255	−119	−231	−26	688	−431
1969	−214	392	178	−47	468	421	−109	490	−23	−794	327
1970	−18	455	437	−56	527	471	−89	819	−22	−818	21
1971	205	590	795	−63	481	418	−90	1 123	−23	−1 330	230
1972	−736	665	−71	−52	407	355	−142	142	−35	477	−584
1973	−2 573	803	−1 770	−68	1 074	1 006	−336	−1 100	−39	1 031	108
1974	−5 241	1 118	−4 123	−92	1 184	1 092	−302	−3 333	−34	3 185	182
1975	−3 245	1 447	−1 798	−102	518	416	−313	−1 695	−36	1 569	162
1976	−3 930	2 532	−1 398	−140	1 100	960	−534	−972	−12	507	477
1977	−2 271	3 306	1 035	−152	−280	−432	−889	−286	11	−3 286	3 561
1978	−1 534	3 777	2 243	−140	138	−2	−1 420	821	−79	−2 655	1 913
1979	−3 326	4 076	750	−130	155	25	−1 777	−1 002	−103	864	241
1980	1 329	3 829	5 158	−82	−1 683	−1 765	−1 653	1 740	−4	−2 157	421
1981	3 238	3 951	7 189	−66	−1 058	−1 124	−1 219	4 846	−79	−5 312	545
1982	1 879	3 198	5 077	−95	−1 273	−1 368	−1 476	2 233	6	−1 233	−1 006
1983	−1 618	4 076	2 458	−89	280	191	−1 391	1 258	75	−3 287	1 954
1984	−5 409	4 491	−918	−94	1 284	1 190	−1 566	−1 294	107	−7 130	8 317
1985	−3 416	6 767	3 351	−120	−877	−997	−2 924	−570	185	−1 657	2 042
1986	−9 617	6 403	−3 214	−156	1 850	1 694	−2 094	−3 614	135	−122	3 601
1987	−11 698	6 813	−4 885	−174	1 091	917	−3 570	−7 538	333	10 764	−3 559
1988	−21 553	4 450	−17 103	−64	817	753	−3 500	−19 850	235	17 201	2 414
1989	−24 724	3 643	−21 081	−138	−654	−792	−4 448	−26 321	270	18 001	8 050
1990	−18 707	4 337	−14 370	−110	−2 869	−2 979	−4 932	−22 281	497	15 083	6 701
1991	−10 223	4 102	−6 121	−63	−3 244	−3 307	−1 231	−10 659	290	5 269	5 100
1992	−13 050	5 482	−7 568	−49	177	128	−5 534	−12 974	421	5 089	7 464
1993	−13 066	6 581	−6 485	35	−226	−191	−5 243	−11 919	309	11 330	280
1994	−11 126	6 379	−4 747	−170	3 518	3 348	−5 369	−6 768	33	2 126	4 609
1995	−12 023	8 481	−3 542	−296	2 397	2 101	−7 574	−9 015	533	5 005	3 477
1996	−13 722	10 272	−3 450	93	1 111	1 204	−4 755	−7 001	1 260	3 959	1 782
1997	−12 342	13 418	1 076	83	3 822	3 905	−5 918	−937	982	−5 136	5 091
1998	−21 813	13 309	−8 504	−10	12 916	12 906	−8 198	−3 796	516	2 219	1 061
1999	−29 051	13 134	−15 917	201	2 221	2 422	−7 383	−20 878	773	20 944	−839
2000	−32 976	13 426	−19 550	150	9 613	9 763	−9 752	−19 539	1 527	24 944	−6 932
2001	−40 620	13 000	−27 620	66	16 122	16 188	−6 606	−18 038	1 411	22 180	−5 553
2002	−46 455	15 166	−31 289	67	21 052	21 119	−8 795	−18 965	1 045	3 536	14 384

1.2 Current account

£ million

		1981	1982	1983	1984	1985	1986	1987	1988	1989	1990	1991
Credits												
Exports of goods and services												
Exports of goods	LQAD	51 034	55 657	60 984	70 565	78 291	72 997	79 531	80 711	92 611	102 313	103 939
Exports of services	KTMQ	16 398	17 051	18 902	21 094	23 783	24 682	27 033	26 843	28 998	31 574	32 001
Total exports of goods and services	KTMW	67 432	72 708	79 886	91 659	102 074	97 679	106 564	107 554	121 609	133 887	135 940
Income												
Compensation of employees	KTMN	238	252	290	323	344	369	413	445	476	543	551
Investment income	HMBN	36 807	43 544	41 632	50 629	51 011	46 431	47 079	55 444	72 604	77 663	75 073
Total income	HMBQ	37 045	43 796	41 922	50 952	51 355	46 800	47 492	55 889	73 080	78 206	75 624
Current transfers												
Central government	FJUM	..	..	..	..	..	1 973	1 475	1 929	1 507	2 050	4 892
Other sectors	FJUN	..	..	..	..	..	4 374	4 412	4 808	5 864	7 376	9 281
Total current transfers	KTND	3 089	3 811	4 226	4 710	4 653	6 347	5 887	6 737	7 371	9 426	14 173
Total	HBOE	**107 566**	**120 315**	**126 034**	**147 321**	**158 082**	**150 826**	**159 943**	**170 180**	**202 060**	**221 519**	**225 737**
Debits												
Imports of goods and services												
Imports of goods	LQBL	47 796	53 778	62 602	75 974	81 707	82 614	91 229	102 264	117 335	121 020	114 162
Imports of services	KTMR	12 447	13 853	14 826	16 603	17 016	18 279	20 220	22 393	25 355	27 237	27 899
Total imports of goods and services	KTMX	60 243	67 631	77 428	92 577	98 723	100 893	111 449	124 657	142 690	148 257	142 061
Income												
Compensation of employees	KTMO	304	347	379	417	464	525	587	509	614	653	614
Investment income	HMBO	37 865	44 817	41 352	49 345	51 888	44 581	45 988	54 627	73 258	80 532	78 317
Total income	HMBR	38 169	45 164	41 731	49 762	52 352	45 106	46 575	55 136	73 872	81 185	78 931
Current transfers												
Central government	FJUO	..	..	..	..	..	1 261	1 449	2 433	2 275	2 125	3 450
Other sectors	FJUP	..	..	..	..	..	7 180	8 008	7 804	9 544	12 233	11 954
Total current transfers	KTNE	4 308	5 287	5 617	6 276	7 577	8 441	9 457	10 237	11 819	14 358	15 404
Total	HBOF	**102 720**	**118 082**	**124 776**	**148 615**	**158 652**	**154 440**	**167 481**	**190 030**	**228 381**	**243 800**	**236 396**
Balances												
Trade in goods and services												
Trade in goods	LQCT	3 238	1 879	−1 618	−5 409	−3 416	−9 617	−11 698	−21 553	−24 724	−18 707	−10 223
Trade in services	KTMS	3 951	3 198	4 076	4 491	6 767	6 403	6 813	4 450	3 643	4 337	4 102
Total trade in goods and services	KTMY	7 189	5 077	2 458	−918	3 351	−3 214	−4 885	−17 103	−21 081	−14 370	−6 121
Income												
Compensation of employees	KTMP	−66	−95	−89	−94	−120	−156	−174	−64	−138	−110	−63
Investment income	HMBM	−1 058	−1 273	280	1 284	−877	1 850	1 091	817	−654	−2 869	−3 244
Total income	HMBP	−1 124	−1 368	191	1 190	−997	1 694	917	753	−792	−2 979	−3 307
Current transfers												
Central government	FJUQ	..	..	..	..	..	712	26	−504	−768	−75	1 442
Other sectors	FJUR	..	..	..	..	..	−2 806	−3 596	−2 996	−3 680	−4 857	−2 673
Total current transfers	KTNF	−1 219	−1 476	−1 391	−1 566	−2 924	−2 094	−3 570	−3 500	−4 448	−4 932	−1 231
Total (Current balance)	HBOG	**4 846**	**2 233**	**1 258**	**−1 294**	**−570**	**−3 614**	**−7 538**	**−19 850**	**−26 321**	**−22 281**	**−10 659**

1.2 Current account
continued

£ million

		1992	1993	1994	1995	1996	1997	1998	1999	2000	2001	2002
Credits												
Exports of goods and services												
Exports of goods	LQAD	107 863	122 229	135 143	153 577	167 196	171 923	164 056	166 166	187 936	190 050	186 257
Exports of services	KTMQ	36 228	41 411	45 365	49 932	56 773	61 104	66 278	72 628	79 071	81 658	86 470
Total exports of goods and services	KTMW	144 091	163 640	180 508	203 509	223 969	233 027	230 334	238 794	267 007	271 708	272 727
Income												
Compensation of employees	KTMN	551	595	681	887	911	1 007	840	960	1 032	1 087	1 121
Investment income	HMBN	66 153	72 333	73 702	87 132	91 621	95 337	103 667	99 729	134 436	141 438	121 954
Total income	HMBQ	66 704	72 928	74 383	88 019	92 532	96 344	104 507	100 689	135 468	142 525	123 075
Current transfers												
Central government	FJUM	2 180	2 826	2 138	1 730	2 828	2 173	1 943	3 542	2 465	4 991	3 544
Other sectors	FJUN	10 295	9 565	9 454	10 751	17 121	10 823	10 527	9 768	8 305	9 153	8 159
Total current transfers	KTND	12 475	12 391	11 592	12 481	19 949	12 996	12 470	13 310	10 770	14 144	11 703
Total	HBOE	**223 270**	**248 959**	**266 483**	**304 009**	**336 450**	**342 367**	**347 311**	**352 793**	**413 245**	**428 377**	**407 505**
Debits												
Imports of goods and services												
Imports of goods	LQBL	120 913	135 295	146 269	165 600	180 918	184 265	185 869	195 217	220 912	230 670	232 712
Imports of services	KTMR	30 746	34 830	38 986	41 451	46 501	47 686	52 969	59 494	65 645	68 658	71 304
Total imports of goods and services	KTMX	151 659	170 125	185 255	207 051	227 419	231 951	238 838	254 711	286 557	299 328	304 016
Income												
Compensation of employees	KTMO	600	560	851	1 183	818	924	850	759	882	1 021	1 054
Investment income	HMBO	65 976	72 559	70 184	84 735	90 510	91 515	90 751	97 508	124 823	125 316	100 902
Total income	HMBR	66 576	73 119	71 035	85 918	91 328	92 439	91 601	98 267	125 705	126 337	101 956
Current transfers												
Central government	FJUO	3 812	4 343	4 977	5 022	5 297	5 260	6 787	7 482	8 015	7 584	9 296
Other sectors	FJUP	14 197	13 291	11 984	15 033	19 407	13 654	13 881	13 211	12 507	13 166	11 202
Total current transfers	KTNE	18 009	17 634	16 961	20 055	24 704	18 914	20 668	20 693	20 522	20 750	20 498
Total	HBOF	**236 244**	**260 878**	**273 251**	**313 024**	**343 451**	**343 304**	**351 107**	**373 671**	**432 784**	**446 415**	**426 470**
Balances												
Trade in goods and services												
Trade in goods	LQCT	−13 050	−13 066	−11 126	−12 023	−13 722	−12 342	−21 813	−29 051	−32 976	−40 620	−46 455
Trade in services	KTMS	5 482	6 581	6 379	8 481	10 272	13 418	13 309	13 134	13 426	13 000	15 166
Total trade in goods and services	KTMY	−7 568	−6 485	−4 747	−3 542	−3 450	1 076	−8 504	−15 917	−19 550	−27 620	−31 289
Income												
Compensation of employees	KTMP	−49	35	−170	−296	93	83	−10	201	150	66	67
Investment income	HMBM	177	−226	3 518	2 397	1 111	3 822	12 916	2 221	9 613	16 122	21 052
Total income	HMBP	128	−191	3 348	2 101	1 204	3 905	12 906	2 422	9 763	16 188	21 119
Current transfers												
Central government	FJUQ	−1 632	−1 517	−2 839	−3 292	−2 469	−3 087	−4 844	−3 940	−5 550	−2 593	−5 752
Other sectors	FJUR	−3 902	−3 726	−2 530	−4 282	−2 286	−2 831	−3 354	−3 443	−4 202	−4 013	−3 043
Total current transfers	KTNF	−5 534	−5 243	−5 369	−7 574	−4 755	−5 918	−8 198	−7 383	−9 752	−6 606	−8 795
Total (Current balance)	HBOG	**−12 974**	**−11 919**	**−6 768**	**−9 015**	**−7 001**	**−937**	**−3 796**	**−20 878**	**−19 539**	**−18 038**	**−18 965**

1.3 Summary of international investment position, financial account and investment income

£ million

		1992	1993	1994	1995	1996	1997	1998	1999	2000	2001	2002
Investment abroad												
International investment position												
Direct investment	HBWD	151.8	172.6	176.1	203.7	201.6	223.3	299.6	428.1	607.4	625.0	644.8
Portfolio investment	HHZZ	327.2	469.8	429.8	499.3	548.2	651.0	703.8	838.3	906.1	942.5	865.3
Other investment	HLXV	639.7	684.4	708.6	808.1	852.6	1 068.2	1 105.5	1 130.4	1 435.0	1 613.1	1 676.5
Reserve assets	LTEB	28.3	29.7	30.7	31.8	27.3	22.8	23.3	22.2	28.8	25.6	25.4
Total	HBQA	1 146.9	1 356.5	1 345.2	1 542.9	1 629.7	1 965.3	2 132.2	2 418.9	2 977.3	3 206.2	3 212.1
Financial account transactions												
Direct investment	-HJYP	11.3	18.2	22.7	28.7	22.3	38.2	73.3	125.0	155.0	43.2	27.8
Portfolio investment	-HHZC	28.6	89.6	−21.8	39.3	59.6	52.0	32.1	21.3	65.5	86.5	0.6
Financial derivatives (net)	-ZPNN	−1.3	−0.2	−2.4	−1.7	−1.0	−1.2	3.0	−2.7	−1.6	−8.4	−1.0
Other investment	-XBMM	31.7	45.3	27.8	47.5	138.7	168.3	19.0	56.8	269.9	173.8	98.1
Reserve assets	-LTCV	−1.4	0.7	1.0	−0.2	−0.5	−2.4	−0.2	−0.6	3.9	−3.1	−0.5
Total	-HBNR	68.9	153.5	27.3	113.6	219.1	255.0	127.3	199.8	492.8	292.0	125.1
Investment income												
Direct investment	HJYW	13.8	17.4	21.9	24.8	28.5	29.4	29.8	33.1	44.9	46.6	49.9
Portfolio investment	HLYX	12.6	16.7	16.4	19.7	20.2	23.8	29.3	25.7	33.0	34.9	31.9
Other investment	AIOP	38.4	36.8	33.8	41.0	41.3	40.7	43.4	39.8	55.5	59.0	39.3
Reserve assets	HHCB	1.5	1.5	1.6	1.7	1.6	1.4	1.1	1.2	1.0	1.0	0.8
Total	HMBN	66.2	72.3	73.7	87.1	91.6	95.3	103.7	99.7	134.4	141.4	122.0
Investment in the UK												
International investment position												
Direct investment	HBWI	130.8	135.9	129.9	146.2	152.6	173.7	213.6	250.3	310.4	380.6	397.5
Portfolio investment	HLXW	247.1	306.9	320.0	406.3	480.0	583.3	692.8	828.9	998.2	954.4	892.6
Other investment	HLYD	756.3	882.3	877.4	1 013.0	1 064.9	1 282.1	1 359.0	1 410.4	1 704.8	1 900.9	1 931.1
Total	HBQB	1 134.2	1 325.1	1 327.3	1 565.5	1 697.5	2 039.1	2 265.5	2 489.5	3 013.4	3 236.0	3 221.3
Financial account transactions												
Direct investment	HJYU	9.4	10.9	7.1	13.8	17.6	22.8	45.1	55.2	80.6	42.7	18.5
Portfolio investment	HHZF	9.6	28.8	30.7	37.3	43.0	26.7	20.9	114.1	164.5	43.9	50.8
Other investment	XBMN	55.0	125.2	−8.3	67.5	162.5	200.4	63.6	51.5	272.6	227.6	59.3
Total	HBNS	74.0	164.9	29.5	118.6	223.1	249.9	129.6	220.8	517.7	314.2	128.6
Investment income												
Direct investment	HJYX	5.6	11.1	10.6	13.8	16.6	14.9	8.6	17.0	27.4	22.8	19.9
Portfolio investment	HLZC	13.3	14.2	17.2	20.6	23.7	26.6	29.1	31.2	30.7	34.3	31.4
Other investment	HLZN	47.1	47.2	42.5	50.3	50.1	50.0	53.0	49.3	66.7	68.2	49.6
Total	HMBO	66.0	72.6	70.2	84.7	90.5	91.5	90.8	97.5	124.8	125.3	100.9
Net investment												
International investment position												
Direct investment	HBWQ	20.9	36.7	46.2	57.5	49.0	49.5	85.9	177.8	297.1	244.4	247.3
Portfolio investment	CGNH	80.1	162.9	109.8	93.0	68.2	67.7	11.0	9.4	−92.2	−11.9	−27.3
Other investment	CGNG	−116.6	−197.9	−168.8	−204.9	−212.3	−213.9	−253.6	−280.0	−269.8	−287.9	−254.6
Reserve assets	LTEB	28.3	29.7	30.7	31.8	27.3	22.8	23.3	22.2	28.8	25.6	25.4
Net investment position	HBQC	12.8	31.4	17.9	−22.6	−67.8	−73.8	−133.2	−70.6	−36.1	−29.8	−9.2
Financial account transactions												
Direct investment	HJYV	−1.8	−7.2	−15.6	−14.9	−4.7	−15.4	−28.3	−69.8	−74.4	−0.5	−9.3
Portfolio investment	HHZD	−19.1	−60.8	52.5	−2.0	−16.6	−25.3	−11.2	92.8	99.0	−42.6	50.2
Financial derivatives	ZPNN	1.3	0.2	2.4	1.7	1.0	1.2	−3.0	2.7	1.6	8.4	1.0
Other investment	HHYR	23.3	79.8	−36.1	20.0	23.8	32.0	44.6	−5.3	2.7	53.8	−38.8
Reserve assets	LTCV	1.4	−0.7	−1.0	0.2	0.5	2.4	0.2	0.6	−3.9	3.1	0.5
Net transactions	HBNT	5.1	11.3	2.1	5.0	4.0	−5.1	2.2	20.9	24.9	22.2	3.5
Investment income												
Direct investment	HJYE	8.2	6.2	11.4	10.9	11.9	14.5	21.3	16.1	17.6	23.8	30.0
Portfolio investment	HLZX	−0.7	2.5	−0.8	−0.9	−3.5	−2.8	0.2	−5.5	2.3	0.6	0.5
Other investment	CGNA	−8.7	−10.4	−8.7	−9.4	−8.8	−9.3	−9.6	−9.5	−11.2	−9.3	−10.3
Reserve assets	HHCB	1.5	1.5	1.6	1.7	1.6	1.4	1.1	1.2	1.0	1.0	0.8
Net earnings	HMBM	0.2	−0.2	3.5	2.4	1.1	3.8	12.9	2.2	9.6	16.1	21.1

Chapter 2
Trade in goods

Summary

The balance on trade in goods has shown a deficit in all but six years over the last century with the value of imports exceeding the value of exports. A surplus on trade in goods has not been recorded since 1982. In the period 1992 to 1997 the deficit settled into the range of £10 billion – £14 billion before widening in every subsequent year.

In 2002 the deficit widened to a record £46.5 billion, driven by a 2 per cent fall in the value of exports to £186.3 billion and a 1 per cent rise in the value of imports to a record £232.7 billion. The deficit with Non-EU countries narrowed from a record £28.9 billion to £26.2 billion with a 6 per cent fall in imports and a 4½ per cent fall in exports. The deficit with EU countries widened from £11.7 billion to £20.2 billion with a 7 per cent rise in imports and a marginal fall in exports.

Figure 2.1

Trade in goods

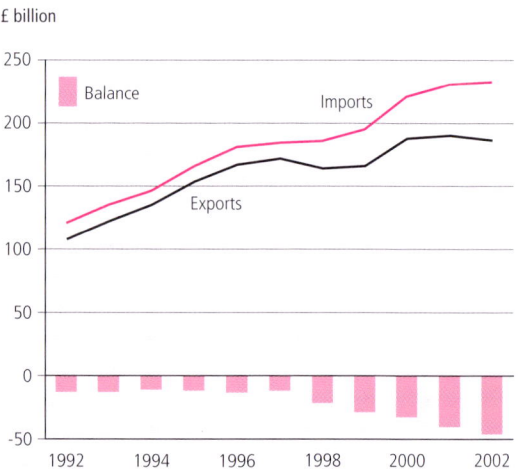

Volume changes

Export volume increased in every year between 1981 and 2001. The growth in exports slowed during the years 1991 to 1993 reflecting a decline in economic activity abroad. Since then there was a period of strong growth between 1994 and 1997 followed by a marked slowdown in 1998. After a slight pick up in growth in 1999 and accelerated growth in 2000 export volume slowed again in 2001 and fell in 2002 as world economic activity slowed. Import volume has also been generally increasing since 1981. However, a downturn in the UK economy resulted in a fall in the volume of imports in 1991. Since then import growth has resumed.

In 2002, export volume fell by 2 per cent and import volume rose by 4 per cent to a record annual level. Export volume fell by 4 per cent to non-EU countries but was only marginally down to EU countries – both down from record levels in 2001. The volume of imports from EU countries rose by 8½ per cent in 2002 while the volume of imports from non-EU countries fell by 1 per cent. Imports from EU countries were at a record annual level in 2002.

Figure 2.2

Export and import volume indices

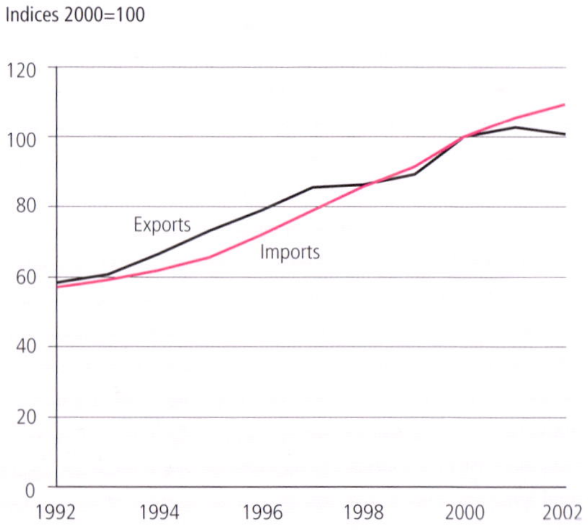

Figure 2.3

Export and import price indices

Indices 2000=100

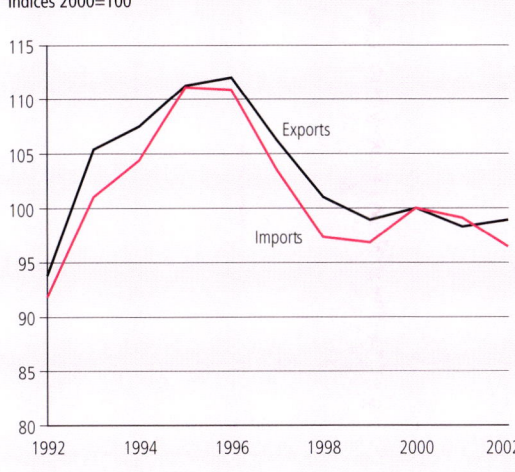

Price changes

Export and import prices rose for nine consecutive years between 1986 and 1995. The largest annual rises, 12 per cent for exports and 10 per cent for imports, occurred between 1992 and 1993 when sterling depreciated sharply following the UK's withdrawal from the Exchange Rate Mechanism (ERM). Both exports and import prices fell significantly during 1997 and 1998. This reflected falls in World commodity prices and the price of crude oil feeding through into the price of manufactured goods. The price of crude oil increased by about 50 per cent in 1999 and by a further 70 per cent in 2000 before falling back in 2001 and 2002.

In 2002, the overall export price index rose by ½ per cent while the import price index was down by 2½ per cent compared to the previous year. Excluding the oil price effect export prices would have risen by ½ per cent in 2002 while import prices would have fallen by 3½ per cent.

Figure 2.4

Trade in oil

£ billion

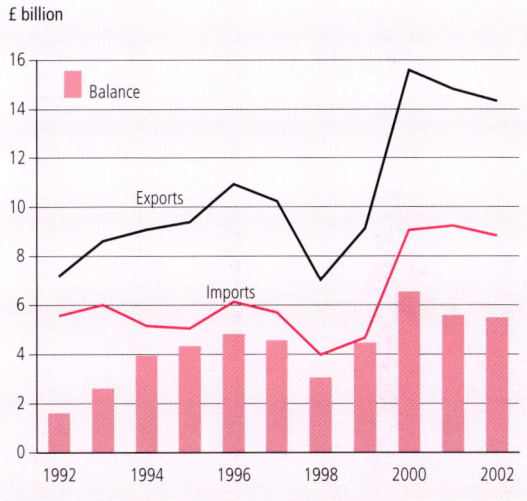

Trade in oil

While the overall balance on trade in goods has shown a deficit every year since 1982, exports of oil consistently exceeded imports of oil in each year since 1980. In 1985 trade in oil showed a record surplus of £8.0 billion as oil prices reached record levels. Disruptions to production in the North Sea subsequently diminished the surplus during the period 1988 to 1991. Until 1996 the annual surplus increased steadily as UK production recovered and World crude oil prices increased. Falling oil prices in 1997 and 1998 then led to a reduction in the surplus to £3.0 billion in 1998 before sharp rises in prices saw the surplus increase to £4.4 billion in 1999 and £6.5 billion in 2000 – the highest surplus since 1985. The fall in the price of crude oil reduced the oil trade surplus to £5.6 billion in 2001 and to £5.5 billion in 2002.

Trade in commodities other than oil

Finished manufactures accounted for an increased share of both total exports and total imports in the last ten years. Their share of total exports rose from 53 per cent in 1992 to 57 per cent in 2002. Imports rose from 53 per cent to 62 per cent over the same ten year period.

Within finished manufactures, the balance on trade in capital goods was in surplus every year between 1992 and 1999. The balance on trade in ships and aircraft was in surplus every year between 1992 and 1997. 2002 saw a record deficit reflecting lower exports and higher imports of aircraft. Trade in motor cars, other consumer goods and intermediate goods has been in deficit in each of the last ten years. The deficit on motor cars fell in 2002 as production picked up after a period of disruption caused by restructuring in the industry in 2001. Within semi-manufactured goods the UK has been a net exporter of chemicals and a net importer of other semi-manufactured goods in each of the last ten years.

In 2002 export growth in volume terms was most prominent in cars which rose by 24 per cent to reach a record level. Import growth, again in volume terms, was particularly strong in other consumer goods which grew by 12 per cent in the year.

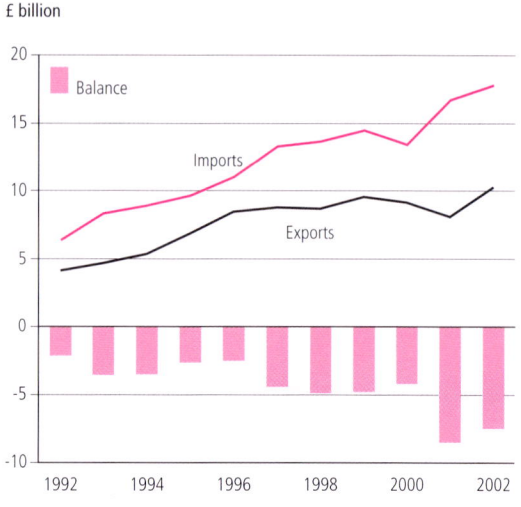

Figure 2.5
Trade in motor cars

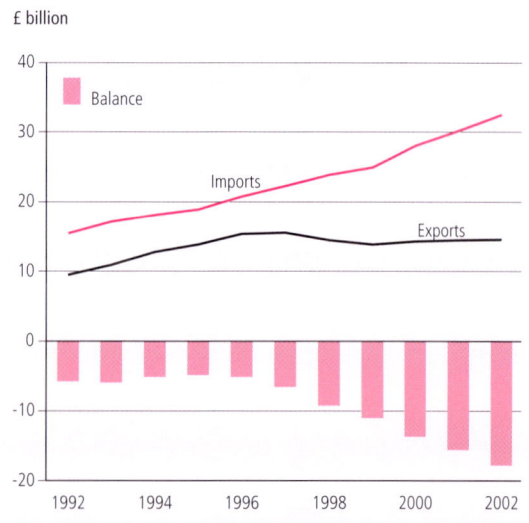

Figure 2.6
Trade in other consumer goods

2.1 Trade in goods
Summary table

£ million

		SITC[1]	1992	1993	1994	1995	1996	1997	1998	1999	2000	2001	2002
Exports													
Food, beverages and tobacco	BQMV	0+1	8 677	9 173	10 039	11 192	11 328	11 103	10 216	9 947	9 908	9 650	9 977
Basic materials	ELBK	2+4	1 950	2 276	2 568	2 946	2 790	2 753	2 512	2 284	2 603	2 579	2 851
Oil													
Crude oil	BQNX	333	4 491	5 169	6 019	6 539	7 508	6 452	4 473	6 148	10 522	10 486	9 795
Oil products	BQNY	334+335	2 681	3 455	3 060	2 845	3 420	3 787	2 545	2 975	5 062	4 323	4 530
Total oil	BOKL	33	7 172	8 624	9 079	9 384	10 928	10 239	7 018	9 123	15 584	14 809	14 325
Coal, gas and electricity	BQNF	32+34+35	307	451	413	558	650	777	495	806	1 473	1 570	1 676
Semi-manufactured goods													
Chemicals	BQOB	5	14 931	17 742	18 806	20 999	22 166	21 901	22 102	23 071	24 992	27 607	28 370
Precious stones and silver	BQOD	667+681.1	1 828	3 048	3 081	3 117	3 609	3 555	2 833	3 633	4 744	4 708	4 725
Other	BQOC	Rest of 6	13 599	14 712	16 493	19 342	19 533	19 120	18 410	16 669	17 929	18 129	17 090
Total semi-manufactured goods	BQMX	5+6	30 358	35 502	38 380	43 458	45 308	44 576	43 345	43 373	47 665	50 444	50 185
Finished manufactured goods													
Motor cars	BQOE	781	4 168	4 690	5 359	6 898	8 450	8 789	8 710	9 585	9 178	8 098	10 291
Other consumer goods[2]	BQOF		9 514	10 951	12 811	13 893	15 391	15 554	14 448	13 840	14 280	14 489	14 559
Intermediate goods[2]	BQOG		22 164	24 630	27 354	31 311	34 320	35 881	35 637	36 659	41 130	42 423	39 966
Capital goods[2]	BQOH		16 470	19 778	23 112	27 499	30 542	32 795	33 654	33 324	37 169	37 974	34 877
Ships and aircraft	BQOI	792+793	5 032	4 495	4 531	4 611	5 536	7 513	6 125	5 730	7 261	6 975	6 477
Total finished manufactured goods	BQMQ	7+8	57 348	64 544	73 167	84 212	94 239	100 532	98 574	99 138	109 018	109 959	106 170
Commodities and transactions not classified according to kind	BOKJ	9	2 051	1 659	1 497	1 827	1 953	1 943	1 896	1 495	1 685	1 039	1 073
Total	LQAD		107 863	122 229	135 143	153 577	167 196	171 923	164 056	166 166	187 936	190 050	186 257
Imports													
Food, beverages and tobacco	BQMW	0+1	12 613	13 300	13 888	15 561	17 422	16 911	17 250	17 787	17 660	18 517	19 324
Basic materials	BQNA	2+4	4 616	5 077	5 539	6 454	6 545	6 273	5 631	5 429	6 307	6 454	5 950
Oil													
Crude oil	BQNM	333	3 634	3 921	3 104	3 093	3 810	3 414	1 967	2 106	4 825	4 877	4 752
Oil products	BQOA	334+335	1 928	2 091	2 038	1 968	2 308	2 265	2 009	2 569	4 223	4 355	4 086
Total oil	BQAQ	33	5 562	6 012	5 142	5 061	6 118	5 679	3 976	4 675	9 048	9 232	8 838
Coal, gas and electricity	BQNG	32+34+35	1 561	1 461	1 200	1 100	1 166	1 145	916	753	968	1 270	1 005
Semi-manufactured goods													
Chemicals	BQOJ	5	11 205	12 980	14 156	17 481	18 095	17 405	17 379	18 619	20 633	22 836	23 881
Precious stones and silver	BQOL	667+681.1	1 957	2 681	2 874	3 352	3 630	3 873	4 025	4 788	5 454	5 260	4 245
Other	BQOK		17 948	19 016	20 970	24 408	25 070	24 134	23 670	22 142	23 778	24 965	24 446
Total semi-manufactured goods	BQMR	5+6	31 110	34 677	38 000	45 241	46 795	45 412	45 074	45 549	49 865	53 061	52 572
Finished manufactured goods													
Motor cars	BQOM	781	6 352	8 273	8 893	9 601	10 978	13 254	13 618	14 433	13 403	16 671	17 782
Other consumer goods[2]	BQON		15 400	17 024	18 019	18 835	20 662	22 237	23 792	24 905	28 011	30 086	32 382
Intermediate goods[2]	BQOO		22 642	25 627	28 408	33 211	38 077	36 506	37 091	41 538	48 455	46 423	44 622
Capital goods[2]	BQOP		15 767	19 135	21 864	25 560	27 434	29 222	30 190	32 256	37 944	38 720	39 205
Ships and aircraft	BQOQ	792+793	3 519	3 283	4 134	3 359	3 956	5 867	6 526	6 093	7 405	8 956	9 580
Total finished manufactured goods	BQMY	7+8	63 680	73 342	81 318	90 566	101 107	107 086	111 217	119 225	135 218	140 856	143 571
Commodities and transactions not classified according to kind	BQAO	9	1 771	1 426	1 182	1 617	1 765	1 759	1 805	1 799	1 846	1 280	1 452
Total	LQBL		120 913	135 295	146 269	165 600	180 918	184 265	185 869	195 217	220 912	230 670	232 712

1 Standard International Trade Classification, Revision 3.

2 Derived from the *Classification by Broad Economic Categories defined in terms of SITC, Revision 3*, published by the United Nations.

2.1 Trade in goods
Summary table
continued

£ million

		SITC[1]	1992	1993	1994	1995	1996	1997	1998	1999	2000	2001	2002
Balances													
Food, beverages and tobacco	BQOS	0+1	−3 936	−4 127	−3 849	−4 369	−6 094	−5 808	−7 034	−7 840	−7 752	−8 867	−9 347
Basic materials	BQOR	2+4	−2 666	−2 801	−2 971	−3 508	−3 755	−3 520	−3 119	−3 145	−3 704	−3 875	−3 099
Oil													
Crude oil	BQMG	333	857	1 248	2 915	3 446	3 698	3 038	2 506	4 042	5 697	5 609	5 043
Oil products	BQMH	334+335	753	1 364	1 022	877	1 112	1 522	536	406	839	−32	444
Total oil	BQNE	33	1 610	2 612	3 937	4 323	4 810	4 560	3 042	4 448	6 536	5 577	5 487
Coal, gas and electricity	BQNH	32+34+35	−1 254	−1 010	−787	−542	−516	−368	−421	53	505	300	671
Semi-manufactured goods													
Chemicals	BQMI	5	3 726	4 762	4 650	3 518	4 071	4 496	4 723	4 452	4 359	4 771	4 489
Precious stones and silver	BQMK	667+681.1	−129	367	207	−235	−21	−318	−1 192	−1 155	−710	−552	480
Other	BQMJ	Rest of 6	−4 349	−4 304	−4 477	−5 066	−5 537	−5 014	−5 260	−5 473	−5 849	−6 836	−7 356
Total semi-manufactured goods	BQOT	5+6	−752	825	380	−1 783	−1 487	−836	−1 729	−2 176	−2 200	−2 617	−2 387
Finished manufactured goods													
Motor cars	BQML	781	−2 184	−3 583	−3 534	−2 703	−2 528	−4 465	−4 908	−4 848	−4 225	−8 573	−7 491
Other consumer goods[2]	BQMM		−5 886	−6 073	−5 208	−4 942	−5 271	−6 683	−9 344	−11 065	−13 731	−15 597	−17 823
Intermediate goods[2]	BQMN		−478	−997	−1 054	−1 900	−3 757	−625	−1 454	−4 879	−7 325	−4 000	−4 656
Capital goods[2]	BQMO		703	643	1 248	1 939	3 108	3 573	3 464	1 068	−775	−746	−4 328
Ships and aircraft	BQMP	792+793	1 513	1 212	397	1 252	1 580	1 646	−401	−363	−144	−1 981	−3 103
Total finished manufactured goods	BQOV	7+8	−6 332	−8 798	−8 151	−6 354	−6 868	−6 554	−12 643	−20 087	−26 200	−30 897	−37 401
Commodities and transactions not classified according to kind	BQOU	9	280	233	315	210	188	184	91	−304	−161	−241	−379
Total	LQCT		−13 050	−13 066	−11 126	−12 023	−13 722	−12 342	−21 813	−29 051	−32 976	−40 620	−46 455

1 Standard International Trade Classification, Revision 3.

2 Derived from the *Classification by Broad Economic Categories defined in terms of SITC, Revision 3*, published by the United Nations.

2.2 Trade in goods: volume indices

2000=100

		SITC[1]	1992	1993	1994	1995	1996	1997	1998	1999	2000	2001	2002
Exports													
Food, beverages and tobacco	BQPP	0+1	82	82	93	100	100	104	102	99	100	96	99
Basic materials	BQPQ	2+4	71	80	88	90	90	94	96	92	100	98	108
Oil													
Crude oil	BOGH	333	80	90	113	114	108	101	104	97	100	110	107
Oil products	BOGO	334+335	64	78	74	62	66	76	65	69	100	90	84
Total oil	BONC	33	73	85	97	92	91	91	88	86	100	104	99
Coal, gas and electricity	BOGP	32+34+35	21	33	33	39	39	50	44	64	100	113	124
Semi-manufactured goods													
Chemicals	BQLB	5	60	65	69	72	76	81	84	92	100	112	117
Precious stones and silver	BQLD	667+681.1	43	64	64	64	75	78	64	81	100	108	133
Other	BQLC	Rest of 6	78	81	86	96	98	100	100	94	100	100	95
Total semi-manufactured goods	BQPR	5+6	65	71	75	80	84	88	88	92	100	107	110
Finished manufactured goods													
Motor cars	BQLE	781	52	51	56	68	83	87	88	97	100	87	108
Other consumer goods[2]	BQLF		69	70	81	86	96	103	99	97	100	101	103
Intermediate goods[2]	BQLG		54	53	59	65	72	79	82	87	100	104	95
Capital goods[2]	BQLH		39	42	49	59	66	75	81	85	100	105	96
Ships and aircraft	BQLI	792+793	81	63	61	61	73	99	82	78	100	93	87
Total finished manufactured goods	BQPS	7+8	52	52	58	66	74	82	84	88	100	102	97
Total	BPBP		58.5	60.7	66.7	73.3	78.9	85.5	86.4	89.2	100.0	102.7	100.8
Imports													
Food, beverages and tobacco	BQPT	0+1	69	68	71	74	81	85	94	99	100	104	108
Basic materials	BQPU	2+4	87	91	91	92	97	98	93	91	100	103	96
Oil													
Crude oil	BQPV	333	135	141	121	110	111	115	105	76	100	113	113
Oil products	BQPW	334+335	107	120	109	106	107	111	112	105	100	114	83
Total oil	ELAM	33	124	133	116	108	109	113	108	90	100	113	99
Coal, gas and electricity	BQPX	32+34+35	116	88	76	70	75	82	76	80	100	103	101
Semi-manufactured goods													
Chemicals	BQLQ	5	53	57	63	69	74	79	83	93	100	111	120
Precious stones and silver	BQLS	667+681.1	48	55	56	64	69	77	78	93	100	106	103
Other	BQLR	Rest of 6	77	78	83	86	90	94	99	97	100	104	105
Total semi-manufactured goods	BQPY	5+6	64	67	72	77	82	86	90	95	100	107	111
Finished manufactured goods													
Motor cars	BQLT	781	60	68	69	68	76	95	99	105	100	130	135
Other consumer goods[2]	BQLU		58	66	67	66	71	79	87	92	100	105	117
Intermediate goods[2]	BQLV		46	46	50	56	65	68	76	87	100	98	97
Capital goods[2]	BQLW		36	40	44	51	56	67	77	84	100	105	113
Ships and aircraft	BQLX	792+793	63	56	66	51	57	88	98	90	100	109	119
Total finished manufactured goods	BQPZ	7+8	48	51	54	58	65	74	82	89	100	105	111
Total	BQBJ		57.1	59.3	61.9	65.7	71.9	79.0	85.7	91.5	100.0	105.4	109.4

1 Standard International Trade Classification, Revision 3.

2 Derived from the *Classification by Broad Economic Categories defined in terms of SITC, Revision 3,* published by the United Nations.

2.3 Trade in goods: price indices

2000=100

		SITC[1]	1992	1993	1994	1995	1996	1997	1998	1999	2000	2001	2002
Exports													
Food, beverages and tobacco	BPAI	0+1	99	108	106	110	112	105	101	101	100	103	103
Basic materials	BPAW	2+4	90	96	103	115	110	105	101	96	100	101	103
Oil													
Crude oil	BQAC	333	54	55	50	54	66	60	40	59	100	90	87
Oil products	BQAD	334+335	75	82	77	85	97	93	77	85	100	94	107
Total oil	BQAL	33	59	61	56	61	73	67	49	65	100	91	93
Coal, gas and electricity	BQAF	32+34+35	88	93	87	96	114	106	77	85	100	94	92
Semi-manufactured goods													
Chemicals	BQLJ	5	95	108	109	115	117	109	106	101	100	99	98
Precious stones and silver	BQLL	667+681.1	90	100	102	103	101	97	93	94	100	92	76
Other	BQLK	Rest of 6	97	104	109	114	112	107	103	99	100	100	101
Total semi-manufactured goods	BQAA	5+6	96	105	109	114	114	107	104	100	100	99	97
Finished manufactured goods													
Motor cars	BQPM	781	88	100	104	110	111	110	108	108	100	100	103
Other consumer goods[2]	BQLM		99	112	115	117	112	106	102	100	100	100	100
Intermediate goods[2]	BQLN		99	112	114	118	117	111	107	102	100	99	102
Capital goods[2]	BQLO		109	122	125	125	124	118	112	105	100	97	97
Ships and aircraft	BQLP	792+793	85	97	102	104	104	104	103	101	100	103	103
Total finished manufactured goods	BQAB	7+8	100	113	116	118	117	112	108	103	100	99	100
Total	BQKR		93.8	105.4	107.5	111.3	112.0	106.2	101.0	98.9	100.0	98.3	98.9
Imports													
Food, beverages and tobacco	ELAN	0+1	100	110	111	118	120	113	105	103	100	101	101
Basic materials	ELAO	2+4	79	86	96	109	106	101	97	95	100	99	99
Oil													
Crude oil	ELAS	333	54	56	52	57	69	60	38	57	100	90	86
Oil products	ELAT	334+335	46	44	45	45	52	49	43	60	100	91	117
Total oil	ELBB	33	51	51	49	52	62	55	40	59	100	90	101
Coal, gas and electricity	ELAU	32+34+35	152	162	154	151	150	135	116	94	100	116	100
Semi-manufactured goods													
Chemicals	BQLY	5	93	105	107	120	118	108	102	97	100	100	98
Precious stones and silver	BQMA	667+681.1	79	93	97	98	100	94	94	95	100	92	75
Other	BQLZ	Rest of 6	96	103	106	118	116	107	101	95	100	101	97
Total semi-manufactured goods	ELAQ	5+6	94	103	106	117	115	106	101	96	100	100	95
Finished manufactured goods													
Motor cars	BQMB	781	82	93	97	105	108	104	103	103	100	96	98
Other consumer goods[2]	BQMC		92	95	98	104	104	101	98	97	100	102	99
Intermediate goods[2]	BQMD		98	108	111	116	115	106	99	99	100	98	94
Capital goods[2]	BQME		104	115	120	120	119	108	101	102	100	97	93
Ships and aircraft	BQMF	792+793	76	80	85	90	93	90	90	91	100	110	108
Total finished manufactured goods	ELAR	7+8	95	103	108	112	111	104	99	99	100	99	96
Total	BQKS		91.8	101.0	104.4	111.1	110.9	103.5	97.3	96.8	100.0	99.1	96.4

1 Standard International Trade Classification, Revision 3.

2 Derived from the *Classification by Broad Economic Categories defined in terms of SITC, Revision 3*, published by the United Nations.

2.4 Adjustments to trade in goods on a balance of payments basis

£ million

		1992	1993	1994	1995	1996	1997	1998	1999	2000	2001	2002
Exports												
Overseas trade statistics (f.o.b.)	HGAA	108 507	119 141	135 186	154 971	169 569	173 082	165 855	168 221	189 666	190 806	187 660
Coverage adjustments												
Second-hand ships	HBYK	277	224	175	208	204	193	219	154	105	134	140
Repairs to ships and aircraft	EPAQ	15	12	12	12	12	12	12	12	12	12	12
Goods not changing ownership	HCLJ	−2 369	−1 009	−1 170	−1 710	−1 972	−2 351	−2 565	−2 291	−2 343	−1 785	−2 789
Goods procured in ports	KTPB	515	636	591	593	659	623	564	645	865	868	899
Industrial gold	DEJO	21	51	34	34	31	22	46	33	33	44	66
Other	BQPO	9	107	174	53	53	56	55	56	57	56	57
Total coverage adjustments	EHHH	−1 532	21	−184	−810	−1 013	−1 445	−1 671	−1 391	−1 271	−671	−1 615
Other adjustments	EPAR	888	3 066	141	−584	−1 360	286	−131	−664	−460	−85	212
Total	LQAD	107 863	122 229	135 143	153 577	167 196	171 923	164 056	166 166	187 936	190 050	186 257
Imports												
Overseas trade statistics (c.i.f.)	HGAD	125 867	136 176	149 888	169 609	186 153	189 107	192 027	199 925	224 415	229 510	228 468
Coverage adjustments												
Second-hand ships	HBTY	32	74	381	235	232	160	185	281	112	165	39
Ships delivered abroad	CGER	205	88	209	186	96	165	217	127	540	535	535
Repairs to ships and aircraft	EPBA	34	8	143	69	9	33	35	15	11	9	26
Goods not changing ownership	HBYS	−2 369	−1 009	−1 170	−1 710	−1 972	−2 351	−2 565	−2 291	−2 343	−1 785	−2 789
Goods procured in ports	KTPC	461	495	553	590	703	789	744	780	1 035	925	866
Industrial gold	DEJP	172	191	221	205	209	194	135	149	164	145	163
Smuggling - alcohol	QHCP	–	–	35	101	272	270	331	266	279	43	..
Smuggling - tobacco	QHCT	–	–	41	121	328	441	693	990	1 072	1 044	..
Other	EHHI	5	29	29	27	25	136	28	13	21	10	..
Total coverage adjustments	EHHJ	−1 459	−124	442	−176	−98	−163	−197	330	891	1 091	91
Valuation adjustments												
Freight	BPGF	−3 081	−3 416	−3 539	−3 628	−3 945	−4 171	−4 362	−4 660	−5 106	−5 423	−5 450
Insurance	ENAG	−378	−418	−433	−496	−522	−556	−548	−594	−654	−666	−652
Total	HCLT	−3 459	−3 834	−3 972	−4 124	−4 467	−4 727	−4 910	−5 254	−5 760	−6 089	−6 102
Other adjustments												
Impact of MTIC fraud	BQHF	–	–	–	–	–	–	–	1 678	2 794	7 060	11 103
Other adjustments	EPBB	−36	3 075	−89	291	−670	48	−1 051	−1 462	−1 428	−902	−848
Total other adjustments	CLAK	−36	3 075	−89	291	−670	48	−1 051	216	1 366	6 158	10 255
Total	LQBL	120 913	135 295	146 269	165 600	180 918	184 265	185 869	195 217	220 912	230 670	232 712

Chapter 3
Trade in services

Summary

A surplus has been recorded for trade in services in every year since 1966. There was a sharp increase in the surplus in 2002, from £13.0 billion in 2001 to £15.2 billion in 2002. Over the year to 2002, exports of services increased by 5.9 per cent (compared to a rise of 3.3 per cent the previous year), while imports grew by 3.9 per cent (compared to an increase of 4.6 per cent in 2001). Of the 11 main product groupings, seven showed surpluses and four (transport, travel, communications and government services) showed deficits. The increase in the surplus was mainly due to a large increase in the balances of insurance services and other business services.

Figure **3.1**

Trade in services

£ billion

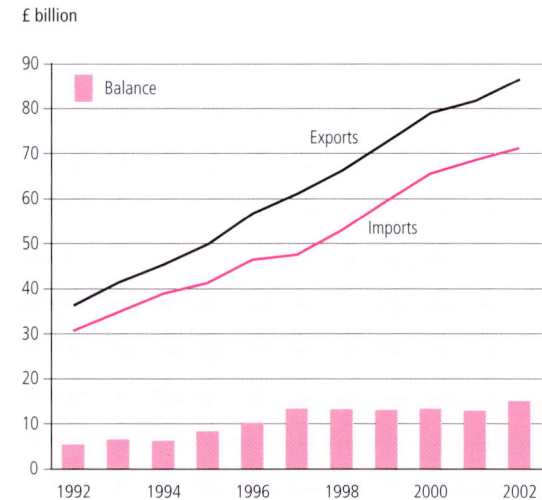

Transportation

Transportation services relate mainly to freight services on exports and imports of goods, and provision of passenger services. They are presented by mode of transport: sea, air and other.

Sea transport was close to balance in 1995, but has recorded deficits every year since. The deficit increased from £0.6 billion in 2001 to £1.2 billion in 2002 reflecting higher imports of freight services from overseas shipping operators.

The UK has recorded a deficit on air transport services in every year since the mid 1980s. The deficit increased from £2.3 billion in 2001 to £2.8 billion in 2002.

Figure **3.2**

Trade in sea and air transport services
Credits less debits
£ billion

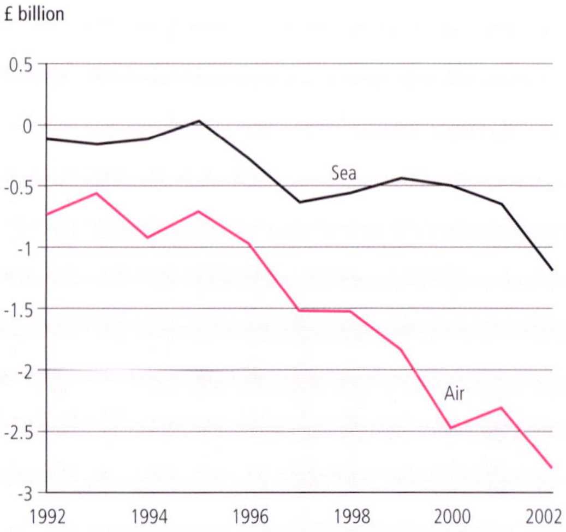

Figure 3.3

Trade in travel services

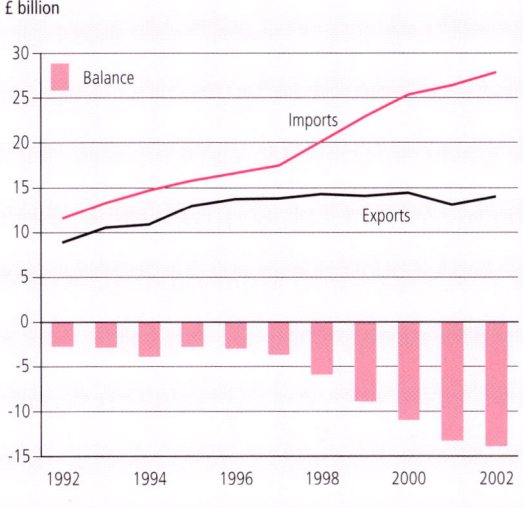

Travel

Travel expenditure by overseas residents in the UK accounts for around 16 per cent of total exports of trade in services, while expenditure by UK residents travelling abroad accounts for around 40 per cent of total imports.

The travel deficit has grown significantly since the late 1980s. The £13.9 billion deficit in 2002 was the highest on record, up from £13.3 billion in 2001. Exports of travel services to overseas visitors to the UK increased by 6.8 per cent in 2002 to £14 billion while imports by UK residents travelling abroad grew by 5.6 per cent to £27.8 billion.

Figure 3.4

Trade in financial services

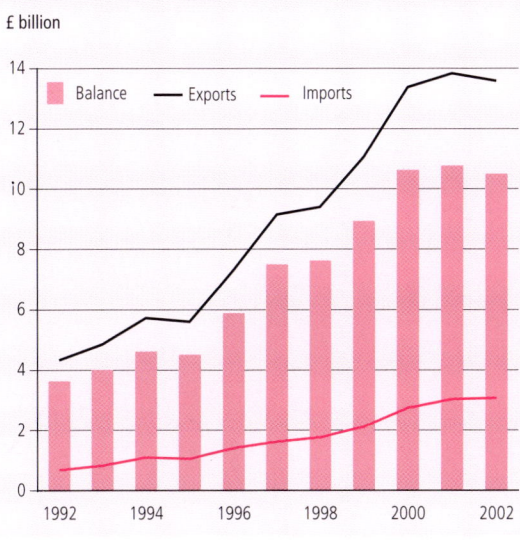

Financial services

Exports and imports of financial services from banks, fund managers, securities dealers etcetera have been presented separately since *Pink Book 2001*. The balance fell slightly in 2002, from £10.8 billion in 2001 to £10.5 billion. A fall of £1.4 billion in the exports of services by UK securities dealers was slightly offset by an increase of £0.3 billion in the exports of services by banks.

Other business services

Other business services covers a broad range of services including operational leasing, trade related services such as merchanting, and consultancy services such as advertising, engineering and legal services. Data for other business services are only available consistent with BPM5 definitions from 1991. Between 1991 and 2002 both exports and imports of other business services have increased fourfold. The balance on other business services increased by 12.9 per cent in 2002 to £13.4 billion: exports increased by £1.8 billion to £25.9 billion, whilst imports only rose by £0.3 billion, to £12.5 billion.

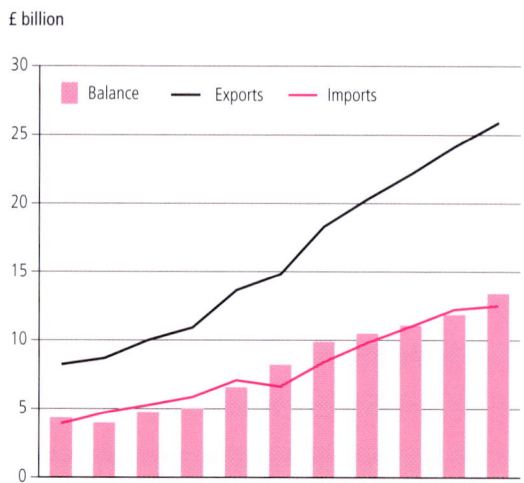

Figure 3.5

Trade in other business services

£ billion

Computer and information services

Both exports and imports of computer services showed strong growth in the late 1990s; the value of exports and imports has trebled since 1995. However, between 2001 and 2002, both exports and imports of computer and information services decreased for the first time since data is available in 1991. Exports fell by 2.5 per cent (compared to an increase of 6.6 per cent in 2001) and imports fell by 5.5 per cent (compared to an increase of 40.2 per cent in 2000).

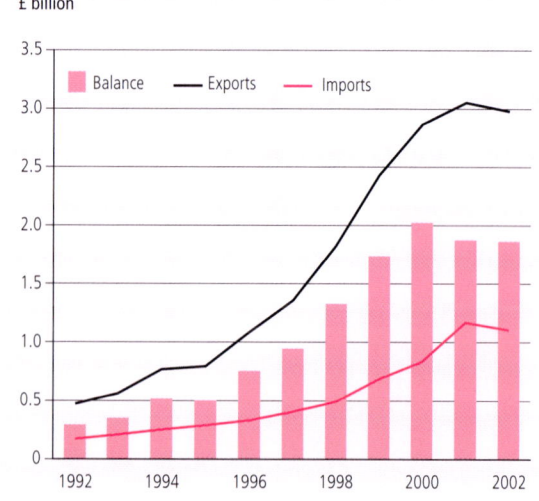

Figure 3.6

Trade in computer and information services

£ billion

3.1 Trade in services
Summary table

£ million

		1992	1993	1994	1995	1996	1997	1998	1999	2000	2001	2002
Exports												
Transportation	FJOD	7 895	8 770	9 492	10 200	10 820	11 229	11 682	11 724	12 615	12 201	12 019
Travel	FJPF	8 841	10 509	10 882	12 990	13 691	13 805	14 302	14 060	14 446	13 110	13 995
Communications	FJPH	895	1 070	1 038	1 009	1 057	1 196	1 289	1 664	1 864	2 054	1 943
Construction	FJPI	87	96	115	130	173	266	332	275	130	174	176
Insurance	FJPJ	1 172	1 854	1 963	2 344	2 656	3 191	2 851	3 997	3 794	4 562	6 922
Financial	FJPK	4 336	4 851	5 733	5 591	7 329	9 153	9 400	11 065	13 379	13 824	13 585
Computer and information	FJPL	469	563	770	795	1 090	1 357	1 826	2 433	2 865	3 053	2 978
Royalties and license fees	FJPM	2 388	2 906	3 468	3 854	4 253	4 148	4 270	5 092	5 389	5 673	5 776
Other business	FJPN	8 247	8 702	10 028	10 906	13 653	14 847	18 313	20 289	22 103	24 127	25 904
Personal, cultural and recreational	FJPR	424	549	571	690	774	820	881	964	1 305	1 358	1 594
Government	FJPU	1 474	1 541	1 305	1 423	1 277	1 092	1 132	1 065	1 181	1 522	1 578
Total	KTMQ	**36 228**	**41 411**	**45 365**	**49 932**	**56 773**	**61 104**	**66 278**	**72 628**	**79 071**	**81 658**	**86 470**
Imports												
Transportation	FJPV	8 671	9 398	10 328	10 733	11 916	13 291	13 799	14 180	15 972	15 757	16 739
Travel	APQA	11 557	13 319	14 728	15 793	16 642	17 443	20 201	22 930	25 385	26 376	27 847
Communications	FJQZ	971	1 274	1 310	1 328	1 340	1 381	1 582	1 805	1 867	1 993	2 025
Construction	FJRA	61	76	83	95	120	168	115	98	55	107	111
Insurance	FJRB	427	427	471	495	567	594	577	575	721	765	756
Financial	FJRE	694	837	1 118	1 073	1 432	1 635	1 771	2 123	2 753	3 046	3 086
Computer and information	FJRF	173	211	253	293	333	405	494	691	838	1 175	1 110
Royalties and license fees	FJRG	2 039	2 403	2 918	3 295	4 042	3 747	4 015	4 285	4 379	4 494	4 440
Other business	FJRH	3 896	4 702	5 266	5 855	7 068	6 615	8 417	9 803	11 006	12 248	12 493
Personal, cultural and recreational	FJRL	193	285	386	493	556	546	489	608	779	724	800
Government	FJRO	2 064	1 898	2 125	1 998	2 485	1 861	1 509	2 396	1 890	1 973	1 897
Total	KTMR	**30 746**	**34 830**	**38 986**	**41 451**	**46 501**	**47 686**	**52 969**	**59 494**	**65 645**	**68 658**	**71 304**
Balances												
Transportation	FJRP	−776	−628	−836	−533	−1 096	−2 062	−2 117	−2 456	−3 357	−3 556	−4 720
Travel	FJSR	−2 716	−2 810	−3 846	−2 803	−2 951	−3 638	−5 899	−8 870	−10 939	−13 266	−13 852
Communications	FJST	−76	−204	−272	−319	−283	−185	−293	−141	−3	61	−82
Construction	FJSU	26	20	32	35	53	98	217	177	75	67	65
Insurance	FJSV	745	1 427	1 492	1 849	2 089	2 597	2 274	3 422	3 073	3 797	6 166
Financial	FJTA	3 642	4 014	4 615	4 518	5 897	7 518	7 629	8 942	10 626	10 778	10 499
Computer and information	FJTB	296	352	517	502	757	952	1 332	1 742	2 027	1 878	1 868
Royalties and license fees	FJTC	349	503	550	559	211	401	255	807	1 010	1 179	1 336
Other business	FJTD	4 351	4 000	4 762	5 051	6 585	8 232	9 896	10 486	11 097	11 879	13 411
Personal, cultural and recreational	FJTH	231	264	185	197	218	274	392	356	526	634	794
Government	FJUL	−590	−357	−820	−575	−1 208	−769	−377	−1 331	−709	−451	−319
Total	KTMS	**5 482**	**6 581**	**6 379**	**8 481**	**10 272**	**13 418**	**13 309**	**13 134**	**13 426**	**13 000**	**15 166**

3.2 Transportation

£ million

		1992	1993	1994	1995	1996	1997	1998	1999	2000	2001	2002
Exports												
Sea transport												
Passenger												
Passenger revenue	FJAL	586	588	594	693	705	697	462	463	630	397	638
Time charter receipts	FJAM	8	8	8	8	9	9	–	9	8	–	9
Total passenger	FJOF	594	596	602	701	714	706	462	472	638	397	647
Freight												
Dry cargo												
Freight on UK exports	HECV	367	384	406	421	409	416	322	375	400	377	501
Freight on cross-trades	HDVI	902	1 129	1 272	1 354	1 345	1 614	1 602	1 511	1 453	1 568	1 571
Time charter receipts	FJAO	97	109	90	125	125	138	109	90	140	101	104
Wet cargo												
Freight on UK exports	HEIX	50	46	66	64	71	68	60	59	98	76	66
Freight on cross-trades	HECX	383	416	502	488	550	536	442	350	458	525	297
Time charter receipts	FJAP	79	96	128	139	120	68	70	87	104	177	112
Total Freight	FJOG	1 878	2 180	2 464	2 591	2 620	2 840	2 605	2 472	2 653	2 824	2 651
Disbursements in the UK	FJAR	840	878	910	946	950	981	1 139	1 063	1 042	1 086	1 008
Total sea transport	FJOE	3 312	3 654	3 976	4 238	4 284	4 527	4 206	4 007	4 333	4 307	4 306
Air transport												
Passenger revenue	FJOJ	2 764	3 163	3 392	3 751	4 110	4 080	4 422	4 402	4 690	4 255	4 162
Freight on UK exports and cross trades	FJOK	275	309	358	361	428	407	408	380	428	365	350
Other												
Disbursements in the UK	FJAX	941	1 018	1 044	983	1 024	1 177	1 565	1 765	1 994	2 167	1 991
Other revenue	HBWB	138	144	154	176	221	242	236	294	303	258	247
Total other	FJOL	1 079	1 162	1 198	1 159	1 245	1 419	1 801	2 059	2 297	2 425	2 238
Total air transport	FJOI	4 118	4 634	4 948	5 271	5 783	5 906	6 631	6 841	7 415	7 045	6 750
Other transport												
Rail												
Passenger	FJOS	–	–	–	71	77	80	108	132	109	113	90
Freight	FJOT	–	–	3	10	11	8	16	17	20	15	12
Total rail	FJOR	–	–	3	81	88	88	124	149	129	128	102
Road												
Passenger	FJOW	–	–	–	–	–	–	–	–	–	–	–
Freight	FJOX	422	443	511	570	629	672	683	690	690	665	805
Total road	FJOV	422	443	511	570	629	672	683	690	690	665	805
Pipeline transport	FJPD	43	39	54	40	36	36	38	37	48	56	56
Total other transport	FJOM	465	482	568	691	753	796	845	876	867	849	963
Total	FJOD	**7 895**	**8 770**	**9 492**	**10 200**	**10 820**	**11 229**	**11 682**	**11 724**	**12 615**	**12 201**	**12 019**

3.2 Transportation
continued

£ million

		1992	1993	1994	1995	1996	1997	1998	1999	2000	2001	2002
Imports												
Sea transport												
Passenger												
Passenger expenditure	FJBP	428	443	483	457	396	486	494	429	413	393	486
Time charter payments	FJBQ	51	55	62	65	70	92	22	24	24	20	20
Total passenger	FJPX	479	498	545	522	466	578	516	453	437	413	506
Freight												
Dry cargo												
Freight on UK imports	HCJO	1 514	1 682	1 761	1 811	1 846	2 008	2 063	2 202	2 531	2 469	2 730
Time charter payments	FJBS	106	118	129	135	145	190	217	122	149	207	401
Wet cargo												
Freight on UK imports	HCNJ	195	237	222	194	221	315	282	415	280	307	343
Time charter payments	FJBT	214	208	200	186	243	161	181	89	172	155	138
Freight on UK coastal routes	HFAA	81	97	92	116	132	135	135	135	172	185	197
Total Freight	FJPY	2 110	2 342	2 404	2 442	2 587	2 809	2 878	2 963	3 304	3 323	3 809
Other												
Disbursements - dry cargo	FJBU	733	865	1 039	1 134	1 375	1 670	1 291	953	1 036	1 184	1 121
Disbursements - wet cargo	FJBW	104	111	102	107	134	104	78	76	55	35	56
Total other	FJPZ	837	976	1 141	1 241	1 509	1 774	1 369	1 029	1 091	1 219	1 177
Total sea transport	FJPW	3 426	3 816	4 090	4 205	4 562	5 161	4 763	4 445	4 832	4 955	5 492
Air transport												
Passenger expenditure	FJQB	2 771	2 894	3 192	3 115	3 505	3 863	4 197	4 650	5 192	4 856	5 209
Freight	FJQC	358	361	375	401	481	543	583	685	740	823	818
Disbursements abroad	FJCA	1 723	1 936	2 298	2 459	2 764	3 015	3 372	3 336	3 951	3 671	3 524
Total air transport	FJQA	4 852	5 191	5 865	5 975	6 750	7 421	8 152	8 671	9 883	9 350	9 551
Other transport												
Rail												
Passenger	FJQK	–	–	2	54	85	98	121	154	167	168	172
Freight	FJQL	–	–	3	13	13	10	21	26	37	43	44
Total rail	FJQJ	–	–	5	67	98	108	142	180	204	211	216
Road												
Passenger	FJQO	–	–	–	–	–	–	–	–	–	–	–
Freight	FJQP	340	337	319	422	457	550	694	836	1 001	1 189	1 428
Total road	FJQN	340	337	319	422	457	550	694	836	1 001	1 189	1 428
Pipeline transport	FJQV	53	54	49	64	49	51	48	48	52	52	52
Total other transport	FJQE	393	391	373	553	604	709	884	1 064	1 257	1 452	1 696
Total	FJPV	**8 671**	**9 398**	**10 328**	**10 733**	**11 916**	**13 291**	**13 799**	**14 180**	**15 972**	**15 757**	**16 739**

3.2 Transportation
continued

£ million

		1992	1993	1994	1995	1996	1997	1998	1999	2000	2001	2002
Balances												
Sea transport												
Passenger	FJRR	115	98	57	179	248	128	−54	19	201	−16	141
Freight												
Dry cargo	FJNJ	−254	−178	−122	−46	−112	−30	−247	−348	−687	−630	−955
Wet cargo	FJNM	103	113	274	311	277	196	109	−8	208	316	−6
Other	FJVC	−81	−97	−92	−116	−132	−135	−135	−135	−172	−185	−197
Total Freight	FJRS	−232	−162	60	149	33	31	−273	−491	−651	−499	−1 158
Other												
Dry cargo	FJVF	−733	−865	−1 039	−1 134	−1 375	−1 670	−1 291	−953	−1 036	−1 184	−1 121
Wet Cargo	FJVG	−104	−111	−102	−107	−134	−104	−78	−76	−55	−35	−56
Other	FJVI	840	878	910	946	950	981	1 139	1 063	1 042	1 086	1 008
Total other	FJRT	3	−98	−231	−295	−559	−793	−230	34	−49	−133	−169
Total sea transport	FJRQ	−114	−162	−114	33	−278	−634	−557	−438	−499	−648	−1 186
of which												
Ships owned or chartered-in by UK residents	FLMZ	1 264	1 419	1 534	1 665	1 367	1 279	1 178	1 580	1 855	1 852	1 562
Ships operated by non-residents	FLNF	−1 378	−1 581	−1 648	−1 632	−1 645	−1 963	−1 835	−2 118	−2 354	−2 532	−2 748
Air transport												
Passenger	FJRV	−7	269	200	636	605	217	225	−248	−502	−601	−1 047
Freight	FJRW	−83	−52	−17	−40	−53	−136	−175	−305	−312	−458	−468
Other	FJRX	−644	−774	−1 100	−1 300	−1 519	−1 596	−1 571	−1 277	−1 654	−1 246	−1 286
Total air transport	FJRU	−734	−557	−917	−704	−967	−1 515	−1 521	−1 830	−2 468	−2 305	−2 801
Other transport												
Rail												
Passenger	FJSE	–	–	−2	17	−8	−18	−13	−22	−58	−55	−82
Freight	FJSF	–	–	–	−3	−2	−2	−5	−9	−17	−28	−32
Total rail	FJSD	–	–	−2	14	−10	−20	−18	−31	−75	−83	−114
Road												
Passenger	FJSI	–	–	–	–	–	–	–	–	–	–	–
Freight	FJSJ	82	106	192	148	172	122	−11	−146	−311	−524	−623
Total road	FJSH	82	106	192	148	172	122	−11	−146	−311	−524	−623
Pipeline transport	FJSP	−10	−15	5	−24	−13	−15	−10	−11	−4	4	4
Total other transport	FJRY	72	91	195	138	149	87	−39	−188	−390	−603	−733
Total	FJRP	−776	−628	−836	−533	−1 096	−2 062	−2 117	−2 456	−3 357	−3 556	−4 720

3.3 Travel

£ million

		1992	1993	1994	1995	1996	1997	1998	1999	2000	2001	2002
Exports												
Business												
Expenditure by seasonal & border workers[1]	FJCQ	–	–	53	52	60	53	132	114	147	163	212
Other	FJNO	2 211	2 489	2 580	3 240	3 246	3 533	3 857	3 998	4 084	3 615	3 671
Total business travel	FJPG	2 211	2 489	2 633	3 292	3 306	3 586	3 989	4 112	4 231	3 778	3 883
Personal												
Health related[2]	FJCX	–	–	91	53	105	112	79	93	66	83	66
Education related	FJDD	1 529	1 774	1 880	2 237	2 512	2 492	2 696	2 534	2 484	2 723	2 367
Other	FJDG	5 101	6 246	6 278	7 408	7 768	7 615	7 538	7 321	7 665	6 526	7 679
Total personal travel	FJTU	6 630	8 020	8 249	9 698	10 385	10 219	10 313	9 948	10 215	9 332	10 112
Total	FJPF	**8 841**	**10 509**	**10 882**	**12 990**	**13 691**	**13 805**	**14 302**	**14 060**	**14 446**	**13 110**	**13 995**
Imports												
Business												
Expenditure by seasonal & border workers[1]	FJDO	–	–	28	71	55	56	118	197	192	215	105
Other	FJNP	2 000	2 364	2 629	3 044	3 435	3 451	4 231	4 352	4 811	4 479	4 356
Total business travel	FJQY	2 000	2 364	2 657	3 115	3 490	3 507	4 349	4 549	5 003	4 694	4 461
Personal												
Health related[2]	FJDT	–	–	9	4	3	11	3	10	19	16	12
Education related	FJDV	63	103	91	106	118	111	133	180	99	108	107
Other	APPW	9 494	10 852	11 971	12 568	13 031	13 814	15 716	18 191	20 264	21 558	23 267
Total personal travel	APQW	9 557	10 955	12 071	12 678	13 152	13 936	15 852	18 381	20 382	21 682	23 386
Total	APQA	11 557	13 319	14 728	15 793	16 642	17 443	20 201	22 930	25 385	26 376	27 847
Balances												
Business												
Expenditure by seasonal & border workers[1]	FJCR	–	–	25	–19	5	–3	14	–83	–45	–52	107
Other	FJCW	211	125	–49	196	–189	82	–374	–354	–727	–864	–685
Total business travel	FJSS	211	125	–24	177	–184	79	–360	–437	–772	–916	–578
Personal												
Health related[2]	FJCY	–	–	82	49	102	101	76	83	47	67	54
Education related	FJDE	1 466	1 671	1 789	2 131	2 394	2 381	2 563	2 354	2 385	2 615	2 260
Other	FJDH	–4 393	–4 606	–5 693	–5 160	–5 263	–6 199	–8 178	–10 870	–12 599	–15 032	–15 588
Total personal travel	FJTW	–2 927	–2 935	–3 822	–2 980	–2 767	–3 717	–5 539	–8 433	–10 167	–12 350	–13 274
Total	FJSR	**–2 716**	**–2 810**	**–3 846**	**–2 803**	**–2 951**	**–3 638**	**–5 899**	**–8 870**	**–10 939**	**–13 266**	**–13 852**

1 There are no firm data for expenditure by seasonal & border workers before 1994, but for continuity some estimates have been included in other business travel.

2 There are no firm data for health related travel before 1994, but for continuity broad estimates have been included in other personal travel.

3.4 Communications services

£ million

		1992	1993	1994	1995	1996	1997	1998	1999	2000	2001	2002
Exports												
Postal and courier services												
Postal services	FJTN	15	80	92	109	85	93	88	109	118	97	110
Courier services	FJTO	20	25	18	24	23	15	13	52	29	80	65
Total postal and courier services	FJED	35	105	110	133	108	108	101	161	147	177	175
Telecommunications services	FJAS	860	965	928	876	949	1 088	1 188	1 503	1 717	1 877	1 768
Total	FJPH	**895**	**1 070**	**1 038**	**1 009**	**1 057**	**1 196**	**1 289**	**1 664**	**1 864**	**2 054**	**1 943**
Imports												
Postal and courier services												
Postal services	FJTP	51	172	198	223	217	200	218	239	260	200	199
Courier services	FJTQ	18	20	19	19	19	14	39	48	18	55	57
Total postal and courier services	FJEI	69	192	217	242	236	214	257	287	278	255	256
Telecommunications services	FJAT	902	1 082	1 093	1 086	1 104	1 167	1 325	1 518	1 589	1 738	1 769
Total	FJQZ	**971**	**1 274**	**1 310**	**1 328**	**1 340**	**1 381**	**1 582**	**1 805**	**1 867**	**1 993**	**2 025**
Balances												
Postal and courier services												
Postal services	FJTR	−36	−92	−106	−114	−132	−107	−130	−130	−142	−103	−89
Courier services	FJTS	2	5	−1	5	4	1	−26	4	11	25	8
Total postal and courier services	FJEE	−34	−87	−107	−109	−128	−106	−156	−126	−131	−78	−81
Telecommunications services	FJAQ	−42	−117	−165	−210	−155	−79	−137	−15	128	139	−1
Total	FJST	**−76**	**−204**	**−272**	**−319**	**−283**	**−185**	**−293**	**−141**	**−3**	**61**	**−82**

3.5 Insurance services

£ million

		1992	1993	1994	1995	1996	1997	1998	1999	2000	2001	2002
Exports												
Life insurance and pension funds	FJEU	188	103	170	238	415	494	838	1 557	1 417	2 174	1 226
Freight insurance	FJJL	14	26	25	2	31	82	76	47	41	49	86
Other direct insurance[1]	FJEW	−221	184	307	562	839	925	439	653	412	−579	2 366
Reinsurance	FJEX	157	389	273	409	339	718	331	−49	−296	1 011	1 192
Auxiliary insurance services (insurance brokers)	FJEY	1 034	1 152	1 188	1 133	1 032	972	1 167	1 789	2 220	1 907	2 052
Total[2]	FJPJ	**1 172**	**1 854**	**1 963**	**2 344**	**2 656**	**3 191**	**2 851**	**3 997**	**3 794**	**4 562**	**6 922**
Imports												
Life insurance and pension funds	FJRC	–	–	–	–	–	–	–	–	–	–	–
Freight insurance	FJRD	427	427	471	495	567	594	577	575	721	765	756
Other direct insurance	FJFC	–	–	–	–	–	–	–	–	–	–	–
Reinsurance	FJFD	–	–	–	–	–	–	–	–	–	–	–
Auxiliary insurance services	FJFE	–	–	–	–	–	–	–	–	–	–	–
Total	FJRB	**427**	**427**	**471**	**495**	**567**	**594**	**577**	**575**	**721**	**765**	**756**
Balances												
Life insurance and pension funds	FJSW	188	103	170	238	415	494	838	1 557	1 417	2 174	1 226
Freight insurance	FJSX	−413	−401	−446	−493	−536	−512	−501	−528	−680	−716	−670
Other direct insurance	FJJM	−221	184	307	562	839	925	439	653	412	−579	2 366
Reinsurance	FJJN	157	389	273	409	339	718	331	−49	−296	1 011	1 192
Auxiliary insurance services	FJJO	1 034	1 152	1 188	1 133	1 032	972	1 167	1 789	2 220	1 907	2 052
Total	FJSV	**745**	**1 427**	**1 492**	**1 849**	**2 089**	**2 597**	**2 274**	**3 422**	**3 073**	**3 797**	**6 166**

1 Other direct insurance by UK insurance companies includes facultative reinsurance on marine, aviation and transport business.
2 Exports of insurance services are net of expenditure abroad by UK insurance companies.

3.6 Financial services

£ million

		1992	1993	1994	1995	1996	1997	1998	1999	2000	2001	2002
Exports												
Monetary financial institutions (banks)												
Commissions and fees	APUP	697	849	996	1 178	1 269	1 778	2 108	2 506	3 041	2 986	3 279
Spread earnings	APVA	941	875	694	788	838	805	576	581	568	549	514
Total monetary financial institutions (banks)	ZXTE	1 638	1 724	1 690	1 966	2 107	2 583	2 684	3 087	3 609	3 535	3 793
Fund managers	FNMM	316	416	451	457	743	904	849	866	868	853	1 022
Securities dealers												
Commissions and fees	CDFI	1 353	1 434	1 955	1 649	2 103	2 761	2 831	3 996	5 632	5 211	4 039
Spread earnings	QZCM	298	522	803	690	934	1 253	1 233	1 209	1 033	1 492	1 267
Total securities dealers	ZXTF	1 651	1 956	2 758	2 339	3 037	4 014	4 064	5 205	6 665	6 703	5 306
Baltic Exchange	APRJ	323	297	282	315	280	340	320	320	336	377	357
Other	ZSHJ	408	458	552	514	1 162	1 312	1 483	1 587	1 901	2 356	3 107
Total	FJPK	4 336	4 851	5 733	5 591	7 329	9 153	9 400	11 065	13 379	13 824	13 585
Imports												
Monetary financial institutions (banks)	APVW	148	214	302	412	463	573	549	733	1 003	1 157	1 475
Fund managers	FNMS	34	41	61	32	150	155	171	143	160	229	214
Securities dealers[1]	RWMG	215	276	418	287	411	506	689	829	1 199	1 296	1 039
Baltic Exchange	APSZ	24	21	20	24	20	24	23	27	39	27	35
Other	ZXTG	273	285	317	318	388	377	339	391	352	337	323
Total	FJRE	694	837	1 118	1 073	1 432	1 635	1 771	2 123	2 753	3 046	3 086
Balances												
Monetary financial institutions	ZXLV	1 490	1 510	1 388	1 554	1 644	2 010	2 135	2 354	2 606	2 378	2 318
Fund managers	ZXLW	282	375	390	425	593	749	678	723	708	624	808
Securities dealers	ZXLX	1 436	1 680	2 340	2 052	2 626	3 508	3 375	4 376	5 466	5 407	4 267
Baltic Exchange	ZXLY	299	276	262	291	260	316	297	293	297	350	322
Other	ZXLZ	135	173	235	196	774	935	1 144	1 196	1 549	2 019	2 784
Total	FJTA	3 642	4 014	4 615	4 518	5 897	7 518	7 629	8 942	10 626	10 778	10 499

1 For securities dealers, the move to a gross presentation means that imports of non-financial services are moved to the other business services accounts (see table 3.9).

3.7 Computer and information services

£ million

		1992	1993	1994	1995	1996	1997	1998	1999	2000	2001	2002
Exports												
Computer services	FJCN	406	491	679	695	956	1 183	1 640	2 056	2 478	2 525	2 556
Information services	FJCO	63	72	91	100	134	174	186	377	387	528	422
Total	FJPL	**469**	**563**	**770**	**795**	**1 090**	**1 357**	**1 826**	**2 433**	**2 865**	**3 053**	**2 978**
Imports												
Computer services	FJDL	147	179	218	253	283	339	473	593	745	859	944
Information services	FJDM	26	32	35	40	50	66	21	98	93	316	166
Total	FJRF	**173**	**211**	**253**	**293**	**333**	**405**	**494**	**691**	**838**	**1 175**	**1 110**
Balances												
Computer Services	FJJP	259	312	461	442	673	844	1 167	1 463	1 733	1 666	1 612
Information services	FJJQ	37	40	56	60	84	108	165	279	294	212	256
Total	FJTB	**296**	**352**	**517**	**502**	**757**	**952**	**1 332**	**1 742**	**2 027**	**1 878**	**1 868**

3.8 Royalties and license fees

£ million

		1992	1993	1994	1995	1996	1997	1998	1999	2000	2001	2002
Exports												
Film and television	FJFO	303	546	716	744	879	705	775	868	934	982	943
Other royalties and license fees	FFVJ	2 085	2 360	2 752	3 110	3 374	3 443	3 495	4 224	4 455	4 691	4 833
Total	FJPM	**2 388**	**2 906**	**3 468**	**3 854**	**4 253**	**4 148**	**4 270**	**5 092**	**5 389**	**5 673**	**5 776**
Imports												
Film and television	FJFQ	393	535	616	763	829	863	882	932	1 020	1 176	1 207
Other royalties and license fees	FFVP	1 646	1 868	2 302	2 532	3 213	2 884	3 133	3 353	3 359	3 318	3 233
Total	FJRG	**2 039**	**2 403**	**2 918**	**3 295**	**4 042**	**3 747**	**4 015**	**4 285**	**4 379**	**4 494**	**4 440**
Balances												
Film and television	FFVV	−90	11	100	−19	50	−158	−107	−64	−86	−194	−264
Other royalties and license fees	FFWB	439	492	450	578	161	559	362	871	1 096	1 373	1 600
Total	FJTC	**349**	**503**	**550**	**559**	**211**	**401**	**255**	**807**	**1 010**	**1 179**	**1 336**

3.9 Other business services

£ million

		1992	1993	1994	1995	1996	1997	1998	1999	2000	2001	2002
Exports												
Merchanting and other trade related services												
Merchanting	FJFS	384	380	459	508	481	314	569	868	679	625	489
Other trade related services	FJFX	362	403	487	547	709	657	732	1 504	1 754	1 878	1 609
Total merchanting and other trade related services	FJPO	746	783	946	1 055	1 190	971	1 301	2 372	2 433	2 503	2 098
Operational leasing services	FJPP	79	94	97	121	129	113	40	92	299	244	187
Miscellaneous business, professional and technical services												
Legal, accounting and management consulting												
Law society	FJGE	496	495	528	537	565	675	824	760	1 171	1 339	1 292
Commercial bar association	FJCP	–	–	35	33	41	47	61	62	61	77	85
Other legal services[1]	FJGD	–	–	–	–	161	202	275	349	288	363	461
Accounting	FJBX	118	129	146	156	178	258	477	603	662	642	701
Business management and management consulting	FJNV	491	538	586	610	668	933	952	1 101	1 083	1 069	2 579
of which Recruitment and training	TVLQ	..	..	..	..	–	–	–	–	–	–	373
Advertising and market research	FJGP	489	536	596	633	717	1 022	1 174	1 150	1 432	1 622	1 796
Research and development	FJDP	659	734	890	986	1 311	1 616	2 300	2 801	2 421	2 930	2 870
Architectural, engineering and other technical services												
North Sea oil and gas	FJCV	382	356	497	358	331	–	–	–	–	–	–
Architectural	FJGT	42	47	51	52	51	83	67	82	76	153	71
Engineering	FJGU	1 330	1 461	1 689	1 843	2 243	2 491	2 987	2 676	2 441	3 239	3 070
Surveying	FJGV	34	37	36	37	37	31	41	45	68	66	64
Other Technical	FJGW	414	457	546	612	807	798	1 083	1 027	1 113	1 220	1 926
Agricultural, mining and on-site processing services	FJHC	13	15	18	21	26	21	52	47	54	41	31
Other miscellaneous business services	FJHH	2 635	2 656	2 901	3 351	4 516	4 715	5 698	6 021	7 221	7 138	7 107
Services between affiliated enterprises, n.i.e.	FJHF	319	364	466	501	682	871	981	1 101	1 280	1 481	1 566
Total miscellaneous business, professional, and technical services	FJPQ	7 422	7 825	8 985	9 730	12 334	13 763	16 972	17 825	19 371	21 380	23 619
Total	FJPN	8 247	8 702	10 028	10 906	13 653	14 847	18 313	20 289	22 103	24 127	25 904
Imports												
Merchanting and other trade related services												
Merchanting	FJHN	56	70	76	88	110	44	65	38	71	55	148
Other trade related services	FJHR	329	410	449	517	652	444	633	884	965	952	766
Total merchanting and other trade related services	FJRI	385	480	525	605	762	488	698	922	1 036	1 007	914
Operational leasing services	FJRJ	147	156	159	163	194	196	193	226	560	478	466
Miscellaneous business, professional and technical services												
Legal, accounting and management consulting												
Legal[1]	FJHX	24	24	24	24	173	209	249	307	490	380	488
Accounting	FJVJ	69	86	93	105	128	98	108	119	213	228	240
Business management and management consulting	FJNW	184	229	242	263	310	327	371	387	456	569	1 329
of which Recruitment and training	TVLV	..	..	..	..	–	–	–	–	–	–	258
Advertising and market research	FJID	305	379	406	443	493	460	581	719	789	841	825
Research and development	FJDQ	389	479	550	639	767	657	753	781	723	661	636
Architectural, engineering and other technical services												
North Sea oil and gas	FJDR	479	484	440	567	442	–	–	–	–	–	–
Architectural	FJIF	4	5	5	5	6	7	12	12	13	35	24
Engineering	FJIG	371	461	497	546	629	909	1 228	977	724	1 075	951
Surveying	FJIH	14	17	18	18	17	36	26	15	55	31	29
Other Technical	FJII	120	149	163	188	232	358	435	410	429	431	464
Agricultural, mining and on-site processing services	FJIN	4	5	5	6	7	7	27	50	71	142	76
Other miscellaneous business services	FJIP	1 195	1 492	1 854	1 954	2 502	2 406	3 017	4 108	4 639	5 301	4 931
Services between affiliated enterprises, n.i.e.	FJHG	206	256	285	329	406	457	719	770	808	1 069	1 120
Total miscellaneous business, professional and technical services	FJRK	3 364	4 066	4 582	5 087	6 112	5 931	7 526	8 655	9 410	10 763	11 113
Total	FJRH	3 896	4 702	5 266	5 855	7 068	6 615	8 417	9 803	11 006	12 248	12 493

1 Other legal services are indistinguishably included within other miscellaneous business services for years before 1996.

3.9 Other business services
continued

£ million

		1992	1993	1994	1995	1996	1997	1998	1999	2000	2001	2002
Balances												
Merchanting and other trade related services												
Merchanting	FJFT	328	310	383	420	371	270	504	830	608	570	341
Other trade related services	FJFY	33	−7	38	30	57	213	99	620	789	926	843
Total merchanting and other trade related services	FJTE	361	303	421	450	428	483	603	1 450	1 397	1 496	1 184
Operational leasing services	FJTF	−68	−62	−62	−42	−65	−83	−153	−134	−261	−234	−279
Miscellaneous business, professional and technical services												
Legal, accounting and management consulting												
Legal	FJGG	472	471	539	546	594	715	911	864	1 030	1 399	1 350
Accounting	FJGI	49	43	53	51	50	160	369	484	449	414	461
Business management and management consulting	FJGK	307	309	344	347	358	606	581	714	627	500	1 250
Advertising and market research	FJGQ	184	157	190	190	224	562	593	431	643	781	971
Research and development	FJGS	270	255	340	347	544	959	1 547	2 020	1 698	2 269	2 234
Architectural, engineering and other technical services	FJGY	1 214	1 242	1 696	1 578	2 143	2 093	2 477	2 416	2 477	3 106	3 663
Agricultural, mining and on-site processing services	FJHD	9	10	13	15	19	14	25	−3	−17	−101	−45
Services between affiliated enterprises, n.i.e.	FJHL	113	108	181	172	276	414	262	331	472	412	446
Other	FJHI	1 440	1 164	1 047	1 397	2 014	2 309	2 681	1 913	2 582	1 837	2 176
Total miscellaneous business, professional, and technical services	FJTG	4 058	3 759	4 403	4 643	6 222	7 832	9 446	9 170	9 961	10 617	12 506
Total	FJTD	**4 351**	**4 000**	**4 762**	**5 051**	**6 585**	**8 232**	**9 896**	**10 486**	**11 097**	**11 879**	**13 411**

3.10 Personal, cultural and recreational services

£ million

		1992	1993	1994	1995	1996	1997	1998	1999	2000	2001	2002
Exports												
Audiovisual and related services												
Film and television	FKJO	253	345	330	422	395	461	480	531	726	737	1 008
Other	FFWH	52	56	67	77	101	152	167	189	252	172	186
Total audiovisual and related services	FJPS	305	401	397	499	496	613	647	720	978	909	1 194
Other personal, cultural and recreational services	FJPT	119	148	174	191	278	207	234	244	327	449	400
Total	FJPR	**424**	**549**	**571**	**690**	**774**	**820**	**881**	**964**	**1 305**	**1 358**	**1 594**
Imports												
Audiovisual and related services												
Film and television	FKJX	134	211	305	400	441	450	411	496	532	512	650
Other	FFWN	13	16	18	20	25	22	35	40	55	46	38
Total audiovisual and related services	FJRM	147	227	323	420	466	472	446	536	587	558	688
Other personal, cultural and recreational services	FJRN	46	58	63	73	90	74	43	72	192	166	112
Total	FJRL	**193**	**285**	**386**	**493**	**556**	**546**	**489**	**608**	**779**	**724**	**800**
Balances												
Audiovisual and related services	FJTI	158	174	74	79	30	141	201	184	391	351	506
Other personal, cultural and recreational services	FJTJ	73	90	111	118	188	133	191	172	135	283	288
Total	FJTH	**231**	**264**	**185**	**197**	**218**	**274**	**392**	**356**	**526**	**634**	**794**

3.11 Government services

£ million

		1992	1993	1994	1995	1996	1997	1998	1999	2000	2001	2002
Exports												
Expenditure by foreign embassies and consulates in the UK	FJUK	365	368	348	367	393	357	371	385	385	389	393
Military units and agencies												
Expenditure by US forces in UK	FJKB	635	520	357	364	328	250	293	247	271	262	262
Other military receipts by UK government	HCOJ	44	196	139	108	91	56	40	29	32	48	67
Total military units and agencies	FJIX	679	716	496	472	419	306	333	276	303	310	329
Other												
EU institutions	FKIE	231	278	239	301	241	240	216	213	226	525	487
Other receipts	HCQO	199	179	222	283	224	189	212	191	267	298	369
Total other	FJJA	430	457	461	584	465	429	428	404	493	823	856
Total	FJPU	**1 474**	**1 541**	**1 305**	**1 423**	**1 277**	**1 092**	**1 132**	**1 065**	**1 181**	**1 522**	**1 578**
Imports												
Expenditure abroad by UK embassies and consulates	FJUJ	91	141	187	194	259	208	177	219	106	142	215
Expenditure abroad by UK military units and agencies	FJJD	1 807	1 624	1 809	1 632	2 030	1 418	1 116	1 972	1 584	1 629	1 494
Civil non-EU services	FJJF	166	133	129	172	196	235	216	205	200	202	188
Total	FJRO	**2 064**	**1 898**	**2 125**	**1 998**	**2 485**	**1 861**	**1 509**	**2 396**	**1 890**	**1 973**	**1 897**
Balances												
Embassies and consulates	FJIW	274	227	161	173	134	149	194	166	279	247	178
Military units and agencies	FJIY	−1 128	−908	−1 313	−1 160	−1 611	−1 112	−783	−1 696	−1 281	−1 319	−1 165
Other	FJJB	264	324	332	412	269	194	212	199	293	621	668
Total	FJUL	**−590**	**−357**	**−820**	**−575**	**−1 208**	**−769**	**−377**	**−1 331**	**−709**	**−451**	**−319**

Chapter 4

Income

Summary

The balance on compensation of employees' earnings and payments has been close to zero in the last ten years, with a small surplus recorded in all years since 1999. The balance on investment income has been in surplus for all years since 1994, following a deficit of £0.2 billion recorded in 1993. From 1999, the investment income surplus has grown strongly, reaching a record surplus of £21.1 billion in 2002. Earnings on direct investment abroad have increased 50 per cent since 1999, reaching a record £49.9 billion in 2002.

Over the last ten years, earnings on investments abroad and investments in the UK have generally increased year on year. In 2002 however, both fell sharply – credits down nearly 14 per cent and debits down almost 20 per cent. This was largely due to cuts in official interest rates, both abroad and in the UK, post September 11th (2001) and throughout 2002, and subsequent falls in interest receipts and payments on loans and deposits. Earnings and payments on other investment are now little changed from earnings recorded in the early 1990s. In contrast, earnings and payments on direct and portfolio investment have both increased strongly since the early 1990s.

In 2002, earnings on direct investment abroad were the largest component of income credits, accounting for 40 per cent of total earnings, compared to only 20 per cent in 1992. The boom in merger and acquisition activity in the late 1990s and in 2000 and subsequent growth in earnings from abroad has been the main driver for this change. Earnings on portfolio investment abroad account for 26 per cent of total earnings from abroad in 2002, compared to 19 per cent in 1992. Other investment income, which is mostly earnings from loans and deposits, now only accounts for 32 per cent of total earnings, down from 58 per cent in 1992. In contrast, the largest component of investment income debits remains other investment, accounting for almost half of all income paid.

An investment income surplus has been recorded in every year since 1994, with a surplus on direct investment every year since 1986. Within portfolio investment, a net surplus on interest receipts and payments on debt securities has largely been offset by net dividend payments on equity securities. Other investment has recorded a net deficit in every year since 1988, reaching £10.3 billion in 2002.

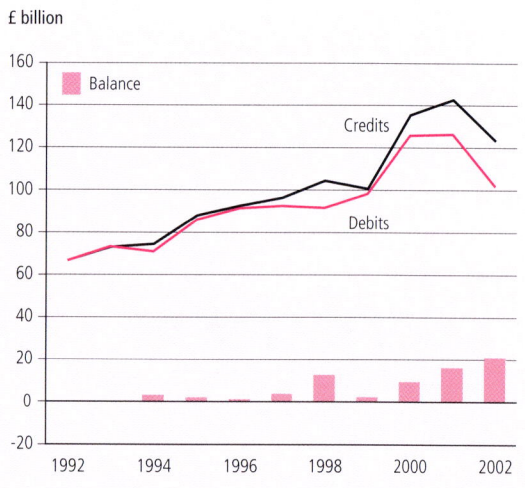

Figure 4.1

Income

£ billion

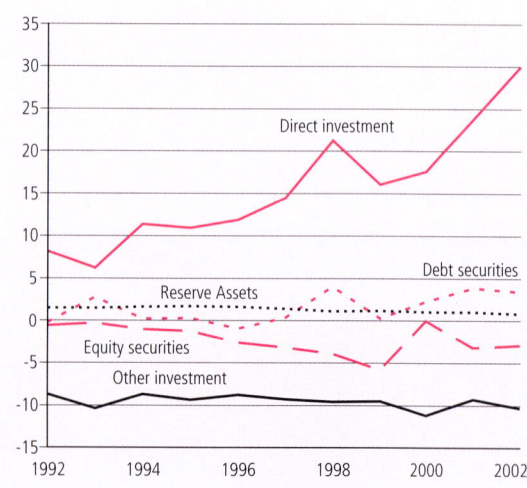

Figure 4.2

Investment income

Credits less debits

£ billion

By sector, the rise in the investment income surplus in the last few years has been largely due to increased net earnings of UK monetary financial institutions (banks and building societies), which have risen from £4.6 billion in 1999 to £14.2 billion in 2002. UK banks net earnings increased on all forms of investment between 1999 and 2002; the surplus on direct investment rose from £0.5 billion to £3.9 billion, the surplus on portfolio investment rose from £6.8 billion to £10.7 billion, and the other investment deficit narrowed from £2.7 billion to £0.4 billion.

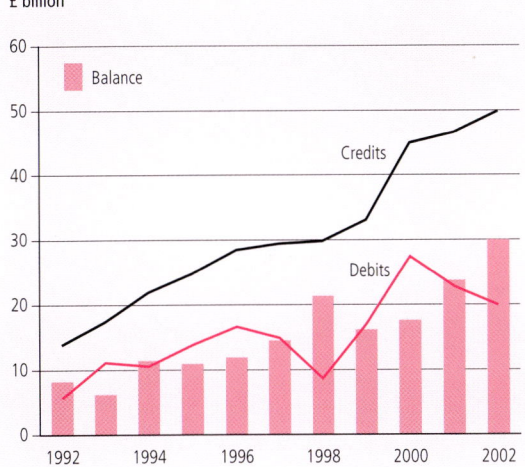

Figure **4.3**

Direct investment income

£ billion

Direct investment

Direct investment income credits have exceeded debits in every year since 1986, increasing to a record £30.0 billion in 2002. In 2002, earnings from direct investment abroad increased to a record £49.9 billion due to higher foreign earnings of UK banks and private non-financial corporations. In contrast, foreign earnings on direct investment in the UK fell for the second consecutive year, to £19.9 billion, mainly due to lower earnings of foreign-owned banks. Foreign banks mainly locate in the UK to be close to the financial markets in London and may have suffered during the difficult trading conditions in 2002. Similarly in 1998, both foreign owned banks and securities dealers recorded losses on their investments in the UK. This generally reflected the turbulent global financial market conditions – notably perturbations from Mexico (1994), South-East Asia (1997), and Russia and Brazil (1998).

Portfolio investment

The UK has generally recorded a deficit on portfolio investment, with a net surplus on debt securities being more than offset by a net deficit on equities. By instrument, the UK has paid out more dividends on equity securities abroad than have been received in all years since 1987. In contrast, the UK has recorded a surplus on debt securities in all but one of the last ten years, with a surplus on earnings from bonds and notes partly offset by a deficit on money market instruments.

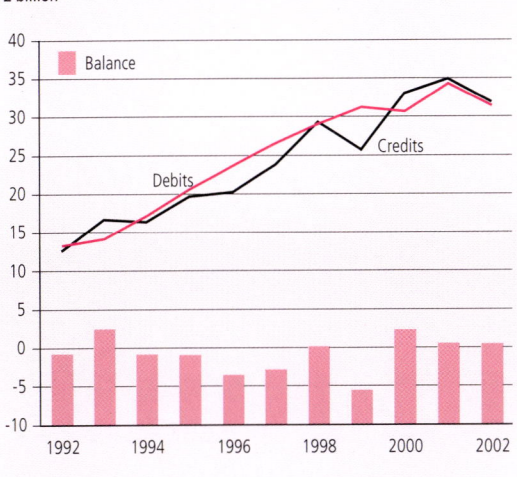

Figure **4.4**

Portfolio investment income

£ billion

A portfolio investment surplus has been recorded in all years since 2000, primarily due to higher UK earnings on portfolio investment abroad – in particular of UK banks and other financial intermediaries. UK monetary financial institutions mainly hold and issue debt (rather than equity) securities, and increased their earnings on debt securities from £13.1 billion in 1999 to £19.0 billion in 2001. In 2002, lower yields on debt securities led to falls in earnings on both debt security assets and liabilities.

By contrast, other financial intermediaries (securities dealers, unit and investment trusts) mainly hold equity rather than debt, which also showed strong earnings growth, from £2.9 billion in 1999 to £4.7 billion in 2000 and £5.1 billion in 2002.

On the debits side, foreign earnings from UK equity continued to rise, reaching a record £13.7 billion in 2002. In contrast, foreign earnings on UK debt securities fell sharply to £17.8 billion, with foreign earnings on money market instruments issued by UK banks down £2.9 billion from 2001 to £4.1 billion in 2002. Foreign earnings on British government stocks were broadly unchanged between 2001 and 2002.

Income | United Kingdom Balance of Payments The Pink Book 2003

Other investment

In 2002 the deficit on other investment widened to £10.3 billion, with a larger fall in interest earned on UK assets than paid out on UK liabilities. Unlike direct and portfolio investment, the earnings from other investment, both abroad and in the UK, were broadly unchanged during the 1990s, with falls in the rates of return on bank deposit and lending activity. In 2000 and 2001 a strong rise in investment in both inward and outward bank deposits led to a strong pick-up in other investment credits and debits. Credits increased from £39.8 billion in 1999 to £59.0 billion in 2001, while debits increased from £49.3 billion to £68.2 billion in the same period. In 2002, earnings on other investment assets and liabilities both fell sharply, primarily due to cuts in official interest rates.

Earnings on deposits and loans abroad by UK banks accounted for 80 per cent of total other investment credits in 2002. The vast majority of these earnings are made from foreign currency, reflecting the international nature of banking in the United Kingdom (as many of the banks trading with the rest of the world are actually branches or subsidiaries of foreign banks). There is a similar picture on the debits side where earnings on deposits with UK banks from abroad constituted around 65 per cent of the total other investment debits, with foreign currency deposits accounting for the vast majority.

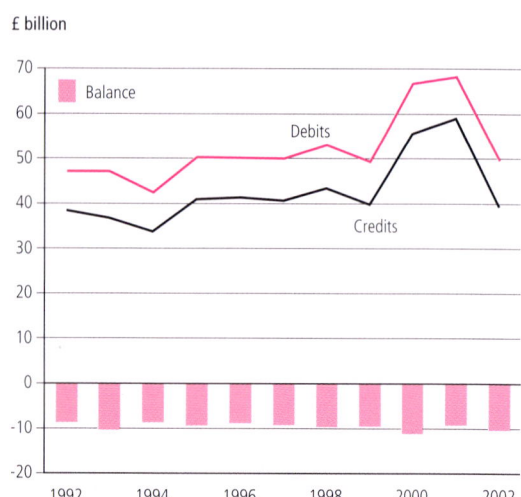

Figure 4.5

Other investment income

£ billion

Sectoral breakdown of investment income

UK banks are the single biggest investing sector in 2002, earning around 45 per cent of total UK investment income credits and paying out 40 per cent of debits. Banks have earned an investment income surplus in every year since 1997, reaching a record £14.2 billion in 2002. Prior to 1997, UK banks recorded a deficit on their international investment activity. By component, UK banks have recorded a growing surplus on their direct and portfolio investment activity and a narrowing deficit on loans and deposits activity. Banks have paid out more than they have received on loans and deposits in all years except 2001, when a small surplus was recorded. When considering the banking sector's overall contribution to the UK's balance of payments, it is important to also include bank's financial service fees and commissions earned from foreign clients – a net £2.3 billion in 2002.

Central government has recorded a net annual deficit of a little over £3 billion in recent years (mostly debits on Gilts), whilst other sectors – private non-financial and non-monetary financial institutions – have historically recorded net surpluses. In 2002, these other sectors recorded a record surplus of £9.4 billion, largely due to strong direct investment earnings from abroad by private non-financial corporations.

Figure 4.6

Investment income of banks
Credits less debits
£ billion

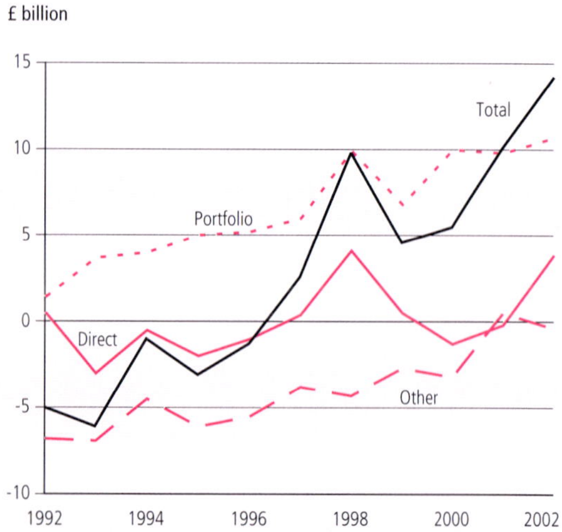

4.1 Income
Summary table

£ million

		1992	1993	1994	1995	1996	1997	1998	1999	2000	2001	2002
Credits												
Compensation of employees	KTMN	551	595	681	887	911	1 007	840	960	1 032	1 087	1 121
Investment income												
Earnings on direct investment abroad	HJYW	13 776	17 378	21 938	24 768	28 506	29 398	29 840	33 060	44 946	46 592	49 881
Earnings on portfolio investment abroad												
Earnings on equity securities	HCPL	3 070	4 110	3 895	4 451	4 768	5 449	6 061	7 773	9 872	9 996	10 741
Earnings on debt securities	HLYW	9 480	12 558	12 505	15 274	15 477	18 377	23 237	17 921	23 101	24 910	21 208
Total portfolio investment	HLYX	12 550	16 668	16 400	19 725	20 245	23 826	29 298	25 694	32 973	34 906	31 949
Earnings on other investment abroad	AIOP	38 371	36 762	33 787	40 953	41 319	40 741	43 397	39 814	55 532	58 979	39 304
Earnings on reserve assets	HHCB	1 456	1 525	1 577	1 686	1 551	1 372	1 132	1 161	985	961	820
Total investment income	HMBN	66 153	72 333	73 702	87 132	91 621	95 337	103 667	99 729	134 436	141 438	121 954
Total	HMBQ	**66 704**	**72 928**	**74 383**	**88 019**	**92 532**	**96 344**	**104 507**	**100 689**	**135 468**	**142 525**	**123 075**
Debits												
Compensation of employees	KTMO	600	560	851	1 183	818	924	850	759	882	1 021	1 054
Investment income												
Foreign earnings on direct investment in the UK	HJYX	5 599	11 150	10 571	13 819	16 630	14 916	8 585	16 968	27 390	22 792	19 892
Foreign earnings on portfolio investment in the UK												
Earnings on equity securities	ZMRB	3 621	4 441	4 895	5 612	7 359	8 601	9 930	13 542	9 899	13 243	13 661
Earnings on debt securities	HLZB	9 657	9 764	12 263	14 988	16 385	17 988	19 210	17 660	20 820	21 033	17 759
Total portfolio investment	HLZC	13 278	14 205	17 158	20 600	23 744	26 589	29 140	31 202	30 719	34 276	31 420
Earnings on other investment in the UK	HLZN	47 099	47 204	42 455	50 316	50 136	50 010	53 026	49 338	66 714	68 248	49 590
Total investment income	HMBO	65 976	72 559	70 184	84 735	90 510	91 515	90 751	97 508	124 823	125 316	100 902
Total	HMBR	**66 576**	**73 119**	**71 035**	**85 918**	**91 328**	**92 439**	**91 601**	**98 267**	**125 705**	**126 337**	**101 956**
Balances (Net earnings)												
Compensation of employees	KTMP	−49	35	−170	−296	93	83	−10	201	150	66	67
Investment income												
Direct investment	HJYE	8 177	6 228	11 367	10 949	11 876	14 482	21 255	16 092	17 556	23 800	29 989
Portfolio investment												
Earnings on equity securities	HLZO	−551	−331	−1 000	−1 161	−2 591	−3 152	−3 869	−5 769	−27	−3 247	−2 920
Earnings on debt securities	HLZP	−177	2 794	242	286	−908	389	4 027	261	2 281	3 877	3 449
Total portfolio investment	HLZX	−728	2 463	−758	−875	−3 499	−2 763	158	−5 508	2 254	630	529
Other investment	CGNA	−8 728	−10 442	−8 668	−9 363	−8 817	−9 269	−9 629	−9 524	−11 182	−9 269	−10 286
Reserve assets	HHCB	1 456	1 525	1 577	1 686	1 551	1 372	1 132	1 161	985	961	820
Total investment income	HMBM	177	−226	3 518	2 397	1 111	3 822	12 916	2 221	9 613	16 122	21 052
Total	HMBP	**128**	**−191**	**3 348**	**2 101**	**1 204**	**3 905**	**12 906**	**2 422**	**9 763**	**16 188**	**21 119**

4.2 Investment income
Sector analysis

£ million

		1992	1993	1994	1995	1996	1997	1998	1999	2000	2001	2002
Credits (Earnings of UK residents on investment abroad)												
Monetary financial institutions												
Banks	CGNB	38 171	37 753	36 989	45 949	48 587	49 302	56 215	50 304	69 368	72 358	54 827
Building societies	GJXE	–	20	63	81	119	103	134	176	292	339	337
Total monetary financial institutions	CGND	38 171	37 773	37 052	46 030	48 706	49 405	56 349	50 480	69 660	72 697	55 164
Central government	CGNY	1 459	1 531	1 585	1 695	1 561	1 380	1 267	1 165	989	965	823
Public corporations	CGNP	87	87	104	118	111	122	137	330	364	443	473
Other sectors	CGNW	26 436	32 942	34 961	39 289	41 243	44 430	45 914	47 754	63 423	67 333	65 494
Total	HMBN	**66 153**	**72 333**	**73 702**	**87 132**	**91 621**	**95 337**	**103 667**	**99 729**	**134 436**	**141 438**	**121 954**
Debits (Foreign earnings on investment in UK)												
Monetary financial institutions (banks and building societies)	CGPN	43 131	43 889	38 008	49 103	50 007	46 820	46 577	45 915	64 194	62 596	40 937
Central government	CGNZ	3 987	4 377	5 209	5 276	5 557	5 824	5 834	5 031	4 593	4 033	3 900
Local authorities	CGOB	54	53	45	38	30	21	16	12	7	4	2
Public corporations	CGOD	55	31	39	43	34	28	20	–	–	–	–
Other sectors	CGSE	18 749	24 209	26 883	30 275	34 882	38 822	38 304	46 550	56 029	58 683	56 063
Total	HMBO	**65 976**	**72 559**	**70 184**	**84 735**	**90 510**	**91 515**	**90 751**	**97 508**	**124 823**	**125 316**	**100 902**
Balances (Net earnings)												
Monetary financial institutions (banks and building societies)	CGSO	–4 960	–6 116	–956	–3 073	–1 301	2 585	9 772	4 565	5 466	10 101	14 227
Central government	CGOE	–2 528	–2 846	–3 624	–3 581	–3 996	–4 444	–4 567	–3 866	–3 604	–3 068	–3 077
Local authorities	-CGOB	–54	–53	–45	–38	–30	–21	–16	–12	–7	–4	–2
Public corporations	CGOF	32	56	65	75	77	94	117	330	364	443	473
Other sectors	CGTX	7 687	8 733	8 078	9 014	6 361	5 608	7 610	1 204	7 394	8 650	9 431
Total	HMBM	**177**	**–226**	**3 518**	**2 397**	**1 111**	**3 822**	**12 916**	**2 221**	**9 613**	**16 122**	**21 052**

4.3 Earnings on direct investment

£ million

		1992	1993	1994	1995	1996	1997	1998	1999	2000	2001	2002
Credits (Earnings of UK residents on direct investment abroad)												
Earnings on equity												
Dividends and distributed branch profits												
Dividends	CNZN	7 242	6 617	6 706	8 808	8 833	11 791	12 246	8 795	14 679	16 600	16 191
Distributed branch profits	HDNG	1 465	581	1 439	1 387	1 670	1 468	1 158	1 278	2 231	2 790	3 012
Total dividends and distributed branch profits	HMAE	8 707	7 198	8 145	10 195	10 503	13 259	13 404	10 073	16 910	19 390	19 203
Reinvested earnings	-HDNY	5 224	10 096	13 827	14 378	17 271	16 112	14 071	21 392	25 178	24 720	28 561
Earnings on property investment	HHBW	66	68	69	44	46	13	10	180	262	359	283
Total earnings on equity	HMAK	13 997	17 362	22 041	24 617	27 820	29 384	27 485	31 645	42 350	44 469	48 047
Earnings on debt [1]	HDNQ	−221	16	−103	151	686	14	2 355	1 415	2 596	2 123	1 834
Total	HJYW	**13 776**	**17 378**	**21 938**	**24 768**	**28 506**	**29 398**	**29 840**	**33 060**	**44 946**	**46 592**	**49 881**
Debits (Foreign earnings on direct investment in the UK)												
Earnings on equity												
Dividends and distributed branch profits												
Dividends	BCEA	3 738	3 498	4 949	5 131	5 895	6 146	6 945	8 198	9 472	10 061	7 391
Distributed branch profits	CYFD	−396	1 465	507	1 354	1 531	787	−2 534	323	2 713	2 285	−1 290
Total dividends and distributed branch profits	HMAH	3 342	4 963	5 456	6 485	7 426	6 933	4 411	8 521	12 185	12 346	6 101
Reinvested earnings	CYFV	121	4 385	3 953	5 254	7 873	6 386	1 522	4 607	10 788	4 912	8 583
Earnings on property investment	HESG	154	178	195	213	219	234	259	1 132	1 213	1 356	1 410
Total earnings on equity	HMAG	3 617	9 526	9 604	11 952	15 518	13 553	6 192	14 260	24 186	18 614	16 094
Earnings on debt [1]	CYFN	1 982	1 624	967	1 867	1 112	1 363	2 393	2 708	3 204	4 178	3 798
Total	HJYX	**5 599**	**11 150**	**10 571**	**13 819**	**16 630**	**14 916**	**8 585**	**16 968**	**27 390**	**22 792**	**19 892**
Balances (Net earnings)												
Earnings on equity												
Dividends and distributed branch profits												
Dividends	LTMA	3 504	3 119	1 757	3 677	2 938	5 645	5 301	597	5 207	6 539	8 800
Distributed branch profits	LTMB	1 861	−884	932	33	139	681	3 692	955	−482	505	4 302
Total dividends and distributed branch profits	HHZA	5 365	2 235	2 689	3 710	3 077	6 326	8 993	1 552	4 725	7 044	13 102
Reinvested earnings	LTMC	5 103	5 711	9 874	9 124	9 398	9 726	12 549	16 785	14 390	19 808	19 978
Earnings on property investment	LTMD	−88	−110	−126	−169	−173	−221	−249	−952	−951	−997	−1 127
Total earnings on equity	HHYY	10 380	7 836	12 437	12 665	12 302	15 831	21 293	17 385	18 164	25 855	31 953
Earnings on debt	HMAM	−2 203	−1 608	−1 070	−1 716	−426	−1 349	−38	−1 293	−608	−2 055	−1 964
Total	HJYE	**8 177**	**6 228**	**11 367**	**10 949**	**11 876**	**14 482**	**21 255**	**16 092**	**17 556**	**23 800**	**29 989**

1 Earnings on debt consists of interest accrued to/from direct investors from/to associated enterprises abroad.

4.4 Earnings on direct investment
Sector analysis

£ million

		1992	1993	1994	1995	1996	1997	1998	1999	2000	2001	2002
Credits (Earnings of UK residents on investment abroad)												
Monetary financial institutions (banks)	HCVU	370	21	789	137	1 409	1 407	1 682	2 613	3 639	4 596	5 067
Insurance companies	CNZD	576	1 045	592	1 608	1 270	1 600	793	1 488	930	829	732
Other financial intermediaries	HCWW	261	1 485	1 373	1 888	2 540	2 547	2 209	2 990	3 017	2 915	3 217
Private non-financial corporations	HCUS	12 553	14 808	19 166	21 109	23 266	23 823	25 136	25 944	37 335	38 226	40 836
Public corporations	HDMG	6	7	6	14	9	12	14	17	17	17	17
Household sector [1]	HHLI	10	12	12	12	12	9	6	8	8	9	12
Total	HJYW	**13 776**	**17 378**	**21 938**	**24 768**	**28 506**	**29 398**	**29 840**	**33 060**	**44 946**	**46 592**	**49 881**
Debits (Foreign earnings on direct investment in UK)												
Monetary financial institutions (banks)	GPAZ	−88	2 971	1 247	2 134	2 379	1 037	−2 433	2 109	4 979	4 802	1 145
Insurance companies	HDPK	−50	228	507	379	881	1 138	1 333	4	612	−770	4
Other financial intermediaries												
Securities dealers	HDQX	358	1 135	−791	269	799	375	−643	1 124	1 495	1 343	1 298
Other	HFBT	61	37	234	127	204	237	415	361	780	829	1 036
Total other financial intermediaries	HFCY	419	1 172	−557	396	1 003	612	−228	1 485	2 275	2 172	2 334
Private non-financial corporations	BCEB	5 318	6 779	9 374	10 910	12 367	12 129	9 913	13 370	19 524	16 588	16 409
Total	HJYX	**5 599**	**11 150**	**10 571**	**13 819**	**16 630**	**14 916**	**8 585**	**16 968**	**27 390**	**22 792**	**19 892**
Balances (Net earnings)												
Monetary financial institutions (banks)	LTME	458	−2 950	−458	−1 997	−970	370	4 115	504	−1 340	−206	3 922
Insurance companies	LTMF	626	817	85	1 229	389	462	−540	1 484	318	1 599	728
Other financial intermediaries	LTMG	−158	313	1 930	1 492	1 537	1 935	2 437	1 505	742	743	883
Private non-financial corporations	LTMH	7 235	8 029	9 792	10 199	10 899	11 694	15 223	12 574	17 811	21 638	24 427
Public corporations	HDMG	6	7	6	14	9	12	14	17	17	17	17
Households	HHLI	10	12	12	12	12	9	6	8	8	9	12
Total	HJYE	**8 177**	**6 228**	**11 367**	**10 949**	**11 876**	**14 482**	**21 255**	**16 092**	**17 556**	**23 800**	**29 989**

1 The household sector includes non-profit institutions serving households.

4.5 Earnings on portfolio investment

£ million

		1992	1993	1994	1995	1996	1997	1998	1999	2000	2001	2002
Credits												
(Earnings of UK residents on portfolio investment abroad)												
Earnings on equity securities (shares) by:												
Monetary financial Institutions (banks)	HHRX	82	171	250	298	414	411	521	609	865	1 261	1 473
Insurance companies and pension funds												
Insurance companies	CGOM	948	1 288	1 146	1 494	1 490	1 511	1 715	1 939	2 237	2 311	2 250
Pension funds	HPDL	1 218	1 408	1 451	1 538	1 544	1 388	2 023	2 132	1 861	1 541	1 605
Total insurance companies and pension funds	CGOX	2 166	2 696	2 597	3 032	3 034	2 899	3 738	4 071	4 098	3 852	3 855
Other financial intermediaries	CGOY	710	1 128	952	990	1 173	1 952	1 610	2 914	4 677	4 576	5 094
Private non-financial corporations	EGMS	4	6	4	6	5	8	9	10	41	122	127
Household sector[1]	HEOG	108	109	92	125	142	179	183	169	191	185	192
Total earnings on equity securities	HCPL	3 070	4 110	3 895	4 451	4 768	5 449	6 061	7 773	9 872	9 996	10 741
Earnings on debt securities												
Earnings on bonds and notes by:												
Monetary financial institutions												
Banks	HHRY	4 188	6 038	6 896	9 429	10 283	11 934	13 369	11 153	15 538	16 066	15 259
Building societies	GJXE	–	20	63	81	119	103	134	176	292	339	337
Total monetary financial institutions	HPCQ	4 188	6 058	6 959	9 510	10 402	12 037	13 503	11 329	15 830	16 405	15 596
Insurance companies and pension funds												
Insurance companies	CGON	590	650	565	733	718	770	1 122	1 075	1 121	1 348	1 306
Pension funds	HPDM	312	300	276	315	361	317	415	509	517	567	614
Total insurance companies and pension funds	CGOZ	902	950	841	1 048	1 079	1 087	1 537	1 584	1 638	1 915	1 920
Other financial intermediaries	CGPA	2 703	3 808	3 059	2 259	2 679	3 759	3 759	2 807	2 762	3 365	1 753
Private non-financial corporations	EGNF	108	142	157	168	156	218	61	54	43	111	110
Household sector[1]	HEOH	929	954	788	1 431	396	336	312	266	286	262	238
Total earnings on bonds and notes	HCPK	8 830	11 912	11 804	14 416	14 712	17 437	19 172	16 040	20 559	22 058	19 617
Earnings on money market instruments by:												
Monetary financial institutions (banks)	HBMX	514	494	524	659	543	700	3 933	1 734	2 292	2 570	1 232
Central government	LSPA	–	–	–	–	–	–	–	–	–	18	26
Other financial intermediaries	NHQV	53	93	91	74	70	113	49	73	131	118	125
Private non-financial corporations	HGBX	83	59	86	125	152	127	83	74	119	146	208
Total earnings on money market instruments	HCHG	650	646	701	858	765	940	4 065	1 881	2 542	2 852	1 591
Total earnings on debt securities	HLYW	9 480	12 558	12 505	15 274	15 477	18 377	23 237	17 921	23 101	24 910	21 208
Total	HLYX	12 550	16 668	16 400	19 725	20 245	23 826	29 298	25 694	32 973	34 906	31 949

1 The household sector includes non-profit institutions serving households.

4.5 Earnings on portfolio investment
continued

£ million

		1992	1993	1994	1995	1996	1997	1998	1999	2000	2001	2002
Debits (Foreign earnings on portfolio investment in the UK)												
Earnings on equity securities (shares) issued by:												
Monetary financial institutions (banks and building societies)	HBQJ	216	252	284	336	441	516	305	296	115	131	106
Other sectors[1]	HBQK	3 405	4 189	4 611	5 276	6 918	8 085	9 625	13 246	9 784	13 112	13 555
Total foreign earnings on UK equity securities	ZMRB	3 621	4 441	4 895	5 612	7 359	8 601	9 930	13 542	9 899	13 243	13 661
Earnings on debt securities												
Earnings on bonds and notes												
Issues by central government												
UK foreign currency bonds and notes	ZMRA	190	583	672	866	817	667	339	311	339	265	128
Earnings on British government stocks by:												
Foreign central banks (exchange reserves)	HESK	1 244	1 139	1 393	1 389	1 339	1 244	1 393	1 244	1 318	1 168	1 292
Other foreign residents	HCEV	1 940	2 383	2 997	2 836	3 232	3 797	4 014	3 417	2 918	2 509	2 402
Total foreign earnings on British government stocks	HENI	3 184	3 522	4 390	4 225	4 571	5 041	5 407	4 661	4 236	3 677	3 694
Total issues by central government	HBQU	3 374	4 105	5 062	5 091	5 388	5 708	5 746	4 972	4 575	3 942	3 822
Local authorities' bonds	HHGH	–	–	–	–	–	–	–	–	–	–	–
Public corporations' bonds	HESY	–	–	–	–	–	–	–	–	–	–	–
Issues by monetary financial institutions (banks and building societies)												
Bonds	HGUV	792	810	1 046	1 304	1 448	1 583	1 540	1 620	1 976	1 895	1 898
European medium term notes and other short-term paper:												
Issued by UK banks	HCEY	297	371	511	745	897	1 025	1 071	1 035	1 138	1 350	1 418
Issued by UK building societies	HCFB	180	159	198	290	234	163	80	54	109	100	86
Total short-term paper	HGMM	477	530	709	1 035	1 131	1 188	1 151	1 089	1 247	1 450	1 504
Total issues by monetary financial institutions	HBOT	1 269	1 340	1 755	2 339	2 579	2 771	2 691	2 709	3 223	3 345	3 402
Issues by other sectors[1]	HGUW	2 466	2 519	3 256	4 057	4 506	4 925	4 793	5 042	6 151	5 898	5 907
Total foreign earnings on UK bonds and notes	HLZA	7 109	7 964	10 073	11 487	12 473	13 404	13 230	12 723	13 949	13 185	13 131
Earnings on money market instruments												
Earnings on treasury bills (issued by central government)												
Sterling treasury bills	XAMR	168	37	26	55	64	31	54	43	4	14	7
Euro treasury bills	HHNV	198	137	95	106	85	67	18	3	–	–	–
Total earnings on treasury bills	HHZU	366	174	121	161	149	98	72	46	4	14	7
Earnings on certificates of deposit (Issued by monetary financial institutions)												
Issued by UK banks	HCEB	1 703	1 221	1 422	2 335	2 612	3 199	4 126	3 163	4 660	6 055	3 449
Issued by UK building societies	HGUY	44	22	37	47	37	26	19	21	35	20	17
Total earnings on certificates of deposit	HCEE	1 747	1 243	1 459	2 382	2 649	3 225	4 145	3 184	4 695	6 075	3 466
Earnings on commercial paper												
Issued by monetary financial institutions												
Issued by UK banks	HCEC	38	51	98	177	275	447	854	621	761	814	561
Issued by UK building societies	HHBC	160	104	119	206	205	140	51	100	161	110	36
Total earnings on mfi issued commercial paper	HCEF	198	155	217	383	480	587	905	721	922	924	597
Issued by other sectors[1]	HHZT	237	228	393	575	634	674	858	986	1 250	835	558
Total earnings on commercial paper	HHBO	435	383	610	958	1 114	1 261	1 763	1 707	2 172	1 759	1 155
Total foreign earnings on UK Money Market Instruments	HLYZ	2 548	1 800	2 190	3 501	3 912	4 584	5 980	4 937	6 871	7 848	4 628
Total foreign earnings on UK debt securities	HLZB	9 657	9 764	12 263	14 988	16 385	17 988	19 210	17 660	20 820	21 033	17 759
Total	HLZC	**13 278**	**14 205**	**17 158**	**20 600**	**23 744**	**26 589**	**29 140**	**31 202**	**30 719**	**34 276**	**31 420**

1 These series relate to non-governmental sectors other than monetary financial institutions.

4.5 Earnings on portfolio investment
continued
£ million

		1992	1993	1994	1995	1996	1997	1998	1999	2000	2001	2002
Balances (net earnings)												
Earnings on equity securities (shares)	HLZO	−551	−331	−1 000	−1 161	−2 591	−3 152	−3 869	−5 769	−27	−3 247	−2 920
Earnings on debt securities												
Earnings on bonds and notes	HLZQ	1 721	3 948	1 731	2 929	2 239	4 033	5 942	3 317	6 610	8 873	6 486
Earnings on money market instruments	HLZR	−1 898	−1 154	−1 489	−2 643	−3 147	−3 644	−1 915	−3 056	−4 329	−4 996	−3 037
Total foreign earnings on UK debt securities	HLZP	−177	2 794	242	286	−908	389	4 027	261	2 281	3 877	3 449
Total	HLZX	**−728**	**2 463**	**−758**	**−875**	**−3 499**	**−2 763**	**158**	**−5 508**	**2 254**	**630**	**529**

1 These series relate to non-governmental sectors other than monetary financial institutions.

4.6 Earnings on portfolio investment
Sector analysis

£ million

		1992	1993	1994	1995	1996	1997	1998	1999	2000	2001	2002
Credits (Earnings of UK residents on portfolio investment abroad)												
Earnings from portfolio investment abroad by UK: Monetary financial institutions												
Banks	AINB	4 784	6 703	7 670	10 386	11 240	13 045	17 823	13 496	18 695	19 897	17 964
Building societies	GJXE	–	20	63	81	119	103	134	176	292	339	337
Total monetary financial institutions	AIND	4 784	6 723	7 733	10 467	11 359	13 148	17 957	13 672	18 987	20 236	18 301
Central government	LSPA	–	–	–	–	–	–	–	–	–	18	26
Insurance companies and pension funds	AINE	3 068	3 646	3 438	4 080	4 113	3 986	5 275	5 655	5 736	5 767	5 775
Other financial intermediaries	AINF	3 466	5 029	4 102	3 323	3 922	5 824	5 418	5 794	7 570	8 059	6 972
Private non-financial corporations	AINI	195	207	247	299	313	353	153	138	203	379	445
Household sector[1]	AINK	1 037	1 063	880	1 556	538	515	495	435	477	447	430
Total	HLYX	**12 550**	**16 668**	**16 400**	**19 725**	**20 245**	**23 826**	**29 298**	**25 694**	**32 973**	**34 906**	**31 949**
Debits (Foreign earnings on portfolio investment in the UK)												
Foreign earnings from portfolio investment in UK:												
Monetary financial institutions (banks and building societies)	HBXI	3 430	2 990	3 715	5 440	6 149	7 099	8 046	6 910	8 955	10 475	7 571
Central government	HBXM	3 740	4 279	5 183	5 252	5 537	5 806	5 818	5 018	4 579	3 956	3 829
Local authorities	HHGH	–	–	–	–	–	–	–	–	–	–	–
Public corporations	HESY	–	–	–	–	–	–	–	–	–	–	–
Other sectors	HBXR	6 108	6 936	8 260	9 908	12 058	13 684	15 276	19 274	17 185	19 845	20 020
Total	HLZC	**13 278**	**14 205**	**17 158**	**20 600**	**23 744**	**26 589**	**29 140**	**31 202**	**30 719**	**34 276**	**31 420**
Balances (Net earnings)												
Monetary financial institutions	LTMI	1 354	3 733	4 018	5 027	5 210	6 049	9 911	6 762	10 032	9 761	10 730
Central government	ZPOF	–3 740	–4 279	–5 183	–5 252	–5 537	–5 806	–5 818	–5 018	–4 579	–3 938	–3 803
Local authorities	-HHGH	–	–	–	–	–	–	–	–	–	–	–
Public corporations	-HESY	–	–	–	–	–	–	–	–	–	–	–
Other sectors	LTMJ	1 658	3 009	407	–650	–3 172	–3 006	–3 935	–7 252	–3 199	–5 193	–6 398
Total	HLZX	**–728**	**2 463**	**–758**	**–875**	**–3 499**	**–2 763**	**158**	**–5 508**	**2 254**	**630**	**529**

1 The household sector includes non-profit institutions serving households.

4.7 Earnings on other investment

£ million

		1992	1993	1994	1995	1996	1997	1998	1999	2000	2001	2002
Credits (Earnings of UK residents on other investment abroad)												
Earnings on trade credit												
Central government	XBGJ	–	–	–	–	–	–	–	–	–	–	–
Other sectors[1]	HGQD	175	122	117	146	138	157	177	–	–	–	–
Total earnings on trade credit	AIOM	175	122	117	146	138	157	177	–	–	–	–
Earnings on loans												
Long-term												
Bank loans under ECGD guarantee	AINM	1 032	745	680	786	708	721	664	594	507	378	235
Inter-government loans by the UK	XBGI	3	6	8	9	10	8	9	4	4	4	3
Loans by Commonwealth Development Corporation (public corporations)	HGEN	81	80	98	104	102	110	123	115	101	100	100
Loans by the Export Credit Guarantee Department	HMNS	..	..	..	..	–	–	–	198	246	326	356
Loans by specialist leasing companies[1]	HBXC	–	–	–	–	–	–	–	–	–	–	–
Total long-term loans	AIOO	1 116	831	786	899	820	839	796	911	858	808	694
Short-term loans	VTUN	179	146	100	81	66	68	54	37	36	36	36
Total earnings on loans	CGKJ	1 295	977	886	980	886	907	850	948	894	844	730
Earnings on deposits												
By UK monetary financial institutions (banks)												
Sterling deposits	CGEJ	4 019	3 459	2 803	3 598	3 995	5 518	6 838	6 341	7 532	7 082	5 418
Foreign currency deposits	HCAT	27 858	26 747	25 022	31 032	31 231	28 606	29 205	27 260	38 995	40 405	26 143
Total deposits by UK banks	CGGT	31 877	30 206	27 825	34 630	35 226	34 124	36 043	33 601	46 527	47 487	31 561
Deposits by securities dealers	HGTD	528	1 785	1 543	1 104	1 272	1 080	789	854	1 376	2 908	1 957
Deposits by other UK residents[1]	CGJK	4 303	3 448	3 155	3 801	3 482	4 135	5 060	4 023	6 187	7 251	4 731
Total earnings on deposits abroad	CGJQ	36 708	35 439	32 523	39 535	39 980	39 339	41 892	38 478	54 090	57 646	38 249
Earnings on other assets (Non-governmental sectors other than monetary financial institutions)												
Trusts and annuities	HHLF	193	224	261	292	315	338	352	388	548	489	325
Foreign currency exchanges	HHKX	–	–	–	–	–	–	–	–	–	–	–
Miscellaneous central government receipts	HPPK	–	–	–	–	–	–	126	–	–	–	–
Total earnings on other assets	CGKM	193	224	261	292	315	338	478	388	548	489	325
Total	AIOP	38 371	36 762	33 787	40 953	41 319	40 741	43 397	39 814	55 532	58 979	39 304

1 These series relate to non-governmental sectors other than monetary financial institutions.

4.7 Earnings on other investment
continued

£ million

		1992	1993	1994	1995	1996	1997	1998	1999	2000	2001	2002
Debits (Foreign earnings on other investment in the UK)												
Earnings on trade credit												
Public corporations	XBGW	–	–	–	–	–	–	–	–	–	–	–
Other sectors [1]	HHLW	94	172	158	150	152	143	140	–	–	–	–
Total earnings on trade credit	CGMA	94	172	158	150	152	143	140	–	–	–	–
Earnings on loans												
Loans to:												
Central government	CGLF	247	98	26	24	20	18	16	13	14	77	71
Local authorities	CGLG	54	53	45	38	30	21	16	12	7	4	2
Public corporations	CGLH	55	31	39	43	34	28	20	–	–	–	–
Securities dealers	CGLI	2 676	5 124	4 377	3 273	3 354	5 293	5 120	4 762	7 502	9 525	7 008
Other[1]	CGMD	3 482	3 218	4 126	4 464	4 352	4 981	5 565	6 375	7 903	10 023	9 032
Total earnings on loans	CGNO	6 514	8 524	8 613	7 842	7 790	10 341	10 737	11 162	15 426	19 629	16 113
Earnings on deposits (Monetary financial institutions)												
Deposits with UK banks												
Sterling deposits	HCEG	8 005	5 444	4 225	5 787	6 118	6 492	8 044	7 132	8 958	8 361	6 807
Foreign currency deposits	HCEH	31 338	32 140	28 437	35 260	34 931	31 837	32 653	29 540	40 992	38 729	25 230
Total deposits with UK banks	HCEQ	39 343	37 584	32 662	41 047	41 049	38 329	40 697	36 672	49 950	47 090	32 037
Deposits with UK building societies	HHLS	446	344	384	482	430	355	267	224	310	229	184
Total earnings on deposits	HMAS	39 789	37 928	33 046	41 529	41 479	38 684	40 964	36 896	50 260	47 319	32 221
Earnings on other liabilities (Non-governmental sectors other than monetary financial institutions)												
Imputed income to foreign households from UK insurance companies technical reserves	HBWS	702	580	638	795	715	842	1 185	1 280	1 028	1 300	1 256
Other liabilities	CGME	–	–	–	–	–	–	–	–	–	–	–
Total earnings on other liabilities	CGMH	702	580	638	795	715	842	1 185	1 280	1 028	1 300	1 256
Total	HLZN	**47 099**	**47 204**	**42 455**	**50 316**	**50 136**	**50 010**	**53 026**	**49 338**	**66 714**	**68 248**	**49 590**
Balances (Net earnings)												
Trade credit	LTMK	81	−50	−41	−4	−14	14	37	–	–	–	–
Loans	LTML	−5 219	−7 547	−7 727	−6 862	−6 904	−9 434	−9 887	−10 214	−14 532	−18 785	−15 383
Currency and deposits	LTMM	−3 081	−2 489	−523	−1 994	−1 499	655	928	1 582	3 830	10 327	6 028
Other investment	LTMN	−509	−356	−377	−503	−400	−504	−707	−892	−480	−811	−931
Total	CGNA	**−8 728**	**−10 442**	**−8 668**	**−9 363**	**−8 817**	**−9 269**	**−9 629**	**−9 524**	**−11 182**	**−9 269**	**−10 286**

1 These series relate to non-governmental sectors other than monetary financial institutions.

4.8 Earnings on other investment
Sector analysis

£ million

		1992	1993	1994	1995	1996	1997	1998	1999	2000	2001	2002
Credits (Earnings of UK residents on other investment abroad)												
Earnings from other investment by UK:													
Monetary financial institutions (banks)	CGMM	33 017	31 029	28 530	35 426	35 938	34 850	36 710	34 195	47 034	47 865	31 796
Central government	CGMN	3	6	8	9	10	8	135	4	4	4	3
Public corporations	ZPOP	81	80	98	104	102	110	123	313	347	426	456
Other sectors	CGMR	5 270	5 647	5 151	5 414	5 269	5 773	6 429	5 302	8 147	10 684	7 049
Total	AIOP	**38 371**	**36 762**	**33 787**	**40 953**	**41 319**	**40 741**	**43 397**	**39 814**	**55 532**	**58 979**	**39 304**
Debits (Foreign earnings on other investment in the UK)												
Foreign earnings from other investment in UK:												
Monetary financial institutions												
Banks	HCEQ	39 343	37 584	32 662	41 047	41 049	38 329	40 697	36 672	49 950	47 090	32 037
Building societies	HHLS	446	344	384	482	430	355	267	224	310	229	184
Total monetary financial institutions	HMAS	39 789	37 928	33 046	41 529	41 479	38 684	40 964	36 896	50 260	47 319	32 221
Central government	CGLF	247	98	26	24	20	18	16	13	14	77	71
Local authorities	CGLG	54	53	45	38	30	21	16	12	7	4	2
Public corporations	CGMV	55	31	39	43	34	28	20	–	–	–	–
Other sectors	CGMZ	6 954	9 094	9 299	8 682	8 573	11 259	12 010	12 417	16 433	20 848	17 296
Total	HLZN	**47 099**	**47 204**	**42 455**	**50 316**	**50 136**	**50 010**	**53 026**	**49 338**	**66 714**	**68 248**	**49 590**
Balances (Net earnings)												
Monetary financial institutions	LTMO	–6 772	–6 899	–4 516	–6 103	–5 541	–3 834	–4 254	–2 701	–3 226	546	–425
Central government	LTMP	–244	–92	–18	–15	–10	–10	119	–9	–10	–73	–68
Local authorities	-CGLG	–54	–53	–45	–38	–30	–21	–16	–12	–7	–4	–2
Public corporations	LTMQ	26	49	59	61	68	82	103	313	347	426	456
Other sectors	LTMR	–1 684	–3 447	–4 148	–3 268	–3 304	–5 486	–5 581	–7 115	–8 286	–10 164	–10 247
Total	CGNA	**–8 728**	**–10 442**	**–8 668**	**–9 363**	**–8 817**	**–9 269**	**–9 629**	**–9 524**	**–11 182**	**–9 269**	**–10 286**

Chapter 5

Current transfers

Summary

The current transfers deficit generally increased through the 1990s, from £1.2 billion in 1991 to a record £9.8 billion in 2000. This was due to an increase in the UK's payments to EU Institutions. After falling to £6.6 billion in 2001, the deficit increased to £8.8 billion in 2002.

The balance on the government sector decreased sharply over the year to 2002, from -£2.6 billion in 2001 to -£5.8 billion. Over the same period, the balance for other sectors transfers improved from -£4.0 billion to -£3.0 billion. Overall receipts from EU Institutions fell by £1.1 billion to £6.3 billion in 2002, while payments increased slightly (from £9.6 billion in 2001 to £10.1 billion in 2002).

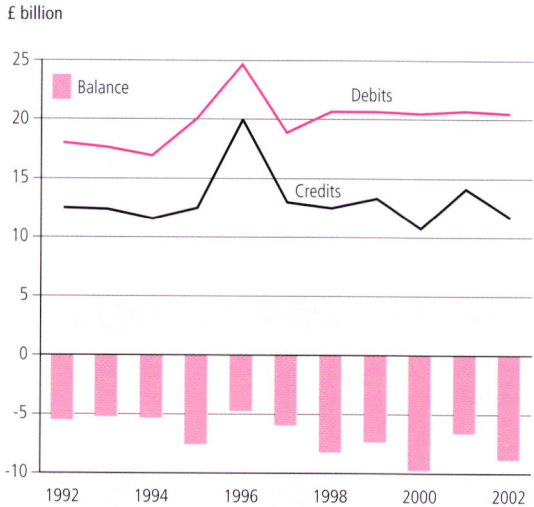

Figure 5.1

Current transfers

£ billion

Central government transfers

Central government transfers include: taxes and social contributions received from non-resident workers and businesses; current transfers with international organisations (e.g. EU Institutions); bilateral aid; social security payments abroad; military grants; and miscellaneous (e.g. Gulf conflict) transfers. For credits, VAT abatement from the EU Institutions decreased by £1.5 billion between 2001 and 2002, to £3.1 billion. For debits, GNP Fourth Resource contributions to EU Institutions increased by £1.4 billion between 2001 and 2002, to £5.3 billion.

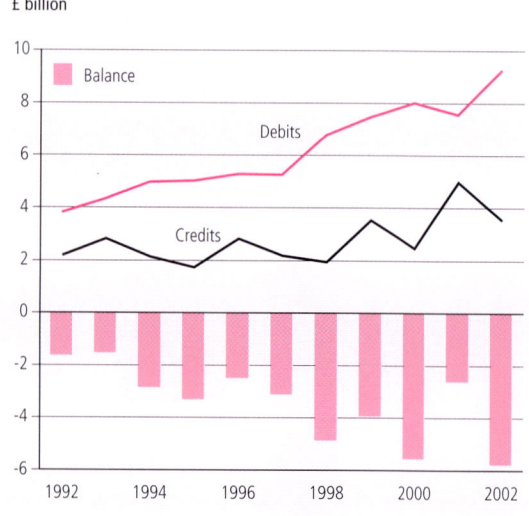

Figure 5.2

Transfers by central government

£ billion

Figure 5.3

Transfers by other sectors

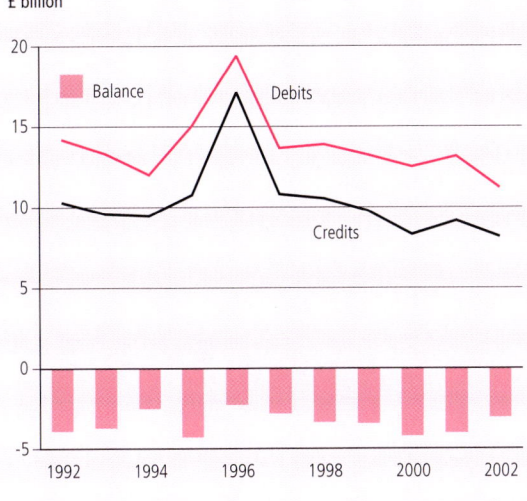

Other sector transfers

Non-government transfers include those EU transfers where the UK government simply acts as the agent for the final beneficiary (e.g. social fund and agricultural guidance fund receipts) or original payer (e.g. VAT based contributions). Other sectors transfers also include: taxes on income and wealth paid by UK workers and outward direct investors to foreign governments; insurance premiums and claims; and other transfers (workers remittances and other private transfers such as gifts). The deficit on other sectors transfers was £3.0 billion in 2002, an improvement from £4.0 billion in 2001.

Figure 5.4

Transfers with EU institutions

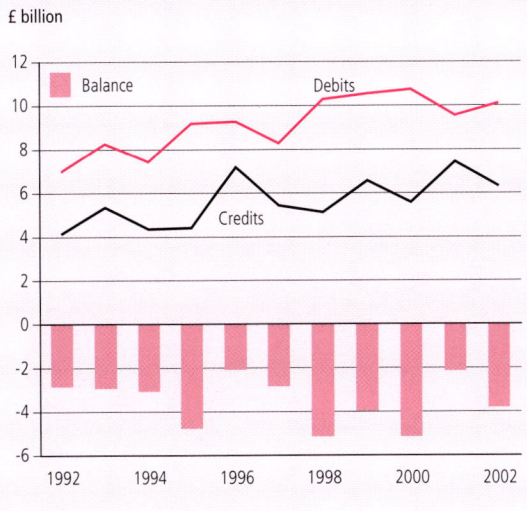

EU Institutions

Transfers with EU institutions constitute the largest single component within current transfers. Transfers with EU institutions showed a deficit in every year from 1991 to 2002; the lowest deficit recorded over this period was £1.2 billion in 1991 and the highest deficit was £5.2 billion in 1998. The deficit with EU institutions increased by £1.7 billion between 2001 and 2002, to £3.8 billion.

5.1 Current transfers

£ million

		1992	1993	1994	1995	1996	1997	1998	1999	2000	2001	2002
Credits												
Central government												
Current taxes on income, wealth etc.	FJKI	259	238	361	472	376	402	530	337	357	398	399
Other taxes on production	FJKH	–	–	–	–	–	–	–	–	–	–	–
Other subsidies on production	FJBC	–	–	–	–	–	–	–	–	–	–	–
Social contributions	FJBH	14	30	25	25	28	32	29	29	24	25	33
Social benefits	FJBL	–	–	–	–	–	–	–	–	–	–	–
EU Institutions:												
(a) Abatement	FKKL	1 881	2 540	1 726	1 208	2 411	1 733	1 377	3 171	2 084	4 560	3 099
(b) Other EU receipts	FKIJ	17	18	26	25	13	6	7	5	–	8	13
Miscellaneous receipts[1]	FKIK	9	–	–	–	–	–	–	–	–	–	–
Total central government	FJUM	2 180	2 826	2 138	1 730	2 828	2 173	1 943	3 542	2 465	4 991	3 544
Other sectors												
Current taxes on income, wealth etc.	FJBJ	–	–	–	–	–	–	–	–	–	–	–
Other taxes on production	FJGC	–	–	–	–	–	–	–	–	–	–	–
Other subsidies on production	FJBA	–	–	–	–	–	–	–	–	–	–	–
Social contributions	FJAB	–	–	–	–	–	–	–	–	–	–	–
EU Institutions:												
(a) Agricultural Guarantee Fund	EBGL	1 742	2 153	2 245	2 392	3 931	3 063	2 935	2 931	2 831	2 484	2 778
(b) Social Fund	HDIZ	437	588	320	755	804	615	783	434	659	370	412
(c) ECSC Grant	FJKP	61	37	45	39	29	5	1	–	–	1	–
Net non-life insurance premiums[2]	NQQP	5 900	4 246	4 145	4 993	9 763	4 423	4 168	3 663	2 144	3 584	2 252
Non-life insurance claims[3]	FJFA	–	–	–	–	5	5	7	10	18	25	19
Other receipts of households[4]	FKIL	2 155	2 541	2 699	2 572	2 589	2 712	2 633	2 730	2 653	2 689	2 698
Total other sectors	FJUN	10 295	9 565	9 454	10 751	17 121	10 823	10 527	9 768	8 305	9 153	8 159
Total	KTND	**12 475**	**12 391**	**11 592**	**12 481**	**19 949**	**12 996**	**12 470**	**13 310**	**10 770**	**14 144**	**11 703**
Of which: Receipts from EU institutions	FKIM	4 138	5 336	4 362	4 419	7 188	5 422	5 103	6 541	5 574	7 423	6 302

1 Includes contributions by other countries towards the UK's cost of the Gulf conflict.
2 Premiums paid to UK insurance companies.
3 Claims paid to UK residents by foreign insurance companies.
4 Includes estimates for workers' remittances and for non-profit institutions serving households.

5.1 Current transfers
continued

£ million

		1992	1993	1994	1995	1996	1997	1998	1999	2000	2001	2002
Debits												
Central government												
Current taxes on income, wealth etc.	FJKK	–	–	–	–	–	–	–	–	–	–	–
Other taxes on production	FJKN	–	–	–	–	–	–	–	–	–	–	–
Other subsidies on production	FJCE	–	–	–	–	–	–	–	–	–	–	–
Social contributions	FJCH	–	–	–	–	–	–	–	–	–	–	–
Social security benefits	FJCK	661	824	899	972	1 029	1 102	1 162	1 183	1 218	1 292	1 388
Contributions to international organisations												
EU Institutions:												
(a) GNP: 4th Resource	HCSO	934	1 608	2 340	1 639	2 488	2 655	3 516	4 403	4 243	3 859	5 259
(b) GNP adjustments	HCSM	–20	–50	–269	187	–34	–197	404	229	136	–1	76
(c) Inter governmental agreements	HCBW	–	–	–	–	–	–	–	–	–	–	–
(d) Other	FKIN	–	2	7	8	8	31	–1	11	6	24	10
Other organisations:												
(a) Military	HDKF	142	74	35	116	112	168	139	118	157	195	192
(b) Multilateral economic assistance	HCHJ	437	355	381	358	273	268	314	245	503	434	539
(c) Other	HCKL	817	750	702	835	633	429	402	479	691	647	459
Bilateral aid:												
(a) Non-project grants	FJKT	346	271	352	249	214	131	142	133	175	185	206
(b) Technical cooperation	FJKU	459	474	516	604	543	644	692	651	859	904	1 038
Military grants	HDJO	36	35	14	54	31	29	17	30	27	45	129
Total central government	FJUO	3 812	4 343	4 977	5 022	5 297	5 260	6 787	7 482	8 015	7 584	9 296
Other sectors												
Current taxes on income, wealth etc.	FJCI	352	393	452	557	610	638	454	682	775	518	638
Other taxes on production	FJLB	–	–	–	–	–	–	–	–	–	–	–
Other subsidies on production	FJCC	–	–	–	–	–	–	–	–	–	–	–
Social contributions	FJBG	–	–	–	–	–	–	–	–	–	–	–
Social benefits	FJCM	–	–	–	–	–	–	–	–	–	–	–
EU Institutions:												
(a) Customs duties and agricultural levies	QYRD	1 943	2 172	2 134	2 458	2 318	2 291	2 076	2 024	2 086	2 069	1 919
(b) Sugar levies	GTBA	47	56	98	55	26	91	42	46	44	31	25
(c) VAT based contributions	HCML	4 356	4 964	4 189	4 635	4 441	3 646	3 758	3 920	4 104	3 624	2 720
(d) VAT adjustments	FSVL	–297	–493	–1 068	210	30	–249	470	–109	100	–49	88
(e) ECSC Production levy	GTBB	7	1	–	–	–	–	–	–	–	–	–
Net non-life insurance premiums[1]	FJDB	–	–	–	–	5	5	7	10	18	25	19
Non-life insurance claims[2]	NQQR	5 900	4 246	4 145	4 993	9 763	4 423	4 168	3 663	2 144	3 584	2 252
Other payments by households[3]	FKIQ	1 889	1 952	2 034	2 125	2 214	2 809	2 906	2 975	3 236	3 364	3 541
Total other sectors	FJUP	14 197	13 291	11 984	15 033	19 407	13 654	13 881	13 211	12 507	13 166	11 202
Total	KTNE	**18 009**	**17 634**	**16 961**	**20 055**	**24 704**	**18 914**	**20 668**	**20 693**	**20 522**	**20 750**	**20 498**
Of which: Payments to EU institutions	FKIR	6 970	8 260	7 431	9 192	9 277	8 268	10 265	10 524	10 719	9 557	10 097

1 Premiums paid by UK residents to foreign insurance companies.
2 Claims paid by UK insurance companies to non-residents.
3 Includes estimates for workers' remittances and for non-profit institutions serving households.

5.1 Current transfers
continued

£ million

		1992	1993	1994	1995	1996	1997	1998	1999	2000	2001	2002
Balances												
Central government												
Current taxes on income, wealth etc.	FJKJ	259	238	361	472	376	402	530	337	357	398	399
Other taxes on production	FJIZ	–	–	–	–	–	–	–	–	–	–	–
Other subsidies on production	FJBD	–	–	–	–	–	–	–	–	–	–	–
Social contributions	FJBI	14	30	25	25	28	32	29	29	24	25	33
Social benefits	FJBM	–661	–824	–899	–972	–1 029	–1 102	–1 162	–1 183	–1 218	–1 292	–1 388
Other current transfers[1]	FJKW	–1 244	–961	–2 326	–2 817	–1 844	–2 419	–4 241	–3 123	–4 713	–1 724	–4 796
Total central government	FJUQ	–1 632	–1 517	–2 839	–3 292	–2 469	–3 087	–4 844	–3 940	–5 550	–2 593	–5 752
Other sectors												
Current taxes on income, wealth etc.	FJHU	–352	–393	–452	–557	–610	–638	–454	–682	–775	–518	–638
Other taxes on production	FJHT	–	–	–	–	–	–	–	–	–	–	–
Other subsidies on production	FJHV	–	–	–	–	–	–	–	–	–	–	–
Social contributions	FJHJ	–	–	–	–	–	–	–	–	–	–	–
Social benefits	FJJG	437	588	320	755	804	615	783	434	659	370	412
Other current transfers[1]	FJLT	–3 987	–3 921	–2 398	–4 480	–2 480	–2 808	–3 683	–3 195	–4 086	–3 865	–2 817
Total other sectors	FJUR	–3 902	–3 726	–2 530	–4 282	–2 286	–2 831	–3 354	–3 443	–4 202	–4 013	–3 043
Total	KTNF	**–5 534**	**–5 243**	**–5 369**	**–7 574**	**–4 755**	**–5 918**	**–8 198**	**–7 383**	**–9 752**	**–6 606**	**–8 795**
Of which: EU institutions	FKIS	–2 832	–2 924	–3 069	–4 773	–2 089	–2 846	–5 162	–3 983	–5 145	–2 134	–3 795

1 Includes an estimate for workers' remittances.

Part 2
Capital account, financial account and International investment position

Chapter 6
Capital account

Summary

The capital account balance remained in surplus between 1991 and 2002, recording a surplus of £1.0 billion in the latest year.
The decrease from £1.5 billion in 2001 was mainly due to a fall in the receipt of capital transfers by Other sectors. In 1994, the surplus was unusually low due to Other sectors debt forgiveness of £0.5 billion.

Figure **6.1**

Capital account

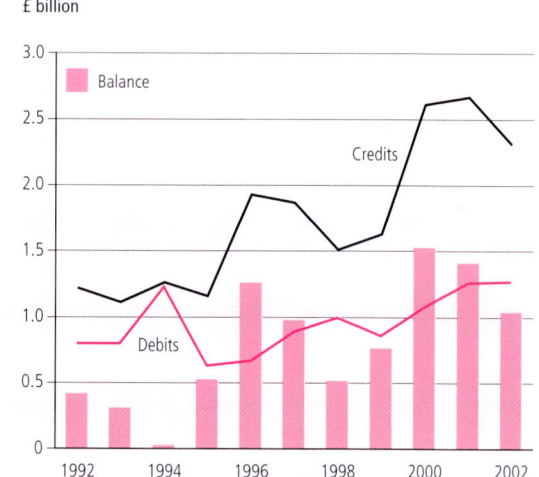

6.1 Capital account

£ million

		1992	1993	1994	1995	1996	1997	1998	1999	2000	2001	2002
Credits												
Capital transfers												
Central government												
Debt forgiveness	FJUU	–	–	–	–	–	–	–	–	–	–	–
Other capital transfers	FJLY	–	–	–	–	–	–	–	–	–	–	–
Total central government	FJMD	–	–	–	–	–	–	–	–	–	–	–
Other sectors												
Migrants' transfers	FJMG	602	584	603	678	703	754	967	1 144	1 371	1 602	1 834
Debt forgiveness	FJNC	–	–	–	–	–	–	–	–	–	–	–
Other capital transfers												
EU Institutions:												
Regional development fund	FKIT	551	425	608	437	620	812	357	285	989	543	296
Agricultural guidance fund	FJXL	71	104	52	48	30	57	56	47	82	26	–
Other capital transfers	EBGO	–	–	–	–	524	178	43	–	–	322	–
Total EU institutions	FKIV	622	529	660	485	1 174	1 047	456	332	1 071	891	296
Total other sectors	FJMU	1 224	1 113	1 263	1 163	1 877	1 801	1 423	1 476	2 442	2 493	2 130
Total capital transfers	FJMX	1 224	1 113	1 263	1 163	1 877	1 801	1 423	1 476	2 442	2 493	2 130
Sales of non-produced, non-financial assets	FJUX	–	–	–	–	49	68	89	152	165	177	181
Total	FKMH	**1 224**	**1 113**	**1 263**	**1 163**	**1 926**	**1 869**	**1 512**	**1 628**	**2 607**	**2 670**	**2 311**
Debits												
Capital transfers												
Central government												
Debt forgiveness	FJUV	20	21	24	28	23	24	146	22	22	18	15
Other capital transfers (project grants)	FJMB	261	201	188	149	143	169	182	171	225	237	263
Total central government	FJME	281	222	212	177	166	193	328	193	247	255	278
Other sectors												
Migrants' transfers	FJMH	522	494	500	453	465	592	531	499	461	430	390
Debt forgiveness												
Monetary financial institutions[1]	FJNF	–	88	518	–	–	–	–	–	–	–	–
Public corporations[1]	HMLY	..	..	..	..	–	–	–	23	231	300	300
Total debt forgiveness	IZZZ	–	88	518	–	–	–	–	23	231	300	300
Other capital transfers	FJMS	–	–	–	–	–	–	–	–	–	–	–
Total other sectors	FJMV	522	582	1 018	453	465	592	531	522	692	730	690
Total capital transfers	FJMY	803	804	1 230	630	631	785	859	715	939	985	968
Purchases of non-produced, non-financial assets	FJUY	–	–	–	–	35	102	137	140	141	274	298
Total	FKMI	**803**	**804**	**1 230**	**630**	**666**	**887**	**996**	**855**	**1 080**	**1 259**	**1 266**
Balances												
Capital transfers												
Central government												
Debt forgiveness	FJUW	−20	−21	−24	−28	−23	−24	−146	−22	−22	−18	−15
Other capital transfers	FJMC	−261	−201	−188	−149	−143	−169	−182	−171	−225	−237	−263
Total central government	FJMF	−281	−222	−212	−177	−166	−193	−328	−193	−247	−255	−278
Other sectors												
Migrants' transfers	FJMI	80	90	103	225	238	162	436	645	910	1 172	1 444
Debt forgiveness	FJNG	–	−88	−518	–	–	–	–	−23	−231	−300	−300
Other capital transfers	FJMT	622	529	660	485	1 174	1 047	456	332	1 071	891	296
Total other sectors	FJMW	702	531	245	710	1 412	1 209	892	954	1 750	1 763	1 440
Total capital transfers	FJMZ	421	309	33	533	1 246	1 016	564	761	1 503	1 508	1 162
Non-produced, non-financial assets	NHSG	–	–	–	–	14	−34	−48	12	24	−97	−117
Total	FKMJ	**421**	**309**	**33**	**533**	**1 260**	**982**	**516**	**773**	**1 527**	**1 411**	**1 045**

1 This series also appears in the Financial Account (see Table 7.7).

Chapter 7
Financial account

Summary

Investments abroad and in the UK have both increased dramatically in the last ten years, reflecting the increased globalisation of the world economy. Growth peaked in 2000 at the height of global merger and acquisition activity, and has since declined to levels of investment seen in the early 1990s. Since 1987 inward investment has exceeded outward investment in every year except 1997. In other words, over this period the United Kingdom generally needed to borrow from abroad to finance a continuing current account deficit. In 1997, when the UK current account was closer to balance, there was net lending to the rest of the world. In 2002, there was net investment in the UK of £3.5 billion.

Volatility in gross financial flows has historically been driven by other investment. The amounts recorded in the gross flows of loans and deposits are as much a consequence of how the transaction is carried out between resident and non-resident banks, as overall market conditions; these transactions largely balance. From 1998 until 2001 cross-border merger and acquisition activity boomed, impacting on direct investment, but also upon portfolio investment flows when such deals have been financed by the issue of equity. 2002 has seen merger and acquisition activity return to levels last seen in the mid-1990s.

With the exception of 1991, there has been net direct investment abroad (net acquisition of assets exceeds net acquisition of liabilities) in every year since 1977. Portfolio investment also generally recorded net investment abroad, although in 1999, 2000 and 2002 there was significant net investment in the UK. In 1999 and 2000 this resulted from substantial UK direct investment acquisitions in foreign telecom and pharmaceutical companies, which was funded by the issue of UK shares to foreign shareholders – this is recorded as portfolio investment in the UK. In 2002, there has been substantial foreign investment in UK money market instruments. Other investment has recorded net inward investment in all years except 1987, 1994, 1999 and 2002. Investment by central government in reserve assets is comparatively small, though quite volatile. Net investment in financial derivatives reflects bank's net settlement receipts or payments from interest rate swaps.

Figure 7.1

Financial account

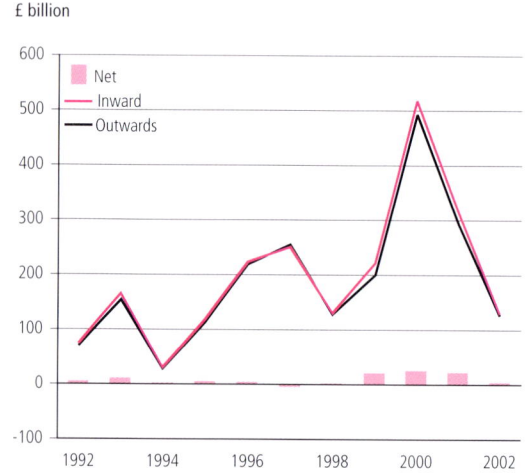

Figure 7.2

UK investment abroad

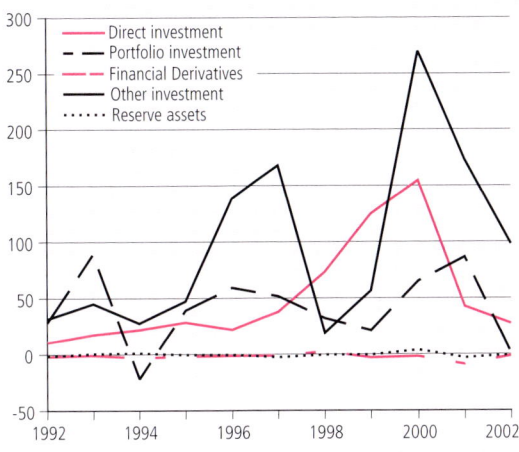

UK investment abroad

UK investment abroad peaked in 2000 at £492.8 billion, with record outward direct investment and other investment. Merger and acquisition activity led to an increase in direct investment abroad from £22.3 billion in 1996 to £155.0 billion in 2000, before falling back to £27.8 billion in 2002. Portfolio investment abroad peaked in 2001 at £86.5 billion, with strong investment by UK securities dealers in foreign equity and UK banks in foreign debt securities. Debt as opposed to equity securities has been the preferred form of investment for UK investment abroad in the last decade. UK residents have made deposits abroad in every year since 1992, peaking in 2000 at £214.0 billion.

Figure 7.3

Foreign investment in the UK

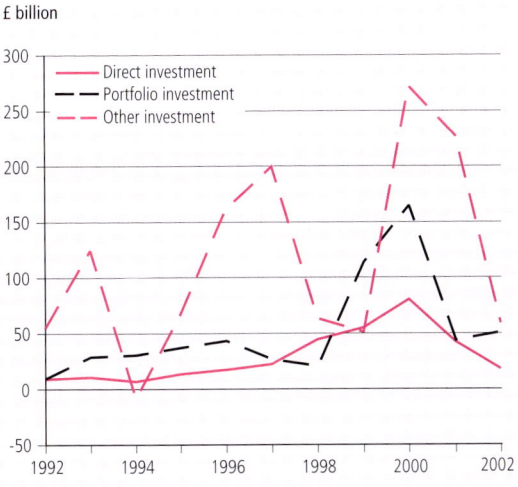

Foreign investment in the UK

Inward direct investment showed a similar pattern to outward investment, with net investment increasing strongly from 1998, peaking at £517.7 billion in 2000 and then declining to £128.6 billion in 2002 (but with continued strong investment into 2001). Inward portfolio investment recorded net investment in all years, with acquisition of equity securities increasing dramatically in 1999 and 2000 – counterparting the direct investment abroad transactions. Again, counterparting the slowdown in outward direct investment activity in 2001, inward investment in UK equity also slowed in 2001 and 2002. There has been non-resident investment in deposits with UK banks in every year except 1991, peaking at £199.8 billion in 2000.

Direct investment

Outward direct investment reached a peak at £155.0 billion in 2000 and has declined to £27.8 billion in 2002. The record direct investment abroad in 2000 was driven by merger and acquisition activity – the largest outward acquisitions were the investment in Mannesmann AG by Vodafone Airtouch for a reported £100 billion and the purchase of Atlantic Richfield Company by BP Amoco plc for a reported £18 billion. These transactions are reflected in the equity capital component on direct investment abroad. Since 1999, reinvested earnings have grown strongly as company profits have also grown. Since 2000, other capital transactions have been very erratic, mainly due to changes in intercompany accounts.

Inward direct investment showed a pattern similar to outward investment, with record direct investment in the UK of £80.6 billion in 2000. The largest inward acquisitions during the year were in the telecommunications sector with France Telecom acquiring Orange Plc for a reported £23.4 billion. In the last two years inward investment has returned to levels of investment seen in the mid-1990s.

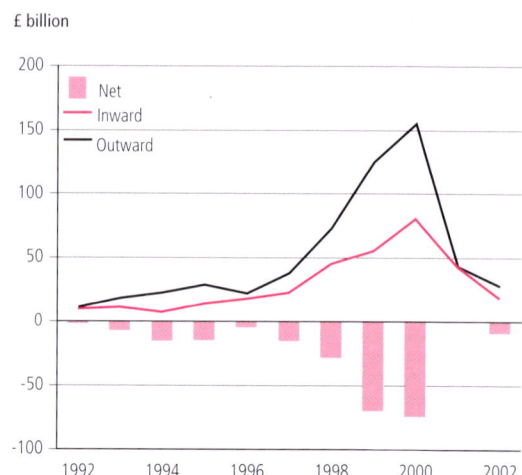

Figure 7.4

Direct investment

£ billion

Portfolio investment

Portfolio investment abroad has shown investment in every year since 1995, although in 2002 investment in foreign debt securities was almost offset by disposals of foreign equity. UK investors have generally invested more in foreign debt than equity in the last decade, although both forms of security showed strong investment in 2000 and 2001. Net disposals of equity securities occurred in three years coinciding with financial shocks: the UK's exit from the Exchange Rate Mechanism in 1992; the South-East Asia crisis in 1997; and the collapse in equity markets in 2002.

There has been inward portfolio investment in every year. In the early 1990s, the majority of investment was in bonds and notes. This switched to UK issued equity in the late 1990s as the counterpart to the outward direct investment. Since 2000, there has also been significant net investment in UK money market instruments. Foreign investors mainly invest in debt securities issued by UK banks and equity securities issued by non-financial sectors.

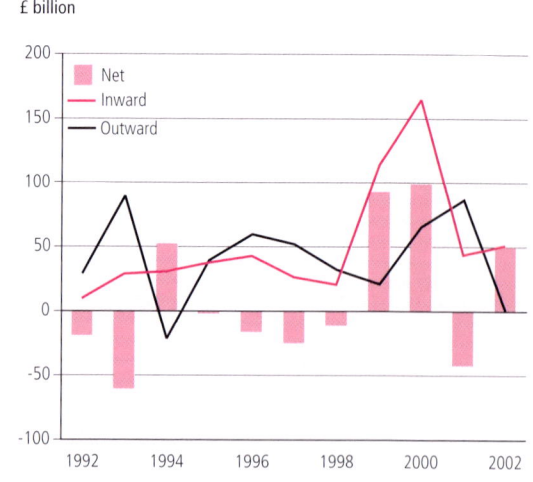

Figure 7.5

Portfolio investment

£ billion

Figure 7.6

Other investment

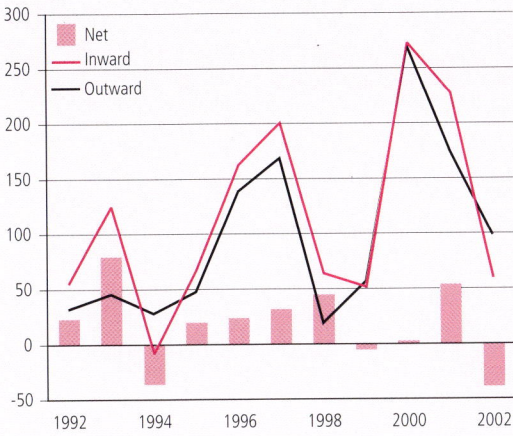

Other investment

Deposits by UK banks, and to a lesser extent securities dealers, constitute the major component of other investment. Loans and deposits by UK banks are carried out predominately in foreign currency. Changes in currency and deposits held abroad by banks are partly influenced by relative exchange rates and interest rates as well as the global financial conditions generally. Transactions in recent years have been very volatile, with UK banks depositing £113.5 billion in 1997 and a record £131.2 billion in 2000, compared to withdrawals of £29.1 billion in 1999.

Other investment in the UK is largely composed of deposits with UK banks and short-term loans to securities dealers and other sectors (principally private non-financial corporations). Loans to the UK reached a record £102.9 billion in 2001, primarily attributable to short-term loans to securities dealers. £30.0 billion of these loans were repaid in 2002. Non-residents deposits with UK banks peaked at £198.6 billion in 2000. falling back to £89.3 billion investment in 2002.

7.1 Financial account
Summary table

£ million

		1992	1993	1994	1995	1996	1997	1998	1999	2000	2001	2002
UK investment abroad (UK assets = net debits)												
Direct investment abroad												
Equity capital	-HJYM	5 447	4 497	7 697	8 079	4 842	21 305	47 185	101 323	147 092	15 693	17 868
Reinvested earnings	-HDNY	5 224	10 096	13 827	14 378	17 271	16 112	14 071	21 392	25 178	24 720	28 561
Other capital transactions	-HMAB	582	3 597	1 170	6 242	175	832	12 075	2 313	-17 275	2 799	-18 617
Total direct investment abroad	-HJYP	11 253	18 190	22 694	28 699	22 288	38 249	73 331	125 028	154 995	43 212	27 812
Portfolio investment abroad												
Equity securities	-HBVI	-3 949	7 938	1 350	8 386	10 289	-4 218	2 721	14 385	20 458	44 431	-2 451
Debt securities	-XBMW	32 586	81 627	-23 159	30 888	49 327	56 215	29 360	6 935	45 042	42 085	3 060
Total portfolio investment abroad	-HHZC	28 637	89 565	-21 809	39 274	59 616	51 997	32 081	21 320	65 500	86 516	609
Financial derivatives (net)	-ZPNN	-1 253	-245	-2 373	-1 667	-963	-1 156	3 043	-2 685	-1 553	-8 417	-1 001
Other investment abroad	-XBMM	31 693	45 329	27 773	47 498	138 681	168 307	19 043	56 791	269 921	173 811	98 123
Reserve assets	-LTCV	-1 407	698	1 045	-200	-510	-2 380	-164	-639	3 915	-3 085	-459
Total	-HBNR	68 923	153 537	27 330	113 604	219 112	255 017	127 334	199 815	492 778	292 037	125 084
Investment in the UK (UK liabilities = net credits)												
Direct investment in the UK												
Equity capital	HJYR	6 560	5 934	3 316	12 756	8 156	11 599	27 895	46 709	59 811	20 409	11 812
Reinvested earnings	CYFV	121	4 385	3 953	5 254	7 873	6 386	1 522	4 607	10 788	4 912	8 583
Other capital transactions	HMAD	2 735	624	-170	-4 179	1 533	4 838	15 637	3 873	9 967	17 374	-1 921
Total direct investment in the UK	HJYU	9 416	10 943	7 099	13 831	17 562	22 823	45 054	55 189	80 566	42 695	18 474
Portfolio investment in the UK												
Equity securities	XBLW	10 276	17 367	4 843	5 111	6 073	4 793	37 785	72 127	113 593	23 065	1 931
Debt securities	XBLX	-697	11 403	25 837	32 204	36 912	21 915	-16 932	41 979	50 950	20 867	48 886
Total portfolio investment in the UK	HHZF	9 579	28 770	30 680	37 315	42 985	26 708	20 853	114 106	164 543	43 932	50 817
Other investment in the UK	XBMN	55 017	125 154	-8 323	67 463	162 524	200 350	63 646	51 464	272 613	227 590	59 329
Total	HBNS	74 012	164 867	29 456	118 609	223 071	249 881	129 553	220 759	517 722	314 217	128 620
Net transactions (net credits *less* net debits)												
Direct investment												
Equity capital	HBWN	1 113	1 437	-4 381	4 677	3 314	-9 706	-19 290	-54 614	-87 281	4 716	-6 056
Reinvested earnings	HBWT	-5 103	-5 711	-9 874	-9 124	-9 398	-9 726	-12 549	-16 785	-14 390	-19 808	-19 978
Other capital transactions	HBWU	2 153	-2 973	-1 340	-10 421	1 358	4 006	3 562	1 560	27 242	14 575	16 696
Total net direct investment	HJYV	-1 837	-7 247	-15 595	-14 868	-4 726	-15 426	-28 277	-69 839	-74 429	-517	-9 338
Portfolio investment												
Equity securities	HBWV	14 225	9 429	3 493	-3 275	-4 216	9 011	35 064	57 742	93 135	-21 366	4 382
Debt securities	HBWX	-33 283	-70 224	48 996	1 316	-12 415	-34 300	-46 292	35 044	5 908	-21 218	45 826
Total net portfolio investment	HHZD	-19 058	-60 795	52 489	-1 959	-16 631	-25 289	-11 228	92 786	99 043	-42 584	50 208
Financial derivatives	ZPNN	1 253	245	2 373	1 667	963	1 156	-3 043	2 685	1 553	8 417	1 001
Other investment	HHYR	23 324	79 825	-36 096	19 965	23 843	32 043	44 603	-5 327	2 692	53 779	-38 794
Reserve assets	LTCV	1 407	-698	-1 045	200	510	2 380	164	639	-3 915	3 085	459
Total	HBNT	5 089	11 330	2 126	5 005	3 959	-5 136	2 219	20 944	24 944	22 180	3 536

7.2 Financial account
Summary table

£ million

		1992	1993	1994	1995	1996	1997	1998	1999	2000	2001	2002
UK investment abroad												
(UK assets = net debits)												
By:												
Monetary financial institutions												
Banks	-HFAM	33 186	32 233	57 062	48 911	85 819	165 973	75 467	6 598	229 288	123 555	60 465
Building societies	HEQN	317	2 237	322	529	−369	2 557	1 334	949	4 382	1 476	−903
Total monetary financial institutions	-HFAQ	33 503	34 470	57 384	49 440	85 450	168 530	76 801	7 547	233 670	125 031	59 562
Central government	-HFAN	−1 005	1 172	1 495	269	1 387	−2 263	−245	−311	4 251	−2 622	403
Public corporations	-HFAO	161	286	110	163	92	122	67	125	400	−138	−125
Other sectors	-HFAP	36 264	117 609	−31 659	63 732	132 183	88 628	50 711	192 454	254 457	169 766	65 244
Total	-HBNR	**68 923**	**153 537**	**27 330**	**113 604**	**219 112**	**255 017**	**127 334**	**199 815**	**492 778**	**292 037**	**125 084**
Investment in the UK												
(UK liabilities = net credits)												
In:												
Monetary financial institutions												
(banks and building societies)	CGUL	23 550	29 657	59 327	48 296	92 343	163 150	34 570	37 914	247 523	143 220	114 333
Central government	HFAR	7 386	14 591	5 813	719	5 299	−4 315	439	−4 434	−245	−3 708	−4 952
Local authorities	HFAS	4	84	−78	−51	13	−53	−87	−106	−188	−118	−52
Public corporations	HFAT	−440	−24	−118	−151	−14	−206	−5	–	–	–	–
Other sectors	GGCJ	43 512	120 559	−35 488	69 796	125 430	91 305	94 636	187 385	270 632	174 823	19 291
Total	HBNS	**74 012**	**164 867**	**29 456**	**118 609**	**223 071**	**249 881**	**129 553**	**220 759**	**517 722**	**314 217**	**128 620**
Net transactions												
(net credits *less* net debits)												
In assets and liabilities of:												
Monetary financial institutions												
(banks and building societies)	GGCK	−9 953	−4 813	1 943	−1 144	6 893	−5 380	−42 231	30 367	13 853	18 189	54 771
Central government	HFAV	8 391	13 419	4 318	450	3 912	−2 052	684	−4 123	−4 496	−1 086	−5 355
Local authorities	HFAS	4	84	−78	−51	13	−53	−87	−106	−188	−118	−52
Public corporations	HFAW	−601	−310	−228	−314	−106	−328	−72	−125	−400	138	125
Other sectors	GGCL	7 248	2 950	−3 829	6 064	−6 753	2 677	43 925	−5 069	16 175	5 057	−45 953
Total	HBNT	**5 089**	**11 330**	**2 126**	**5 005**	**3 959**	**−5 136**	**2 219**	**20 944**	**24 944**	**22 180**	**3 536**

7.3 Direct investment

£ million

		1992	1993	1994	1995	1996	1997	1998	1999	2000	2001	2002
Direct investment abroad (UK assets = net debits)												
Equity capital												
Claims on affiliated enterprises (net acquisition of ordinary shares)												
Purchases of ordinary shares	-HDOA	7 976	6 932	12 637	11 655	12 703	25 476	60 627	114 693	181 488	40 601	27 492
Sales of ordinary shares	-HDOC	-2 764	-2 465	-4 786	-3 840	-7 672	-4 041	-13 677	-13 620	-34 693	-25 071	-10 252
Total claims on affiliated enterprises	-HJYL	5 212	4 467	7 851	7 815	5 031	21 435	46 950	101 073	146 795	15 530	17 240
Net acquisition of property	-HHVG	235	30	-154	264	-189	-130	235	250	297	163	628
Total equity capital	-HJYM	5 447	4 497	7 697	8 079	4 842	21 305	47 185	101 323	147 092	15 693	17 868
Reinvested earnings	-HDNY	5 224	10 096	13 827	14 378	17 271	16 112	14 071	21 392	25 178	24 720	28 561
Other capital transactions												
Claims on affiliated enterprises												
Debt securities issued by affiliated enterprises												
Purchases of debt securities	-HDOD	–	–	1 777	1 175	89	529	396	636	952	2 199	1 741
Sales of debt securities	-HDOE	–	–	–	–	-52	-117	-315	-578	-496	-26	-51
Other claims on affiliated enterprises												
Change in inter-company accounts	-HDOF	2 905	3 550	1 267	4 631	2 506	5 040	20 721	15 806	15 110	8 159	-36
Change in branch indebtedness	-HDOI	685	174	1 047	669	500	1 053	1 493	-483	-3 360	5 838	3 087
Total claims on affiliated enterprises	-HJYN	3 590	3 724	4 091	6 475	3 043	6 505	22 295	15 381	12 206	16 170	4 741
Liabilities to affiliated enterprises												
Change in inter-company accounts	-HDOG	-2 162	292	-2 922	-10	-3 292	-5 299	-8 453	-14 340	-28 278	-12 651	-21 708
Change in branch indebtedness	-HDOJ	-846	-419	1	-223	424	-374	-1 767	1 272	-1 203	-720	-1 650
Total liabilities to affiliated enterprises	-HJYO	-3 008	-127	-2 921	-233	-2 868	-5 673	-10 220	-13 068	-29 481	-13 371	-23 358
Total other capital transactions	-HMAB	582	3 597	1 170	6 242	175	832	12 075	2 313	-17 275	2 799	-18 617
Total	-HJYP	11 253	18 190	22 694	28 699	22 288	38 249	73 331	125 028	154 995	43 212	27 812
Direct investment in the UK (UK liabilities = net credits)												
Equity capital												
Liabilities to direct investors												
Quoted ordinary shares												
Purchases of quoted ordinary shares	CYFY	246	651	389	4 255	6 510	7 434	24 660	40 393	16 253	5 441	7 039
Sales of quoted ordinary shares	CYFZ	–	–	-612	-191	-1 206	-1 293	-4 336	-10 526	-2 038	-1 166	-853
Unquoted ordinary shares												
Purchases of unquoted ordinary shares	CYGA	7 363	6 152	3 923	11 755	3 039	5 055	7 147	20 721	48 154	18 171	10 276
Sales of unquoted ordinary shares	CYGB	-1 350	-1 329	-856	-3 287	-800	-447	-274	-4 692	-4 187	-2 490	-5 398
Total liabilities to direct investors	HJYQ	6 259	5 474	2 844	12 532	7 543	10 749	27 197	45 896	58 182	19 956	11 064
Net acquisition of property	CGLO	301	460	472	224	613	850	698	813	1 629	453	748
Total equity capital	HJYR	6 560	5 934	3 316	12 756	8 156	11 599	27 895	46 709	59 811	20 409	11 812
Reinvested earnings	CYFV	121	4 385	3 953	5 254	7 873	6 386	1 522	4 607	10 788	4 912	8 583
Other capital transactions												
Claims on direct investors												
Change in inter-company accounts	CYGF	-689	-1 987	-2 791	-4 441	-423	-3 591	-11 199	-13 266	-2 495	4 124	-1 246
Change in branch indebtedness	CYGK	-49	-30	-50	-5	-74	735	144	105	-272	-501	–
Total claims on direct investors	HJYS	-738	-2 017	-2 841	-4 446	-497	-2 856	-11 055	-13 161	-2 767	3 623	-1 246
Liabilities to direct investors												
Debt securities issued by affiliated enterprises												
Purchases of debt securities	CYGC	176	32	174	540	3	1 516	783	558	710	915	756
Sales of debt securities	CYGD	–	-135	-21	–	–	-22	-183	-567	-183	-313	-179
Other liabilities to direct investors												
Change in inter-company accounts	CYGH	3 251	2 614	2 478	-315	1 915	5 571	25 700	17 253	11 338	12 868	-1 202
Change in branch indebtedness	CYGL	46	130	40	42	112	629	392	-210	869	281	-50
Total liabilities to direct investors	HJYT	3 473	2 641	2 671	267	2 030	7 694	26 692	17 034	12 734	13 751	-675
Total other capital transactions	HMAD	2 735	624	-170	-4 179	1 533	4 838	15 637	3 873	9 967	17 374	-1 921
Total	HJYU	9 416	10 943	7 099	13 831	17 562	22 823	45 054	55 189	80 566	42 695	18 474

7.3 Direct investment
continued

£ million

		1992	1993	1994	1995	1996	1997	1998	1999	2000	2001	2002
Net transactions (net credits less net debits)												
Equity capital												
Net acquisition of ordinary shares	LTMS	1 047	1 007	−5 007	4 717	2 512	−10 686	−19 753	−55 177	−88 613	4 426	−6 176
Net acquisition of property	LTMT	66	430	626	−40	802	980	463	563	1 332	290	120
Total equity capital	HBWN	1 113	1 437	−4 381	4 677	3 314	−9 706	−19 290	−54 614	−87 281	4 716	−6 056
Reinvested earnings	HBWT	−5 103	−5 711	−9 874	−9 124	−9 398	−9 726	−12 549	−16 785	−14 390	−19 808	−19 978
Other capital transactions	HBWU	2 153	−2 973	−1 340	−10 421	1 358	4 006	3 562	1 560	27 242	14 575	16 696
Total	HJYV	−1 837	−7 247	−15 595	−14 868	−4 726	−15 426	−28 277	−69 839	−74 429	−517	−9 338

7.4 Direct investment
Sector analysis

£ million

		1992	1993	1994	1995	1996	1997	1998	1999	2000	2001	2002
Direct investment abroad (UK assets = net debits)												
By:												
UK Monetary financial institutions (banks)	-HCWJ	1 374	1 261	2 310	1 820	1 444	169	971	1 028	3 378	4 497	3 050
Insurance companies	-CNZE	239	1 122	−409	2 343	506	3 137	969	−2 135	2 166	−780	−349
Other financial intermediaries	-HCXL	634	1 425	1 498	1 977	2 631	5 711	11 676	8 469	9 716	4 576	5 294
Private non-financial corporations	-HCVH	8 890	14 140	19 162	22 463	17 684	29 132	59 663	117 330	139 101	34 833	19 704
Public corporations	-HDND	84	210	101	64	−9	68	20	280	574	25	50
Household sector[1]	-AAQN	32	32	32	32	32	32	32	56	60	61	63
Total	-HJYP	11 253	18 190	22 694	28 699	22 288	38 249	73 331	125 028	154 995	43 212	27 812
Direct investment in the UK (UK liabilities = net credits)												
In:												
Monetary financial institutions (banks)	GPBQ	1 032	2 027	1 008	2 092	2 458	3 494	678	1 616	4 133	3 303	1 984
Insurance companies	HDQI	88	197	−38	−144	1 615	891	−138	1 763	2 492	1 142	−198
Other financial intermediaries												
Securities dealers	HDRU	244	1 085	−682	356	905	338	−1 188	836	1 919	942	726
Other	HFCL	66	−120	143	1 453	87	−34	9 865	−232	5 792	3 664	4 870
Total other financial intermediaries	HFDR	310	965	−539	1 809	992	304	8 677	604	7 711	4 606	5 596
Private non-financial corporations	BCEC	7 986	7 754	6 668	10 074	12 497	18 134	35 837	51 206	66 230	33 644	11 092
Total	HJYU	9 416	10 943	7 099	13 831	17 562	22 823	45 054	55 189	80 566	42 695	18 474
Net transaction (net credits less net debits)												
In assets and liabilities of:												
Monetary financial institutions	LTMU	−342	766	−1 302	272	1 014	3 325	−293	588	755	−1 194	−1 066
Insurance companies	LTMV	−151	−925	371	−2 487	1 109	−2 246	−1 107	3 898	326	1 922	151
Other financial intermediaries	LTMW	−324	−460	−2 037	−168	−1 639	−5 407	−2 999	−7 865	−2 005	30	302
Private non-financial corporations	LTMX	−904	−6 386	−12 494	−12 389	−5 187	−10 998	−23 826	−66 124	−72 871	−1 189	−8 612
Public corporations	HDND	−84	−210	−101	−64	9	−68	−20	−280	−574	−25	−50
Household sector[1]	AAQN	−32	−32	−32	−32	−32	−32	−32	−56	−60	−61	−63
Total	HJYV	−1 837	−7 247	−15 595	−14 868	−4 726	−15 426	−28 277	−69 839	−74 429	−517	−9 338

1 The household sector includes non-profit institutions serving households.

7.5 Portfolio investment

£ million

		1992	1993	1994	1995	1996	1997	1998	1999	2000	2001	2002
Portfolio investment abroad (UK assets = net debits)												
Transactions in equity securities (shares) by:													
Monetary financial Institutions (banks)	-VTWC	−612	272	1 607	161	4 570	−3 138	4 549	100	7 195	−1 287	−11 767
Insurance companies and pension funds												
Insurance companies	-HBHM	−1 354	4 399	3 654	3 688	3 147	1 335	1 015	3 111	−4 297	6 520	3 768
Pension funds	-HBHO	−478	1 579	−5 250	−1 884	2 828	−3 326	2 073	−518	−12 798	11 720	15 562
Total insurance companies and pension funds	-HBRD	−1 832	5 978	−1 596	1 804	5 975	−1 991	3 088	2 593	−17 095	18 240	19 330
Other financial intermediaries												
Securities dealers	-HGLG	−812	−1 637	−3 311	3 600	−3 058	810	−7 634	5 783	13 673	24 128	−12 440
Unit and Investment Trusts	-HBHQ	−487	3 539	4 148	3 178	2 724	919	3 567	6 468	9 968	3 913	3 329
Other	-HBRC	−166	−241	−369	−290	−456	−831	−833	−1 300	−1 446	−1 077	−851
Total other financial intermediaries	-HBRE	−1 465	1 661	468	6 488	−790	898	−4 900	10 951	22 195	26 964	−9 962
Private non-financial corporations	-XBNL	−105	141	55	−222	188	−62	84	241	9 047	444	−52
Household sector[1]	HALH	65	−114	816	155	346	75	−100	500	−884	70	–
Total transactions in equity securities	-HBVI	−3 949	7 938	1 350	8 386	10 289	−4 218	2 721	14 385	20 458	44 431	−2 451
Transactions in debt securities												
Transactions in bonds and notes by:												
Monetary financial institutions												
Banks	-VTWA	13 577	34 426	12 474	23 672	19 034	17 442	43 090	11 011	34 007	37 604	3 825
Building societies	RYWJ	48	661	355	496	67	691	1 417	1 099	2 464	854	−338
Total monetary financial institutions	-HPCP	13 625	35 087	12 829	24 168	19 101	18 133	44 507	12 110	36 471	38 458	3 487
Insurance companies and pension funds												
Insurance companies	-HBHN	3 187	−227	231	1 052	4 096	3 614	11 615	7 103	5 363	8 200	9 226
Pension funds	-HBHP	708	355	357	732	1 650	4 696	3 581	2 933	5 875	1 267	−3 532
Total insurance companies and pension funds	-HBRF	3 895	128	588	1 784	5 746	8 310	15 196	10 036	11 238	9 467	5 694
Other financial intermediaries												
Securities dealers	CGFO	13 381	39 772	−32 564	3 039	26 584	22 318	−33 645	−28 883	−1 935	−19 589	−3 863
Unit and investment trusts	-HBHR	197	316	−128	−133	351	195	1 452	1 121	664	1 478	720
Other	-HBRG	−17	−33	−25	−22	−35	45	−154	−38	−36	−57	−51
Total other financial intermediaries	-HBRH	13 561	40 055	−32 717	2 884	26 900	22 558	−32 347	−27 800	−1 307	−18 168	−3 194
Private non-financial corporations	-XBNM	675	174	666	−135	840	−2 370	553	−1 299	1 179	566	300
Household sector[1]	HBRI	140	−59	−77	−556	−1 586	186	184	−380	256	88	88
Total transactions in bonds and notes	-HEPK	31 896	75 385	−18 711	28 145	51 001	46 817	28 093	−7 333	47 837	30 411	6 375
Transactions in Money Market Instruments												
Transactions in commercial paper by:												
Monetary financial institutions:												
Banks	-HBXH	2 385	2 619	−4 229	2 233	−3 547	7 295	4 112	9 729	−963	6 700	−3 980
Building societies	TAIH	39	535	−135	−339	14	254	−169	66	899	635	−564
Central government	-RUUR	–	–	–	–	–	–	–	–	–	456	329
Insurance companies and pension funds	-HBVK	65	51	19	178	292	617	−1 558	243	−106	−159	70
Other financial intermediaries	-HGIS	−606	1 963	−296	420	1 182	635	−815	504	−2 077	2 505	−646
Private non-financial corporations	-HBRL	−535	912	73	−2	390	327	−956	722	1 110	1 912	1 109
Total transactions in commercial paper	-HGLU	1 348	6 080	−4 568	2 490	−1 669	9 128	614	11 264	−1 137	12 049	−3 682
Transactions in certificates of deposit by:												
Monetary financial institutions												
(Building societies)	TAIF	–	20	36	−25	2	261	210	−71	409	37	563
Other financial intermediaries	-RZUV	−658	142	84	278	−7	9	443	3 075	−2 067	−412	−196
Total transactions in certificates of deposit	HEPH	−658	162	120	253	−5	270	653	3 004	−1 658	−375	367
Total transactions in Money Market Instruments	-HHZM	690	6 242	−4 448	2 743	−1 674	9 398	1 267	14 268	−2 795	11 674	−3 315
Total transactions in debt securities	-XBMW	32 586	81 627	−23 159	30 888	49 327	56 215	29 360	6 935	45 042	42 085	3 060
Total	-HHZC	28 637	89 565	−21 809	39 274	59 616	51 997	32 081	21 320	65 500	86 516	609

1 The household sector includes non-profit institutions serving households.

United Kingdom Balance of Payments The Pink Book 2003 — Financial account

7.5 Portfolio investment
continued
£ million

		1992	1993	1994	1995	1996	1997	1998	1999	2000	2001	2002
Portfolio investment in the UK (UK liabilities = net credits)												
Transactions in equity securities (shares) issued by:													
Monetary financial Institutions (banks and building societies)	HBQG	568	372	−517	−914	−1 173	−2 172	−2 470	−847	1 267	−8 117	−4 188
Other sectors[1]	HBQH	9 708	16 995	5 360	6 025	7 246	6 965	40 255	72 974	112 326	31 182	6 119
Total transactions in equity securities	XBLW	10 276	17 367	4 843	5 111	6 073	4 793	37 785	72 127	113 593	23 065	1 931
Transactions in debt securities												
Transactions in bonds and notes												
Issues by central government												
UK foreign currency bonds and notes	HEZP	4 676	1 225	2 774	101	−1 632	−3 058	−1 660	241	988	−3 342	−3 085
Other central government bonds	HHJM	−	−	−	−	−	−	−	−	−	−	−
Transactions in British government stocks (gilts) by:												
Foreign central banks (exchange reserves)	AING	2 561	1 462	2 017	−250	261	−1 586	1 692	489	1 049	1 094	1 725
Other foreign residents	VTWG	1 589	14 890	520	−879	7 604	2 244	1 802	−6 017	−2 338	−2 040	−2 986
Total transactions in British government stocks	HEPC	4 150	16 352	2 537	−1 129	7 865	658	3 494	−5 528	−1 289	−946	−1 261
Total issues by central government	HBRX	8 826	17 577	5 311	−1 028	6 233	−2 400	1 834	−5 287	−301	−4 288	−4 346
Local authorities' bonds	HBQT	−	−	−	−	−	−	−	−	−	−	−
Public corporations' bonds	HCEW	−10	−6	−2	−7	−	−	−	−	−	−	−
Issues by monetary financial Institutions (banks and building societies)												
Bonds	HBRY	841	1 746	2 704	3 233	2 998	3 139	−1 163	6 574	1 905	360	4 940
European medium term notes and other short-term paper:												
Issued by UK banks	HCEZ	1 034	3 037	4 353	1 572	5 585	3 137	1 881	4 244	891	3 425	1 706
Issued by UK building societies	HCFC	336	884	2 066	−399	−315	−116	−140	252	1 814	630	69
Total	HBRV	1 370	3 921	6 419	1 173	5 270	3 021	1 741	4 496	2 705	4 055	1 775
Total monetary financial institutions	HMBD	2 211	5 667	9 123	4 406	8 268	6 160	578	11 070	4 610	4 415	6 715
Issues by other sectors[1]	HBRT	2 623	5 433	8 419	10 063	9 331	9 776	−3 622	20 465	5 928	1 118	15 377
Total transactions in bonds and notes	XBLY	13 650	28 671	22 851	13 434	23 832	13 536	−1 210	26 248	10 237	1 245	17 746
Transactions in Money Market Instruments												
Transactions in treasury bills (issued by central government)												
Sterling treasury bills	AARB	−1 222	−438	−199	853	−663	−183	−820	637	−251	305	116
Euro treasury bills	HHNW	−1 194	133	59	471	425	−729	−913	−227	−	−	−
Total treasury bills	HHZO	−2 416	−305	−140	1 324	−238	−912	−1 733	410	−251	305	116
Transactions in certificates of deposit (issued by UK monetary financial institutions)												
Issued by banks	HBRS	−6 503	−16 909	1 066	12 718	9 906	5 547	−16 985	11 500	34 653	19 911	5 250
Issued by building societies	HBHH	−181	−15	107	−	23	157	−25	−6	301	−50	264
Total certificates of deposit	HBQX	−6 684	−16 924	1 173	12 718	9 929	5 704	−17 010	11 494	34 954	19 861	5 514
Transactions in commercial paper												
Issued by UK monetary financial Institutions												
Banks	HBHI	−4 830	413	328	708	2 174	1 800	257	296	2 542	−599	14 950
Building societies	HBHL	294	−1 802	−673	2 768	−643	204	335	1 748	768	−182	−332
Total monetary financial institutions	HBRU	−4 536	−1 389	−345	3 476	1 531	2 004	592	2 044	3 310	−781	14 618
Issued by other sectors[1]	HHZN	−711	1 350	2 298	1 252	1 858	1 583	2 429	1 783	2 700	237	10 892
Total transactions in commercial paper	HBQW	−5 247	−39	1 953	4 728	3 389	3 587	3 021	3 827	6 010	−544	25 510
Total transactions in Money Market Instruments	HHZE	−14 347	−17 268	2 986	18 770	13 080	8 379	−15 722	15 731	40 713	19 622	31 140
Total transactions in debt securities	XBLX	−697	11 403	25 837	32 204	36 912	21 915	−16 932	41 979	50 950	20 867	48 886
Total	HHZF	9 579	28 770	30 680	37 315	42 985	26 708	20 853	114 106	164 543	43 932	50 817

1 These series relate to non-governmental sectors other than monetary financial institutions.

7.5 Portfolio investment
continued

£ million

		1992	1993	1994	1995	1996	1997	1998	1999	2000	2001	2002
Net transactions (net credits less net debits)												
Equity securities (shares)	HBWV	14 225	9 429	3 493	−3 275	−4 216	9 011	35 064	57 742	93 135	−21 366	4 382
Debt securities												
Bonds and notes	LTMY	−18 246	−46 714	41 562	−14 711	−27 169	−33 281	−29 303	33 581	−37 600	−29 166	11 371
Money Market Instruments	LTMZ	−15 037	−23 510	7 434	16 027	14 754	−1 019	−16 989	1 463	43 508	7 948	34 455
Total debt securities	HBWX	−33 283	−70 224	48 996	1 316	−12 415	−34 300	−46 292	35 044	5 908	−21 218	45 826
Total	HHZD	**−19 058**	**−60 795**	**52 489**	**−1 959**	**−16 631**	**−25 289**	**−11 228**	**92 786**	**99 043**	**−42 584**	**50 208**

7.6 Portfolio investment
Sector analysis

£ million

		1992	1993	1994	1995	1996	1997	1998	1999	2000	2001	2002
Portfolio investment abroad (UK assets = net debits)												
Investment by:												
Monetary financial institutions												
Banks	-HBWF	15 350	37 317	9 852	26 066	20 057	21 599	51 751	20 840	40 239	43 017	−11 922
Building societies	HEPI	87	1 216	256	132	83	1 206	1 458	1 094	3 772	1 526	−339
Total monetary financial institutions	-HBRJ	15 437	38 533	10 108	26 198	20 140	22 805	53 209	21 934	44 011	44 543	−12 261
Central government	-RUUR	–	–	–	–	–	–	–	–	–	–	–
Insurance companies and pension funds	-HBRO	2 128	6 157	−989	3 766	12 013	6 936	16 726	12 872	−5 963	27 548	25 094
Other financial intermediaries	-HBRP	10 832	43 821	−32 461	10 070	27 285	24 100	−37 619	−13 270	16 744	10 889	−13 998
Private non-financial corporations	-HBRQ	35	1 227	794	−359	1 418	−2 105	−319	−336	11 336	2 922	1 357
Household sector[1]	-HBRR	205	−173	739	−401	−1 240	261	84	120	−628	158	88
Total	-HHZC	**28 637**	**89 565**	**−21 809**	**39 274**	**59 616**	**51 997**	**32 081**	**21 320**	**65 500**	**86 516**	**609**
Portfolio investment in the UK (UK liabilities = net credits)												
Investment in securities issued by:												
Monetary financial institutions (banks and building societies)	CGPH	−8 441	−12 274	9 434	19 686	18 555	11 696	−18 310	23 761	44 141	15 378	22 659
Central government	HBSO	6 410	17 272	5 171	296	5 995	−3 312	101	−4 877	−552	−3 983	−4 230
Local authorities	HBQT	–	–	–	–	–	–	–	–	–	–	–
Public corporations	HCEW	−10	−6	−2	−7	–	–	–	–	–	–	–
Other sectors	CGPL	11 620	23 778	16 077	17 340	18 435	18 324	39 062	95 222	120 954	32 537	32 388
Total	HHZF	**9 579**	**28 770**	**30 680**	**37 315**	**42 985**	**26 708**	**20 853**	**114 106**	**164 543**	**43 932**	**50 817**
Net transactions net credits less net debits)												
In assets and liabilities of:												
Monetary financial institutions	LTNA	−23 878	−50 807	−674	−6 512	−1 585	−11 109	−71 519	1 827	130	−29 165	34 920
Central government	ZPOG	6 410	17 272	5 171	296	5 995	−3 312	101	−4 877	−552	−4 439	−4 559
Local authorities	HBQT	–	–	–	–	–	–	–	–	–	–	–
Public corporations	HCEW	−10	−6	−2	−7	–	–	–	–	–	–	–
Other sectors	LTNB	−1 580	−27 254	47 994	4 264	−21 041	−10 868	60 190	95 836	99 465	−8 980	19 847
Total	HHZD	**−19 058**	**−60 795**	**52 489**	**−1 959**	**−16 631**	**−25 289**	**−11 228**	**92 786**	**99 043**	**−42 584**	**50 208**

1 The household sector includes non-profit institutions serving households.

Financial account   United Kingdom Balance of Payments The Pink Book 2003

7.7 Other investment

£ million

		1992	1993	1994	1995	1996	1997	1998	1999	2000	2001	2002
Other investment abroad (UK assets = net debits)												
Trade credit												
Long-term												
Central government	-XBMC	340	400	400	400	400	–	–	–	–	–	–
Other sectors[1]	-HCQK	332	30	–103	–407	–19	–	–	–	–	–	–
Total long-term trade credit	-HBRZ	672	430	297	–7	381	–	–	–	–	–	–
Short-term												
Other sectors[1]	-XBMF	–49	47	–190	49	1 698	–635	–1 119	102	–42	–315	559
Total trade credit	-XBMB	623	477	107	42	2 079	–635	–1 119	102	–42	–315	559
Loans												
Long-term												
Bank loans under ECGD guarantee	-HGBS	–862	–513	291	1 128	–626	643	–7	–355	–1 476	187	–1 017
Inter-government loans by the UK	-HEUC	–32	–57	–53	–59	–44	–51	–176	–19	–27	–20	–19
Loans by Commonwealth Development Corporation (public corporations)	-HETB	77	76	9	99	101	54	47	25	2	–	–
Loans by the Export Credit Guarantee Department	HMNR	–	–	–	–	–	–	–	–180	–176	–163	–175
Loans by specialist leasing companies[1]	-HGKU	–	–	–	–	–	–	–	–	–	–	–
Total long-term loans	-HBSG	–817	–494	247	1 168	–569	646	–136	–529	–1 677	4	–1 211
Short-term loans												
By monetary financial institutions												
By banks												
Sterling loans	NFBE	1 602	–456	–945	619	4 802	3 342	–613	2 621	1 869	4 863	4 768
Foreign currency loans	ZPON	3 605	–7 002	–2 810	11 183	34 157	27 803	1 581	14 299	55 631	43 228	12 416
Total banks	HEQO	5 207	–7 458	–3 755	11 802	38 959	31 145	968	16 920	57 500	48 091	17 184
By building societies	NFBG	–	4	5	–	–9	–	–	–	–	1	3
Total monetary financial institutions	ZPOL	5 207	–7 454	–3 750	11 802	38 950	31 145	968	16 920	57 500	48 092	17 187
By other sectors	-XBLN	226	274	–126	34	125	8	–133	3	–	–	–
Total short-term loans	VTUL	5 433	–7 180	–3 876	11 836	39 075	31 153	835	16 923	57 500	48 092	17 187
Total loans	-XBMG	4 616	–7 674	–3 629	13 004	38 506	31 799	699	16 394	55 823	48 096	15 976
Currency and deposits												
Transactions in foreign notes and coin												
Monetary financial institutions (banks)	TAAG	–14	42	22	–5	35	42	30	–63	–44	1	21
Other sectors[1]	-HETF	–17	40	1	34	50	76	10	40	28	–4	14
Total foreign notes and coin	HEOV	–31	82	23	29	85	118	40	–23	–16	–3	35
Deposits abroad by UK residents												
Deposits by monetary financial institutions												
Deposits by banks												
Sterling deposits	-HBQY	8 640	8 689	–247	893	3 726	28 254	6 032	–12 470	20 713	7 296	–6 612
Foreign currency deposits	-HBQZ	4 744	–6 772	51 480	8 874	23 187	85 277	12 679	–16 617	110 531	28 883	60 762
Total deposits by UK banks	-XBMI	13 384	1 917	51 233	9 767	26 913	113 531	18 711	–29 087	131 244	36 179	54 150
Deposits by building societies	TAID	230	1 017	61	397	–443	1 351	–124	–145	610	–51	–567
Total deposits by monetary financial institutions	HCES	13 614	2 934	51 294	10 164	26 470	114 882	18 587	–29 232	131 854	36 128	53 583

1 These series relate to non-governmental sectors other than monetary financial institutions.

7.7 Other investment
continued

£ million

		1992	1993	1994	1995	1996	1997	1998	1999	2000	2001	2002
Other investment abroad - *continued*												
Currency and deposits - *continued*												
Deposits abroad by UK residents - *continued*												
Deposits by securities dealers	-HGTF	14 471	45 636	–22 393	18 328	61 179	5 660	–6 117	45 920	47 567	58 756	–10 896
Deposits by other UK residents[1]	-HBSI	–1 698	3 827	2 782	5 799	8 817	16 315	6 858	23 306	34 603	31 422	38 614
Total deposits abroad by UK residents	-HBXV	26 387	52 397	31 683	34 291	96 466	136 857	19 328	39 994	214 024	126 306	81 301
Total currency and deposits	-HBVN	26 356	52 479	31 706	34 320	96 551	136 975	19 368	39 971	214 008	126 303	81 336
Other assets												
Central government subscriptions to international organisations												
Regional development banks	-HEUD	34	42	75	65	56	60	65	50	50	53	69
European Investment Bank (EIB)	-HEUE	22	23	14	16	16	–	–	–	–	–	–
Other subscriptions	-HEUF	12	14	1	4	9	3	2	41	3	3	21
Total central government subscriptions	-HGLR	68	79	90	85	81	63	67	91	53	56	90
Other short-term central government assets	-LOEL	26	52	13	43	1 460	105	28	256	310	–29	462
Total central government	-LOES	94	131	103	128	1 541	168	95	347	363	27	552
Debt forgiveness (monetary financial institutions)[2]	-FJNF	–	–88	–518	–	–	–	–	–	–	–	–
Other sectors (excluding monetary financial institutions)												
Long-term assets	-HHZH	–	–	–	–	–	–	–	–	–	–	–
Short-term assets												
Public corporations assets abroad	-HBSR	–	–	–	–	–	–	–	–	–	–	–
Public corporations debt forgiveness	HMLW	–	–	–	–	–	–	–	–23	–231	–300	–300
Other[1]	-HBSK	4	4	4	4	4	–	–	–	–	–	–
Total short-term assets	-HHZI	4	4	4	4	4	–	–	–23	–231	–300	–300
Total other sectors	-XBLP	4	4	4	4	4	–	–	–23	–231	–300	–300
Total other assets	-XBMK	98	47	–411	132	1 545	168	95	324	132	–273	252
Total	-XBMM	31 693	45 329	27 773	47 498	138 681	168 307	19 043	56 791	269 921	173 811	98 123

1 This series relates to non-governmental sectors other than monetary financial institutions.
2 This series also appears in the capital account (see Table 6.1).

7.7 Other investment
continued

£ million

		1992	1993	1994	1995	1996	1997	1998	1999	2000	2001	2002
Other investment in the UK (UK liabilities = net credits)												
Trade credit												
Long-term[1]	CGJF	198	335	357	265	18	–	–	–	–	–	–
Short-term[1]	XBLQ	–29	–3	8	–2	13	–7	–	–	–	–	–
Total trade credit	XBMO	169	332	365	263	31	–7	–	–	–	–	–
Loans												
Long-term												
Drawings by:												
Central government	HBSP	40	–	–	–	–	–	–	–	–	–	–
Local authorities	HBSQ	135	217	76	120	150	58	9	17	–	–	–
Public corporations	HHYT	–	–	–	–	–	–	–	–	–	–	–
Other [1]	HIBY	–	–	–	–	–	–	–	–	–	–	–
Total long-term drawings	HBST	175	217	76	120	150	58	9	17	–	–	–
Repayments from:												
Central government	HBSW	–133	–127	–131	–103	–99	–254	–91	–105	–114	–46	–48
Local authorities	HBSX	–129	–140	–163	–174	–139	–109	–96	–123	–188	–118	–52
Public corporations	HHYU	–430	–18	–116	–144	–14	–206	–5	–	–	–	–
Other [1]	HIBZ	–177	–56	–1	–1	–	–	–	–	–	–	–
Total long-term repayments	HBSY	–869	–341	–411	–422	–252	–569	–192	–228	–302	–164	–100
Total long-term loans	HBSZ	–694	–124	–335	–302	–102	–511	–183	–211	–302	–164	–100
Short-term loans to:												
Central government	HBTA	1 289	–2 825	–	–	–	–	–	–	–	–	–
Local authorities	HBTB	–2	7	9	3	2	–2	–	–	–	–	–
Public corporations	HIAW	–	–	–	–	–	–	–	–	–	–	–
Securities dealers	HBTD	18 276	78 614	–58 541	34 398	73 904	32 764	14 901	28 746	59 410	62 790	–37 602
Other [1]	HBSS	4 338	8 680	783	5 074	10 117	20 609	–3 728	10 424	12 873	40 226	7 655
Total short-term loans	HBTC	23 901	84 476	–57 749	39 475	84 023	53 371	11 173	39 170	72 283	103 016	–29 947
Total loans	XBMP	23 207	84 352	–58 084	39 173	83 921	52 860	10 990	38 959	71 981	102 852	–30 047
Currency and deposits												
Sterling notes and coin												
Notes (issued by Bank of England)	HLYV	53	65	85	60	32	45	98	77	67	–31	72
Coins (issued by Royal Mint)	HMAT	6	6	10	6	3	5	11	8	8	–3	8
Total notes and coin	AASD	59	71	95	66	35	50	109	85	75	–34	80
Deposits from abroad with UK residents												
Deposits with monetary financial institutions												
Deposits with banks												
Sterling deposits	NWXP	4 670	–1 401	6 550	10 248	–431	16 550	13 800	23 179	32 508	16 381	11 186
Foreign currency deposits	NFAS	25 313	39 616	40 805	15 766	70 488	131 530	37 421	–11 261	166 107	107 666	78 124
Total deposits with banks	HBWA	29 983	38 215	47 355	26 014	70 057	148 080	51 221	11 918	198 615	124 047	89 310
Deposits with building societies	NEWS	923	1 624	1 445	444	1 241	–165	883	542	567	523	308
Total deposits with UK monetary financial institutions	HDKE	30 906	39 839	48 800	26 458	71 298	147 915	52 104	12 460	199 182	124 570	89 618
Deposit liabilities of UK central government	HEUN	–188	21	950	484	–608	–759	304	693	527	–178	–24
Total deposits from abroad with UK residents	HBXY	30 718	39 860	49 750	26 942	70 690	147 156	52 408	13 153	199 709	124 392	89 594
Total currency and deposits	HMAO	30 777	39 931	49 845	27 008	70 725	147 206	52 517	13 238	199 784	124 358	89 674

1 These series relate to non-governmental sectors other than monetary financial institutions.

7.7 Other investment
continued

£ million

		1992	1993	1994	1995	1996	1997	1998	1999	2000	2001	2002
Other investment in the UK - *continued*												
Other liabilities												
Long-term												
Net equity of foreign households in life insurance reserves and in pension funds	QZEP	6	−1	−3	−2	−2	−2	−2	−2	−4	−5	−1
Prepayments of premiums and reserves against outstanding claims	NQMC	928	296	493	973	6 793	264	3	−602	942	−141	316
Total long-term liabilities	VTUG	934	295	490	971	6 791	262	1	−604	938	−146	315
Short-term	HJYF	−70	244	−939	48	1 056	29	138	−129	−90	526	−613
Total other liabilities	XBMX	864	539	−449	1 019	7 847	291	139	−733	848	380	−298
Total	XBMN	55 017	125 154	−8 323	67 463	162 524	200 350	63 646	51 464	272 613	227 590	59 329
Net transactions (net credits less net debits)												
Trade credit	LTNC	−480	−197	245	221	−2 048	628	1 119	−102	42	315	−559
Loans	LTND	18 591	92 026	−54 455	26 169	45 415	21 061	10 291	22 565	16 158	54 756	−46 023
Deposits	LTNE	4 421	−12 548	18 139	−7 312	−25 826	10 231	33 149	−26 733	−14 224	−1 945	8 338
Other	LTNF	792	544	−25	887	6 302	123	44	−1 057	716	653	−550
Total	HHYR	23 324	79 825	−36 096	19 965	23 843	32 043	44 603	−5 327	2 692	53 779	−38 794

7.8 Other investment
Sector analysis

£ million

		1992	1993	1994	1995	1996	1997	1998	1999	2000	2001	2002
Other investment abroad (UK assets = net debits)												
Investment by:												
Monetary financial institutions												
Banks	-HBSL	17 715	-6 100	47 273	22 692	65 281	145 361	19 702	-12 585	187 224	84 458	70 338
Building societies	HEQR	230	1 021	66	397	-452	1 351	-124	-145	610	-50	-564
Total monetary financial institutions	HCET	17 945	-5 079	47 339	23 089	64 829	146 712	19 578	-12 730	187 834	84 408	69 774
Central government	-HBSM	402	474	450	469	1 897	117	-81	328	336	7	533
Public corporations	-HBSV	77	76	9	99	101	54	47	-155	-174	-163	-175
Other sectors	-HBSN	13 269	49 858	-20 025	23 841	71 854	21 424	-501	69 348	81 925	89 559	27 991
Total	-XBMM	**31 693**	**45 329**	**27 773**	**47 498**	**138 681**	**168 307**	**19 043**	**56 791**	**269 921**	**173 811**	**98 123**
Other investment in the UK (UK liabilities = net credits)												
Investment in:												
Monetary financial institutions												
Banks	CGOT	30 036	38 280	47 440	26 074	70 089	148 125	51 319	11 995	198 682	124 016	89 382
Building societies	NEWS	923	1 624	1 445	444	1 241	-165	883	542	567	523	308
Total monetary financial institutions	HBWG	30 959	39 904	48 885	26 518	71 330	147 960	52 202	12 537	199 249	124 539	89 690
Central government	HBWH	976	-2 681	642	423	-696	-1 003	338	443	307	275	-722
Local authorities	HBWJ	4	84	-78	-51	13	-53	-87	-106	-188	-118	-52
Public corporations	HBWL	-430	-18	-116	-144	-14	-206	-5	–	–	–	–
Other sectors	HBWM	23 508	87 865	-57 656	40 717	91 891	53 652	11 198	38 590	73 245	102 894	-29 587
Total	XBMN	**55 017**	**125 154**	**-8 323**	**67 463**	**162 524**	**200 350**	**63 646**	**51 464**	**272 613**	**227 590**	**59 329**
Net transactions (net credits less net debits)												
In assets and liabilities of:												
Monetary financial institutions												
Banks	LTNG	12 321	44 380	167	3 382	4 808	2 764	31 617	24 580	11 458	39 558	19 044
Building societies	LTNH	693	603	1 379	47	1 693	-1 516	1 007	687	-43	573	872
Total monetary financial institutions	LTNI	13 014	44 983	1 546	3 429	6 501	1 248	32 624	25 267	11 415	40 131	19 916
Central government	LTNJ	574	-3 155	192	-46	-2 593	-1 120	419	115	-29	268	-1 255
Local authorities	HBWJ	4	84	-78	-51	13	-53	-87	-106	-188	-118	-52
Public corporations	LTNK	-507	-94	-125	-243	-115	-260	-52	155	174	163	175
Other sectors	LTNL	10 239	38 007	-37 631	16 876	20 037	32 228	11 699	-30 758	-8 680	13 335	-57 578
Total	HHYR	**23 324**	**79 825**	**-36 096**	**19 965**	**23 843**	**32 043**	**44 603**	**-5 327**	**2 692**	**53 779**	**-38 794**

7.9 Reserve assets
Central government sector
Net debits

£ million

		1992	1993	1994	1995	1996	1997	1998	1999	2000	2001	2002
Monetary gold	-HBOX	−269	−212	756	−72	−23	1 115	931	−412	−883	−786	−266
Special drawing rights	-HBOY	−693	−250	176	−48	−31	84	−16	38	−73	−22	26
Reserve position in the Fund	-HBOZ	274	−138	27	622	57	410	751	626	−478	633	469
Foreign Exchange												
Currency and deposits												
With central banks	-HBPC	..	..	..	..	−418	−675	−1 822	239	−368	6	95
With other banks	-HBPD	..	..	..	..	1 509	400	−733	2 312	6	−900	−863
Total currency and deposits	-HBPB	..	..	..	..	1 091	−275	−2 555	2 551	−363	−892	−767
Securities												
Bonds and notes	-HBPG	..	..	..	..	−1 108	−2 937	−214	−3 105	5 418	−1 838	2 280
Money market instruments	-HBPH	..	..	..	..	−496	−777	939	−337	244	−185	−2 043
Total securities	-HBPE	..	..	..	..	−1 604	−3 714	725	−3 442	5 662	−2 023	237
Total foreign exchange	-HBPA	−719	1 298	86	−701	−513	−3 989	−1 830	−891	5 299	−2 915	−530
Other claims	-HBPI	−	−	−	−	−	−	−	−	50	5	−158
Total	-LTCV	−1 407	698	1 045	−200	−510	−2 380	−164	−639	3 915	−3 085	−459

Chapter 8

International Investment Position

Summary

The international investment position is the balance sheet of the stock of external assets and liabilities. Between 1966 and 1994 the UK's assets tended to exceed its liabilities, by up to a record £86.4 billion in 1986. From 1995 however, the UK has recorded a net liability position in every year, reaching a record £133.2 billion in 1998. Since then the net liability position has fallen to £9.2 billion in 2002, equivalent to less than 1 per cent of GDP.

The value of UK assets and liabilities grew most rapidly between 1996 and 2001, when they broadly doubled. This period corresponded with a surge in cross-border investment, much of it associated with merger and acquisition activity. During this period, total assets increased to £3206 billion and total liabilities increased to £3236 billion at end 2001. In 2002, the level of assets and liabilities changed little as investment abroad and in the UK has largely been offset by falls in the value of global equity markets, leading to lower equity security assets and liabilities.

Around half of all UK assets at end 2002 were held by banks. Foreign investment in UK banks also accounted for around half of all UK liabilities, down from around three-quarters in the late 1980s. UK banks' liabilities have consistently exceeded their assets in the last ten years, reaching a record £136.4 billion in 2002.

UK assets include reserve assets held by central government. Reserves are mainly held in the form of foreign exchange – in particular bonds and notes. In the years for which detailed data are available, bonds and notes accounted for around half of the total reserve assets, and monetary gold accounted for around a sixth of total assets (although this declined to around 10 per cent in the last few years). Reserve assets in 2002 account for less than 1 per cent of total UK assets, down from around 4 per cent in the late 1980s.

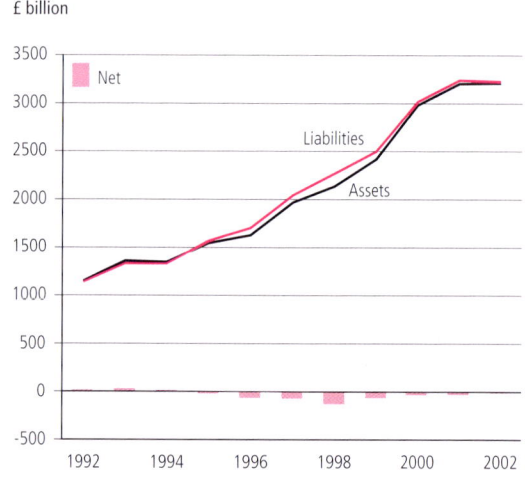

Figure **8.1**

International investment position

£ billion

Figure 8.2

UK assets

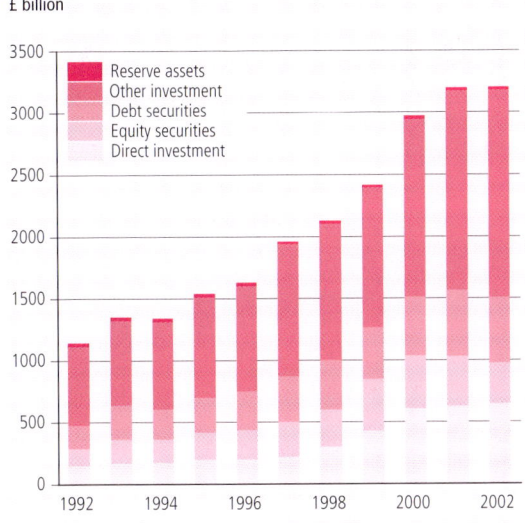

UK assets

The proportion of direct investment abroad remained fairly constant through much of the 1990s at around 12 per cent of total UK assets. Between 1998 and 2000 it increased to over 20 per cent, reflecting the high level of merger and acquisition activity by UK companies in those years. It has remained at 20 per cent since 2000. Portfolio investment assets increased rapidly in the late 1980s and early 1990s, to reach around a third of total UK assets in 1993. This proportion remained fairly stable until 1999, since when it has declined to 27 per cent in 2002, mainly due to the falls in world stock markets in these years. The proportion of other investment assets gradually declined from around 60 per cent in the late 1980s to 47 per cent of total assets in 1999, since when it has increased to 52 per cent, probably due to the relative security of such assets in times of financial turmoil.

Figure 8.3

UK liabilities

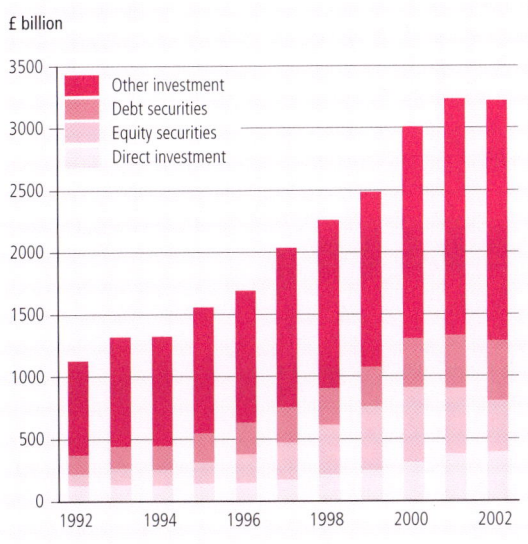

UK liabilities

Direct investment in the UK accounted for around 10 per cent of the total value of UK liabilities throughout the last decade. Portfolio investment increased from just over 20 per cent in 1990 to 33 per cent in 2000, before falling back in 2001. The increase in portfolio liabilities was mainly in equity, reflecting the counterpart to the big outward direct investment acquisitions in recent years. The proportion declined to 28 per cent in 2002 partly due to substantially reduced outward merger and acquisition activity, but also as a result of stock market falls reducing the value of UK equity. As for assets, the share of the value of other investment liabilities in the UK fell from around two-thirds in 1990 to less than 57 per cent in 2000, since when it has increased to 60 per cent at end 2002.

Direct investment

The strongest growth in UK assets has been in direct investment abroad. Between 1992 and 2002, UK direct investment assets increased from £151.8 billion to £644.8 billion. UK private non-financial corporations (PNFC's) accounted for 85 per cent of UK direct investment assets at end 2002, banks accounted for less than 5 per cent and other financial intermediaries a further 7 per cent. The value of PNFC's assets trebled between 1997 and 2000, reflecting the substantial foreign acquisitions by UK oil and telecom companies in this period.

The growth in inward direct investment has not been as spectacular as for outward in the last 10 years, roughly trebling between 1992 and 2002 to £397.5 billion. PNFC's share of the value of total foreign direct investment liabilities fell from around 85 per cent in 1990 to 75 per cent in 1997, since when it has increased to 80 per cent. The increase in the late 1990s was driven by inward investment in UK oil, pharmaceutical and telecom companies. Direct investment in UK banks accounted for only 7 per cent of inward investment in 2002, down from 12 per cent in 1997.

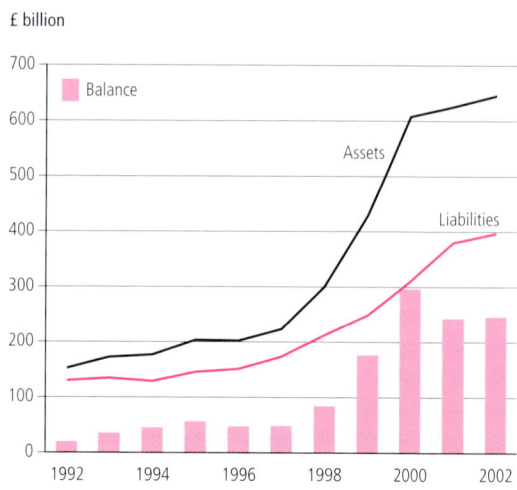

Figure 8.4
Direct investment
£ billion

Portfolio investment

Between 1992 and 2001 UK portfolio investment assets increased from £327.2 billion to £942.5 billion, since when it has fallen back to £865.3 billion. The value of investment in equity securities increased threefold to £429.3 billion between 1992 and 2000, since when they have declined nearly 25 per cent to £333.6 billion. The value of foreign debt securities held by UK investors also almost trebled between 1992 and 2002, with most of the growth between 1996 and 2001. UK banks hold two thirds of total UK debt securities assets, but less than 1 per cent of total equity security assets. UK insurance companies, pension funds and other financial intermediaries hold the vast majority of UK equity assets and over a quarter of UK debt security assets.

The total value of UK portfolio investment liabilities has declined for the second consecutive year to £892.6 billion at the end of 2002. Previously the value of UK portfolio investment liabilities had risen every year since 1990. The falls in the last two years do not reflect any disinvestment in UK issued securities, but rather a fall in the price of UK equity on the London stock exchange. Partly offsetting the falls in equity, the total value of foreign investment in debt securities has continued to rise, reaching £482.8 billion in 2002, up almost 15 per cent compared to the level of investment at the end of 2001. Investment in short-term instruments continues to grow strongly, with investment in commercial paper issued by UK banks doubling to £28.9 billion in 2002.

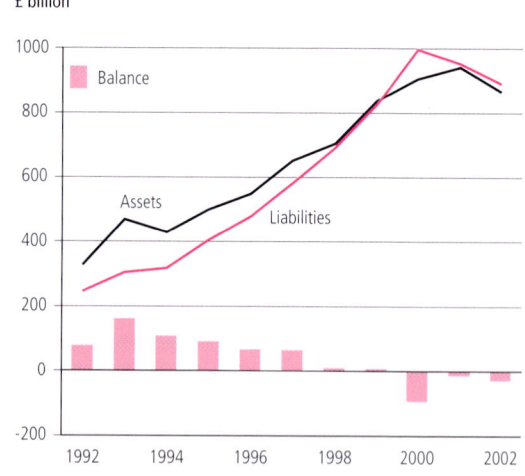

Figure 8.5
Portfolio investment
£ billion

Other investment

Other investment accounts for over half of total UK external assets and although the growth in the last 10 years has not been as strong as portfolio and direct investment, it has shown substantial increases in the level of investment since 1999. UK banks deposits and short term loans to abroad accounted for 70 per cent of total other investment abroad in 2002; this proportion has declined from around 80 per cent of total other investment in the late 1980s. The bulk of UK bank deposits abroad were in foreign currencies: only 11 per cent was held in sterling at end 2002. There has been strong growth in the value of deposits abroad by non-bank sectors in the last two years.

Deposits from abroad held with UK banks represent the largest item in other investment liabilities, although these have declined over the period 1992 to 2002, to 74 per cent in 2002. Of total deposits with UK banks of £1434.6 billion in 2002, only 16 per cent were held in sterling. The fall in the proportionate value of deposits with banks is largely the result of the increase in short term loans to UK securities dealers and other non-bank sectors – increasing from £117.7 billion in 1992 to £475.8 billion by end 2002.

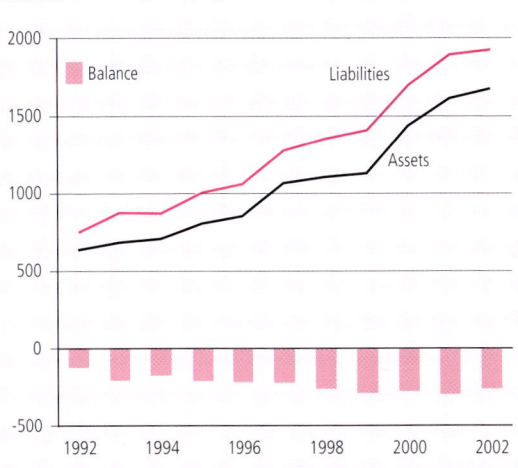

Figure **8.6**

Other investment

£ billion

8.1 International investment position
Summary table
Balance sheets valued at end of year

£ billion

		1992	1993	1994	1995	1996	1997	1998	1999	2000	2001	2002
UK Assets												
Direct investment abroad												
Equity capital and reinvested earnings	CGMO	145.0	162.4	164.8	188.0	190.9	214.2	273.7	402.1	575.0	590.7	630.8
Other capital assets	HBUW	6.8	10.2	11.4	15.7	10.7	9.0	25.9	26.0	32.5	34.2	14.0
Total direct investment abroad	HBWD	151.8	172.6	176.1	203.7	201.6	223.3	299.6	428.1	607.4	625.0	644.8
Portfolio investment abroad												
Equity securities	HEPX	138.8	194.0	186.8	217.0	238.3	282.3	303.7	419.9	429.3	409.7	333.6
Debt securities	HHZX	188.3	275.7	243.0	282.3	309.9	368.6	400.2	418.4	476.8	532.8	531.7
Total portfolio investment abroad	HHZZ	327.2	469.8	429.8	499.3	548.2	651.0	703.8	838.3	906.1	942.5	865.3
Other investment abroad	HLXV	639.7	684.4	708.6	808.1	852.6	1 068.2	1 105.5	1 130.4	1 435.0	1 613.1	1 676.5
Reserve assets	LTEB	28.3	29.7	30.7	31.8	27.3	22.8	23.3	22.2	28.8	25.6	25.4
Total	HBQA	**1 146.9**	**1 356.5**	**1 345.2**	**1 542.9**	**1 629.7**	**1 965.3**	**2 132.2**	**2 418.9**	**2 977.3**	**3 206.2**	**3 212.1**
UK Liabilities												
Direct investment in the UK												
Equity capital and reinvested earnings	HBUY	93.7	98.9	98.7	118.9	120.6	134.3	159.8	192.4	240.6	283.1	302.1
Other capital liabilities	HBVC	37.2	37.0	31.2	27.3	32.1	39.4	53.8	57.9	69.8	97.5	95.4
Total direct investment in the UK	HBWI	130.8	135.9	129.9	146.2	152.6	173.7	213.6	250.3	310.4	380.6	397.5
Portfolio investment in the UK												
Equity securities	HLXX	92.8	133.7	126.1	172.7	226.1	301.9	402.1	509.8	604.4	529.5	409.8
Debt securities	HLXY	154.3	173.2	193.8	233.6	253.9	281.4	290.7	319.0	393.8	424.9	482.8
Total portfolio investment in the UK	HLXW	247.1	306.9	320.0	406.3	480.0	583.3	692.8	828.9	998.2	954.4	892.6
Other investment in the UK	HLYD	756.3	882.3	877.4	1 013.0	1 064.9	1 282.1	1 359.0	1 410.4	1 704.8	1 900.9	1 931.1
Total	HBQB	**1 134.2**	**1 325.1**	**1 327.3**	**1 565.5**	**1 697.5**	**2 039.1**	**2 265.5**	**2 489.5**	**3 013.4**	**3 236.1**	**3 221.3**
Net International Investment Position												
Direct investment												
Equity capital and reinvested earnings	HBSH	51.3	63.5	66.0	69.0	70.3	80.0	113.9	209.7	334.4	307.7	328.7
Other capital	CGKF	−30.4	−26.8	−19.8	−11.5	−21.4	−30.4	−27.9	−31.9	−37.3	−63.3	−81.4
Total net direct investment	HBWQ	20.9	36.7	46.2	57.5	49.0	49.5	85.9	177.8	297.1	244.4	247.3
Portfolio investment												
Equity securities	CGNE	46.0	60.3	60.7	44.3	12.2	−19.5	−98.4	−90.0	−175.1	−119.8	−76.2
Debt securities	CGNF	34.1	102.6	49.1	48.7	56.0	87.2	109.5	99.4	82.9	107.9	48.9
Total net portfolio investment	CGNH	80.1	162.9	109.8	93.0	68.2	67.7	11.0	9.4	−92.2	−11.9	−27.3
Other investment	CGNG	−116.6	−197.9	−168.8	−204.9	−212.3	−213.9	−253.6	−280.0	−269.8	−287.9	−254.6
Reserve assets	LTEB	28.3	29.7	30.7	31.8	27.3	22.8	23.3	22.2	28.8	25.6	25.4
Total	HBQC	**12.8**	**31.4**	**17.9**	**−22.6**	**−67.8**	**−73.8**	**−133.2**	**−70.6**	**−36.1**	**−29.8**	**−9.2**
Allocations of Special Drawing Rights to the UK by the IMF	HEVP	1.7	1.8	1.8	1.8	1.6	1.6	1.6	1.6	1.7	1.7	1.6

8.2 International investment position
Sector analysis
Balance sheets valued at end of year

£ billion

		1992	1993	1994	1995	1996	1997	1998	1999	2000	2001	2002
UK Assets												
Monetary financial institutions												
Banks	CGNI	617.9	652.6	704.0	805.5	798.9	1 030.1	1 140.0	1 132.2	1 411.5	1 522.4	1 561.8
Building societies	VTXF	0.6	2.9	3.2	3.4	3.1	2.9	4.3	5.0	8.5	10.0	9.1
Total monetary financial institutions	CGNJ	618.6	655.5	707.2	808.9	801.9	1 033.0	1 144.3	1 137.2	1 419.9	1 532.3	1 570.9
Central government	CGNK	36.4	38.3	39.7	41.2	38.7	34.4	34.8	25.7	32.7	29.6	29.9
Public corporations	CGNL	1.3	1.6	1.7	1.9	1.9	2.0	1.9	4.5	4.7	4.7	4.7
Other sectors	CGNM	490.7	661.1	596.6	690.8	787.1	896.0	951.3	1 251.5	1 519.9	1 639.6	1 606.6
Total	HBQA	**1 146.9**	**1 356.5**	**1 345.2**	**1 542.9**	**1 629.7**	**1 965.3**	**2 132.2**	**2 418.9**	**2 977.3**	**3 206.2**	**3 212.1**
UK Liabilities												
UK Monetary financial institutions (banks and building societies)	HBYJ	716.5	746.6	805.6	919.9	916.5	1 113.0	1 182.6	1 197.2	1 485.8	1 623.3	1 707.3
Central government	CGOG	44.9	62.6	61.5	65.7	69.2	67.9	76.4	63.7	65.6	59.8	58.7
Local authorities	CGOH	1.2	1.3	1.2	1.2	1.2	1.1	1.2	1.1	0.8	0.7	0.6
Public corporations	CGOI	0.2	0.1	0.3	0.2	0.2	–	–	–	–	–	–
Other sectors	HCON	371.5	514.6	458.7	578.5	710.3	857.1	1 005.3	1 227.7	1 461.2	1 552.1	1 454.7
Total	HBQB	**1 134.2**	**1 325.1**	**1 327.3**	**1 565.5**	**1 697.5**	**2 039.1**	**2 265.5**	**2 489.5**	**3 013.4**	**3 236.0**	**3 221.3**
Net International Investment Position												
Monetary financial institutions (banks and building societies)	HDIJ	−97.9	−91.1	−98.4	−111.0	−114.6	−80.0	−38.3	−60.0	−65.9	−91.0	−136.4
Central government	CGOK	−8.5	−24.3	−21.8	−24.4	−30.5	−33.5	−41.6	−37.9	−32.9	−30.3	−28.8
Local authorities	-CGOH	−1.2	−1.3	−1.2	−1.2	−1.2	−1.1	−1.2	−1.1	−0.8	−0.7	−0.6
Public corporations	CGOL	1.2	1.5	1.4	1.7	1.7	2.0	1.9	4.5	4.7	4.7	4.7
Other sectors	HDKB	119.2	146.5	137.9	112.3	76.8	38.8	−54.0	23.9	58.7	87.5	151.9
Total	HBQC	**12.8**	**31.4**	**17.9**	**−22.6**	**−67.8**	**−73.8**	**−133.2**	**−70.6**	**−36.1**	**−29.8**	**−9.2**

8.3 Direct investment
Balance sheets valued at end of year

£ billion

		1992	1993	1994	1995	1996	1997	1998	1999	2000	2001	2002
Direct investment abroad												
(UK assets)												
Equity capital and reinvested earnings												
Ordinary share capital and reinvested earnings	CVWF	141.6	159.2	162.1	185.4	188.5	212.3	271.9	399.8	570.6	586.8	627.3
Holdings of property	HCHP	3.4	3.2	2.7	2.6	2.4	1.9	1.8	2.3	4.3	4.0	3.5
Total equity capital and reinvested earnings	CGMO	145.0	162.4	164.8	188.0	190.9	214.2	273.7	402.1	575.0	590.7	630.8
Other capital												
Claims on affiliated enterprises												
Debt securities issued by affiliated enterprises	CVWG	–	–	1.8	3.0	1.5	2.9	6.3	8.8	28.1	25.5	25.0
Other claims on affiliated enterprises												
Inter-company balance	CVOK	35.3	40.1	39.8	45.9	44.8	47.7	66.1	71.4	80.7	92.2	91.2
Branch indebtedness balance	CVOP	4.2	3.7	4.8	5.9	5.7	6.3	10.4	10.2	7.9	13.2	15.0
Total claims on affiliated enterprises	CGLS	39.5	43.8	46.4	54.8	52.0	57.0	82.8	90.3	116.8	130.8	131.2
Liabilities to affiliated enterprises												
Inter-company balance	-CVOL	−31.4	−32.1	−33.7	−37.0	−40.3	−47.1	−53.2	−61.8	−79.1	−92.2	−111.6
Branch indebtedness balance	-CVOQ	−1.3	−1.5	−1.3	−2.0	−1.0	−0.8	−3.7	−2.5	−5.2	−4.4	−5.6
Total liabilities to affiliated enterprises	-HHDJ	−32.7	−33.7	−35.0	−39.1	−41.3	−48.0	−56.9	−64.4	−84.3	−96.6	−117.2
Total other capital assets	HBUW	6.8	10.2	11.4	15.7	10.7	9.0	25.9	26.0	32.5	34.2	14.0
Total	HBWD	**151.8**	**172.6**	**176.1**	**203.7**	**201.6**	**223.3**	**299.6**	**428.1**	**607.4**	**625.0**	**644.8**
Direct investment in the UK												
(UK liabilities)												
Equity capital and reinvested earnings												
Share capital and reinvested earnings												
Quoted share capital and reinvested earnings	CVVB	–	–	–	–	–	–	–	–	–	–	–
Unquoted share capital and reinvested earnings	CVVC	86.5	91.3	90.3	110.2	111.3	124.1	149.0	180.7	227.1	269.1	287.4
Total share capital and reinvested earnings	HBUX	86.5	91.3	90.3	110.2	111.3	124.1	149.0	180.7	227.1	269.1	287.4
Holdings of UK property	HCQM	7.2	7.6	8.5	8.7	9.3	10.2	10.9	11.7	13.5	14.0	14.7
Total equity capital and reinvested earnings	HBUY	93.7	98.9	98.7	118.9	120.6	134.3	159.8	192.4	240.6	283.1	302.1
Other capital												
Liabilities to direct investors												
Debt securities issued by affiliated enterprises	CVVD	3.2	3.3	3.9	4.2	6.3	6.7	6.6	7.0	11.0	11.5	11.9
Other liabilities to direct investors												
Inter-company balance	CVVJ	43.0	40.1	37.9	38.9	43.4	53.4	78.4	96.0	103.8	128.0	126.8
Branch indebtedness balance	CVVM	4.8	5.4	4.3	4.4	6.2	7.4	8.1	6.8	8.5	9.0	9.0
Total liabilities to direct investors	HBVB	51.0	48.8	46.2	47.5	55.9	67.5	93.2	109.8	123.2	148.5	147.6
Claims on direct investors												
Inter-company balance	-CVVI	−13.2	−11.4	−14.9	−20.1	−23.7	−27.7	−39.2	−51.8	−51.3	−48.3	−49.6
Branch indebtedness balance	-CVVL	−0.6	−0.5	−0.1	−0.1	−0.2	−0.3	−0.2	−0.1	−2.1	−2.7	−2.7
Total claims on direct investors	-HBVA	−13.9	−11.8	−15.0	−20.2	−23.9	−28.0	−39.4	−51.9	−53.4	−51.0	−52.2
Total other capital liabilities	HBVC	37.2	37.0	31.2	27.3	32.1	39.4	53.8	57.9	69.8	97.5	95.4
Total	HBWI	**130.8**	**135.9**	**129.9**	**146.2**	**152.6**	**173.7**	**213.6**	**250.3**	**310.4**	**380.6**	**397.5**
Net international investment position												
(UK assets less UK liabilities)												
Equity capital												
Ordinary share capital and reinvested earnings	LTNM	55.0	67.9	71.8	75.1	77.3	88.2	123.0	219.1	343.5	317.7	339.9
Holdings of property	LTNN	−3.7	−4.4	−5.8	−6.1	−6.9	−8.2	−9.1	−9.4	−9.2	−10.0	−11.2
Total equity capital and reinvested earnings	HBSH	51.3	63.5	66.0	69.0	70.3	80.0	113.9	209.7	334.4	307.7	328.7
Total other capital	CGKF	−30.4	−26.8	−19.8	−11.5	−21.4	−30.4	−27.9	−31.9	−37.3	−63.3	−81.4
Total	HBWQ	**20.9**	**36.7**	**46.2**	**57.5**	**49.0**	**49.5**	**85.9**	**177.8**	**297.1**	**244.4**	**247.3**

8.4 Direct investment Sector analysis
Balance sheets valued at end of year

£ billion

		1992	1993	1994	1995	1996	1997	1998	1999	2000	2001	2002
Direct investment abroad (UK assets)												
By:												
Monetary financial institutions (banks)	CVKH	2.9	3.9	6.2	5.8	5.3	3.2	9.9	11.7	18.1	24.8	27.7
Insurance companies	DPYH	12.7	14.5	12.3	17.0	17.5	22.5	22.0	21.2	24.3	23.5	21.8
Other financial intermediaries	CVWH	1.0	8.6	7.5	9.3	11.5	15.8	26.9	26.8	34.9	37.8	43.4
Private non-financial corporations	CVLX	134.0	144.3	148.8	170.1	165.9	180.6	239.5	366.7	527.9	536.5	549.4
Public corporations	CVOF	0.4	0.6	0.7	0.8	0.7	0.8	0.8	1.1	1.7	1.7	1.8
Household sector[1]	AQHH	0.8	0.6	0.6	0.7	0.7	0.3	0.5	0.6	0.6	0.7	0.8
Total	HBWD	**151.8**	**172.6**	**176.1**	**203.7**	**201.6**	**223.3**	**299.6**	**428.1**	**607.4**	**625.0**	**644.8**
Direct investment in the UK (UK liabilities)												
In:												
Monetary financial institutions (banks)	CVJW	10.7	13.0	13.4	15.4	17.8	21.3	20.3	19.8	26.0	27.1	27.5
Insurance companies	CVSM	4.2	4.1	3.1	3.1	6.8	9.0	9.4	13.7	11.7	13.5	13.3
Other financial intermediaries												
Securities dealers	CVTC	4.3	6.9	6.2	7.1	8.0	8.4	7.2	8.2	9.5	10.9	11.7
Other	CVTS	1.3	1.1	1.4	2.2	2.8	4.9	8.1	7.4	15.8	19.5	24.3
Total other financial intermediaries	CVUI	5.7	8.0	7.6	9.4	10.8	13.3	15.2	15.6	25.2	30.4	36.0
Private non-financial corporations	CVKW	110.3	110.9	105.9	118.3	117.2	130.2	168.7	201.3	247.4	309.7	320.7
Total	HBWI	**130.8**	**135.9**	**129.9**	**146.2**	**152.6**	**173.7**	**213.6**	**250.3**	**310.4**	**380.6**	**397.5**
Net international investment position (UK assets less UK liabilities)												
Monetary financial institutions	LTNO	−7.8	−9.1	−7.2	−9.5	−12.5	−18.1	−10.5	−8.1	−8.0	−2.3	0.2
Insurance companies	LTNP	8.5	10.5	9.2	13.9	10.6	13.4	12.6	7.6	12.6	10.1	8.5
Other financial intermediares	LTNQ	−4.7	0.6	−0.1	–	0.7	2.6	11.7	11.2	9.7	7.4	7.4
Private non-financial corporations	LTNR	23.7	33.4	43.0	51.7	48.7	50.4	70.8	165.5	280.4	226.8	228.7
Public corporations	CVOF	0.4	0.6	0.7	0.8	0.7	0.8	0.8	1.1	1.7	1.7	1.8
Household sector[1]	AQHH	0.8	0.6	0.6	0.7	0.7	0.3	0.5	0.6	0.6	0.7	0.8
Total	HBWQ	**20.9**	**36.7**	**46.2**	**57.5**	**49.0**	**49.5**	**85.9**	**177.8**	**297.1**	**244.4**	**247.3**

1 The household sector includes non-profit institutions serving households.

8.5 Portfolio investment
Balance sheets valued at end of year

£ billion

		1992	1993	1994	1995	1996	1997	1998	1999	2000	2001	2002
Portfolio investment abroad (UK assets)												
Investment in equity securities (shares) by:													
Monetary financial Institutions (banks)	VTWF	3.6	2.0	3.5	4.8	5.0	2.7	8.8	6.8	19.7	14.3	2.7
Insurance companies and pension funds												
Insurance companies	CGPB	31.8	48.5	47.3	59.9	62.0	72.3	77.3	115.7	100.7	106.2	86.1
Pension funds	ZPOR	63.3	84.1	74.8	82.2	84.2	104.2	108.9	148.3	135.5	127.9	114.8
Total insurance companies and pension funds	CGPV	95.1	132.6	122.1	142.0	146.2	176.5	186.2	264.0	236.2	234.1	201.0
Other financial intermediaries													
Securities dealers	HCEA	−0.2	1.2	0.8	4.3	8.5	31.4	27.0	38.3	49.3	51.9	39.4
Unit and Investment Trusts	CGSN	33.8	49.8	51.3	55.5	68.4	60.7	69.0	93.6	99.1	88.0	73.8
Other	CGTV	–	–	–	–	–	–	–	–	–	–	–
Total other financial intermediaries	HDIG	33.6	51.0	52.1	59.8	76.9	92.1	96.0	131.8	148.4	139.8	113.3
Private non-financial corporations	XBNN	0.2	0.4	0.4	0.3	0.5	0.5	0.7	1.1	10.0	8.5	6.7
Household sector[1]	HFLX	6.3	8.1	8.7	10.1	9.8	10.6	11.9	16.1	15.0	13.0	9.9
Total investment in equity securities	HEPX	138.8	194.0	186.8	217.0	238.3	282.3	303.7	419.9	429.3	409.7	333.6
Investment in debt securities													
Investment in bonds and notes by:													
Monetary financial institutions													
Banks	VTWJ	72.0	109.8	119.4	144.9	154.7	181.9	224.8	239.0	282.8	312.9	325.9
Building societies	HPEG	–	0.7	1.1	1.6	1.6	1.6	3.0	4.1	5.8	6.7	6.3
Total monetary financial institutions	HPCO	72.1	110.6	120.5	146.5	156.4	183.5	227.8	243.1	288.7	319.6	332.3
Insurance companies and pension funds													
Insurance companies	CGTU	17.5	18.9	16.4	19.8	22.5	24.4	41.4	37.8	39.8	55.9	61.1
Pension funds	JIRX	17.1	16.6	15.9	16.7	22.3	21.6	23.9	36.4	44.2	49.9	44.8
Total insurance companies and pension funds	HBUM	34.7	35.5	32.4	36.6	44.9	46.0	65.3	74.1	84.0	105.8	105.8
Other financial intermediaries													
Securities dealers	HCDZ	54.0	94.5	58.6	61.4	80.4	103.4	68.1	45.6	45.2	34.9	28.4
Unit and investment trusts	HBXZ	2.2	2.4	2.8	4.3	3.0	3.6	4.7	5.8	6.8	8.4	7.7
Other	HCNA	–	–	–	–	–	0.1	–	–	–	–	–
Total other financial intermediaries	HCOR	56.2	96.9	61.4	65.6	83.5	107.1	72.8	51.4	52.1	43.3	36.0
Private non-financial corporations	XBNK	1.8	2.0	2.6	2.5	3.1	0.8	1.4	0.4	1.6	2.0	2.2
Household sector[1]	HCJC	9.3	10.4	10.7	11.9	6.4	6.7	7.1	6.9	7.5	7.6	7.7
Total investment in bonds and notes	HEPW	174.1	255.4	227.5	263.1	294.2	344.2	374.4	376.0	433.8	478.3	484.1
Investment in Money Market Instruments													
Investment in commercial paper by:													
Monetary financial institutions													
Banks	HBMW	12.2	14.8	10.1	13.2	8.6	16.6	21.3	31.3	33.2	39.7	32.3
Building societies	TAIG	–	0.6	0.4	0.1	0.1	0.3	0.2	0.2	1.1	1.8	1.2
Central government	LSPI	–	–	–	–	–	–	–	–	–	0.5	0.8
Insurance companies and pension funds	HBXX	0.8	0.9	0.9	1.1	1.4	2.0	1.1	1.4	1.3	1.1	1.2
Other financial intermediaries	HGRJ	0.4	2.2	2.1	2.6	3.3	3.0	1.1	4.1	2.2	4.7	4.2
Private non-financial corporations	HFBN	0.8	1.7	1.7	1.7	1.8	2.1	1.2	1.9	3.0	4.9	6.0
Total investment in commercial paper	HGRK	14.2	20.1	15.2	18.7	15.2	24.0	24.8	38.9	40.8	52.6	45.5
Investment in certificates of deposit													
Monetary financial institutions													
(Building societies)	TAIE	–	–	0.1	–	–	–	0.2	0.1	0.6	0.6	1.2
Other financial intermediaries	CDHB	–	0.2	0.2	0.5	0.5	0.5	0.8	3.4	1.6	1.2	0.9
Total transactions in certificates of deposit	VTWN	–	0.2	0.3	0.5	0.5	0.5	1.0	3.6	2.2	1.8	2.1
Total investment in Money Market Instruments	HLYR	14.3	20.3	15.4	19.2	15.7	24.5	25.8	42.5	43.0	54.5	47.6
Total investment in debt securities	HHZX	188.3	275.7	243.0	282.3	309.9	368.6	400.2	418.4	476.8	532.8	531.7
Total	HHZZ	**327.2**	**469.8**	**429.8**	**499.3**	**548.2**	**651.0**	**703.8**	**838.3**	**906.1**	**942.5**	**865.3**

1 The household sector includes non-profit institutions serving households.

8.5 Portfolio investment
Balance sheets valued at end of year

continued

£ billion

		1992	1993	1994	1995	1996	1997	1998	1999	2000	2001	2002
Portfolio investment in the UK (UK liabilities)												
Investment in equity securities (shares) issued by:												
Monetary financial Institutions (banks and building societies)	HBQD	2.6	4.7	4.4	6.3	9.7	14.8	10.7	9.2	5.8	5.2	2.7
Other sectors[1]	HBQE	90.2	129.1	121.8	166.4	216.3	287.1	391.4	500.6	598.6	524.3	407.1
Total investment in equity securities	HLXX	92.8	133.7	126.1	172.7	226.1	301.9	402.1	509.8	604.4	529.5	409.8
Investment in debt securities												
Investment in bonds and notes												
Issues by central government												
UK foreign currency bonds and notes	HEWE	8.4	9.5	12.4	13.1	10.0	6.4	5.1	4.7	6.5	3.3	0.7
Investment in British government stocks by:												
Foreign central banks (exchange reserves)	HCCH	11.4	14.5	14.1	14.7	14.7	14.1	18.0	16.7	18.1	18.7	20.9
Other foreign residents	HEQF	17.4	34.2	30.1	31.2	38.8	43.8	50.9	39.6	37.8	34.2	34.3
Total investment in British government stocks	HEWD	28.8	48.7	44.2	45.9	53.5	58.0	68.8	56.2	55.9	53.0	55.2
Total issues by central government	HHGF	37.3	58.2	56.6	58.9	63.5	64.4	73.9	60.9	62.4	56.3	55.8
Local authorities' bonds	HHGG	–	–	–	–	–	–	–	–	–	–	–
Public corporations' bonds	HEWM	–	–	–	–	–	–	–	–	–	–	–
Issues by monetary financial Institutions (banks and building societies)												
Bonds	HMBL	10.3	12.6	16.4	20.4	22.1	25.4	28.6	33.6	39.0	41.4	51.2
European medium term notes and other short-term paper:												
Issued by UK banks	HCFA	7.0	10.2	13.9	15.5	19.6	24.9	27.7	33.5	35.8	39.2	40.4
Issued by UK building societies	HCFD	2.6	3.5	5.6	5.1	4.4	1.3	1.1	1.2	2.6	3.3	3.2
Total	HHGI	9.6	13.7	19.6	20.7	24.0	26.3	28.9	34.7	38.4	42.5	43.6
Total monetary financial institutions	HMBF	19.9	26.3	36.0	41.1	46.1	51.7	57.4	68.3	77.4	83.9	94.9
Issues by other sectors[1]	HHGJ	32.0	39.2	51.2	63.6	68.8	79.1	89.0	104.5	121.3	129.0	159.5
Total investment in bonds and notes	HLXZ	89.1	123.7	143.8	163.7	178.4	195.2	220.3	233.8	261.1	269.2	310.3
Investment in Money Market Instruments												
Investment in treasury bills (issued by central government)												
Sterling treasury bills	ACQJ	1.2	0.7	0.5	1.4	1.0	0.6	0.2	0.2	–	0.1	0.3
Euro treasury bills	HHNX	1.3	1.2	1.3	1.8	2.0	1.1	0.2	–	–	–	–
Total treasury bills	HLYU	2.5	1.9	1.8	3.2	3.0	1.8	0.4	0.2	–	0.1	0.3
Investment in certificates of deposit (issued by monetary financial institutions)												
Issued by UK banks	HHGK	48.6	33.6	33.0	46.3	51.1	59.1	41.6	53.9	92.8	115.0	109.6
Issued by UK building societies	HHGL	0.6	0.6	0.8	0.6	0.6	0.2	0.3	0.5	0.5	0.4	0.6
Total certificates of deposit	HHGM	49.2	34.2	33.8	46.9	51.7	59.3	42.0	54.4	93.3	115.3	110.3
Investment in commercial paper												
Issued by UK monetary financial Institutions												
UK banks	HHGN	2.4	2.8	3.0	4.7	6.3	11.1	11.4	10.1	14.7	14.9	28.9
Building societies	HHGO	4.2	2.4	1.7	3.9	3.2	0.7	1.0	2.7	2.9	2.8	2.4
Total monetary financial institutions	HHGP	6.6	5.2	4.8	8.6	9.5	11.8	12.4	12.8	17.7	17.7	31.4
Issued by other sectors[1]	HLYQ	6.8	8.2	9.6	11.2	11.3	13.4	15.6	17.8	21.7	22.5	30.7
Total investment in commercial paper	HHGR	13.4	13.4	14.4	19.8	20.8	25.2	28.0	30.6	39.4	40.2	62.0
Total investment in Money Market Instruments	HLYB	65.1	49.5	50.0	69.9	75.5	86.3	70.4	85.3	132.7	155.7	172.6
Total investment in debt securities	HLXY	154.3	173.2	193.8	233.6	253.9	281.4	290.7	319.0	393.8	424.9	482.8
Total	HLXW	**247.1**	**306.9**	**320.0**	**406.3**	**480.0**	**583.3**	**692.8**	**828.9**	**998.2**	**954.4**	**892.6**

1 These series relate to non-governmental sectors other than monetary financial institutions.

International investment position United Kingdom Balance of Payments The Pink Book 2003

8.5 Portfolio investment
Balance sheets valued at end of year

continued
£ billion

		1992	1993	1994	1995	1996	1997	1998	1999	2000	2001	2002
Net international investment position (UK assets less UK liabilities)												
Equity securities	CGNE	46.0	60.3	60.7	44.3	12.2	−19.5	−98.4	−90.0	−175.1	−119.8	−76.2
Debt securities												
Bonds and notes	LTNS	85.0	131.7	83.7	99.4	115.8	149.0	154.0	142.2	172.7	209.1	173.8
Money market instruments	LTNT	−50.9	−29.2	−34.5	−50.7	−59.8	−61.8	−44.6	−42.8	−89.8	−101.2	−125.0
Total debt securities	CGNF	34.1	102.6	49.1	48.7	56.0	87.2	109.5	99.4	82.9	107.9	48.9
Total	CGNH	**80.1**	**162.9**	**109.8**	**93.0**	**68.2**	**67.7**	**11.0**	**9.4**	**−92.2**	**−11.9**	**−27.3**

8.6 Portfolio investment
Sector analysis
Balance sheets valued at end of year

£ billion

		1992	1993	1994	1995	1996	1997	1998	1999	2000	2001	2002
Portfolio investment abroad (UK assets)												
Investment by:												
Monetary financial institutions												
Banks	HBRW	87.9	126.6	133.0	163.0	168.3	201.1	254.8	277.1	335.8	367.0	360.9
Building societies	VTWM	0.1	1.3	1.6	1.7	1.7	1.9	3.4	4.5	7.5	9.0	8.7
Total monetary financial institutions	HHGQ	88.0	127.9	134.5	164.6	170.1	203.1	258.2	281.6	343.2	376.0	369.6
Central government	LSPI	–	–	–	–	–	–	–	–	–	0.5	0.8
Insurance companies and pension funds	HHHH	130.5	169.0	155.4	179.7	192.4	224.4	252.7	339.5	321.4	341.0	308.0
Other financial intermediaries	HHNH	90.3	150.3	115.8	128.6	164.2	202.7	170.7	190.8	204.3	189.1	154.4
Private non-financial corporations	AIMH	2.8	4.1	4.7	4.5	5.4	3.4	3.2	3.4	14.7	15.3	14.9
Household sector[1]	AINA	15.6	18.5	19.4	22.0	16.2	17.3	19.0	23.0	22.4	20.7	17.7
Total	HHZZ	**327.2**	**469.8**	**429.8**	**499.3**	**548.2**	**651.0**	**703.8**	**838.3**	**906.1**	**942.5**	**865.3**
Portfolio investment in the UK (UK liabilities)												
Investment in securities issued by:												
Monetary financial institutions (banks and building societies)	CGPC	78.3	70.3	79.0	103.0	117.1	137.6	122.5	144.8	194.2	222.2	239.2
Central government	HHGS	39.7	60.1	58.4	62.2	66.5	66.1	74.3	61.1	62.4	56.4	56.1
Local authorities	HHGG	–	–	–	–	–	–	–	–	–	–	–
Public corporations	HEWM	–	–	–	–	–	–	–	–	–	–	–
Other sectors	CGPG	129.0	176.4	182.6	241.2	296.4	379.6	496.0	623.0	741.7	675.8	597.3
Total	HLXW	**247.1**	**306.9**	**320.0**	**406.3**	**480.0**	**583.3**	**692.8**	**828.9**	**998.2**	**954.4**	**892.6**
Net international investment position (UK assets less UK liabilities)												
Monetary financial institutions	LTNU	9.6	57.6	55.6	61.7	53.0	65.5	135.7	136.9	149.1	153.8	130.4
Central government	ZPOH	−39.7	−60.1	−58.4	−62.2	−66.5	−66.1	−74.3	−61.1	−62.4	−56.0	−55.3
Local authorities	HHGG	–	–	–	–	–	–	–	–	–	–	–
Public corporations	-HEWM	–	–	–	–	–	–	–	–	–	–	–
Other sectors	LTNV	110.2	165.4	112.7	93.5	81.7	68.3	−50.3	−66.3	−178.8	−109.8	−102.4
Total	CGNH	**80.1**	**162.9**	**109.8**	**93.0**	**68.2**	**67.7**	**11.0**	**9.4**	**−92.2**	**−11.9**	**−27.3**

1 The household sector includes non-profit institutions serving households.

8.7 Other investment
Balance sheets valued at end of year

£ billion

		1992	1993	1994	1995	1996	1997	1998	1999	2000	2001	2002
Other investment abroad (UK assets)												
Trade credit												
Long-term												
Central government	ZPOC	6.6	7.0	7.4	7.8	8.2	8.2	8.2	–	–	–	–
Other sectors[1]	HCLK	1.2	1.1	1.1	0.5	0.5	0.5	0.5	–	–	–	–
Total long-term trade credit	HHGU	7.8	8.1	8.5	8.3	8.7	8.7	8.7	–	–	–	–
Short-term												
Other sectors[1]	HLXU	1.7	1.8	1.5	1.6	3.2	2.6	1.4	0.5	0.4	0.1	0.7
Total trade credit	HLXP	9.5	9.8	10.0	9.9	11.9	11.3	10.1	0.5	0.4	0.1	0.7
Loans												
Long-term												
Bank loans under ECGD guarantee	HCFQ	5.4	4.9	5.0	6.3	5.2	5.8	6.0	6.0	4.8	5.1	3.8
Inter-government loans by the UK and other central government assets	HCFN	0.7	0.7	0.6	0.6	0.5	0.5	0.3	0.3	0.3	0.2	0.2
Loans by Commonwealth Development Corporation (public corporations)	HEWZ	0.9	1.0	1.0	1.1	1.2	1.2	1.1	1.1	0.5	0.4	0.4
Loans by the Export Credit Guarantee Department	HMLX	–	–	–	–	–	–	–	2.3	2.5	2.6	2.6
Loans by specialist leasing companies[1]	HGIH	–	–	–	–	–	–	–	–	–	–	–
Total long-term loans	HFAX	7.1	6.6	6.7	8.0	6.9	7.4	7.3	9.6	8.1	8.3	7.0
Short-term loans												
By monetary financial institutions												
By banks												
Sterling loans	NLHN	14.8	14.3	13.2	13.9	18.7	24.0	23.4	26.1	27.6	32.3	37.6
Foreign currency loans	ZPOO	99.8	92.4	87.5	110.9	127.8	168.6	180.1	189.1	252.5	290.9	291.0
Total banks	HEQS	114.6	106.7	100.7	124.8	146.5	192.6	203.5	215.3	280.1	323.2	328.6
By building societies	NLHP	–	–	–	–	–	–	–	–	–	–	–
Total monetary financial institutions	ZPOM	114.6	106.7	100.7	124.8	146.5	192.6	203.5	215.3	280.1	323.2	328.6
By other sectors	HLXI	0.8	1.1	1.0	0.6	0.7	0.7	0.6	0.5	0.5	0.5	0.5
Total short-term loans	VTUM	115.4	107.7	101.7	125.4	147.2	193.3	204.0	215.8	280.6	323.8	329.1
Total loans	HLXQ	122.4	114.3	108.4	133.4	154.2	200.7	211.4	225.5	288.7	332.1	336.1
Currency and deposits												
Foreign notes and coin												
Monetary financial institutions (banks)	TAAF	–	0.1	0.1	0.1	0.1	0.1	0.2	0.1	0.1	0.1	0.1
Other sectors[1]	CGML	0.2	0.2	0.2	0.3	0.3	0.3	0.3	0.4	0.4	0.4	0.4
Total foreign notes and coin	HEOX	0.2	0.3	0.3	0.4	0.4	0.5	0.5	0.5	0.5	0.5	0.5
Deposits abroad by UK residents												
Deposits by monetary financial institutions												
Deposits by banks												
Sterling deposits	HFBB	28.6	38.1	40.0	42.9	47.0	83.2	89.2	75.6	94.8	102.1	94.6
Foreign currency deposits	HFBG	378.4	372.4	419.0	462.6	426.3	544.1	576.5	546.4	677.8	700.1	746.1
Total deposits by UK banks	HLXL	407.1	410.5	459.0	505.5	473.4	627.3	665.7	621.9	772.7	802.2	840.7
Deposits by building societies	TAIC	0.5	1.6	1.6	1.8	1.3	1.0	0.9	0.5	1.0	0.9	0.4
Total deposits by monetary financial institutions	VTWL	407.6	412.1	460.6	507.3	474.7	628.3	666.5	622.4	773.7	803.2	841.1
Deposits by securities dealers	HGUX	38.4	80.3	59.0	79.2	129.8	129.1	111.5	152.2	206.1	261.9	243.7
Deposits by other UK residents[1]	HHGW	60.5	66.2	68.7	76.5	78.5	95.2	102.0	125.3	160.9	210.6	249.1
Total deposits abroad	HBXS	506.4	558.6	588.3	663.0	683.0	852.6	880.0	899.9	1 140.6	1 275.7	1 333.8
Total currency and deposits	HBVS	506.6	558.9	588.6	663.3	683.3	853.1	880.5	900.4	1 141.1	1 276.1	1 334.3

1 These series relate to non-governmental sectors other than monetary financial institutions.

8.7 Other investment
Balance sheets valued at end of year

continued

£ billion

		1992	1993	1994	1995	1996	1997	1998	1999	2000	2001	2002
Other investment abroad - *continued* (UK assets)												
Other assets												
Central government assets												
Central government subscriptions to international organisations												
Regional development banks	HEXW	0.6	0.6	0.7	0.8	0.8	0.9	1.0	1.0	1.1	1.1	1.2
European Investment Bank (EIB)	HEXX	0.3	0.4	0.4	0.4	0.4	0.4	0.4	0.4	0.4	0.4	0.4
Other subscriptions	HEXZ	0.3	0.3	0.3	0.3	0.3	0.3	0.3	0.4	0.4	0.4	0.4
Total central government subscriptions	HLXO	1.2	1.3	1.4	1.5	1.6	1.6	1.7	1.8	1.8	1.9	2.0
Other long-term central government assets	XBJL	–	–	–	–	–	–	–	–	–	–	–
Other short-term central government assets	LOEM	–0.5	–0.4	–0.4	–0.4	1.1	1.2	1.2	1.5	1.8	1.7	2.2
Total central government	LOET	0.8	0.9	1.0	1.1	2.7	2.8	2.9	3.3	3.6	3.7	4.2
Other sectors assets												
Long-term assets[1]	HLXM	–	–	–	–	–	–	–	–	–	–	–
Short-term assets												
Public corporations assets abroad	HGJM	–	–	–	–	–	–	–	–	–	–	–
Other[1]	HHGY	0.4	0.5	0.6	0.4	0.5	0.4	0.5	0.8	1.1	1.1	1.2
Total short-term assets	HLXJ	0.4	0.5	0.6	0.4	0.5	0.4	0.5	0.8	1.1	1.1	1.2
Total other sectors	HLXN	0.4	0.5	0.6	0.4	0.5	0.4	0.5	0.8	1.1	1.1	1.2
Total other assets	HLXS	1.1	1.4	1.6	1.5	3.2	3.2	3.4	4.0	4.7	4.8	5.4
Total	HLXV	**639.7**	**684.4**	**708.6**	**808.1**	**852.6**	**1 068.2**	**1 105.5**	**1 130.4**	**1 435.0**	**1 613.1**	**1 676.5**

1 These series relate to non-governmental sectors other than monetary financial institutions.

8.7 Other investment
Balance sheets valued at end of year
continued

£ billion

		1992	1993	1994	1995	1996	1997	1998	1999	2000	2001	2002
Other investment in the UK (UK liabilities)												
Trade credit												
Long-term [1]	HBWC	0.5	0.8	1.2	1.5	1.5	1.5	1.5	–	–	–	–
Short-term [1]	HCGB	1.3	1.3	1.3	1.3	1.2	1.2	1.2	1.0	1.1	1.1	1.0
Total trade credit	HLYL	1.8	2.2	2.5	2.7	2.7	2.7	2.7	1.0	1.1	1.1	1.0
Loans												
Long-term loans to:												
Central government	HHGZ	1.4	1.3	1.1	1.0	0.8	0.6	0.4	0.4	0.6	0.5	0.4
Local authorities	HHHA	1.2	1.3	1.2	1.2	1.2	1.1	1.2	1.1	0.8	0.7	0.6
Public corporations	HHHB	0.2	0.1	0.3	0.2	0.2	–	–	–	–	–	–
Other [1]	AQBX	0.4	0.4	–	–	–	–	–	–	–	–	–
Total long-term loans	HHHC	3.2	3.1	2.6	2.3	2.2	1.7	1.6	1.4	1.4	1.2	1.0
Short-term loans to:												
Central government	HHHD	2.8	–	–	–	–	–	–	–	–	–	–
Local authorities	HHHE	–	–	–	–	–	–	–	–	–	–	–
Securities dealers	HHHF	61.1	135.7	79.2	113.4	178.0	204.3	198.3	235.7	280.6	340.6	294.8
Other [1]	HHHG	50.7	69.7	70.8	81.5	83.2	102.0	99.5	122.8	142.2	170.3	180.1
Total short-term loans	HHHJ	114.5	205.4	150.0	194.9	261.2	306.3	297.8	358.5	422.8	510.9	474.8
Total loans	HLYI	117.7	208.5	152.5	197.2	263.4	308.0	299.4	359.9	424.1	512.1	475.8
Currency and deposits												
Sterling notes and coin												
Notes (issued by Bank of England)	HLVG	0.5	0.6	0.7	0.7	0.7	0.8	0.9	1.0	1.0	1.0	1.1
Coins (issued by Royal Mint)	HLVH	0.1	0.1	0.1	0.1	0.1	0.1	0.1	0.1	0.1	0.1	0.1
Total notes and coin	APME	0.6	0.6	0.7	0.8	0.8	0.9	1.0	1.1	1.1	1.1	1.2
Deposits from abroad with UK residents												
Deposits with monetary financial institutions												
Deposits with banks												
Sterling deposits	NLCZ	87.3	86.2	92.8	103.7	106.5	134.4	147.2	167.5	200.4	215.9	228.0
Foreign currency deposits	NLDA	534.2	569.5	611.3	688.2	664.6	814.9	886.7	859.0	1 060.0	1 152.5	1 206.6
Total deposits with banks	CGEH	621.5	655.7	704.1	791.9	771.1	949.3	1 033.9	1 026.5	1 260.4	1 368.4	1 434.6
Deposits with building societies	NLDB	5.4	7.0	8.5	8.9	9.9	4.0	4.9	5.2	4.1	4.6	4.9
Total deposits with UK monetary financial institutions	HDKG	626.9	662.7	712.6	800.8	781.0	953.4	1 038.8	1 031.7	1 264.6	1 373.0	1 439.5
Deposit liabilities of UK central government	HEYH	0.2	0.2	1.2	1.7	1.1	0.3	0.6	1.3	1.8	1.7	1.6
Total deposits from abroad with UK residents	HBYA	627.1	663.0	713.8	802.5	782.1	953.7	1 039.5	1 033.0	1 266.4	1 374.7	1 441.1
Total currency and deposits	HLVI	627.7	663.6	714.5	803.3	782.9	954.6	1 040.4	1 034.1	1 267.5	1 375.8	1 442.3
Other liabilities												
Long-term												
Net equity of foreign households in life insurance reserves and in pension funds	VTUE	0.2	0.2	0.2	0.2	0.2	0.2	0.2	0.2	0.2	0.2	0.2
Prepayments of premiums and reserves against oustanding claims	NQLR	8.2	7.0	7.8	9.5	14.7	15.5	15.0	14.1	10.8	10.1	10.8
Total long-term liabilities[1]	VTUF	8.4	7.2	7.9	9.6	14.8	15.7	15.2	14.3	11.0	10.4	11.0
Short-term[1]	HBMV	0.7	0.9	–	–	1.1	1.1	1.3	1.1	1.1	1.6	1.0
Total other liabilities	HLYM	9.1	8.1	7.9	9.7	16.0	16.8	16.5	15.4	12.0	11.9	12.0
Total	HLYD	756.3	882.3	877.4	1 013.0	1 064.9	1 282.1	1 359.0	1 410.4	1 704.8	1 900.9	1 931.1

1 These series relate to non-governmental sectors other than monetary financial institutions.

8.7 Other investment
Balance sheets valued at end of year

continued
£ billion

		1992	1993	1994	1995	1996	1997	1998	1999	2000	2001	2002
Net international investment position (UK assets less UK liabilities)												
Trade credit	LTNW	7.2	7.2	7.1	7.2	9.2	8.6	7.4	−0.5	−0.7	−1.0	−0.3
Loans	LTNX	4.8	−94.1	−44.2	−63.9	−109.2	−107.3	−88.0	−134.4	−135.4	−180.0	−139.7
Currency and deposits	LTNY	−121.0	−104.7	−125.9	−140.0	−99.5	−101.5	−159.9	−133.7	−126.5	−99.7	−108.0
Other	LTNZ	−7.5	−6.3	−5.9	−8.2	−12.8	−13.7	−13.1	−11.4	−7.3	−7.2	−6.5
Total	CGNG	**−116.6**	**−197.9**	**−168.8**	**−204.9**	**−212.3**	**−213.9**	**−253.6**	**−280.0**	**−269.8**	**−287.9**	**−254.6**

8.8 Other investment
Sector analysis
Balance sheets valued at end of year

£ billion

		1992	1993	1994	1995	1996	1997	1998	1999	2000	2001	2002
Other investment abroad (UK assets)												
Investment by:												
Monetary financial institutions												
Banks	CGEI	527.1	522.1	564.8	636.7	625.2	825.8	875.3	843.4	1 057.6	1 130.6	1 173.2
Building societies	HEQT	0.5	1.6	1.6	1.8	1.3	1.0	0.9	0.5	1.0	0.9	0.4
Total monetary financial institutions	VTXD	527.6	523.7	566.4	638.4	626.6	826.8	876.2	843.9	1 058.6	1 131.6	1 173.5
Central government	CGEN	8.1	8.6	9.0	9.5	11.4	11.5	11.4	3.5	3.9	3.9	4.4
Public corporations	CGEO	0.9	1.0	1.0	1.1	1.2	1.2	1.1	3.4	3.0	3.0	3.0
Other sectors	CGGH	103.1	151.1	132.1	159.1	213.4	228.8	216.8	279.6	369.4	474.6	495.6
Total	HLXV	**639.7**	**684.4**	**708.6**	**808.1**	**852.6**	**1 068.2**	**1 105.5**	**1 130.4**	**1 435.0**	**1 613.1**	**1 676.5**
Other investment in the UK (UK liabilities)												
Investment in:												
Monetary financial institutions												
Banks	CGOV	622.0	656.3	704.8	792.7	771.8	950.1	1 034.8	1 027.4	1 261.5	1 369.4	1 435.6
Building societies	NLDB	5.4	7.0	8.5	8.9	9.9	4.0	4.9	5.2	4.1	4.6	4.9
Total monetary financial institutions	CGHB	627.4	663.3	713.2	801.6	781.7	954.2	1 039.7	1 032.7	1 265.6	1 374.0	1 440.6
Central government	CGHG	5.1	2.5	3.1	3.5	2.7	1.8	2.1	2.5	3.2	3.4	2.6
Local authorities	CGHX	1.2	1.3	1.2	1.2	1.2	1.1	1.2	1.1	0.8	0.7	0.6
Public corporations	ZPOX	..	..	..	0.2	0.2	–	–	–	–	–	–
Other sectors	CGNC	122.4	215.2	159.6	206.5	279.0	325.1	316.0	374.2	435.2	522.8	487.3
Total	HLYD	**756.3**	**882.3**	**877.4**	**1 013.0**	**1 064.9**	**1 282.1**	**1 359.0**	**1 410.4**	**1 704.8**	**1 900.9**	**1 931.1**
Net international investment position (UK assets less UK liabilities)												
Monetary financial institutions												
Banks	LTOA	−94.9	−134.1	−140.0	−156.0	−146.6	−124.3	−159.5	−184.1	−203.8	−238.8	−262.4
Building societies	LTOB	−4.8	−5.4	−6.8	−7.1	−8.6	−3.0	−4.1	−4.7	−3.1	−3.7	−4.6
Total monetary financial institutions	LTOC	−99.8	−139.6	−146.8	−163.1	−155.2	−127.4	−163.6	−188.8	−207.0	−242.5	−267.0
Central government	LTOD	3.0	6.1	5.9	6.0	8.7	9.8	9.3	1.0	0.7	0.5	1.8
Local authorities	-CGHX	−1.2	−1.3	−1.2	−1.2	−1.2	−1.1	−1.2	−1.1	−0.8	−0.7	−0.6
Public corporations	LTOE	0.8	0.9	0.7	0.9	1.0	1.2	1.1	3.4	3.0	3.0	3.0
Other sectors	LTOF	−19.3	−64.1	−27.4	−47.5	−65.6	−96.3	−99.2	−94.6	−65.8	−48.2	8.3
Total	CGNG	**−116.6**	**−197.9**	**−168.8**	**−204.9**	**−212.3**	**−213.9**	**−253.6**	**−280.0**	**−269.8**	**−287.9**	**−254.6**

8.9 Reserve assets
Central government sector
Balance sheets valued at end of year

£ billion

		1992	1993	1994	1995	1996	1997	1998	1999	2000	2001	2002
Monetary gold	HCGD	4.1	4.9	4.5	4.6	4.0	3.2	4.0	3.7	2.9	2.2	2.1
Special drawing rights	HCGE	0.4	0.2	0.3	0.3	0.2	0.3	0.3	0.3	0.2	0.2	0.2
Reserve position in the Fund	HCGF	1.3	1.3	1.3	1.6	1.4	1.8	2.6	3.3	2.9	3.5	3.8
Foreign exchange												
Currency and deposits												
With central banks	CGDE	..	..	..	3.5	2.9	3.0	0.8	0.4	0.1	0.1	0.2
With other banks	CGDF	..	..	..	2.2	3.1	2.9	2.6	5.0	3.7	2.8	1.9
Total currency and deposits	CGDD	..	..	..	5.7	5.9	5.9	3.4	5.5	3.7	2.9	2.1
Securities												
Bonds and notes	CGDH	..	..	..	17.0	14.1	10.6	10.9	7.6	16.7	14.4	16.8
Money market instruments	CGDL	–	–	–	2.6	1.7	1.0	2.1	1.8	2.3	2.2	0.2
Total securities	CGDG	..	..	..	19.6	15.8	11.6	13.0	9.5	19.0	16.6	17.0
Total foreign exchange	HCGG	22.5	23.4	24.6	25.3	21.7	17.6	16.4	14.9	22.7	19.4	19.1
Other claims	CGDM	–	–	–	–	–	–	–	–	0.1	0.4	0.2
Total	LTEB	28.3	29.7	30.7	31.8	27.3	22.8	23.3	22.2	28.8	25.6	25.4

FD Financial derivatives[1]
Balance sheets valued at end of year

£ billion

		1998	1999	2000	2001	2002
Financial derivatives assets						
UK banks' assets						
Sterling	ZPNP	27.9	29.4	49.8	43.5	56.7
Foreign currency	ZPNQ	370.5	360.8	340.6	481.0	626.2
Total UK banks	ZPNA	398.3	390.2	390.5	524.5	682.8
UK securities dealers' assets						
Sterling	RUVI	2.8	4.6	3.2	13.2	20.2
Foreign currency	RUVJ	42.4	58.0	52.6	51.9	87.9
Total UK securities dealers	RVAP	45.2	62.6	55.7	65.1	108.2
Total	ZPNC	443.6	452.8	446.2	589.6	791.0
Financial derivative liabilities						
UK banks' liabilities						
Sterling	ZPNR	34.7	36.1	48.2	43.8	57.1
Foreign currency	ZPNS	362.2	351.9	351.8	485.8	631.5
Total UK banks	ZPNB	396.9	388.0	400.0	529.6	688.7
UK securities dealers' liabilities						
Sterling	RUXE	3.1	5.3	4.3	13.6	21.2
Foreign currency	RUXF	40.4	51.9	46.5	50.2	90.8
Total UK securities dealers	RVAV	43.5	57.1	50.9	63.8	112.0
Total	ZPND	440.4	445.1	450.9	593.4	800.6
Net international investment position						
Banks	ZPNE	1.5	2.2	−9.5	−5.1	−5.8
Securities dealers	ZPNF	1.7	5.5	4.9	1.3	−3.8
Total	ZPNG	3.2	7.7	−4.6	−3.8	−9.7

1 The data in this table are not included in the main aggregates of the UK's international investment position as the data are developmental. Work is continuing to validate and improve the estimates and to obtain more information on the type of derivatives traded.

Part 3
Geographical breakdown

Chapter 9
Geographical breakdown of current account

The tables appearing in this chapter show a geographical breakdown of the current account. The data cover 63 individual countries as well as international organisations. These estimates are generally less firmly based than the world totals, and data for earlier years are less reliable than recent figures. In some cases estimates are unavailable for the first few years.

Current account by region

Current account surpluses were recorded with America and Australasia & Oceania in all years since 1992. The current account surplus with America increased by £6.2 billion to a record £17.0 billion in 2002, due to a decrease in the imports of goods from the region, and an increase in the exports of services. There was a surplus with Asia for the years 1995 to 1997 but an overall deficit in 1992 to 1994 and 1998 to 2002. The current account deficit with Asia narrowed to £10.9 billion in 2002 from £15.7 billion in 2001, largely due to lower imports of goods.

In 2002, over half of current account transactions, around 60 per cent of total credits and total debits, were with **Europe.** European Union (EU) countries accounted for around 85 per cent of the total current account flows with Europe and around half of total current account transactions. Trade in goods accounted for just over half of the current account flows with Europe, with income accounting for around a quarter.

The continent of **America** accounted for almost a quarter of total credits and around a fifth of debits. Income accounted for around two-fifths of current account flows with America. The United States of America (USA) was the most significant country, representing around 80 per cent of total current account credits and debits in the region.

Asia accounted for 13 per cent of UK current account credits in 2002, down from 18 per cent in 1992, largely due to lower income receipts. Debits remained relatively stable at around 16 per cent throughout the period. The largest component of current account debits was imports of goods, which at £39.8 billion represent 63 per cent of the total debits with the region in 2002. Asia accounted for 23 per cent of the world income credits and debits in 1992 but this has fallen over subsequent years to around 13 per cent in 2002. The single largest contributing country in Asia is Japan, representing almost 25 per cent of the total current account and nearly 40 per cent of income credits with Asia.

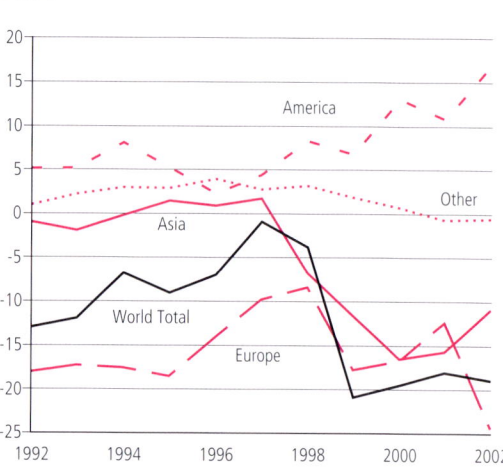

Figure **9.1**

Current account
Credits less debits
£ billion

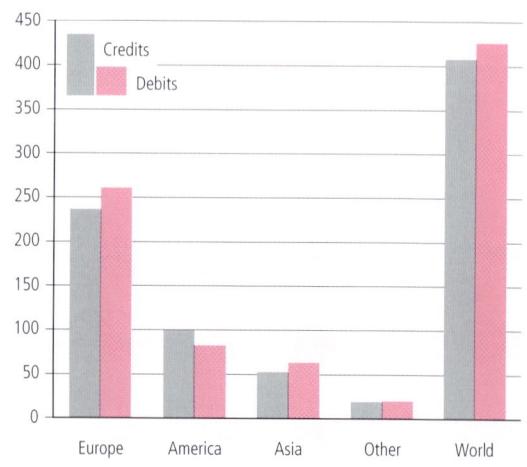

Figure **9.2**

Current account by continent, 2002
£ billion

The current account with **Africa** had been in surplus until 1999, with the first deficit being recorded in 2000. In 2001 this deficit doubled from £1.1 billion to £2.0 billion, and has stabilised in 2002. These deficits have mainly been driven by higher imports of goods by the UK.

Current account with EU, USA and Japan

A current account deficit has been recorded with the EU in every year since 1992, with the exception of 2001. Broadly speaking, surpluses on the income account are offset by deficits on all the remaining components of the current account. In 2002 the balance with the EU deteriorated to reach a record deficit of £15.5 billion, largely due to a rise in imports of goods from EU countries, and a lower income surplus.

The current account balance with the EU was in deficit by around £8.0 billion between 1992 and 1996. This deficit fell to £1.9 billion in 1998, increasing again in 1999 to £8.7 billion. Following a narrowing of the deficit to £4.7 billion in 2000, there was a surplus of £1.1 billion in 2001, the only year in which a surplus has been recorded. In 2002 the current account worsened dramatically, to a record deficit of £15.5 billion.

Net income received from the EU grew significantly from -£0.2 billion in 1992 to £16.8 billion in 2001, before falling back to £12.9 billion in 2002. The trade in goods deficit with the EU increased sharply in the last two years, reaching £20.2 billion in 2002, an increase of £8.6 billion on the previous year. These figures include the revisions made to include the effects of missing trader intra-Community VAT fraud – this has led to significant increases to data on imports from the EU from 1999 onwards. The deficit on current transfers was erratic throughout the period, starting at the lowest position in 1992 at £2.7 billion and increasing to a peak of £5.1 billion in 2000. The latest position shows a deficit of £3.8 billion, an increase of £1.8 billion on the 2001 figure. The main components of current transfers are payments to and receipts from EU institutions.

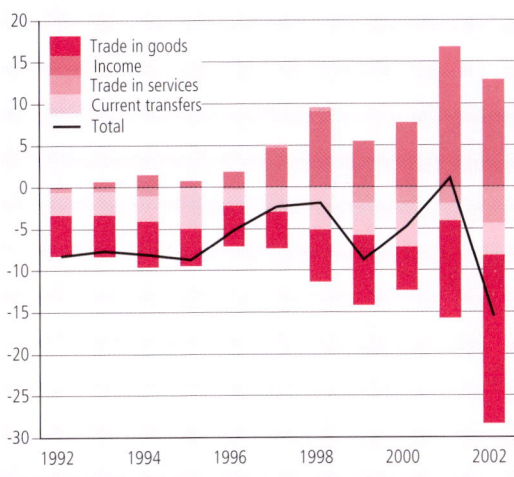

Figure 9.3

Current account with the European Union

Credits less debits

£ billion

The USA is consistently the single largest counterpart country within the UK's balance of payments, representing 19 per cent of current account credits and 15 per cent of debits in 2002. There has been a current account surplus with the USA in each year since 1992. Prior to 2000 these were typically between £2.0 billion and £4.0 billion, whereas the most recent periods have seen significantly higher surpluses. Following a downturn in 2001, the latest period shows a record surplus of £12.2 billion.

Transactions with Japan were relatively stable and in deficit over the period 1992 to 1999. However in 2000 this position worsened to give a current account deficit of £6.0 billion – an increase of £1.6 billion over the previous year. The deficit fell to £4.8 billion in 2001 and again to £2.9 billion in the latest year, mainly due to lower imports of goods.

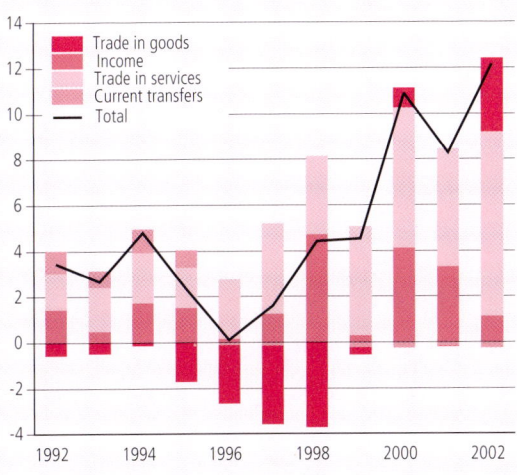

Figure 9.4

Current account with the USA

Credits less debits

£ billion

Current account in 2002: the largest balances

When ranking individual countries by the size of the current account balance in 2002 the largest surpluses were recorded with: the United States of America (£12.2 billion), the Republic of Ireland (£3.6 billion), the Netherlands (£2.7 billion), Australia (£2.7 billion) and Sweden (£1.0 billion).

The current account has been in surplus with the USA since the geographic split of the data began in 1992, reaching a record surplus of £12.2 billion in 2002. Credits exceeded debits in income (£1.1 billion), trade in services (£8.1 billion) and trade in goods (£3.2 billion), and were offset slightly by a deficit in current transfers (£0.3 billion). In 2002 transactions with the United States of America accounted for 19 per cent of global current account credits and 15 per cent of debits.

The surpluses with the Netherlands, Australia and Sweden are all driven by a positive balance on investment income; the surplus with Ireland is largely due to exports of goods and services.

When ranking individual countries by the size of the current account balance, the largest deficits were recorded with: Germany (£7.7 billion), China (£4.9 billion), Spain (£4.2 billion), Japan (£2.9 billion) and Hong Kong (£2.8 billion).

The largest current account deficit was with Germany, with imports of goods exceeding exports of goods (£10.2 billion) being partly offset by surpluses on trade in services (£0.7 billion) and income (£1.7 billion) Current transfers remained in balance.

The deficits with China, Spain, Japan and Hong Kong are all a result of trading deficits. A deficit on trade in services is the main factor in the balance with Spain; the remaining deficits are largely due to high levels of UK imports of goods from these nations.

Figure 9.5

Current account: largest 5 surpluses in 2002

£ billion

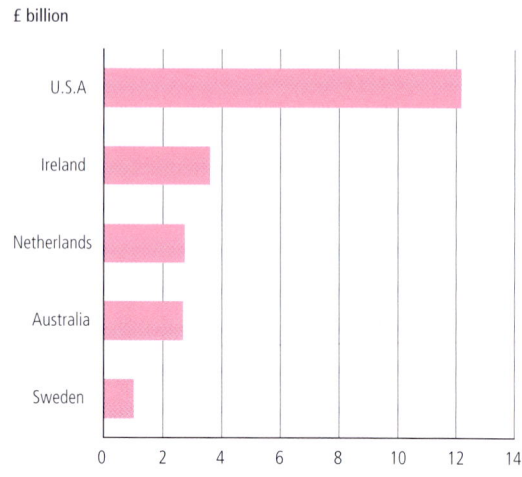

Figure 9.6

Current account: largest 5 deficits in 2002

£ billion

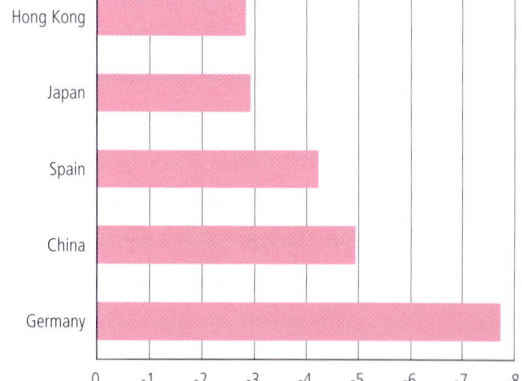

United Kingdom Balance of Payments The Pink Book 2003

Geographical breakdown of current account

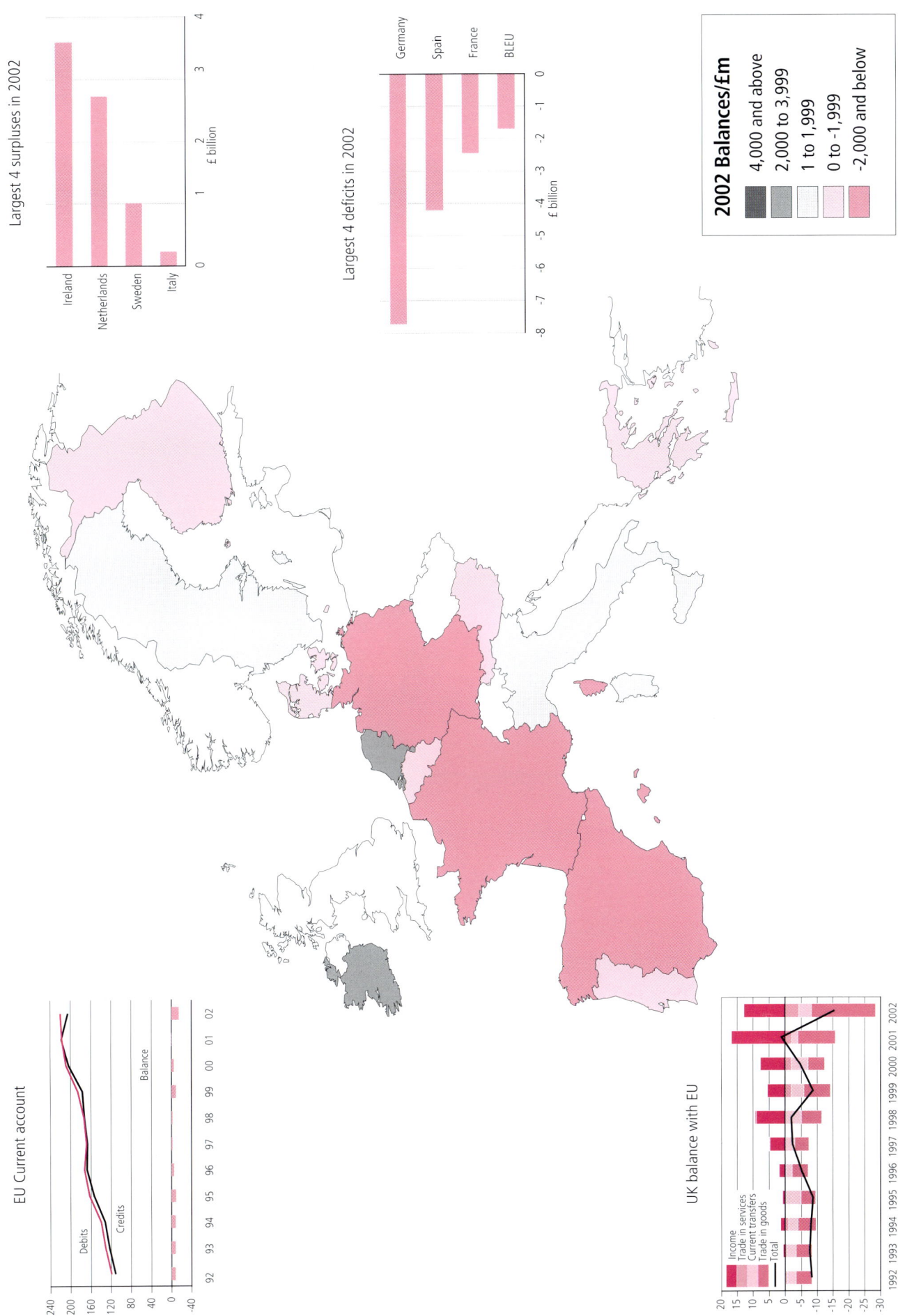

Geographical breakdown of current account

United Kingdom Balance of Payments The Pink Book 2003

Proportion of Total 2002 Credits

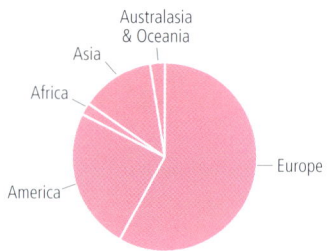

EU

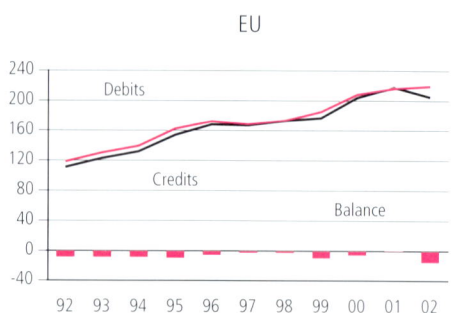

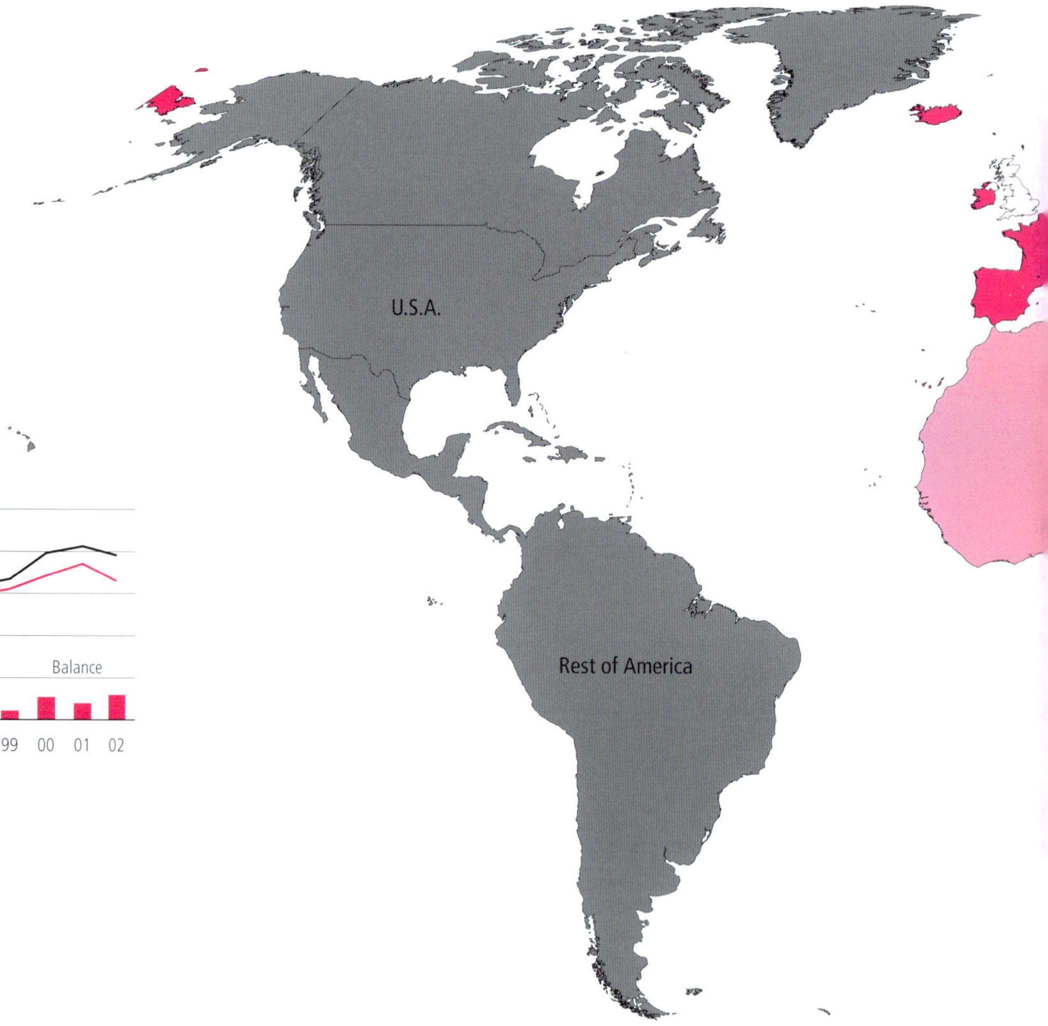

USA

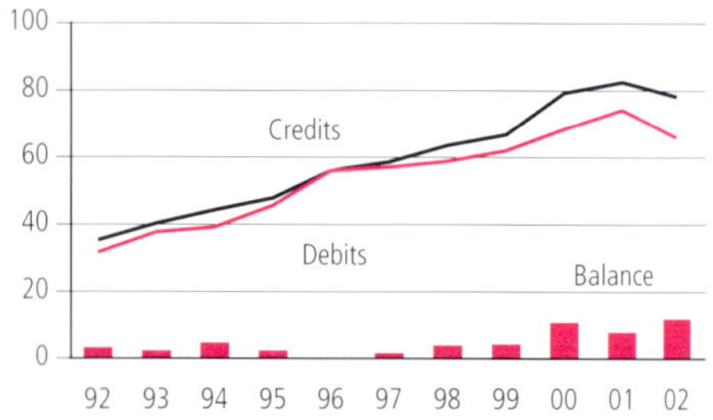

Total America

2002 Balances/£m
- 4,000 and above
- 2,000 to 3,999
- 1 to 1,999
- 0 to -1,999
- -2,000 to -3,999
- -4,000 or below

118

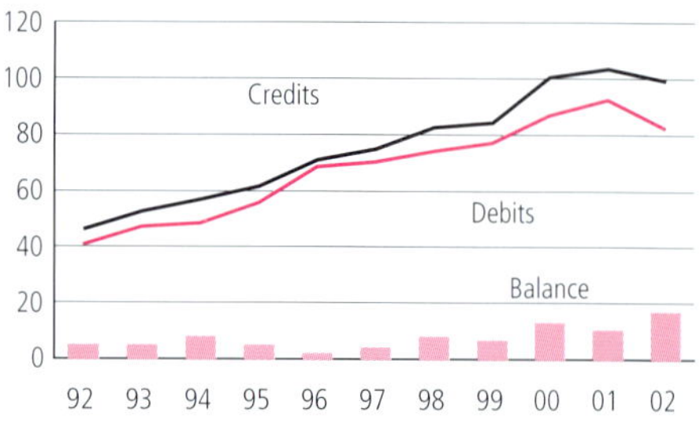

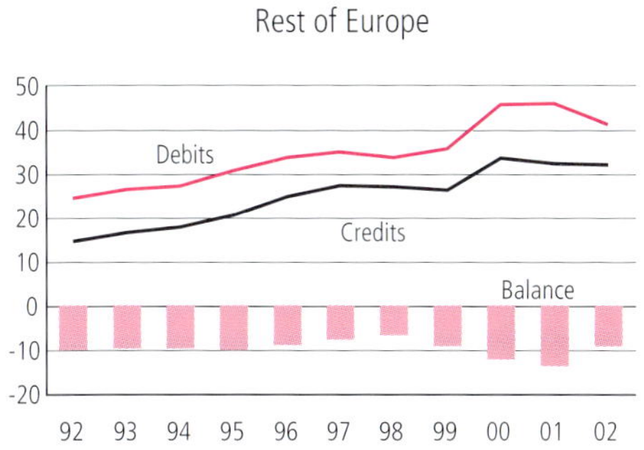

United Kingdom Balance of Payments The Pink Book 2003

Geographical breakdown of current account

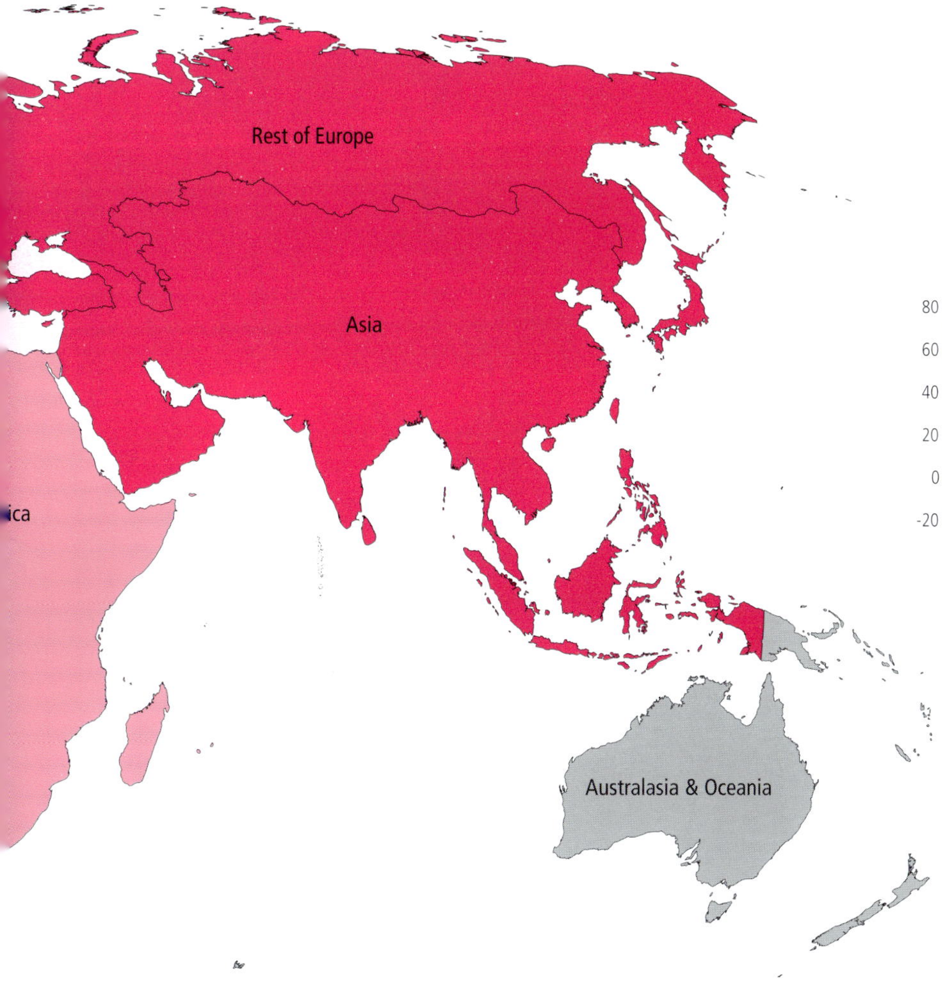

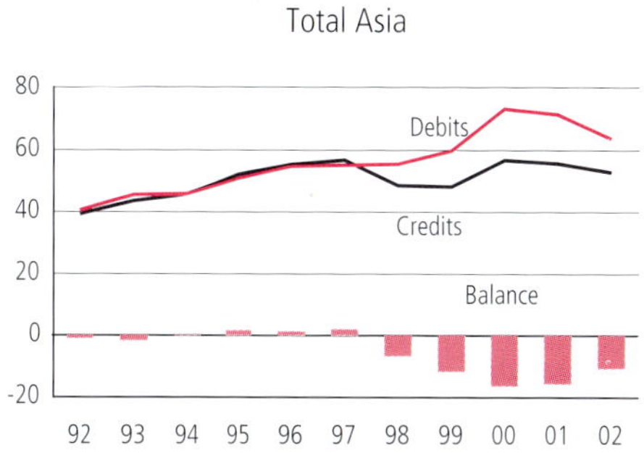

Rest of Europe

Proportion of Total 2002 Debits

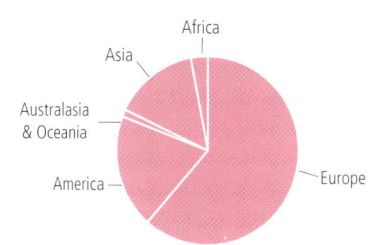

Total Asia

Total Africa

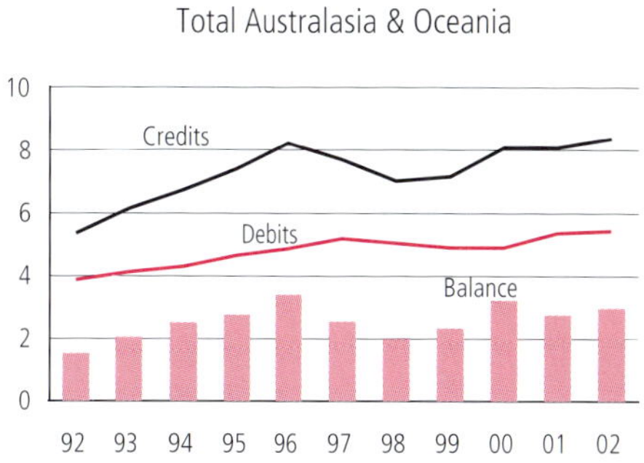

Total Australasia & Oceania

9.1 Current account
Summary transactions in 2002

£ million

	Trade in goods	Trade in services	Income	Current transfers	**Current account**
Credits					
Europe					
European Union (EU)					
Austria	1 263	370	592	32	2 257
Belgium and Luxembourg	10 534	2 391	5 496	239	18 660
Denmark	2 724	1 207	855	35	4 821
Finland	1 439	782	633	14	2 868
France	18 720	5 274	7 308	295	31 597
Germany	22 020	6 571	9 669	418	38 678
Greece	1 193	677	778	42	2 690
Ireland	15 385	3 341	4 358	134	23 218
Italy	8 493	2 604	4 893	104	16 094
Netherlands	13 984	4 127	14 056	327	32 494
Portugal	1 516	452	845	19	2 832
Spain	8 473	2 362	2 339	95	13 269
Sweden	3 867	1 349	1 929	90	7 235
European Central Bank	–	2	–	–	2
EU Institutions	–	539	622	6 302	7 463
Total EU	109 611	32 048	54 373	8 146	204 178
European Free Trade Association (EFTA)					
Iceland	131	47	26	34	238
Liechtenstein	2	42	21	1	66
Norway	1 691	1 305	804	71	3 871
Switzerland	3 074	3 324	5 120	64	11 582
Total EFTA	4 898	4 718	5 971	170	15 757
Other Europe					
Albania	19	6	–	–	25
Belarus	32	4	–	–	36
Bulgaria	131	55	55	8	249
Croatia	94	48	18	2	162
Czech Republic	1 029	167	127	2	1 325
Estonia	100	14	2	–	116
Hungary	747	188	333	8	1 276
Latvia	75	39	4	5	123
Lithuania	148	33	4	–	185
Poland	1 313	313	241	12	1 879
Romania	426	60	53	11	550
Russia	980	527	382	13	1 902
Slovakia	199	23	24	3	249
Slovenia	181	35	57	5	278
Turkey	1 286	345	338	31	2 000
Ukraine	182	218	1	–	401
Yugoslavia	62	27	1	2	92
Other	660	1 453	3 386	15	5 514
Total Europe	**122 173**	**40 321**	**65 370**	**8 433**	**236 297**
America					
Argentina	127	126	201	8	462
Brazil	880	311	541	12	1 744
Canada	3 106	1 492	1 712	173	6 483
Chile	115	101	236	7	459
Colombia	83	115	231	13	442
Mexico	704	269	461	21	1 455
United States of America	28 192	21 297	27 504	1 264	78 257
Uruguay	30	25	14	–	69
Venezuela	307	119	46	9	481
Other Central American Countries	691	1 966	5 796	135	8 588
Other	410	220	304	10	944
Total America	**34 645**	**26 041**	**37 046**	**1 652**	**99 384**
Asia					
China	1 493	703	348	10	2 554
Hong Kong	2 410	979	1 773	30	5 192
India	1 754	661	492	20	2 927
Indonesia	324	227	193	18	762
Iran	397	181	38	2	618
Israel	1 428	475	55	29	1 987
Japan	3 588	3 489	5 610	104	12 791
Malaysia	876	475	542	18	1 911
Pakistan	240	223	106	3	572
Philippines	352	137	131	8	628
Saudi Arabia	1 387	643	196	484	2 710
Singapore	1 443	1 069	2 600	10	5 122
South Korea	1 462	495	523	14	2 494
Taiwan	847	378	328	11	1 564
Thailand	529	232	176	6	943
Residual Gulf	2 618	2 571	1 397	165	6 751
Other Near & Middle East	498	316	129	294	1 237
Other	509	1 063	264	40	1 876
Total Asia	**22 155**	**14 317**	**14 901**	**1 266**	**52 639**
Australasia & Oceania					
Australia	2 119	1 881	2 658	177	6 835
New Zealand	310	345	430	54	1 139
Other	55	206	143	2	406
Total Australasia & Oceania	**2 484**	**2 432**	**3 231**	**233**	**8 380**
Africa					
Egypt	461	263	89	3	816
Morocco	346	66	22	2	436
South Africa	1 597	987	1 147	69	3 800
Other North Africa	478	248	99	11	836
Other	1 918	1 720	710	34	4 382
Total Africa	**4 800**	**3 284**	**2 067**	**119**	**10 270**
International Organisations	–	75	454	–	529
World Total	**186 257**	**86 470**	**123 075**	**11 703**	**407 505**

9.1 Current account
Summary transactions in 2002
continued

£ million

	Trade in goods	Trade in services	Income	Current transfers	Current account
Debits					
Europe					
European Union (EU)					
Austria	2 380	654	530	24	3 588
Belgium and Luxembourg	13 099	1 902	5 280	93	20 374
Denmark	3 567	797	869	32	5 265
Finland	2 780	338	329	13	3 460
France	20 329	7 720	5 708	308	34 065
Germany	32 262	5 829	7 967	356	46 414
Greece	586	1 750	393	41	2 770
Ireland	13 008	2 203	3 901	502	19 614
Italy	10 642	2 934	2 144	141	15 861
Netherlands	16 043	3 333	10 215	168	29 759
Portugal	1 751	1 036	204	40	3 031
Spain	9 097	7 083	1 180	136	17 496
Sweden	4 314	778	1 092	34	6 218
European Central Bank	–	1	–	–	1
EU Institutions	–	12	1 650	10 097	11 759
Total EU	129 858	36 370	41 462	11 985	219 675
European Free Trade Association (EFTA)					
Iceland	287	40	14	5	346
Liechtenstein	22	1	326	1	350
Norway	5 175	704	367	53	6 299
Switzerland	4 576	1 499	6 187	109	12 371
Total EFTA	10 060	2 244	6 894	168	19 366
Other Europe					
Albania	2	12	64	12	90
Belarus	31	3	15	11	60
Bulgaria	115	74	26	14	229
Croatia	68	37	139	6	250
Czech Republic	1 240	199	64	10	1 513
Estonia	323	15	3	–	341
Hungary	843	119	30	19	1 011
Latvia	474	17	6	2	499
Lithuania	259	32	4	15	310
Poland	1 255	214	92	49	1 610
Romania	510	82	27	20	639
Russia	1 940	322	258	20	2 540
Slovakia	208	23	15	6	252
Slovenia	167	17	23	4	211
Turkey	2 152	610	75	38	2 875
Ukraine	142	17	67	15	241
Yugoslavia	30	31	45	31	137
Other	673	2 507	5 561	199	8 940
Total Europe	**150 350**	**42 945**	**54 870**	**12 624**	**260 789**
America					
Argentina	236	101	4	16	357
Brazil	1 357	196	56	55	1 664
Canada	3 537	1 141	963	276	5 917
Chile	458	41	21	11	531
Colombia	210	36	17	19	282
Mexico	502	283	75	24	884
United States of America	24 973	13 208	26 378	1 522	66 081
Uruguay	47	21	1	1	70
Venezuela	182	33	43	10	268
Other Central American Countries	761	1 053	2 675	435	4 924
Other	847	297	177	101	1 422
Total America	**33 110**	**16 410**	**30 410**	**2 470**	**82 400**
Asia					
China	6 695	451	218	125	7 489
Hong Kong	5 533	620	1 756	121	8 030
India	1 795	671	415	544	3 425
Indonesia	1 001	141	55	45	1 242
Iran	33	18	96	24	171
Israel	873	307	161	38	1 379
Japan	8 248	1 390	5 976	106	15 720
Malaysia	1 724	205	114	44	2 087
Pakistan	469	336	180	229	1 214
Philippines	939	81	37	31	1 088
Saudi Arabia	671	899	560	47	2 177
Singapore	1 948	378	1 738	81	4 145
South Korea	2 789	168	32	15	3 004
Taiwan	2 375	174	320	11	2 880
Thailand	1 545	448	90	37	2 120
Residual Gulf Arabian Countries	1 219	464	1 350	86	3 119
Other Near & Middle Eastern	188	195	231	82	696
Other	1 713	911	336	613	3 573
Total Asia	**39 758**	**7 857**	**13 665**	**2 279**	**63 559**
Australasia & Oceania					
Australia	1 727	1 408	773	239	4 147
New Zealand	533	320	110	67	1 030
Other	96	38	96	21	251
Total Australasia & Oceania	**2 356**	**1 766**	**979**	**327**	**5 428**
Africa					
Egypt	414	255	137	26	832
Morocco	452	144	37	8	641
South Africa	2 673	600	551	283	4 107
Other North Africa	586	203	128	12	929
Other	3 013	1 084	5 954	1 279	5 954
Total Africa	**7 138**	**2 286**	**1 431**	**1 608**	**12 463**
International Organisations	–	40	601	1 190	1 831
World total	**232 712**	**71 304**	**101 956**	**20 498**	**426 470**

9.1 Current account
Summary transactions in 2002
continued

£ million

	Trade in goods	Trade in services	Income	Current transfers	Current account
Balances					
Europe					
European Union (EU)					
Austria	−1 117	−284	62	8	−1 331
Belgium and Luxembourg	−2 565	489	216	146	−1 714
Denmark	−843	410	−14	3	−444
Finland	−1 341	444	304	1	−592
France	−1 609	−2 446	1 600	−13	−2 468
Germany	−10 242	742	1 702	62	−7 736
Greece	607	−1 073	385	1	−80
Ireland	2 377	1 138	457	−368	3 604
Italy	−2 149	−330	2 749	−37	233
Netherlands	−2 059	794	3 841	159	2 735
Portugal	−235	−584	641	−21	−199
Spain	−624	−4 721	1 159	−41	−4 227
Sweden	−447	571	837	56	1 017
European Central Bank	–	1	–	–	1
EU Institutions	–	527	−1 028	−3 795	−4 296
Total EU	−20 247	−4 322	12 911	−3 839	−15 497
European Free Trade Association (EFTA)					
Iceland	−156	7	12	29	−108
Liechtenstein	−20	41	−305	–	−284
Norway	−3 484	601	437	18	−2 428
Switzerland	−1 502	1 825	−1 067	−45	−789
Total EFTA	−5 162	2 474	−923	2	−3 609
Other Europe					
Albania	17	−6	−64	−12	−65
Belarus	1	1	−15	−11	−24
Bulgaria	16	−19	29	−6	20
Croatia	26	11	−121	−4	−88
Czech Republic	−211	−32	63	−8	−188
Estonia	−223	−1	−1	–	−225
Hungary	−96	69	303	−11	265
Latvia	−399	22	−2	3	−376
Lithuania	−111	1	–	−15	−125
Poland	58	99	149	−37	269
Romania	−84	−22	26	−9	−89
Russia	−960	205	124	−7	−638
Slovakia	−9	–	9	−3	−3
Slovenia	14	18	34	1	67
Turkey	−866	−265	263	−7	−875
Ukraine	40	201	−66	−15	160
Yugoslavia	32	−4	−44	−29	−45
Other	−13	−1 054	−2 175	−184	−3 426
Total Europe	**−28 177**	**−2 624**	**10 500**	**−4 191**	**−24 492**
America					
Argentina	−109	25	197	−8	105
Brazil	−477	115	485	−43	80
Canada	−431	351	749	−103	566
Chile	−343	60	215	−4	−72
Colombia	−127	79	214	−6	160
Mexico	202	−14	386	−3	571
USA	3 219	8 089	1 126	−258	12 176
Uruguay	−17	4	13	−1	−1
Venezuela	125	86	3	−1	213
Other Central American Countries	−70	913	3 121	−300	3 664
Other America	−437	−77	127	−91	−478
Total America	**1 535**	**9 631**	**6 636**	**−818**	**16 984**
Asia					
China	−5 202	252	130	−115	−4 935
Hong Kong	−3 123	359	17	−91	−2 838
India	−41	−10	77	−524	−498
Indonesia	−677	86	138	−27	−480
Iran	364	163	−58	−22	447
Israel	555	168	−106	−9	608
Japan	−4 660	2 099	−366	−2	−2 929
Malaysia	−848	270	428	−26	−176
Pakistan	−229	−113	−74	−226	−642
Philippines	−587	56	94	−23	−460
Saudi Arabia	716	−256	−364	437	533
Singapore	−505	691	862	−71	977
South Korea	−1 327	327	491	−1	−510
Taiwan	−1 528	204	8	–	−1 316
Thailand	−1 016	−216	86	−31	−1 177
Residual Gulf Arabian Countries	1 399	2 107	47	79	3 632
Other Near & Middle Eastern Countries	310	121	−102	212	541
Other	−1 204	152	−72	−573	−1 697
Total Asia	**−17 603**	**6 460**	**1 236**	**−1 013**	**−10 920**
Australasia & Oceania					
Australia	392	473	1 885	−62	2 688
New Zealand	−223	25	320	−13	109
Other	−41	168	47	−19	155
Total Australasia & Oceania	**128**	**666**	**2 252**	**−94**	**2 952**
Africa					
Egypt	47	8	−48	−23	−16
Morocco	−106	−78	−15	−6	−205
South Africa	−1 076	387	596	−214	−307
Other North Africa	−108	45	−29	−1	−93
Other	−1 095	636	−2 175	−1 245	−1 572
Total Africa	**−2 338**	**998**	**636**	**−1 489**	**−2 193**
International Organisations	–	35	−147	−1 190	−1 302
World total	**−46 455**	**15 166**	**21 119**	**−8 795**	**−18 965**

9.2 Current account

£ million

		1992	1993	1994	1995	1996	1997	1998	1999	2000	2001	2002
Credits												
Europe												
European Union (EU)												
Austria	CUGP	1 418	1 563	1 748	1 983	2 187	2 023	2 187	2 147	2 340	2 333	2 257
Belgium and Luxembourg	CTFH	9 143	10 914	11 229	12 981	13 691	13 829	14 439	15 249	19 159	19 471	18 660
Denmark	LEQR	2 595	2 749	2 807	3 286	3 782	3 729	4 190	3 989	4 646	4 557	4 821
Finland	LEUD	1 797	2 031	2 287	2 790	2 949	2 648	2 444	2 421	3 033	3 110	2 868
France	LEUM	18 017	19 813	21 516	24 723	26 840	25 826	26 849	27 854	31 775	34 066	31 597
Germany	LEQI	22 482	26 290	28 284	34 301	34 798	33 797	34 259	34 626	40 141	42 369	38 678
Greece	LEUV	1 400	1 519	1 651	1 962	2 589	2 787	2 432	2 805	3 092	2 716	2 690
Ireland	BFLV	8 285	9 166	10 320	11 696	13 076	14 209	14 986	16 357	19 155	22 306	23 218
Italy	BFOD	12 071	12 264	13 049	14 917	15 365	15 575	18 071	15 784	17 673	17 605	16 094
Netherlands	BFQF	16 039	16 210	18 533	22 150	24 339	25 723	25 361	27 109	32 772	36 409	32 494
Portugal	BFSH	1 686	1 958	1 893	2 236	2 539	2 479	2 649	2 752	2 780	2 850	2 832
Spain	LEST	6 566	6 990	7 740	9 210	10 740	10 668	11 398	11 701	13 153	13 129	13 269
Sweden	BFTI	4 476	5 198	5 457	6 549	7 209	7 134	7 294	7 068	8 022	7 963	7 235
European Central Bank	ZWVF	–	–	–	–	–	–	–	–	3	12	2
EU Institutions	CSFH	4 870	5 909	4 902	5 006	7 578	5 830	5 610	6 995	6 188	8 452	7 463
Total EU	LEPZ	110 845	122 574	131 416	153 790	167 682	166 257	172 169	176 857	203 932	217 348	204 178
European Free Trade Association (EFTA)												
Iceland	BFNH	193	241	193	215	268	268	274	255	333	284	238
Liechtenstein	BFPE	..	..	..	68	94	78	63	74	89	71	66
Norway	BFQO	2 626	2 916	3 561	3 502	3 834	4 260	4 574	3 913	4 111	3 882	3 871
Switzerland	LEOY	5 535	6 389	6 305	7 506	8 773	8 616	8 760	9 573	13 068	12 284	11 582
Total EFTA	CTFQ	8 404	9 590	10 100	11 291	12 969	13 222	13 671	13 815	17 601	16 521	15 757
Other Europe												
Albania	ZWVG	4	6	6	8	14	8	8	15	9	29	25
Belarus	ZWVH	..	14	14	28	33	42	33	30	59	37	36
Bulgaria	ZWVI	157	168	110	134	116	139	116	165	168	250	249
Croatia	ZWVJ	..	82	185	277	172	144	131	133	126	150	162
Czech Republic	LEPQ	..	365	483	731	956	966	1 011	1 013	1 228	1 467	1 325
Estonia	ZWVK	11	15	23	38	67	95	86	70	112	100	116
Hungary	BFKO	309	348	393	453	604	762	755	875	1 265	1 155	1 276
Latvia	ZWVM	24	45	58	79	106	117	114	97	119	113	123
Lithuania	ZWVN	12	21	33	62	107	135	127	114	159	187	185
Poland	BFRY	761	919	947	1 246	1 671	1 736	1 556	1 549	1 730	1 976	1 879
Romania	ZWVO	79	114	153	217	282	269	286	330	446	488	550
Russia	BFSQ	..	803	1 106	1 309	1 541	1 851	1 662	1 035	1 371	1 838	1 902
Slovakia	ZWVP	..	30	68	124	190	230	169	182	246	295	249
Slovenia	ZWVQ	..	64	100	133	147	174	163	215	227	292	278
Turkey	BFUJ	1 016	1 412	1 175	1 525	2 021	2 284	2 189	1 963	2 664	2 003	2 000
Ukraine	ZWVR	..	104	124	151	194	201	238	173	200	237	401
Yugoslavia	BFWC	..	54	37	48	102	123	61	70	130	95	92
Other	LEVW	..	2 531	2 708	2 917	3 562	4 954	4 764	4 639	5 713	5 067	5 514
Total Europe	LERA	125 550	139 259	149 239	174 561	192 536	193 709	199 309	203 340	237 505	249 648	236 297
America												
Argentina	ZWVT	573	738	765	781	930	1 105	1 095	720	970	871	462
Brazil	LENO	1 066	1 359	1 669	1 998	2 257	2 137	2 114	1 455	1 670	1 654	1 744
Canada	LEOP	3 794	4 255	4 544	4 796	5 180	5 409	5 911	6 045	7 354	7 392	6 483
Chile	ZWVU	410	459	516	568	587	565	498	399	480	440	459
Colombia	ZWVV	207	242	376	287	388	350	309	281	499	493	442
Mexico	BFPN	1 405	1 379	1 255	1 063	959	1 164	1 116	1 359	1 419	1 271	1 455
United States of America	BFVB	35 311	40 386	44 106	47 899	55 956	58 530	63 368	66 682	79 192	82 344	78 257
Uruguay	ZWVW	66	72	80	87	105	115	102	82	80	72	69
Venezuela	ZWVX	499	545	426	400	456	427	293	278	228	615	481
Other Central American Countries	JISS	1 756	1 938	2 085	2 114	2 818	3 112	6 760	6 202	7 748	7 747	8 588
Other	LEVE	981	1 092	1 176	1 398	1 394	1 897	925	885	750	703	944
Total America	LESK	46 068	52 465	56 998	61 391	71 030	74 811	82 491	84 388	100 390	103 602	99 384
Asia												
China	LEPH	666	1 013	1 183	1 195	1 196	1 380	1 383	1 935	2 229	2 824	2 554
Hong Kong	BFJR	4 825	5 470	5 964	6 596	7 265	6 829	5 772	5 110	5 382	5 144	5 192
India	BFMY	1 513	1 795	2 033	2 411	2 380	2 445	2 152	2 361	3 111	3 016	2 927
Indonesia	BFKX	573	578	659	891	1 266	1 238	841	740	769	762	762
Iran	ZWWA	769	665	427	507	573	515	450	370	463	619	618
Israel	BFMP	860	1 220	1 449	1 528	1 746	1 655	1 481	1 922	2 048	1 975	1 987
Japan	BFOM	12 870	12 596	12 613	15 148	14 473	13 873	12 745	13 654	16 523	15 235	12 791
Malaysia	BFPW	1 315	1 749	2 191	2 091	2 140	2 216	1 598	1 762	1 807	1 864	1 911
Pakistan	BFRP	555	598	651	689	746	681	567	592	514	646	572
Philippines	BFRG	386	517	571	698	675	859	549	476	647	724	628
Saudi Arabia	BFSZ	3 525	3 452	3 301	3 597	4 692	6 071	5 025	4 167	4 605	4 232	2 710
Singapore	BFTR	3 382	3 895	4 387	5 185	5 346	5 237	3 977	4 234	5 527	5 417	5 122
South Korea	BFOV	1 079	1 259	1 518	1 862	2 219	2 282	1 532	1 673	2 173	2 200	2 494
Taiwan	BFUS	774	978	1 049	1 340	1 382	1 489	1 287	1 318	1 566	1 498	1 564
Thailand	BFUA	792	1 045	1 216	1 415	1 520	1 368	690	784	1 001	1 106	943
Residual Gulf Arabian Countries	JITT	2 785	3 381	3 226	3 728	4 046	4 606	5 252	4 490	5 350	5 371	6 751
Other Near & Middle Eastern Countries	ZWWC	..	737	724	793	953	1 095	1 017	976	1 099	1 270	1 237
Other	LEWF	6 571	2 428	2 309	2 270	2 592	2 857	2 019	1 430	1 807	1 736	1 876
Total Asia	LETC	39 252	43 376	45 471	51 944	55 210	56 696	48 337	47 994	56 621	55 639	52 639
Australasia & Oceania												
Australia	CWBG	4 190	4 808	5 274	5 812	6 510	6 244	5 542	5 902	6 962	6 868	6 835
New Zealand	BFQX	937	1 073	1 217	1 293	1 323	1 152	998	1 131	989	1 091	1 139
Other	LEVN	214	235	253	289	391	315	474	137	151	109	406
Total Australasia & Oceania	LETU	5 341	6 116	6 744	7 394	8 224	7 711	7 014	7 170	8 102	8 068	8 380
Africa												
Egypt	ZWWE	383	488	498	521	597	693	523	849	1 034	1 029	816
Morocco	ZWWF	207	259	279	357	390	413	424	433	498	485	436
South Africa	BFWU	2 255	2 460	2 881	3 354	3 533	3 341	3 303	3 475	3 667	4 089	3 800
Other North Africa	JIRU	589	657	579	606	620	795	836	565	779	894	836
Other	LEWO	3 295	3 553	3 497	3 592	4 094	3 933	4 678	4 162	4 154	4 347	4 382
Total Africa	LERS	6 729	7 417	7 734	8 430	9 234	9 175	9 764	9 484	10 132	10 844	10 270
International Organisations	CTEY	330	326	297	289	216	265	399	416	491	574	529
World total	HBOE	223 270	248 959	266 483	304 009	336 450	342 367	347 311	352 793	413 245	428 377	407 505

9.2 Current account
continued

£ million

Debits

		1992	1993	1994	1995	1996	1997	1998	1999	2000	2001	2002
Europe												
European Union (EU)												
Austria	CUGW	1 816	1 934	2 021	2 080	2 311	2 622	2 399	2 304	2 453	3 040	3 588
Belgium and Luxembourg	CTFI	9 906	11 412	12 067	14 192	14 858	14 578	15 695	16 254	17 762	19 618	20 374
Denmark	LEQS	3 157	3 207	3 136	3 320	3 963	3 965	3 712	3 815	4 454	4 591	5 265
Finland	LEUE	2 201	2 418	2 843	3 201	3 458	3 316	2 885	2 993	3 621	3 739	3 460
France	LEUN	19 662	22 386	24 210	27 390	27 569	28 522	29 840	32 562	34 078	34 881	34 065
Germany	LEQJ	28 430	31 097	33 324	40 040	41 108	37 898	36 895	39 671	45 696	45 406	46 414
Greece	LEUW	1 588	1 550	1 730	1 981	2 079	2 110	2 002	2 417	2 794	2 846	2 770
Ireland	BFLW	7 098	7 792	8 462	10 308	11 905	12 183	12 749	13 408	16 054	18 901	19 614
Italy	BFOE	9 638	9 912	11 070	12 421	14 386	15 417	15 750	14 908	15 256	15 879	15 861
Netherlands	BFQG	15 162	15 000	16 403	18 845	20 303	18 666	19 725	22 634	30 742	30 832	29 759
Portugal	BFSI	2 139	2 263	2 210	2 609	2 861	2 911	2 787	2 952	2 927	2 925	3 031
Spain	LESU	5 999	7 324	8 240	9 895	11 028	10 871	12 306	13 007	13 458	15 520	17 496
Sweden	BFTJ	4 790	5 173	5 742	6 364	7 081	6 543	6 165	6 883	7 142	6 852	6 218
European Central Bank	ZWWI	–	–	–	–	–	–	–	1	1	1	1
EU Institutions	CSFI	7 528	8 817	8 076	9 886	9 959	9 014	11 152	11 744	12 199	11 263	11 759
Total EU	LEQA	119 114	130 285	139 534	162 532	172 869	168 616	174 062	185 553	208 637	216 294	219 675
European Free Trade Association (EFTA)												
Iceland	BFNI	268	275	271	279	315	271	304	317	445	343	346
Liechtenstein	BFPF	..	..	..	137	154	157	159	107	139	333	350
Norway	BFQP	4 571	4 936	4 723	5 303	5 866	6 009	4 077	4 244	6 706	6 867	6 299
Switzerland	LEOZ	10 837	12 023	12 228	13 156	13 544	12 734	12 308	14 341	18 172	15 871	12 371
Total EFTA	CTFR	15 792	17 351	17 338	18 875	19 879	19 171	16 848	19 009	25 462	23 414	19 366
Other Europe												
Albania	ZWWJ	29	31	47	58	53	63	115	109	92	91	90
Belarus	ZWWK	..	33	58	74	64	73	97	80	77	49	60
Bulgaria	ZWWL	115	137	153	217	201	211	188	172	192	183	229
Croatia	ZWWM	..	87	118	121	130	129	266	242	222	265	250
Czech Republic	LEPR	..	345	423	507	624	730	801	800	1 067	1 363	1 513
Estonia	ZWWN	45	55	108	166	193	211	213	229	369	308	341
Hungary	BFKP	258	257	353	501	561	645	715	832	854	864	1 011
Latvia	ZWWP	81	119	286	247	360	410	362	331	459	456	499
Lithuania	ZWWQ	79	176	206	227	244	211	208	214	285	264	310
Poland	BFRZ	538	657	766	924	874	1 061	1 050	1 011	1 367	1 584	1 610
Romania	ZWWR	150	183	255	284	305	354	333	355	453	559	639
Russia	BFSR	..	1 123	1 192	1 341	1 662	1 919	1 762	1 682	2 189	2 663	2 540
Slovakia	ZWWS	..	51	143	200	163	167	189	193	212	227	252
Slovenia	ZWWT	..	86	142	169	160	163	194	179	189	199	211
Turkey	BFUK	869	1 085	1 207	1 562	1 780	1 709	1 767	1 815	2 075	2 355	2 875
Ukraine	ZWWU	..	56	78	92	94	132	149	140	135	187	241
Yugoslavia	BFWD	..	68	120	137	187	209	97	92	140	136	137
Other	LEVX	..	4 403	4 259	4 884	6 205	7 335	8 330	8 114	9 789	10 588	8 940
Total Europe	LERB	143 638	156 588	166 786	193 118	206 608	203 519	207 746	221 152	254 265	262 049	260 789
America												
Argentina	ZWWW	103	170	197	276	368	375	338	346	409	405	357
Brazil	LENP	992	1 051	1 054	1 302	1 523	1 365	1 317	1 269	1 490	1 688	1 664
Canada	LEOQ	3 588	3 662	3 958	4 412	4 635	4 512	4 721	5 464	6 818	6 115	5 917
Chile	ZWWX	328	427	380	516	592	563	455	396	503	532	531
Colombia	ZWWY	318	322	301	289	439	315	326	275	326	418	282
Mexico	BFPO	390	381	412	490	620	687	750	799	1 088	1 277	884
United States of America	BFVC	31 876	37 729	39 293	45 567	55 847	56 925	58 944	62 146	68 298	74 058	66 081
Uruguay	ZWWZ	86	77	87	81	99	103	45	54	60	59	70
Venezuela	ZWXA	207	183	200	265	269	208	177	205	278	269	268
Other Central American Countries	JIST	1 862	1 966	1 861	1 792	2 833	3 283	6 019	5 447	6 716	6 177	4 924
Other	LEVF	1 211	1 336	1 200	1 152	1 528	2 048	1 150	1 231	1 327	1 824	1 422
Total America	LESL	40 961	47 304	48 943	56 142	68 753	70 384	74 242	77 632	87 313	92 822	82 400
Asia												
China	LEPI	1 312	1 636	1 974	2 252	2 520	2 811	3 304	3 879	5 511	6 520	7 489
Hong Kong	BFJS	4 911	5 517	5 589	6 024	6 327	6 402	6 962	8 392	9 846	9 493	8 030
India	BFMZ	1 385	1 676	2 029	2 201	2 562	2 744	2 617	2 741	3 050	3 567	3 425
Indonesia	BFKY	819	976	1 031	1 162	1 318	1 192	1 102	1 207	1 332	1 385	1 242
Iran	ZWXD	344	408	305	317	346	196	162	155	292	337	171
Israel	BFMQ	784	872	920	1 079	1 245	1 379	1 370	1 511	1 583	1 598	1 379
Japan	BFON	13 888	15 075	15 624	17 476	17 230	16 532	17 399	18 113	22 565	20 031	15 720
Malaysia	BFPX	1 352	1 716	1 643	1 965	2 932	2 647	2 379	2 446	2 868	2 432	2 087
Pakistan	BFRQ	510	562	643	661	711	779	723	746	796	949	1 214
Philippines	BFRH	357	388	365	461	1 011	900	1 010	1 172	1 462	1 372	1 088
Saudi Arabia	BFTA	2 928	3 270	2 501	2 684	2 500	2 630	2 197	1 939	2 317	2 613	2 177
Singapore	BFTS	2 778	3 479	3 564	4 176	4 639	4 780	4 079	4 727	5 388	4 856	4 145
South Korea	BFOW	1 071	1 227	1 249	1 776	2 253	2 524	2 551	3 035	3 697	3 121	3 004
Taiwan	BFUT	1 770	1 945	1 858	1 947	2 282	2 536	2 476	2 882	3 854	3 322	2 880
Thailand	BFUB	887	1 029	1 194	1 400	1 509	1 513	1 618	1 636	2 089	2 236	2 120
Residual Gulf Arabian Countries	JITU	1 719	1 688	1 533	1 459	1 506	1 678	2 306	2 204	2 819	3 445	3 119
Other Near & Middle Eastern Countries	ZWXF	..	626	530	525	476	516	405	446	584	677	696
Other	LEWG	5 565	3 208	3 147	2 944	2 966	3 203	2 442	2 435	3 093	3 414	3 573
Total Asia	LETD	40 228	45 298	45 699	50 509	54 333	54 962	55 102	59 666	73 146	71 368	63 559
Australasia & Oceania												
Australia	CWBO	2 935	3 049	3 105	3 361	3 455	3 883	3 896	3 784	3 753	4 039	4 147
New Zealand	BFQY	685	802	919	986	1 094	1 050	1 000	891	949	1 016	1 030
Other	LEVO	233	249	246	294	306	241	135	184	183	286	251
Total Australasia & Oceania	LETV	3 853	4 100	4 270	4 641	4 855	5 174	5 031	4 859	4 885	5 341	5 428
Africa												
Egypt	ZWXH	1 060	1 280	1 211	1 226	1 154	938	679	715	962	964	832
Morocco	ZWXI	208	276	308	343	409	470	490	535	612	631	641
South Africa	BFWV	1 340	1 575	1 479	1 760	1 984	2 185	2 497	3 124	4 012	4 411	4 107
Other North Africa	JIRV	707	643	637	734	643	755	679	575	1 072	955	929
Other	LEWP	2 483	2 306	2 505	2 830	3 274	3 641	3 476	4 186	4 552	5 894	5 954
Total Africa	LERT	5 798	6 080	6 140	6 893	7 464	7 989	7 821	9 135	11 210	12 855	12 463
International Organisations	CTEZ	1 766	1 508	1 413	1 721	1 438	1 275	1 163	1 227	1 965	1 980	1 831
World total	HBOF	236 244	260 878	273 251	313 024	343 451	343 304	351 107	373 671	432 784	446 415	426 470

9.2 Current account
continued

£ million

		1992	1993	1994	1995	1996	1997	1998	1999	2000	2001	2002
Balances												
Europe												
European Union (EU)												
Austria	CUGX	−398	−371	−273	−97	−124	−599	−212	−157	−113	−707	−1 331
Belgium and Luxembourg	CTFJ	−763	−498	−838	−1 211	−1 167	−749	−1 256	−1 005	1 397	−147	−1 714
Denmark	LEQT	−562	−458	−329	−34	−181	−236	478	174	192	−34	−444
Finland	LEUF	−404	−387	−556	−411	−509	−668	−441	−572	−588	−629	−592
France	LEUO	−1 645	−2 573	−2 694	−2 667	−729	−2 696	−2 991	−4 708	−2 303	−815	−2 468
Germany	LEQK	−5 948	−4 807	−5 040	−5 739	−6 310	−4 101	−2 636	−5 045	−5 555	−3 037	−7 736
Greece	LEUX	−188	−31	−79	−19	510	677	430	388	298	−130	−80
Ireland	BFLX	1 187	1 374	1 858	1 388	1 171	2 026	2 237	2 949	3 101	3 405	3 604
Italy	BFOF	2 433	2 352	1 979	2 496	979	158	2 321	876	2 417	1 726	233
Netherlands	BFQH	877	1 210	2 130	3 305	4 036	7 057	5 636	4 475	2 030	5 577	2 735
Portugal	BFSJ	−453	−305	−317	−373	−322	−432	−138	−200	−147	−75	−199
Spain	LESV	567	−334	−500	−685	−288	−203	−908	−1 306	−305	−2 391	−4 227
Sweden	BPTK	−314	25	−285	185	128	591	1 129	185	880	1 111	1 017
European Central Bank	ZWXL	–	–	–	–	–	–	–	−1	2	11	1
EU Institutions	CSFJ	−2 658	−2 908	−3 174	−4 880	−2 381	−3 184	−5 542	−4 749	−6 011	−2 811	−4 296
Total EU	LEQB	−8 269	−7 711	−8 118	−8 742	−5 187	−2 359	−1 893	−8 696	−4 705	1 054	−15 497
European Free Trade Association (EFTA)												
Iceland	BFNJ	−75	−34	−78	−64	−47	−3	−30	−62	−112	−59	−108
Liechtenstein	BFPG	..	..	..	−69	−60	−79	−96	−33	−50	−262	−284
Norway	BFQQ	−1 945	−2 020	−1 162	−1 801	−2 032	−1 749	497	−331	−2 595	−2 985	−2 428
Switzerland	LEPA	−5 302	−5 634	−5 923	−5 650	−4 771	−4 118	−3 548	−4 768	−5 104	−3 587	−789
Total EFTA	CTFS	−7 388	−7 761	−7 238	−7 584	−6 910	−5 949	−3 177	−5 194	−7 861	−6 893	−3 609
Other Europe												
Albania	ZWXM	−25	−25	−41	−50	−39	−55	−107	−94	−83	−62	−65
Belarus	ZWXN	..	−19	−44	−46	−31	−31	−64	−50	−18	−12	−24
Bulgaria	ZWXO	42	31	−43	−83	−85	−72	−72	−7	−24	67	20
Croatia	ZWXP	..	−5	67	156	42	15	−135	−109	−96	−115	−88
Czech Republic	LEPS	..	20	60	224	332	236	210	213	161	104	−188
Estonia	ZWXQ	−34	−40	−85	−128	−126	−116	−127	−159	−257	−208	−225
Hungary	BFKQ	51	91	40	−48	43	117	40	43	411	291	265
Latvia	ZWXS	−57	−74	−228	−168	−254	−293	−248	−234	−340	−343	−376
Lithuania	ZWXT	−67	−155	−173	−165	−137	−76	−81	−100	−126	−77	−125
Poland	BFSA	223	262	181	322	797	675	506	538	363	392	269
Romania	ZWXU	−71	−69	−102	−67	−23	−85	−47	−25	−7	−71	−89
Russia	BFSS	..	−320	−86	−32	−121	−68	−100	−647	−818	−825	−638
Slovakia	ZWXV	..	−21	−75	−76	27	63	−20	−11	34	68	−3
Slovenia	ZWXW	..	−22	−42	−36	−13	11	−31	36	38	93	67
Turkey	BFUL	147	327	−32	−37	241	575	422	148	589	−352	−875
Ukraine	ZWXX	..	48	46	59	100	69	89	33	65	50	160
Yugoslavia	BFWE	..	−14	−83	−89	−85	−86	−36	−22	−10	−41	−45
Other	LEVY	..	−1 872	−1 551	−1 967	−2 643	−2 381	−3 566	−3 475	−4 076	−5 521	−3 426
Total Europe	LERC	−18 088	−17 329	−17 547	−18 557	−14 072	−9 810	−8 437	−17 812	−16 760	−12 401	−24 492
America												
Argentina	ZWXZ	470	568	568	505	562	730	757	374	561	466	105
Brazil	LENQ	74	308	615	696	734	772	797	186	180	−34	80
Canada	LEOR	206	593	586	384	545	897	1 190	581	536	1 277	566
Chile	ZWYA	82	32	136	52	−5	2	43	3	−23	−92	−72
Colombia	ZWYB	−111	−80	75	−2	−51	35	−17	6	173	75	160
Mexico	BFPP	1 015	998	843	573	339	477	366	560	331	−6	571
United States of America	BFVD	3 435	2 657	4 813	2 332	109	1 605	4 424	4 536	10 894	8 286	12 176
Uruguay	ZWYC	−20	−5	−7	6	6	12	57	28	20	13	−1
Venezuela	ZWYD	292	362	226	135	187	219	116	73	−50	346	213
Other Central American Countries	JISU	−106	−28	224	322	−15	−171	741	755	1 032	1 570	3 664
Other	LEVG	−230	−244	−24	246	−134	−151	−225	−346	−577	−1 121	−478
Total America	LESM	5 107	5 161	8 055	5 249	2 277	4 427	8 249	6 756	13 077	10 780	16 984
Asia												
China	LEPJ	−646	−623	−791	−1 057	−1 324	−1 431	−1 921	−1 944	−3 282	−3 696	−4 935
Hong Kong	BFJT	−86	−47	375	572	938	427	−1 190	−3 282	−4 464	−4 349	−2 838
India	BFNA	128	119	4	210	−182	−299	−465	−380	61	−551	−498
Indonesia	BFKZ	−246	−398	−372	−271	−52	46	−261	−467	−563	−623	−480
Iran	ZWYG	425	257	122	190	227	319	288	215	171	282	447
Israel	BFMR	76	348	529	449	501	276	111	411	465	377	608
Japan	BFOO	−1 018	−2 479	−3 011	−2 328	−2 757	−2 659	−4 654	−4 459	−6 042	−4 796	−2 929
Malaysia	BFPY	−37	33	548	126	−792	−431	−781	−684	−1 061	−568	−176
Pakistan	BFRR	45	36	8	28	35	−98	−156	−154	−282	−303	−642
Philippines	BFRI	29	129	206	237	−336	−41	−461	−696	−815	−648	−460
Saudi Arabia	BFTB	597	182	800	913	2 192	3 441	2 828	2 228	2 288	1 619	533
Singapore	BFTT	604	416	823	1 009	707	457	−102	−493	139	561	977
South Korea	BFOX	8	32	269	86	−34	−242	−1 019	−1 362	−1 524	−921	−510
Taiwan	BFUU	−996	−967	−809	−607	−900	−1 047	−1 189	−1 564	−2 187	−1 824	−1 316
Thailand	BFUC	−95	16	22	15	11	−145	−928	−852	−1 088	−1 130	−1 177
Residual Gulf Arabian Countries	JITV	1 066	1 693	1 693	2 269	2 540	2 928	2 946	2 286	2 531	1 926	3 632
Other Near & Middle Eastern Countries	ZWYI	..	111	194	268	477	579	612	530	515	593	541
Other	LEWH	1 006	−780	−838	−674	−374	−346	−423	−1 005	−1 286	−1 678	−1 697
Total Asia	LETE	−976	−1 922	−228	1 435	877	1 734	−6 765	−11 672	−16 525	−15 729	−10 920
Australasia & Oceania												
Australia	CWJK	1 255	1 759	2 169	2 451	3 055	2 361	1 646	2 118	3 209	2 829	2 688
New Zealand	BFQZ	252	271	298	307	229	102	−2	240	40	75	109
Other	LEVP	−19	−14	7	−5	85	74	339	−47	−32	−177	155
Total Australasia & Oceania	LETW	1 488	2 016	2 474	2 753	3 369	2 537	1 983	2 311	3 217	2 727	2 952
Africa												
Egypt	ZWYK	−677	−792	−713	−705	−557	−245	−156	134	72	65	−16
Morocco	ZWYL	−1	−17	−29	14	−19	−57	−66	−102	−114	−146	−205
South Africa	BFWW	915	885	1 402	1 594	1 549	1 156	806	351	−345	−322	−307
Other North Africa	JIRW	−118	14	−58	−128	−23	40	157	−10	−293	−61	−93
Other	LEWQ	812	1 247	992	762	820	292	1 202	−24	−398	−1 547	−1 572
Total Africa	LERU	931	1 337	1 594	1 537	1 770	1 186	1 943	349	−1 078	−2 011	−2 193
International Organisations	CTFA	−1 436	−1 182	−1 116	−1 432	−1 222	−1 010	−764	−811	−1 474	−1 406	−1 302
World total	HBOG	−12 974	−11 919	−6 768	−9 015	−7 001	−937	−3 796	−20 878	−19 539	−18 038	−18 965

9.3 Trade in goods and services

£ million

		1992	1993	1994	1995	1996	1997	1998	1999	2000	2001	2002
Exports												
Europe												
European Union (EU)												
Austria	LGHT	995	1 156	1 317	1 446	1 615	1 453	1 527	1 544	1 530	1 590	1 633
Belgium and Luxembourg	LGHU	6 594	8 170	8 507	9 748	10 017	10 091	10 340	11 448	12 660	12 245	12 925
Denmark	LGHV	1 945	2 059	2 279	2 617	3 065	2 953	3 072	3 006	3 472	3 427	3 931
Finland	LGHW	1 275	1 424	1 644	2 100	2 371	2 107	1 959	1 998	2 412	2 459	2 221
France	LGHX	13 718	14 751	16 398	18 290	20 411	20 076	20 545	21 515	23 849	24 915	23 994
Germany	LGHY	18 316	19 674	21 263	24 587	25 207	25 338	25 660	25 847	29 193	30 187	28 591
Greece	LGHZ	1 140	1 322	1 380	1 555	1 680	1 659	1 717	1 928	2 042	1 851	1 870
Ireland	LGIA	6 808	7 552	8 685	9 750	10 879	11 647	12 103	13 259	15 101	17 235	18 726
Italy	LGIB	7 497	7 537	8 416	9 567	9 943	10 248	10 922	10 487	11 031	11 082	11 097
Netherlands	LGIC	9 972	9 804	11 490	14 444	15 930	16 747	16 121	17 571	19 545	19 125	18 111
Portugal	LGID	1 433	1 671	1 588	1 820	2 053	2 068	2 161	2 270	2 076	2 024	1 968
Spain	LGIE	5 441	5 538	6 252	7 336	8 171	8 125	8 887	9 548	10 503	10 429	10 835
Sweden	LGIF	3 124	3 636	4 196	5 053	5 438	5 593	5 726	5 423	5 796	5 514	5 216
European Central Bank	ZWLL	–	–	–	–	–	–	–	–	3	12	2
EU Institutions	LGIG	584	360	316	376	247	245	226	231	244	538	539
Total EU	LHRU	78 842	84 654	93 731	108 689	117 027	118 350	120 966	126 075	139 457	142 633	141 659
European Free Trade Association (EFTA)												
Iceland	LGII	129	183	154	178	202	212	206	190	265	215	178
Liechtenstein	LGIJ	..	..	..	15	19	20	25	33	42	30	44
Norway	LGIK	2 053	2 311	2 989	2 920	3 097	3 568	3 855	3 117	3 017	2 799	2 996
Switzerland	LGIL	2 652	3 280	3 489	3 991	5 048	4 930	5 181	5 129	5 551	6 594	6 398
Total EFTA	LGIM	4 835	5 775	6 633	7 104	8 366	8 730	9 267	8 469	8 875	9 638	9 616
Other Europe												
Albania	ZWLP	4	6	6	8	14	7	8	15	9	29	25
Belarus	ZWLS	..	14	14	28	33	42	33	30	59	36	36
Bulgaria	ZWLR	63	91	95	110	100	98	95	117	128	164	186
Croatia	ZWMC	..	53	157	244	156	124	118	119	109	122	142
Czech Republic	LGIN	..	362	459	678	833	829	893	886	1 097	1 264	1 196
Estonia	ZWLX	9	12	20	34	63	79	73	65	110	92	114
Hungary	XUXI	188	244	307	347	424	544	579	627	816	823	935
Latvia	ZWMF	13	22	36	50	95	112	102	94	115	111	114
Lithuania	ZWME	12	21	33	62	102	126	123	110	150	179	181
Poland	LGIO	700	861	881	1 123	1 544	1 588	1 458	1 439	1 583	1 643	1 626
Romania	ZWMH	74	105	143	195	240	244	262	286	426	410	486
Russia	LGIP	..	775	1 003	1 181	1 349	1 588	1 361	823	1 074	1 327	1 507
Slovakia	ZWMJ	..	25	66	100	139	161	127	142	195	259	222
Slovenia	ZWMI	..	64	100	133	147	166	141	160	179	191	216
Turkey	LGIQ	833	1 220	989	1 365	1 803	2 058	1 885	1 588	2 138	1 543	1 631
Ukraine	ZWMK	..	96	114	140	186	200	222	170	199	233	400
Yugoslavia	ZWMN	..	8	9	15	45	74	61	66	127	92	89
Other	ZWLM	..	1 213	1 349	1 565	2 049	2 328	1 609	1 794	1 974	1 904	2 113
Total Europe	LGIS	87 597	95 621	106 145	123 171	134 715	137 448	139 383	143 075	158 820	162 693	162 494
America												
Argentina	ZWLQ	177	253	312	318	449	602	665	457	474	465	253
Brazil	LGIT	453	631	756	930	1 122	1 322	1 313	1 101	1 115	1 182	1 191
Canada	LGIU	2 391	2 747	2 836	2 738	2 941	3 283	3 537	3 928	4 911	4 855	4 598
Chile	ZWLT	153	183	201	213	215	267	293	221	214	244	216
Colombia	ZWLU	122	165	300	214	250	229	241	159	164	239	198
Mexico	LGIV	406	456	517	409	429	592	677	792	943	968	973
United States of America	LGIW	20 389	24 631	27 044	28 507	32 917	35 199	36 219	41 388	48 191	47 855	49 489
Uruguay	ZWML	38	53	60	63	73	86	79	75	64	59	55
Venezuela	ZWMM	221	264	236	216	224	256	314	274	308	426	426
Other Central American Countries	ZWLW	971	1 144	1 415	1 413	1 392	1 698	2 145	1 958	2 294	2 113	2 657
Other	ZWLZ	457	536	714	903	751	918	839	829	651	666	630
Total America	LGIY	25 778	31 063	34 391	35 924	40 763	44 452	46 322	51 182	59 329	59 072	60 686
Asia												
China	LGIZ	568	923	1 057	1 038	976	1 143	1 156	1 659	1 911	2 267	2 196
Hong Kong	LGJA	2 187	2 903	3 149	3 415	3 814	4 099	3 613	3 304	3 643	3 670	3 389
India	LGJB	1 247	1 513	1 753	2 101	2 093	2 144	1 723	1 958	2 606	2 465	2 415
Indonesia	LGJC	437	476	527	732	1 000	898	565	553	603	516	551
Iran	ZWMD	630	553	342	387	444	445	410	330	410	575	578
Israel	LGJD	791	1 161	1 395	1 454	1 579	1 541	1 387	1 821	1 966	1 880	1 903
Japan	LGJE	3 608	4 347	5 007	6 045	6 593	6 527	5 700	6 217	6 903	7 000	7 077
Malaysia	LGJF	953	1 359	1 770	1 670	1 668	1 706	1 211	1 317	1 293	1 417	1 351
Pakistan	LGJG	511	564	610	630	671	550	467	515	380	500	463
Philippines	LGJH	275	396	452	571	497	734	393	363	460	557	489
Saudi Arabia	LGJI	3 406	3 309	3 135	3 410	4 093	5 440	4 338	3 441	3 825	3 477	2 030
Singapore	LGJJ	1 467	1 840	2 246	2 551	2 610	2 548	2 144	2 681	2 656	2 801	2 512
South Korea	LGJK	923	1 116	1 344	1 578	1 768	1 699	1 150	1 352	1 737	1 696	1 957
Taiwan	LGJL	665	855	904	1 183	1 186	1 302	1 098	1 114	1 297	1 178	1 225
Thailand	LGJM	670	909	1 032	1 179	1 229	1 138	611	667	773	816	761
Residual Gulf Arabian Countries	ZWMA	2 355	2 968	2 782	3 248	3 475	3 935	3 612	3 234	3 636	3 810	5 189
Other Near & Middle Eastern Countries	ZWMB	..	473	473	500	563	643	638	604	615	772	814
Other	ZWLN	..	2 051	1 898	1 790	2 086	2 316	1 783	1 243	1 448	1 441	1 572
Total Asia	LGJO	22 598	27 716	29 876	33 482	36 345	38 808	31 999	32 373	36 162	36 838	36 472
Australasia & Oceania												
Australia	LGJP	2 299	2 687	3 116	3 373	3 921	3 945	3 612	3 744	4 282	4 175	4 000
New Zealand	LGJQ	450	553	680	716	728	686	654	681	609	610	655
Other	LGJR	70	82	71	84	157	145	89	100	127	106	261
Total Australasia & Oceania	LGJS	2 819	3 322	3 867	4 173	4 806	4 776	4 355	4 525	5 018	4 891	4 916
Africa												
Egypt	ZWLY	307	410	443	450	515	609	602	810	767	766	724
Morocco	ZWMG	155	207	237	309	324	384	405	406	467	453	412
South Africa	LGJT	1 608	1 810	2 214	2 568	2 591	2 456	2 430	2 380	2 381	2 621	2 584
Other North Africa	ZWLV	397	489	435	472	512	695	723	496	672	742	726
Other	ZWLO	2 668	2 870	2 772	2 832	3 328	3 327	4 076	3 515	3 350	3 578	3 638
Total Africa	LGJV	5 135	5 786	6 101	6 631	7 270	7 471	8 236	7 607	7 637	8 160	8 084
International Organisations	LGJW	164	132	128	128	70	72	39	32	41	54	75
World total	KTMW	144 091	163 640	180 508	203 509	223 969	233 027	230 334	238 794	267 007	271 708	272 727

9.3 Trade in goods and services
continued

£ million

		1992	1993	1994	1995	1996	1997	1998	1999	2000	2001	2002
Imports												
Europe												
European Union (EU)												
Austria	LGJY	1 234	1 328	1 405	1 306	1 529	1 722	1 848	1 877	1 855	2 357	3 034
Belgium and Luxembourg	LGJZ	6 312	7 488	7 867	9 201	10 358	10 673	11 201	11 910	12 624	13 974	15 001
Denmark	LGKA	2 603	2 440	2 522	2 572	2 887	2 883	2 743	2 969	3 355	3 639	4 364
Finland	LGKB	1 744	2 009	2 423	2 651	2 892	2 737	2 553	2 690	3 224	3 357	3 118
France	LGKC	14 988	16 748	18 732	20 401	21 154	22 796	23 707	25 186	26 405	27 865	28 049
Germany	LGKD	21 570	22 942	25 251	29 693	31 632	29 131	28 847	31 597	33 765	35 547	38 091
Greece	LGKE	1 241	1 247	1 438	1 470	1 221	1 202	1 261	1 724	1 939	2 167	2 336
Ireland	LGKF	5 679	6 285	6 859	8 139	8 758	8 930	9 432	10 771	12 472	14 333	15 211
Italy	LGKG	7 508	7 650	8 709	9 498	10 746	11 492	12 052	11 912	12 274	12 744	13 576
Netherlands	LGKH	10 966	10 373	11 747	13 260	14 390	14 184	15 470	16 106	18 271	18 351	19 376
Portugal	LGKI	1 671	1 779	1 852	2 123	2 398	2 488	2 502	2 709	2 643	2 602	2 787
Spain	LGKJ	5 121	5 892	6 814	7 889	8 737	8 999	10 240	11 518	12 101	13 888	16 180
Sweden	LGKK	3 564	3 975	4 674	5 053	5 437	5 252	4 939	5 430	5 780	5 494	5 092
European Central Bank	ZWNR	–	–	–	–	–	–	–	–	1	1	1
EU Institutions	LGKL	–	1	1	1	2	1	9	6	2	4	12
Total EU	LHRV	84 201	90 157	100 294	113 257	122 141	122 490	126 804	136 406	146 711	156 323	166 228
European Free Trade Association (EFTA)												
Iceland	LGKN	252	260	258	267	300	260	292	304	432	330	327
Liechtenstein	LGKO	..	..	..	5	17	26	49	29	28	32	23
Norway	LGKP	4 330	4 615	4 305	4 862	5 319	5 242	3 940	4 037	6 076	6 193	5 879
Switzerland	LGKQ	4 418	5 261	5 644	6 058	6 452	5 731	6 137	6 764	7 017	6 073	6 075
Total EFTA	LGKR	9 000	10 136	10 207	11 192	12 088	11 259	10 418	11 134	13 553	12 628	12 304
Other Europe												
Albania	ZWNV	1	1	1	1	1	2	1	7	7	7	14
Belarus	ZWNY	..	5	14	20	16	15	25	21	36	20	34
Bulgaria	ZWNX	66	92	89	130	134	115	95	98	116	137	189
Croatia	ZWOI	..	56	71	62	69	60	70	55	62	100	105
Czech Republic	LGKS	..	318	372	404	441	538	683	696	942	1 255	1 439
Estonia	ZWOD	13	23	62	109	144	148	154	188	338	299	338
Hungary	ZWOJ	154	189	283	400	459	527	607	734	769	817	962
Latvia	ZWOM	27	70	221	166	297	336	295	281	424	440	491
Lithuania	ZWOL	49	140	152	165	181	142	146	162	250	240	291
Poland	LGKT	425	526	626	732	657	733	804	838	1 141	1 385	1 469
Romania	ZWOO	81	114	166	186	201	217	241	297	392	513	592
Russia	LGKU	..	1 010	1 010	1 154	1 388	1 623	1 638	1 469	1 704	2 259	2 262
Slovakia	ZWOQ	..	13	69	75	76	80	101	128	164	201	231
Slovenia	ZWOP	..	58	98	115	112	105	110	116	148	163	184
Turkey	LGKV	633	872	987	1 240	1 452	1 487	1 573	1 688	1 920	2 170	2 762
Ukraine	ZWOR	..	17	23	26	28	50	63	55	77	83	159
Yugoslavia	ZWOU	..	9	10	8	23	43	39	43	44	53	61
Other	ZWNS	..	1 606	1 779	1 565	2 140	2 265	2 287	2 328	2 781	3 147	3 180
Total Europe	LGKX	97 413	105 412	116 534	131 007	142 048	142 235	146 154	156 744	171 579	182 240	193 295
America												
Argentina	ZWNW	142	165	199	270	308	290	262	279	302	325	337
Brazil	LGKY	878	927	955	1 004	1 053	1 036	1 032	1 072	1 278	1 503	1 553
Canada	LGKZ	2 478	2 506	2 656	3 082	3 096	3 375	3 496	4 040	5 085	4 885	4 678
Chile	ZWNZ	208	252	204	302	381	391	369	363	483	492	499
Colombia	ZWOA	128	182	198	178	226	197	255	222	268	347	246
Mexico	LGLA	174	196	276	347	417	526	558	614	844	1 011	785
United States of America	LGLB	19 373	23 180	25 003	28 449	32 839	34 707	36 504	36 913	41 183	42 720	38 181
Uruguay	ZWOS	47	46	51	60	74	72	59	44	42	44	68
Venezuela	ZWOT	141	134	141	210	200	166	146	182	250	213	215
Other Central American Countries	ZWOC	866	1 033	1 112	1 106	1 417	1 430	1 645	1 642	2 314	1 751	1 814
Other	ZWOF	469	558	545	559	744	634	616	855	997	1 518	1 144
Total America	LGLD	24 904	29 179	31 340	35 567	40 755	42 824	44 942	46 226	53 046	54 809	49 520
Asia												
China	LGLE	969	1 402	1 742	1 997	2 256	2 564	3 056	3 619	5 101	6 082	7 146
Hong Kong	LGLF	2 766	3 465	3 680	3 848	4 380	4 753	4 920	5 548	6 484	6 360	6 153
India	LGLG	1 061	1 372	1 596	1 719	1 894	1 975	1 867	2 018	2 223	2 539	2 466
Indonesia	LGLH	622	806	884	982	1 020	992	961	1 075	1 204	1 239	1 142
Iran	ZWOK	159	240	135	121	110	40	51	48	66	55	51
Israel	LGLI	589	660	747	879	953	1 108	1 171	1 291	1 338	1 321	1 180
Japan	LGLJ	7 667	8 871	9 451	10 251	9 804	10 141	10 308	10 368	11 767	10 866	9 638
Malaysia	LGLK	1 171	1 517	1 360	1 614	2 450	2 174	2 144	2 149	2 511	2 147	1 929
Pakistan	LGLL	376	448	499	508	505	526	504	544	589	640	805
Philippines	LGLM	270	318	297	397	910	781	910	1 061	1 351	1 287	1 020
Saudi Arabia	LGLN	1 241	1 653	1 138	1 044	1 003	1 283	1 219	1 252	1 489	1 554	1 570
Singapore	LGLO	1 490	1 975	2 306	2 455	2 726	2 936	2 662	2 687	2 717	2 406	2 326
South Korea	LGLP	951	1 108	1 152	1 607	2 051	2 302	2 340	2 928	3 550	2 920	2 957
Taiwan	LGLQ	1 369	1 629	1 610	1 728	2 102	2 362	2 357	2 758	3 710	2 956	2 549
Thailand	LGLR	768	952	1 096	1 255	1 342	1 353	1 519	1 536	1 934	2 010	1 993
Residual Gulf Arabian Countries	ZWOG	866	913	908	814	894	1 025	1 274	1 244	1 444	1 579	1 683
Other Near & Middle Eastern Countries	ZWOH	..	183	188	176	170	147	145	201	273	310	383
Other	ZWNT	..	1 703	1 825	1 631	1 891	1 943	1 852	1 892	2 455	2 521	2 624
Total Asia	LGLT	23 622	29 247	30 614	33 026	36 461	38 405	39 260	42 219	50 206	48 792	47 615
Australasia & Oceania												
Australia	LGLU	1 497	1 561	1 728	1 776	2 083	2 259	2 373	2 396	2 808	3 096	3 135
New Zealand	LGLV	544	635	700	747	821	786	742	786	785	818	853
Other	LGLW	136	170	169	215	269	196	148	148	147	116	134
Total Australasia & Oceania	LGLX	2 177	2 366	2 597	2 738	3 173	3 241	3 263	3 330	3 740	4 030	4 122
Africa												
Egypt	ZWOE	231	293	370	382	397	351	355	439	649	699	669
Morocco	ZWON	151	217	239	290	332	405	447	493	576	581	596
South Africa	LGLY	1 041	1 229	1 191	1 409	1 586	1 780	1 878	2 108	3 075	3 411	3 273
Other North Africa	ZWOB	427	462	461	504	467	467	521	455	905	757	789
Other	ZWNU	1 595	1 638	1 832	2 044	2 128	2 176	1 953	2 641	2 702	3 948	4 097
Total Africa	LGMA	3 445	3 839	4 093	4 629	4 910	5 179	5 154	6 136	7 907	9 396	9 424
International Organisations	LGMB	98	82	77	84	72	67	65	56	79	61	40
World total	KTMX	151 659	170 125	185 255	207 051	227 419	231 951	238 838	254 711	286 557	299 328	304 016

9.3 Trade in goods and services
continued

£ million

		1992	1993	1994	1995	1996	1997	1998	1999	2000	2001	2002
Balances												
Europe												
European Union (EU)												
Austria	LGMD	−239	−172	−88	140	86	−269	−321	−333	−325	−767	−1 401
Belgium and Luxembourg	LGME	282	682	640	547	−341	−582	−861	−462	36	−1 729	−2 076
Denmark	LGMF	−658	−381	−243	45	178	70	329	37	117	−212	−433
Finland	LGMG	−469	−585	−779	−551	−521	−630	−594	−692	−812	−898	−897
France	LGMH	−1 270	−1 997	−2 334	−2 111	−743	−2 720	−3 162	−3 671	−2 556	−2 950	−4 055
Germany	LGMI	−3 254	−3 268	−3 988	−5 106	−6 425	−3 793	−3 187	−5 750	−4 572	−5 360	−9 500
Greece	LGMJ	−101	75	−58	85	459	457	456	204	103	−316	−466
Ireland	LGMK	1 129	1 267	1 826	1 611	2 121	2 717	2 671	2 488	2 629	2 902	3 515
Italy	LGML	−11	−113	−293	69	−803	−1 244	−1 130	−1 425	−1 243	−1 662	−2 479
Netherlands	LGMM	−994	−569	−257	1 184	1 540	2 563	651	1 465	1 274	774	−1 265
Portugal	LGMN	−238	−108	−264	−303	−345	−420	−341	−439	−567	−578	−819
Spain	LGMO	320	−354	−562	−553	−566	−874	−1 353	−1 970	−1 598	−3 459	−5 345
Sweden	LGMP	−440	−339	−478	–	1	341	787	−7	16	20	124
European Central Bank	ZWSE	–	–	–	–	–	–	–	−1	2	11	1
EU Institutions	LGMQ	584	359	315	375	245	244	217	225	242	534	527
Total EU	LHRW	−5 359	−5 503	−6 563	−4 568	−5 114	−4 140	−5 838	−10 331	−7 254	−13 690	−24 569
European Free Trade Association (EFTA)												
Iceland	LGMS	−123	−77	−104	−89	−98	−48	−86	−114	−167	−115	−149
Liechtenstein	LGMT	..	..	..	10	2	−6	−24	4	14	−2	21
Norway	LGMU	−2 277	−2 304	−1 316	−1 942	−2 222	−1 674	−85	−920	−3 059	−3 394	−2 883
Switzerland	LGMV	−1 766	−1 981	−2 155	−2 067	−1 404	−801	−956	−1 635	−1 466	521	323
Total EFTA	LGMW	−4 165	−4 361	−3 574	−4 088	−3 722	−2 529	−1 151	−2 665	−4 678	−2 990	−2 688
Other Europe												
Albania	ZWSI	3	5	5	7	13	5	7	8	2	22	11
Belarus	ZWSL	..	9	–	8	17	27	8	9	23	16	2
Bulgaria	ZWSK	−3	−1	6	−20	−34	−17	–	19	12	27	−3
Croatia	ZWSV	..	−3	86	182	87	64	48	64	47	22	37
Czech Republic	LGMX	..	44	87	274	392	291	210	190	155	9	−243
Estonia	ZWSQ	−4	−11	−42	−75	−81	−69	−81	−123	−228	−207	−224
Hungary	ZWSW	34	55	24	−53	−35	17	−28	−107	47	6	−27
Latvia	ZWSZ	−14	−48	−185	−116	−202	−224	−193	−187	−309	−329	−377
Lithuania	ZWSY	−37	−119	−119	−103	−79	−16	−23	−52	−100	−61	−110
Poland	LGMY	275	335	255	391	887	855	654	601	442	258	157
Romania	ZWTB	−7	−9	−23	9	39	27	21	−11	34	−103	−106
Russia	LGMZ	..	−235	−7	27	−39	−35	−277	−646	−630	−932	−755
Slovakia	ZWTD	..	12	−3	25	63	81	26	14	31	58	−9
Slovenia	ZWTC	..	6	2	18	35	61	31	44	31	28	32
Turkey	LGNA	200	348	2	125	351	571	312	−100	218	−627	−1 131
Ukraine	ZWTE	..	79	91	114	158	150	159	115	122	150	241
Yugoslavia	ZWTH	..	−1	−1	7	22	31	22	23	83	39	28
Other	ZWSF	..	−393	−430	–	−91	63	−678	−534	−807	−1 243	−1 067
Total Europe	LGNC	−9 816	−9 791	−10 389	−7 836	−7 333	−4 787	−6 771	−13 669	−12 759	−19 547	−30 801
America												
Argentina	ZWSJ	35	88	113	48	141	312	403	178	172	140	−84
Brazil	LGND	−425	−296	−199	−74	69	286	281	29	−163	−321	−362
Canada	LGNE	−87	241	180	−344	−155	−92	41	−112	−174	−30	−80
Chile	ZWSM	−55	−69	−3	−89	−166	−124	−76	−142	−269	−248	−283
Colombia	ZWSN	−6	−17	102	36	24	32	−14	−63	−104	−108	−48
Mexico	LGNF	232	260	241	62	12	66	119	178	99	−43	188
United States of America	LGNG	1 016	1 451	2 041	58	78	492	−285	4 475	7 008	5 135	11 308
Uruguay	ZWTF	−9	7	9	3	−1	14	20	31	22	15	−13
Venezuela	ZWTG	80	130	95	6	24	90	168	92	58	213	211
Other Central American Countries	ZWSP	105	111	303	307	−25	268	500	316	−20	362	843
Other	ZWSS	−12	−22	169	344	7	284	223	−26	−346	−852	−514
Total America	LGNI	**874**	**1 884**	**3 051**	**357**	**8**	**1 628**	**1 380**	**4 956**	**6 283**	**4 263**	**11 166**
Asia												
China	LGNJ	−401	−479	−685	−959	−1 280	−1 421	−1 900	−1 960	−3 190	−3 815	−4 950
Hong Kong	LGNK	−579	−562	−531	−433	−566	−654	−1 307	−2 244	−2 841	−2 690	−2 764
India	LGNL	186	141	157	382	199	169	−144	−60	383	−74	−51
Indonesia	LGNM	−185	−330	−357	−250	−20	−94	−396	−522	−601	−723	−591
Iran	ZWSX	471	313	207	266	334	405	359	282	344	520	527
Israel	LGNN	202	469	648	575	626	433	216	530	628	559	723
Japan	LGNO	−4 059	−4 524	−4 444	−4 206	−3 211	−3 614	−4 608	−4 151	−4 864	−3 866	−2 561
Malaysia	LGNP	−218	−158	410	56	−782	−468	−933	−832	−1 218	−730	−578
Pakistan	LGNQ	135	116	111	122	166	24	−37	−29	−209	−140	−342
Philippines	LGNR	5	78	155	174	−413	−47	−517	−698	−891	−730	−531
Saudi Arabia	LGNS	2 165	1 656	1 997	2 366	3 090	4 157	3 119	2 189	2 336	1 923	460
Singapore	LGNT	−23	−135	−60	96	−116	−388	−518	−6	−61	395	186
South Korea	LGNU	−28	8	192	−29	−283	−603	−1 190	−1 576	−1 813	−1 224	−1 000
Taiwan	LGNV	−704	−774	−706	−545	−916	−1 060	−1 259	−1 644	−2 413	−1 778	−1 324
Thailand	LGNW	−98	−43	−64	−76	−113	−215	−908	−869	−1 161	−1 194	−1 232
Residual Gulf Arabian Countries	ZWST	1 489	2 055	1 874	2 434	2 581	2 910	2 338	1 990	2 192	2 231	3 506
Other Near & Middle Eastern Countries	ZWSU	..	290	285	324	393	496	493	403	342	462	431
Other	ZWSG	..	348	73	159	195	373	−69	−649	−1 007	−1 080	−1 052
Total Asia	LGNY	−1 024	−1 531	−738	456	−116	403	−7 261	−9 846	−14 044	−11 954	−11 143
Australasia & Oceania												
Australia	LGNZ	802	1 126	1 388	1 597	1 838	1 686	1 239	1 348	1 474	1 079	865
New Zealand	LGOA	−94	−82	−20	−31	−93	−100	−88	−105	−176	−208	−198
Other	LGOB	−66	−88	−98	−131	−112	−51	−59	−48	−20	−10	127
Total Australasia & Oceania	LGOC	**642**	**956**	**1 270**	**1 435**	**1 633**	**1 535**	**1 092**	**1 195**	**1 278**	**861**	**794**
Africa												
Egypt	ZWSR	76	117	73	68	118	258	247	371	118	67	55
Morocco	ZWTA	4	−10	−2	19	−8	−21	−42	−87	−109	−128	−184
South Africa	LGOD	567	581	1 023	1 159	1 005	676	552	272	−694	−790	−689
Other North Africa	ZWSO	−30	27	−26	−32	45	228	202	41	−233	−15	−63
Other	ZWSH	1 073	1 232	940	788	1 200	1 151	2 123	874	648	−370	−459
Total Africa	LGOF	**1 690**	**1 947**	**2 008**	**2 002**	**2 360**	**2 292**	**3 082**	**1 471**	**−270**	**−1 236**	**−1 340**
International Organisations	LGOG	66	50	51	44	−2	5	−26	−24	−38	−7	35
World total	KTMY	**−7 568**	**−6 485**	**−4 747**	**−3 542**	**−3 450**	**1 076**	**−8 504**	**−15 917**	**−19 550**	**−27 620**	**−31 289**

9.4 Trade in goods

£ million

		1992	1993	1994	1995	1996	1997	1998	1999	2000	2001	2002
Exports												
Europe												
European Union (EU)												
Austria	QBRY	795	918	1 052	1 122	1 263	1 159	1 190	1 168	1 146	1 224	1 263
Belgium and Luxembourg	QBSB	5 706	7 150	7 367	8 298	8 522	8 451	8 445	9 241	10 322	9 893	10 534
Denmark	QBSE	1 557	1 618	1 821	2 108	2 214	2 093	2 057	2 054	2 315	2 267	2 724
Finland	QBSH	995	1 121	1 316	1 716	1 810	1 570	1 434	1 354	1 471	1 610	1 439
France	QDJA	11 493	12 215	13 655	15 265	17 093	16 601	16 449	16 907	18 577	19 243	18 720
Germany	QDJD	15 185	16 097	17 339	20 242	20 715	20 685	20 590	20 464	22 789	23 647	22 020
Greece	QDJG	776	929	933	1 038	1 147	1 047	1 045	1 153	1 229	1 112	1 193
Ireland	QDJJ	5 733	6 369	7 163	7 794	8 661	9 357	9 604	10 783	12 372	13 829	15 385
Italy	QDJM	6 137	6 094	6 836	7 883	8 027	8 214	8 608	7 831	8 429	8 400	8 493
Netherlands	QDJP	8 491	8 121	9 593	12 346	13 484	13 923	12 983	13 632	15 167	14 596	13 984
Portugal	QDJT	1 164	1 376	1 259	1 469	1 677	1 752	1 722	1 712	1 660	1 578	1 516
Spain	QDJW	4 509	4 494	5 131	6 098	6 725	6 745	7 171	7 526	8 302	8 361	8 473
Sweden	QDJZ	2 435	2 900	3 411	4 157	4 420	4 451	4 392	4 035	4 211	3 950	3 867
European Central Bank	QARP	–	–	–	–	–	–	–	–	–	–	–
EU Institutions	EOAY	–	–	–	–	–	–	–	–	–	–	–
Total EU	ENJF	64 976	69 402	76 876	89 536	95 758	96 048	95 690	97 860	107 990	109 710	109 611
European Free Trade Association (EFTA)												
Iceland	QDKW	92	148	110	137	152	157	158	159	193	154	131
Liechtenstein	EPOW	..	..	..	13	14	10	4	2	6	3	2
Norway	QDKZ	1 409	1 505	2 047	1 993	2 039	2 609	2 658	1 999	2 018	1 862	1 691
Switzerland	QDLC	1 839	2 282	2 480	2 727	3 166	2 955	2 892	2 768	3 061	3 578	3 074
Total EFTA	EPOT	3 340	3 935	4 637	4 870	5 371	5 731	5 712	4 928	5 278	5 597	4 898
Other Europe												
Albania	QAMC	4	6	6	8	14	7	8	12	7	24	19
Belarus	QAME	..	11	11	23	27	35	32	27	37	33	32
Bulgaria	QAMF	59	86	89	103	88	78	81	76	86	123	131
Croatia	QAMM	..	44	147	232	137	105	106	80	72	88	94
Czech Republic	QDLF	..	290	383	574	719	709	698	738	934	1 088	1 029
Estonia	QAMN	6	8	16	30	56	64	68	51	98	83	100
Hungary	QDLI	157	209	263	299	351	435	486	490	616	621	747
Latvia	QAMO	8	17	31	41	82	85	86	69	84	85	75
Lithuania	QAMP	6	14	25	51	84	107	116	95	133	137	148
Poland	QDLL	589	732	716	953	1 358	1 354	1 178	1 177	1 304	1 310	1 313
Romania	QAMQ	64	94	129	179	213	213	233	243	383	344	426
Russia	QDLO	..	561	728	874	1 018	1 233	929	532	668	903	980
Slovakia	QAMR	..	11	48	78	106	132	103	112	157	206	199
Slovenia	QAMS	..	58	93	123	131	149	136	139	157	160	181
Turkey	QDLR	690	1 047	821	1 150	1 545	1 734	1 562	1 198	1 800	1 179	1 286
Ukraine	QAMT	..	76	88	113	145	166	166	147	156	206	182
Yugoslavia	QAMW	..	4	4	8	34	37	43	29	32	52	62
Other	BOQE	..	619	569	714	693	682	604	620	713	730	660
Total Europe	EPLM	71 115	77 224	85 680	99 959	107 930	109 104	108 037	108 623	120 705	122 679	122 173
America												
Argentina	QAOM	118	183	232	235	335	486	458	293	288	268	127
Brazil	QDLU	270	422	539	677	853	1 030	899	739	775	819	880
Canada	QATH	1 637	1 848	1 935	1 806	1 963	2 146	2 147	2 532	3 487	3 239	3 106
Chile	QAMG	121	145	160	172	168	211	171	115	115	132	115
Colombia	QAML	75	107	238	146	182	170	175	107	101	105	83
Mexico	QDLX	302	336	393	276	316	428	516	577	675	689	704
United States of America	QAMH	12 640	15 403	17 081	17 899	19 753	20 853	21 082	24 040	29 276	29 561	28 192
Uruguay	QAMU	32	47	53	56	66	78	68	66	57	49	30
Venezuela	QAMV	191	228	199	178	182	206	242	205	222	318	307
Other Central American Countries	BOQQ	505	588	797	798	669	758	785	922	979	690	691
Other	BOQT	308	367	531	724	555	655	589	596	431	442	410
Total America	EPLO	16 199	19 674	22 158	22 967	25 042	27 021	27 132	30 192	36 406	36 312	34 645
Asia												
China	QDMA	425	755	868	830	741	922	860	1 211	1 468	1 735	1 493
Hong Kong	QDMD	1 597	2 177	2 356	2 666	2 943	3 215	2 671	2 312	2 673	2 717	2 410
India	QDMG	937	1 155	1 340	1 691	1 718	1 576	1 242	1 450	2 058	1 797	1 754
Indonesia	QDMJ	315	333	371	518	809	674	369	385	404	313	324
Iran	QAON	587	502	293	330	385	380	320	237	292	432	397
Israel	QDMM	583	895	1 060	1 114	1 277	1 178	1 079	1 295	1 516	1 376	1 428
Japan	QAMJ	2 172	2 673	3 047	3 818	4 296	4 180	3 127	3 300	3 672	3 743	3 588
Malaysia	QDMP	633	985	1 346	1 195	1 169	1 206	677	934	907	1 045	876
Pakistan	QDMS	308	336	362	343	347	271	228	221	207	234	240
Philippines	QDMV	202	313	364	435	398	601	301	239	273	397	352
Saudi Arabia	QDMY	1 969	1 844	1 534	1 625	2 425	3 656	2 605	1 481	1 557	1 523	1 387
Singapore	QDNB	1 137	1 459	1 811	2 077	2 158	2 047	1 598	1 597	1 625	1 613	1 443
South Korea	QDNE	644	805	987	1 162	1 314	1 222	666	949	1 350	1 284	1 462
Taiwan	QDNH	552	681	752	966	945	1 036	867	865	1 015	890	847
Thailand	QDNK	473	677	769	839	981	863	386	463	582	601	529
Residual Gulf Arabian Countries	BOQW	1 848	2 345	2 187	2 570	2 756	3 127	2 640	2 258	2 586	2 750	2 618
Other Near & Middle Eastern Countries	QARJ	..	378	382	394	456	498	466	406	393	486	498
Other	BORB	..	1 013	911	699	1 005	1 186	771	592	644	572	509
Total Asia	EPLP	15 339	19 326	20 740	23 272	26 123	27 838	20 873	20 195	23 222	23 508	22 155
Australasia & Oceania												
Australia	QDNN	1 340	1 611	1 957	2 141	2 492	2 454	2 188	2 155	2 699	2 344	2 119
New Zealand	QDNQ	258	335	422	440	474	409	336	324	305	314	310
Other	EGIZ	48	57	48	55	54	84	42	38	43	42	55
Total Australasia & Oceania	EPLQ	1 646	2 003	2 427	2 636	3 020	2 947	2 566	2 517	3 047	2 700	2 484
Africa												
Egypt	QDNT	251	347	378	385	434	501	505	539	498	458	461
Morocco	QAOO	124	173	200	273	284	356	348	359	407	373	346
South Africa	QDNW	1 071	1 149	1 452	1 840	1 894	1 646	1 520	1 281	1 413	1 558	1 597
Other North Africa	BORU	311	397	332	372	390	451	440	386	419	447	478
Other	BOQH	1 807	1 936	1 776	1 873	2 079	2 059	2 635	2 074	1 819	2 015	1 918
Total Africa	EPLN	3 564	4 002	4 138	4 743	5 081	5 013	5 448	4 639	4 556	4 851	4 800
International Organisations	EPLR	–	–	–	–	–	–	–	–	–	–	–
World total	LQAD	107 863	122 229	135 143	153 577	167 196	171 923	164 056	166 166	187 936	190 050	186 257

9.4 Trade in goods
continued

£ million

Imports

		1992	1993	1994	1995	1996	1997	1998	1999	2000	2001	2002
Europe												
European Union (EU)												
Austria	QBRZ	920	958	1 027	925	1 172	1 393	1 411	1 453	1 410	1 888	2 380
Belgium and Luxembourg	QBSC	5 601	6 678	7 121	8 130	9 026	9 390	9 831	10 156	10 927	12 131	13 099
Denmark	QBSF	2 326	2 133	2 170	2 199	2 393	2 316	2 156	2 342	2 631	2 921	3 567
Finland	QBTG	1 636	1 880	2 271	2 500	2 682	2 544	2 328	2 364	2 765	2 961	2 780
France	QDJB	11 945	13 430	15 037	16 457	16 873	18 020	17 956	18 415	18 642	20 114	20 329
Germany	QDJE	18 588	19 891	21 860	26 234	27 597	25 632	25 095	26 817	28 461	29 882	32 262
Greece	QDJH	370	315	348	429	401	396	363	399	443	482	586
Ireland	QDJK	4 945	5 449	5 897	7 045	7 342	7 391	7 802	8 708	10 261	12 135	13 008
Italy	QDJN	6 609	6 660	7 496	8 264	8 900	9 548	9 744	9 385	9 516	9 852	10 642
Netherlands	QDJQ	9 676	8 973	10 064	11 516	12 596	12 328	13 408	13 772	15 379	15 384	16 043
Portugal	QDJU	1 141	1 235	1 283	1 467	1 686	1 763	1 790	1 822	1 734	1 623	1 751
Spain	QDJX	2 952	3 266	3 678	4 356	5 120	5 102	5 738	5 967	6 140	7 347	9 097
Sweden	QDKA	3 201	3 566	4 196	4 537	4 840	4 693	4 361	4 649	4 950	4 665	4 314
European Central Bank	QARQ	–	–	–	–	–	–	–	–	–	–	–
EU Institutions	EOBS	–	–	–	–	–	–	–	–	–	–	–
Total EU	ENJO	69 910	74 434	82 448	94 059	100 628	100 516	101 983	106 249	113 259	121 385	129 858
European Free Trade Association (EFTA)												
Iceland	QDKX	233	242	233	243	255	229	251	282	365	286	287
Liechtenstein	EPOX	..	..	..	4	17	26	20	23	22	25	22
Norway	QDLA	3 798	4 027	3 711	4 182	4 751	4 666	3 440	3 546	5 563	5 596	5 175
Switzerland	QDLD	3 830	4 590	4 677	4 983	5 183	4 636	4 755	5 341	5 485	4 604	4 576
Total EFTA	EPOU	7 861	8 859	8 621	9 412	10 206	9 557	8 466	9 192	11 435	10 511	10 060
Other Europe												
Albania	QAMX	–	–	–	–	–	2	–	1	2	–	2
Belarus	QAMY	..	3	11	18	13	14	20	20	34	18	31
Bulgaria	QAMZ	48	74	68	112	111	88	74	68	85	97	115
Croatia	QANC	..	29	40	36	36	34	40	39	41	51	68
Czech Republic	QDLG	..	234	271	313	353	450	555	571	800	1 094	1 240
Estonia	QAND	9	19	57	105	139	147	150	184	306	280	323
Hungary	QDLJ	112	145	232	358	402	465	535	656	683	706	843
Latvia	QANE	24	67	217	163	294	331	290	270	400	433	474
Lithuania	QANF	47	138	150	163	178	140	140	158	245	232	259
Poland	QDLM	338	429	533	615	570	597	653	662	905	1 164	1 255
Romania	QANG	60	91	141	165	174	195	222	249	333	444	510
Russia	QDLP	..	792	781	917	1 222	1 418	1 406	1 324	1 496	2 061	1 940
Slovakia	QANH	..	2	56	64	62	71	71	101	136	176	208
Slovenia	QANI	..	52	91	109	104	95	100	104	122	148	167
Turkey	QDLS	446	515	610	770	892	990	1 103	1 204	1 450	1 692	2 152
Ukraine	QANJ	..	12	17	21	22	37	50	47	64	71	142
Yugoslavia	QANM	..	–	–	–	12	30	30	14	23	23	30
Other	BOQF	..	300	269	317	378	345	407	522	547	662	673
Total Europe	EPMM	79 974	86 195	94 613	107 717	115 796	115 522	116 295	121 635	132 366	141 248	150 350
America												
Argentina	QAOP	116	136	167	240	273	258	198	190	181	210	236
Brazil	QDLV	830	872	891	937	942	911	883	910	1 114	1 283	1 357
Canada	QATI	1 824	1 805	1 827	2 304	2 409	2 480	2 519	3 026	4 009	3 693	3 537
Chile	QANA	194	237	188	285	359	374	329	328	451	467	458
Colombia	QANB	119	170	186	165	203	178	199	191	231	311	210
Mexico	QDLY	149	160	233	290	326	371	366	395	613	686	502
United States of America	QAMI	13 221	15 886	17 233	19 620	22 287	24 329	24 785	24 360	28 416	29 588	24 973
Uruguay	QANK	46	45	50	59	73	70	53	40	36	36	47
Venezuela	QANL	128	119	125	194	181	150	115	144	207	161	182
Other Central American Countries	BOQR	460	521	556	546	678	680	712	871	1 044	617	761
Other	BOQU	297	351	318	333	413	388	410	542	700	1 228	847
Total America	EPMO	17 384	20 302	21 774	24 973	28 144	30 189	30 569	30 997	37 002	38 280	33 110
Asia												
China	QDMB	891	1 279	1 592	1 841	2 110	2 379	2 816	3 384	4 826	5 773	6 695
Hong Kong	QDME	2 242	2 894	2 988	3 358	3 904	4 146	4 391	4 909	5 917	5 787	5 533
India	QDMH	808	1 050	1 249	1 362	1 542	1 546	1 382	1 426	1 651	1 824	1 795
Indonesia	QDMK	501	665	728	814	852	862	854	931	1 081	1 128	1 001
Iran	QAOQ	152	232	124	113	102	29	32	33	30	28	33
Israel	QDMN	454	530	555	658	796	839	875	996	1 025	947	873
Japan	QAMK	7 051	8 140	8 584	9 288	8 545	9 031	9 124	9 118	10 214	9 146	8 248
Malaysia	QDMQ	1 032	1 350	1 166	1 414	2 280	1 931	1 892	1 961	2 288	1 950	1 724
Pakistan	QDMT	256	312	348	347	375	362	340	318	363	426	469
Philippines	QDMW	225	266	237	334	858	726	855	983	1 155	1 163	939
Saudi Arabia	QDMZ	900	1 208	757	645	654	841	791	783	977	931	671
Singapore	QDNC	1 113	1 558	1 836	2 097	2 465	2 585	2 343	2 348	2 395	2 079	1 948
South Korea	QDNF	890	1 029	1 068	1 506	1 935	2 147	2 201	2 784	3 416	2 776	2 789
Taiwan	QDNI	1 305	1 561	1 535	1 640	2 001	2 230	2 217	2 626	3 561	2 801	2 375
Thailand	QDNL	600	746	884	987	1 140	1 166	1 264	1 291	1 602	1 617	1 545
Residual Gulf Arabian Countries	BOQX	606	604	546	496	597	734	847	833	1 109	1 141	1 219
Other Near & Middle Eastern Countries	QARK	..	132	129	124	123	87	81	135	118	133	188
Other	BORD	..	870	851	779	1 065	1 138	1 117	1 217	1 596	1 677	1 713
Total Asia	EPMP	19 548	24 426	25 177	27 803	31 344	32 779	33 422	36 076	43 324	41 327	39 758
Australasia & Oceania												
Australia	QDNO	953	954	1 035	1 070	1 230	1 320	1 363	1 338	1 543	1 791	1 727
New Zealand	QDNR	405	474	527	556	602	555	517	565	544	549	533
Other	HFKF	128	144	152	188	203	164	124	122	124	94	96
Total Australasia & Oceania	EPMQ	1 486	1 572	1 714	1 814	2 035	2 039	2 004	2 025	2 211	2 434	2 356
Africa												
Egypt	QDNU	130	180	245	236	271	256	277	255	411	408	414
Morocco	QAOR	115	178	196	241	290	331	349	383	454	444	452
South Africa	QDNX	811	964	941	1 057	1 170	1 323	1 351	1 636	2 553	2 861	2 673
Other North Africa	BORW	349	374	363	391	367	323	280	333	699	516	586
Other	BOQJ	1 116	1 104	1 246	1 368	1 501	1 503	1 322	1 877	1 892	3 152	3 013
Total Africa	EPMN	2 521	2 800	2 991	3 293	3 599	3 736	3 579	4 484	6 009	7 381	7 138
International Organisations	EPMR	–	–	–	–	–	–	–	–	–	–	–
World total	LQBL	120 913	135 295	146 269	165 600	180 918	184 265	185 869	195 217	220 912	230 670	232 712

9.4 Trade in goods
continued

£ million

		1992	1993	1994	1995	1996	1997	1998	1999	2000	2001	2002
Balances												
Europe												
European Union (EU)												
Austria	QBSA	−125	−40	25	197	91	−234	−221	−285	−264	−664	−1 117
Belgium and Luxembourg	QBSD	105	472	246	168	−504	−939	−1 386	−915	−605	−2 238	−2 565
Denmark	QBSG	−769	−515	−349	−91	−179	−223	−99	−288	−316	−654	−843
Finland	QBTL	−641	−759	−955	−784	−872	−974	−894	−1 010	−1 294	−1 351	−1 341
France	QDJC	−452	−1 215	−1 382	−1 192	220	−1 419	−1 507	−1 508	−65	−871	−1 609
Germany	QDJF	−3 403	−3 794	−4 521	−5 992	−6 882	−4 947	−4 505	−6 353	−5 672	−6 235	−10 242
Greece	QDJI	406	614	585	609	746	651	682	754	786	630	607
Ireland	QDJL	788	920	1 266	749	1 319	1 966	1 802	2 075	2 111	1 694	2 377
Italy	QDJO	−472	−566	−660	−381	−873	−1 334	−1 136	−1 554	−1 087	−1 452	−2 149
Netherlands	QDJR	−1 185	−852	−471	830	888	1 595	−425	−140	−212	−788	−2 059
Portugal	QDJV	23	141	−24	2	−9	−11	−68	−110	−74	−45	−235
Spain	QDJY	1 557	1 228	1 453	1 742	1 605	1 643	1 433	1 559	2 162	1 014	−624
Sweden	QDKV	−766	−666	−785	−380	−420	−242	31	−614	−739	−715	−447
European Central Bank	QARR	–	–	–	–	–	–	–	–	–	–	–
EU Institutions	EOCM	–	–	–	–	–	–	–	–	–	–	–
Total EU	ENJX	−4 934	−5 032	−5 572	−4 523	−4 870	−4 468	−6 293	−8 389	−5 269	−11 675	−20 247
European Free Trade Association (EFTA)												
Iceland	QDKY	−141	−94	−123	−106	−103	−72	−93	−123	−172	−132	−156
Liechtenstein	EPOY	..	..	..	9	−3	−16	−16	−21	−16	−22	−20
Norway	QDLB	−2 389	−2 522	−1 664	−2 189	−2 712	−2 057	−782	−1 547	−3 545	−3 734	−3 484
Switzerland	QDLE	−1 991	−2 308	−2 197	−2 256	−2 017	−1 681	−1 863	−2 573	−2 424	−1 026	−1 502
Total EFTA	EPOV	−4 521	−4 924	−3 984	−4 542	−4 835	−3 826	−2 754	−4 264	−6 157	−4 914	−5 162
Other Europe												
Albania	QANN	4	6	6	8	14	5	8	11	5	24	17
Belarus	QANO	..	8	–	5	14	21	12	7	3	15	1
Bulgaria	QANP	11	12	21	−9	−23	−10	7	8	1	26	16
Croatia	QANS	..	15	107	196	101	71	66	41	31	37	26
Czech Republic	QDLH	..	56	112	261	366	259	143	167	134	−6	−211
Estonia	QANT	−3	−11	−41	−75	−83	−83	−82	−133	−208	−197	−223
Hungary	QDLK	45	64	31	−59	−51	−30	−49	−166	−67	−85	−96
Latvia	QANU	−16	−50	−186	−122	−212	−246	−204	−201	−316	−348	−399
Lithuania	QANV	−41	−124	−125	−112	−94	−33	−24	−63	−112	−95	−111
Poland	QDLN	251	303	183	338	788	757	525	515	399	146	58
Romania	QAOD	4	3	−12	14	39	18	11	−6	50	−100	−84
Russia	QDLQ	..	−231	−53	−43	−204	−185	−477	−792	−828	−1 158	−960
Slovakia	QAOG	..	9	−8	14	44	61	32	11	21	30	−9
Slovenia	QAOH	..	6	2	14	27	54	36	35	35	12	14
Turkey	QDLT	244	532	211	380	653	744	459	−6	350	−513	−866
Ukraine	QAOI	..	64	71	92	123	129	116	100	92	135	40
Yugoslavia	QAOL	..	4	4	8	22	7	13	15	9	29	32
Other	BOQG	..	319	300	397	315	337	197	98	166	68	−13
Total Europe	EPNM	**−8 859**	**−8 971**	**−8 933**	**−7 758**	**−7 866**	**−6 418**	**−8 258**	**−13 012**	**−11 661**	**−18 569**	**−28 177**
America												
Argentina	QAOS	2	47	65	−5	62	228	260	103	107	58	−109
Brazil	QDLW	−560	−450	−352	−260	−89	119	16	−171	−339	−464	−477
Canada	QBRV	−187	43	108	−498	−446	−334	−372	−494	−522	−454	−431
Chile	QANQ	−73	−92	−28	−113	−191	−163	−158	−213	−336	−335	−343
Colombia	QANR	−44	−63	52	−19	−21	−8	−24	−84	−130	−206	−127
Mexico	QDLZ	153	176	160	−14	−10	57	150	182	62	3	202
United States of America	QBRP	−581	−483	−152	−1 721	−2 534	−3 476	−3 703	−320	860	−27	3 219
Uruguay	QAOJ	−14	2	3	−3	−7	8	15	26	21	13	−17
Venezuela	QAOK	63	109	74	−16	1	56	127	61	15	157	125
Other Central American Countries	BOQS	45	67	241	252	−9	78	73	51	−65	73	−70
Other	BOQV	11	16	213	391	142	267	179	54	−269	−786	−437
Total America	EPNO	**−1 185**	**−628**	**384**	**−2 006**	**−3 102**	**−3 168**	**−3 437**	**−805**	**−596**	**−1 968**	**1 535**
Asia												
China	QDMC	−466	−524	−724	−1 011	−1 369	−1 457	−1 956	−2 173	−3 358	−4 038	−5 202
Hong Kong	QDMF	−645	−717	−632	−692	−961	−931	−1 720	−2 597	−3 244	−3 070	−3 123
India	QDMI	129	105	91	329	176	30	−140	24	407	−27	−41
Indonesia	QDML	−186	−332	−357	−296	−43	−188	−485	−546	−677	−815	−677
Iran	QAOT	435	270	169	217	283	351	288	204	262	404	364
Israel	QDMO	129	365	503	456	481	339	204	299	491	429	555
Japan	QBRR	−4 879	−5 467	−5 537	−5 470	−4 249	−4 851	−5 997	−5 818	−6 542	−5 403	−4 660
Malaysia	QDMR	−399	−365	180	−219	−1 111	−725	−1 215	−1 027	−1 381	−905	−848
Pakistan	QDMU	52	24	14	−4	−28	−91	−112	−97	−156	−192	−229
Philippines	QDMX	−23	47	127	101	−460	−125	−554	−744	−882	−766	−587
Saudi Arabia	QDNA	1 069	636	777	980	1 771	2 815	1 814	698	580	592	716
Singapore	QDND	24	−99	−25	−20	−307	−538	−745	−751	−770	−466	−505
South Korea	QDNG	−246	−224	−81	−344	−621	−925	−1 535	−1 835	−2 066	−1 492	−1 327
Taiwan	QDNJ	−753	−880	−783	−674	−1 056	−1 194	−1 350	−1 761	−2 546	−1 911	−1 528
Thailand	QDNM	−127	−69	−115	−148	−159	−303	−878	−828	−1 020	−1 016	−1 016
Residual Gulf Arabian Countries	BORA	1 242	1 741	1 641	2 074	2 159	2 393	1 793	1 425	1 477	1 609	1 399
Other Near & Middle Eastern Countries	QARL	..	246	253	270	333	411	385	271	275	353	310
Other	BORE	..	143	60	−80	−60	48	−346	−625	−952	−1 105	−1 204
Total Asia	EPNP	**−4 209**	**−5 100**	**−4 437**	**−4 531**	**−5 221**	**−4 941**	**−12 549**	**−15 881**	**−20 102**	**−17 819**	**−17 603**
Australasia & Oceania												
Australia	QDNP	387	657	922	1 071	1 262	1 134	825	817	1 156	553	392
New Zealand	QDNS	−147	−139	−105	−116	−128	−146	−181	−241	−239	−235	−223
Other	HFKK	−80	−87	−104	−133	−149	−80	−82	−84	−81	−52	−41
Total Australasia & Oceania	EPNQ	**160**	**431**	**713**	**822**	**985**	**908**	**562**	**492**	**836**	**266**	**128**
Africa												
Egypt	QDNV	121	167	133	149	163	245	228	284	87	50	47
Morocco	QAOU	9	−5	4	32	−6	25	−1	−24	−47	−71	−106
South Africa	QDNY	260	185	511	783	724	323	169	−355	−1 140	−1 303	−1 076
Other North Africa	BORX	−38	23	−31	−19	23	128	160	53	−280	−69	−108
Other	BOQK	691	832	530	505	578	556	1 313	197	−73	−1 137	−1 095
Total Africa	EPNN	**1 043**	**1 202**	**1 147**	**1 450**	**1 482**	**1 277**	**1 869**	**155**	**−1 453**	**−2 530**	**−2 338**
International Organisations	EPNR	–	–	–	–	–	–	–	–	–	–	–
World total	LQCT	**−13 050**	**−13 066**	**−11 126**	**−12 023**	**−13 722**	**−12 342**	**−21 813**	**−29 051**	**−32 976**	**−40 620**	**−46 455**

9.5 Trade in services

£ million

		1992	1993	1994	1995	1996	1997	1998	1999	2000	2001	2002
Exports												
Europe												
European Union (EU)												
Austria	FYVC	200	238	265	324	352	294	337	376	384	366	370
Belgium and Luxembourg	FYVD	888	1 020	1 140	1 450	1 495	1 640	1 895	2 207	2 338	2 352	2 391
Denmark	FYVE	388	441	458	509	851	860	1 015	952	1 157	1 160	1 207
Finland	FYVF	280	303	328	384	561	537	525	644	941	849	782
France	FYVG	2 225	2 536	2 743	3 025	3 318	3 475	4 096	4 608	5 272	5 672	5 274
Germany	FYVH	3 131	3 577	3 924	4 345	4 492	4 653	5 070	5 383	6 404	6 540	6 571
Greece	FYVI	364	393	447	517	533	612	672	775	813	739	677
Ireland	FYVJ	1 075	1 183	1 522	1 956	2 218	2 290	2 499	2 476	2 729	3 406	3 341
Italy	FYVK	1 360	1 443	1 580	1 684	1 916	2 034	2 314	2 656	2 602	2 682	2 604
Netherlands	FYVL	1 481	1 683	1 897	2 098	2 446	2 824	3 138	3 939	4 378	4 529	4 127
Portugal	FYVM	269	295	329	351	376	316	439	558	416	446	452
Spain	FYVN	932	1 044	1 121	1 238	1 446	1 380	1 716	2 022	2 201	2 068	2 362
Sweden	FYVO	689	736	785	896	1 018	1 142	1 334	1 388	1 585	1 564	1 349
European Central Bank	KNWZ	–	–	–	–	–	–	–	–	3	12	2
EU Institutions	FYVP	584	360	316	376	247	245	226	231	244	538	539
Total EU	LGOL	13 866	15 252	16 855	19 153	21 269	22 302	25 276	28 215	31 467	32 923	32 048
European Free Trade Association (EFTA)												
Iceland	FYVR	37	35	44	41	50	55	48	31	72	61	47
Liechtenstein	FYVS	1	1	1	2	5	10	21	31	36	27	42
Norway	FYVT	644	806	942	927	1 058	959	1 197	1 118	999	937	1 305
Switzerland	FYVU	813	998	1 009	1 264	1 882	1 975	2 289	2 361	2 490	3 016	3 324
Total EFTA	FYVV	1 495	1 840	1 996	2 234	2 995	2 999	3 555	3 541	3 597	4 041	4 718
Other Europe												
Albania	ZWKM	–	–	–	–	–	–	–	3	2	5	6
Belarus	ZWKP	3	3	3	5	6	7	1	3	22	3	4
Bulgaria	ZWKO	4	5	6	7	12	20	14	41	42	41	55
Croatia	ZWKZ	9	9	10	12	19	19	12	39	37	34	48
Czech Republic	FYVW	65	72	76	104	114	120	195	148	163	176	167
Estonia	ZWKU	3	4	4	4	7	15	5	14	12	9	14
Hungary	GYWV	31	35	44	48	73	109	93	137	200	202	188
Latvia	ZWLC	5	5	5	9	13	27	16	25	31	26	39
Lithuania	ZWLB	6	7	8	11	18	19	7	15	17	42	33
Poland	FYVX	111	129	165	170	186	234	280	262	279	333	313
Romania	ZWLE	10	11	14	16	27	31	29	43	43	66	60
Russia	FYVY	170	214	275	307	331	355	432	291	406	424	527
Slovakia	ZWLG	13	14	18	22	33	29	24	30	38	53	23
Slovenia	ZWLF	5	6	7	10	16	17	5	21	22	31	35
Turkey	FYVZ	143	173	168	215	258	324	323	390	338	364	345
Ukraine	ZWLH	18	20	26	27	41	34	56	23	43	27	218
Yugoslavia	ZWLK	3	4	5	7	11	37	18	37	95	40	27
Other	ZWKJ	522	594	780	851	1 356	1 646	1 005	1 174	1 261	1 174	1 453
Total Europe	FYWB	**16 482**	**18 397**	**20 465**	**23 212**	**26 785**	**28 344**	**31 346**	**34 452**	**38 115**	**40 014**	**40 321**
America												
Argentina	ZWKN	59	70	80	83	114	116	207	164	186	197	126
Brazil	FYWC	183	209	217	253	269	292	414	362	340	363	311
Canada	FYWD	754	899	901	932	978	1 137	1 390	1 396	1 424	1 616	1 492
Chile	ZWKQ	32	38	41	41	47	56	122	106	99	112	101
Colombia	ZWKR	47	58	62	68	68	59	66	52	63	134	115
Mexico	FYWE	104	120	124	133	113	164	161	215	268	279	269
United States of America	FYWF	7 749	9 228	9 963	10 608	13 164	14 346	15 137	17 348	18 915	18 294	21 297
Uruguay	ZWLI	6	6	7	7	7	8	11	9	7	10	25
Venezuela	ZWLJ	30	36	37	38	42	50	72	69	86	108	119
Other Central American Countries	ZWKT	466	556	618	615	723	940	1 360	1 036	1 315	1 423	1 966
Other	ZWKW	149	169	183	179	196	263	250	233	220	224	220
Total America	FYWH	**9 579**	**11 389**	**12 233**	**12 957**	**15 721**	**17 431**	**19 190**	**20 990**	**22 923**	**22 760**	**26 041**
Asia												
China	FYWI	143	168	189	208	235	221	296	448	443	532	703
Hong Kong	FYWJ	590	726	793	749	871	884	942	992	970	953	979
India	FYWK	310	358	413	410	375	568	481	508	548	668	661
Indonesia	FYWL	122	143	156	214	191	224	196	168	199	203	227
Iran	ZWLA	43	51	49	57	59	65	90	93	118	143	181
Israel	FYWM	208	266	335	340	302	363	308	526	450	504	475
Japan	FYWN	1 436	1 674	1 960	2 227	2 297	2 347	2 573	2 917	3 231	3 257	3 489
Malaysia	FYWO	320	374	424	475	499	500	534	383	386	372	475
Pakistan	FYWP	203	228	248	287	324	279	239	294	173	266	223
Philippines	FYWQ	73	83	88	136	99	133	92	124	187	160	137
Saudi Arabia	FYWR	1 437	1 465	1 601	1 785	1 668	1 784	1 733	1 960	2 268	1 954	643
Singapore	FYWS	330	381	435	474	452	501	546	1 084	1 031	1 188	1 069
South Korea	FYWT	279	311	357	416	454	477	484	403	387	412	495
Taiwan	FYWU	113	174	152	217	241	266	231	249	282	288	378
Thailand	FYWV	197	232	263	340	248	275	225	204	191	215	232
Residual Gulf Arabian Countries	ZWKX	507	623	595	678	719	808	972	976	1 050	1 060	2 571
Other Near & Middle Eastern Countries	ZWKY	78	95	91	106	107	145	172	198	222	286	316
Other Asian Countries	ZWKK	870	1 038	987	1 091	1 081	1 130	1 012	651	804	869	1 063
Total Asia	FYWX	**7 259**	**8 390**	**9 136**	**10 210**	**10 222**	**10 970**	**11 126**	**12 178**	**12 940**	**13 330**	**14 317**
Australasia & Oceania												
Australia	FYWY	959	1 076	1 159	1 232	1 429	1 491	1 424	1 589	1 583	1 831	1 881
New Zealand	FYWZ	192	218	258	276	254	277	318	357	304	296	345
Other	FYXA	22	25	23	29	103	61	47	62	84	64	206
Total Australasia & Oceania	FYXB	**1 173**	**1 319**	**1 440**	**1 537**	**1 786**	**1 829**	**1 789**	**2 008**	**1 971**	**2 191**	**2 432**
Africa												
Egypt	ZWKV	56	63	65	65	81	108	97	271	269	308	263
Morocco	ZWLD	31	34	37	36	40	28	57	47	60	80	66
South Africa	FYXC	537	661	762	728	697	810	910	1 099	968	1 063	987
Other North Africa	ZWKS	86	92	103	100	122	244	283	110	253	295	248
Other	ZWKL	861	934	996	959	1 249	1 268	1 441	1 441	1 531	1 563	1 720
Total Africa	FYXE	**1 571**	**1 784**	**1 963**	**1 888**	**2 189**	**2 458**	**2 788**	**2 968**	**3 081**	**3 309**	**3 284**
International Organisations	FYXF	164	132	128	128	70	72	39	32	41	54	75
World total	KTMQ	**36 228**	**41 411**	**45 365**	**49 932**	**56 773**	**61 104**	**66 278**	**72 628**	**79 071**	**81 658**	**86 470**

United Kingdom Balance of Payments The Pink Book 2003 — Geographical breakdown of current account

9.5 Trade in services
continued
£ million

		1992	1993	1994	1995	1996	1997	1998	1999	2000	2001	2002
Imports												
Europe												
European Union (EU)												
Austria	GGOR	314	370	378	381	357	329	437	424	445	469	654
Belgium and Luxembourg	GGOS	711	810	746	1 071	1 332	1 283	1 370	1 754	1 697	1 843	1 902
Denmark	GGOT	277	307	352	373	494	567	587	627	724	718	797
Finland	GGOU	108	129	152	151	210	193	225	326	459	396	338
France	GGOV	3 043	3 318	3 695	3 944	4 281	4 776	5 751	6 771	7 763	7 751	7 720
Germany	GGOW	2 982	3 051	3 391	3 459	4 035	3 499	3 752	4 780	5 304	5 665	5 829
Greece	GGOX	871	932	1 090	1 041	820	806	898	1 325	1 496	1 685	1 750
Ireland	GGOY	734	836	962	1 094	1 416	1 539	1 630	2 063	2 211	2 198	2 203
Italy	GGOZ	899	990	1 213	1 234	1 846	1 944	2 308	2 527	2 758	2 892	2 934
Netherlands	GGPA	1 290	1 400	1 683	1 744	1 794	1 856	2 062	2 334	2 892	2 967	3 333
Portugal	GGPB	530	544	569	656	712	725	712	887	909	979	1 036
Spain	GGPC	2 169	2 626	3 136	3 533	3 617	3 897	4 502	5 551	5 961	6 541	7 083
Sweden	GGPD	363	409	478	516	597	559	578	781	830	829	778
European Central Bank	KOFJ	–	–	–	–	–	–	–	1	1	1	1
EU Institutions	GGPE	–	1	1	1	2	1	9	6	2	4	12
Total EU	LGON	14 291	15 723	17 846	19 198	21 513	21 974	24 821	30 157	33 452	34 938	36 370
European Free Trade Association (EFTA)												
Iceland	GGPG	19	18	25	24	45	31	41	22	67	44	40
Liechtenstein	GGPH	–	–	–	1	–	–	29	6	6	7	1
Norway	GGPI	532	588	594	680	568	576	500	491	513	597	704
Switzerland	GGPJ	588	671	967	1 075	1 269	1 095	1 382	1 423	1 532	1 469	1 499
Total EFTA	GGPK	1 139	1 277	1 586	1 780	1 882	1 702	1 952	1 942	2 118	2 117	2 244
Other Europe												
Albania	ZWMS	1	1	1	1	1	–	1	6	5	7	12
Belarus	ZWMV	2	2	3	2	3	1	5	1	2	2	3
Bulgaria	ZWMU	18	18	21	18	23	27	21	30	31	40	74
Croatia	ZWNF	26	27	31	26	33	26	30	16	21	49	37
Czech Republic	GGPL	68	84	101	91	88	88	128	125	142	161	199
Estonia	ZWNA	4	4	5	4	5	1	4	4	32	19	15
Hungary	GYXH	42	44	51	42	57	62	72	78	86	111	119
Latvia	ZWNI	3	3	4	3	3	5	5	11	24	7	17
Lithuania	ZWNH	2	2	2	2	3	2	6	4	5	8	32
Poland	GGPM	87	97	93	117	87	136	151	176	236	221	214
Romania	ZWNK	21	23	25	21	27	22	19	48	59	69	82
Russia	GGPN	206	218	229	237	166	205	232	145	208	198	322
Slovakia	ZWNM	11	11	13	11	14	9	30	27	28	25	23
Slovenia	ZWNL	6	6	7	6	8	10	10	12	26	15	17
Turkey	GGPO	187	357	377	470	560	497	470	484	470	478	610
Ukraine	ZWNN	5	5	6	5	6	13	13	8	13	12	17
Yugoslavia	ZWNQ	9	9	10	8	11	13	9	29	21	30	31
Other	ZWMP	1 311	1 306	1 510	1 248	1 762	1 920	1 880	1 806	2 234	2 485	2 507
Total Europe	GGPQ	**17 439**	**19 217**	**21 921**	**23 290**	**26 252**	**26 713**	**29 859**	**35 109**	**39 213**	**40 992**	**42 945**
America												
Argentina	ZWMT	26	29	32	30	35	32	64	89	121	115	101
Brazil	GGPR	48	55	64	67	111	125	149	162	164	220	196
Canada	GGPS	654	701	829	778	687	895	977	1 014	1 076	1 192	1 141
Chile	ZWMW	14	15	16	17	22	17	40	35	32	25	41
Colombia	ZWMX	9	12	12	13	23	19	56	31	37	36	36
Mexico	GGPT	25	36	43	57	91	155	192	219	231	325	283
United States of America	GGPU	6 152	7 294	7 770	8 829	10 552	10 378	11 719	12 553	12 767	13 132	13 208
Uruguay	ZWNO	1	1	1	1	1	2	6	4	6	8	21
Venezuela	ZWNP	13	15	16	16	19	16	31	38	43	52	33
Other Central American Countries	ZWMZ	406	512	556	560	739	750	933	771	1 270	1 134	1 053
Other	ZWNC	172	207	227	226	331	246	206	313	297	290	297
Total America	GGPW	**7 520**	**8 877**	**9 566**	**10 594**	**12 611**	**12 635**	**14 373**	**15 229**	**16 044**	**16 529**	**16 410**
Asia												
China	GGPX	78	123	150	156	146	185	240	235	275	309	451
Hong Kong	GGPY	524	571	692	490	476	607	529	639	567	573	620
India	GGPZ	253	322	347	357	352	429	485	592	572	715	671
Indonesia	GGQA	121	141	156	168	168	130	107	144	123	111	141
Iran	ZWNG	7	8	11	8	8	11	19	15	36	27	18
Israel	GGQB	135	162	192	221	157	269	296	295	313	374	307
Japan	GGQC	616	731	867	963	1 259	1 110	1 184	1 250	1 553	1 720	1 390
Malaysia	GGQD	139	167	194	200	170	243	252	188	223	197	205
Pakistan	GGQE	120	136	151	161	130	164	164	226	226	214	336
Philippines	GGQF	45	52	60	63	52	55	55	78	196	124	81
Saudi Arabia	GGQG	341	445	381	399	349	442	428	469	512	623	899
Singapore	GGQH	377	417	470	358	261	351	319	339	322	327	378
South Korea	GGQI	61	79	84	101	116	155	139	144	134	144	168
Taiwan	GGQJ	64	68	75	88	101	132	140	132	149	155	174
Thailand	GGQK	168	206	212	268	202	187	255	245	332	393	448
Residual Gulf Arabian Countries	ZWND	260	309	362	318	297	291	427	411	335	438	464
Other Near & Middle Eastern Countries	ZWNE	42	51	59	52	47	60	64	66	155	177	195
Other	ZWMQ	723	833	974	852	826	805	735	675	859	844	911
Total Asia	GGQM	**4 074**	**4 821**	**5 437**	**5 223**	**5 117**	**5 626**	**5 838**	**6 143**	**6 882**	**7 465**	**7 857**
Australasia & Oceania												
Australia	GGQN	544	607	693	706	853	939	1 010	1 058	1 265	1 305	1 408
New Zealand	GGQO	139	161	173	191	219	231	225	221	241	269	320
Other	GGQP	8	26	17	27	66	32	24	26	23	22	38
Total Australasia & Oceania	GGQQ	**691**	**794**	**883**	**924**	**1 138**	**1 202**	**1 259**	**1 305**	**1 529**	**1 596**	**1 766**
Africa												
Egypt	ZWNB	101	113	125	146	126	95	78	184	238	291	255
Morocco	ZWNJ	36	39	43	49	42	74	98	110	122	137	144
South Africa	GGQR	230	265	250	352	416	457	527	472	522	550	600
Other North Africa	ZWMY	78	88	98	113	100	144	241	122	206	241	203
Other	ZWMR	479	534	586	676	627	673	631	764	810	796	1 084
Total Africa	GGQT	**924**	**1 039**	**1 102**	**1 336**	**1 311**	**1 443**	**1 575**	**1 652**	**1 898**	**2 015**	**2 286**
International Organisations	GGQU	98	82	77	84	72	67	65	56	79	61	40
World total	KTMR	**30 746**	**34 830**	**38 986**	**41 451**	**46 501**	**47 686**	**52 969**	**59 494**	**65 645**	**68 658**	**71 304**

9.5 Trade in services
continued
£ million

		1992	1993	1994	1995	1996	1997	1998	1999	2000	2001	2002
Balances												
Europe												
European Union (EU)												
Austria	GGQW	−114	−132	−113	−57	−5	−35	−100	−48	−61	−103	−284
Belgium and Luxembourg	GGQX	177	210	394	379	163	357	525	453	641	509	489
Denmark	GGQY	111	134	106	136	357	293	428	325	433	442	410
Finland	GGQZ	172	174	176	233	351	344	300	318	482	453	444
France	GGRA	−818	−782	−952	−919	−963	−1 301	−1 655	−2 163	−2 491	−2 079	−2 446
Germany	GGRB	149	526	533	886	457	1 154	1 318	603	1 100	875	742
Greece	GGRC	−507	−539	−643	−524	−287	−194	−226	−550	−683	−946	−1 073
Ireland	GGRD	341	347	560	862	802	751	869	413	518	1 208	1 138
Italy	GGRE	461	453	367	450	70	90	6	129	−156	−210	−330
Netherlands	GGRF	191	283	214	354	652	968	1 076	1 605	1 486	1 562	794
Portugal	GGRG	−261	−249	−240	−305	−336	−409	−273	−329	−493	−533	−584
Spain	GGRH	−1 237	−1 582	−2 015	−2 295	−2 171	−2 517	−2 786	−3 529	−3 760	−4 473	−4 721
Sweden	GGRI	326	327	307	380	421	583	756	607	755	735	571
European Central Bank	ZWTI	–	–	–	–	–	–	–	−1	2	11	1
EU Institutions	GGRJ	584	359	315	375	245	244	217	225	242	534	527
Total EU	LGOV	−425	−471	−991	−45	−244	328	455	−1 942	−1 985	−2 015	−4 322
European Free Trade Association (EFTA)												
Iceland	GGRL	18	17	19	17	5	24	7	9	5	17	7
Liechtenstein	GGRM	1	1	1	1	5	10	−8	25	30	20	41
Norway	GGRN	112	218	348	247	490	383	697	627	486	340	601
Switzerland	GGRO	225	327	42	189	613	880	907	938	958	1 547	1 825
Total EFTA	GGRP	356	563	410	454	1 113	1 297	1 603	1 599	1 479	1 924	2 474
Other Europe												
Albania	ZWTM	−1	−1	−1	−1	−1	–	−1	−3	−3	−2	−6
Belarus	ZWTP	1	1	–	3	3	6	−4	2	20	1	1
Bulgaria	ZWTO	−14	−13	−15	−11	−11	−7	−7	11	11	1	−19
Croatia	ZWTZ	−17	−18	−21	−14	−14	−7	−18	23	16	−15	11
Czech Republic	GGRQ	−3	−12	−25	13	26	32	67	23	21	15	−32
Estonia	ZWTU	−1	–	−1	–	2	14	1	10	−20	−10	−1
Hungary	GYXT	−11	−9	−7	6	16	47	21	59	114	91	69
Latvia	ZWUC	2	2	1	6	10	22	11	14	7	19	22
Lithuania	ZWUB	4	5	6	9	15	17	1	11	12	34	1
Poland	GGRR	24	32	72	53	99	98	129	86	43	112	99
Romania	ZWUE	−11	−12	−11	−5	–	9	10	−5	−16	−3	−22
Russia	GGRS	−36	−4	46	70	165	150	200	146	198	226	205
Slovakia	ZWUG	2	3	5	11	19	20	−6	3	10	28	–
Slovenia	ZWUF	−1	–	–	4	8	7	−5	9	−4	16	18
Turkey	GGRT	−44	−184	−209	−255	−302	−173	−147	−94	−132	−114	−265
Ukraine	ZWUH	13	15	20	22	35	21	43	15	30	15	201
Yugoslavia	ZWUK	−6	−5	−5	−1	–	24	9	8	74	10	−4
Other	ZWTJ	−789	−712	−730	−397	−406	−274	−875	−632	−973	−1 311	−1 054
Total Europe	GGRV	**−957**	**−820**	**−1 456**	**−78**	**533**	**1 631**	**1 487**	**−657**	**−1 098**	**−978**	**−2 624**
America												
Argentina	ZWTN	33	41	48	53	79	84	143	75	65	82	25
Brazil	GGRW	135	154	153	186	158	167	265	200	176	143	115
Canada	GGRX	100	198	72	154	291	242	413	382	348	424	351
Chile	ZWTQ	18	23	25	24	25	39	82	71	67	87	60
Colombia	ZWTR	38	46	50	55	45	40	10	21	26	98	79
Mexico	GGRY	79	84	81	76	22	9	−31	−4	37	−46	−14
United States of America	GGRZ	1 597	1 934	2 193	1 779	2 612	3 968	3 418	4 795	6 148	5 162	8 089
Uruguay	ZWUI	5	5	6	6	6	6	5	5	1	2	4
Venezuela	ZWUJ	17	21	21	22	23	34	41	31	43	56	86
Other Central American Countries	ZWTT	60	44	62	55	−16	190	427	265	45	289	913
Other	ZWTW	−23	−38	−44	−47	−135	17	44	−80	−77	−66	−77
Total America	GGSB	**2 059**	**2 512**	**2 667**	**2 363**	**3 110**	**4 796**	**4 817**	**5 761**	**6 879**	**6 231**	**9 631**
Asia												
China	GGSC	65	45	39	52	89	36	56	213	168	223	252
Hong Kong	GGSD	66	155	101	259	395	277	413	353	403	380	359
India	GGSE	57	36	66	53	23	139	−4	−84	−24	−47	−10
Indonesia	GGSF	1	2	–	46	23	94	89	24	76	92	86
Iran	ZWUA	36	43	38	49	51	54	71	78	82	116	163
Israel	GGSG	73	104	143	119	145	94	12	231	137	130	168
Japan	GGSH	820	943	1 093	1 264	1 038	1 237	1 389	1 667	1 678	1 537	2 099
Malaysia	GGSI	181	207	230	275	329	257	282	195	163	175	270
Pakistan	GGSJ	83	92	97	126	194	115	75	68	−53	52	−113
Philippines	GGSK	28	31	28	73	47	78	37	46	−9	36	56
Saudi Arabia	GGSL	1 096	1 020	1 220	1 386	1 319	1 342	1 305	1 491	1 756	1 331	−256
Singapore	GGSM	−47	−36	−35	116	191	150	227	745	709	861	691
South Korea	GGSN	218	232	273	315	338	322	345	259	253	268	327
Taiwan	GGSO	49	106	77	129	140	134	91	117	133	133	204
Thailand	GGSP	29	26	51	72	46	88	−30	−41	−141	−178	−216
Residual Gulf Arabian Countries	ZWTX	247	314	233	360	422	517	545	565	715	622	2 107
Other Near & Middle Eastern Countries	ZWTY	36	44	32	54	60	85	108	132	67	109	121
Other	ZWTK	147	205	13	239	255	325	277	−24	−55	25	152
Total Asia	GGSR	**3 185**	**3 569**	**3 699**	**4 987**	**5 105**	**5 344**	**5 288**	**6 035**	**6 058**	**5 865**	**6 460**
Australasia & Oceania												
Australia	GGSS	415	469	466	526	576	552	414	531	318	526	473
New Zealand	GGST	53	57	85	85	35	46	93	136	63	27	25
Other	GGSU	14	−1	6	2	37	29	23	36	61	42	168
Total Australasia & Oceania	GGSV	**482**	**525**	**557**	**613**	**648**	**627**	**530**	**703**	**442**	**595**	**666**
Africa												
Egypt	ZWTV	−45	−50	−60	−81	−45	13	19	87	31	17	8
Morocco	ZWUD	−5	−5	−6	−13	−2	−46	−41	−63	−62	−57	−78
South Africa	GGSW	307	396	512	376	281	353	383	627	446	513	387
Other North Africa	ZWTS	8	4	5	−13	22	100	42	−12	47	54	45
Other	ZWTL	382	400	410	283	622	595	810	677	721	767	636
Total Africa	GGSY	**647**	**745**	**861**	**552**	**878**	**1 015**	**1 213**	**1 316**	**1 183**	**1 294**	**998**
International Organisations	GGSZ	66	50	51	44	−2	5	−26	−24	−38	−7	35
World total	KTMS	**5 482**	**6 581**	**6 379**	**8 481**	**10 272**	**13 418**	**13 309**	**13 134**	**13 426**	**13 000**	**15 166**

9.6 Income

£ million

		1992	1993	1994	1995	1996	1997	1998	1999	2000	2001	2002
Credits												
Europe												
European Union (EU)												
Austria	CUGY	417	400	424	531	530	535	625	568	780	712	592
Belgium and Luxembourg	CTFK	2 490	2 635	2 593	3 113	3 407	3 517	3 847	3 556	6 275	7 008	5 496
Denmark	LEQU	644	654	507	612	625	724	1 071	941	1 146	1 100	855
Finland	LEUG	516	607	631	656	542	519	467	405	597	635	633
France	LEUP	3 910	4 697	4 860	6 001	5 905	5 410	5 944	6 013	7 648	8 819	7 308
Germany	LEQL	3 748	6 176	6 592	9 225	8 948	7 994	8 117	8 324	10 557	11 785	9 669
Greece	LEUY	222	139	198	348	799	1 069	655	824	1 010	823	778
Ireland	BFLY	1 280	1 399	1 426	1 707	1 916	2 395	2 717	2 946	3 940	4 906	4 358
Italy	BFOG	4 457	4 616	4 466	5 187	5 085	5 152	6 978	5 145	6 539	6 401	4 893
Netherlands	BFQI	5 175	5 888	6 378	7 097	7 990	8 642	8 896	9 216	12 904	16 968	14 056
Portugal	BFSK	253	258	287	394	460	392	469	464	676	812	845
Spain	LESW	1 046	1 359	1 411	1 784	2 409	2 427	2 391	2 043	2 559	2 602	2 339
Sweden	BFTL	1 352	1 508	1 191	1 417	1 600	1 428	1 459	1 542	2 137	2 355	1 929
European Central Bank	ZWYO	–	–	–	–	–	–	–	–	–	–	–
EU Institutions	CSFK	148	213	224	211	143	163	281	223	370	491	622
Total EU	LEQC	25 658	30 549	31 188	38 283	40 359	40 367	43 917	42 210	57 138	65 417	54 373
European Free Trade Association (EFTA)												
Iceland	BFNQ	60	55	36	32	25	20	32	29	35	35	26
Liechtenstein	BFPH	47	41	38	51	64	52	34	38	45	39	21
Norway	BFQR	533	553	525	531	588	606	636	719	1 033	1 021	804
Switzerland	LEPB	2 400	2 789	2 774	3 289	3 530	3 578	3 472	4 351	7 458	5 621	5 120
Total EFTA	CTFT	3 040	3 438	3 373	3 903	4 207	4 256	4 174	5 137	8 571	6 716	5 971
Other Europe												
Albania	ZWYP	–	–	–	–	–	–	–	–	–	–	–
Belarus	ZWYQ	–	–	–	–	–	–	–	–	–	–	–
Bulgaria	ZWYR	94	77	15	24	16	41	21	48	38	86	55
Croatia	ZWYS	4	4	4	4	4	14	9	11	15	26	18
Czech Republic	LEPT	–2	–1	21	49	109	130	113	123	125	201	127
Estonia	ZWYT	1	1	1	2	3	13	13	5	2	8	2
Hungary	BFKR	121	104	86	106	180	218	175	248	448	331	333
Latvia	ZWYU	–	–	–	2	–	1	8	–	2	–	4
Lithuania	ZWYV	–	–	–	–	5	8	4	4	9	7	4
Poland	BFSB	52	49	57	114	111	119	91	105	144	331	241
Romania	ZWYW	5	9	10	22	42	25	22	42	20	78	53
Russia	BFST	5	7	82	105	130	234	269	189	287	498	382
Slovakia	ZWYX	2	5	2	24	51	69	37	36	51	34	24
Slovenia	ZWYY	–	–	–	–	–	8	22	55	48	101	57
Turkey	BFUM	159	170	164	136	158	190	268	340	498	429	338
Ukraine	ZWYZ	10	8	10	11	8	–	16	3	–	4	1
Yugoslavia	BFWF	67	46	28	33	57	49	–	1	1	1	1
Other	LEVZ	1 721	1 216	1 261	1 229	1 463	2 601	3 130	2 826	3 727	3 131	3 386
Total Europe	LERD	30 937	35 682	36 302	44 047	46 903	48 343	52 289	51 383	71 124	77 399	65 370
America												
Argentina	ZWZB	377	469	440	449	437	484	410	248	488	395	201
Brazil	LENR	596	716	902	1 053	1 079	790	776	333	545	457	541
Canada	LEOS	1 155	1 279	1 404	1 817	1 609	1 820	2 078	1 848	2 269	2 333	1 712
Chile	ZWZC	243	264	305	345	339	283	190	166	259	185	236
Colombia	ZWZD	56	52	55	51	68	92	41	98	321	228	231
Mexico	BFPQ	971	900	718	630	455	535	404	537	458	282	461
United States of America	BFVE	11 908	13 494	14 476	16 639	18 645	21 125	25 048	23 428	29 793	32 105	27 504
Uruguay	ZWZE	28	19	20	24	32	29	23	7	16	13	14
Venezuela	ZWZF	258	264	175	169	184	149	–48	–15	–88	178	46
Other Central American Countries	JISP	531	577	484	515	822	1 153	4 362	4 017	5 310	5 477	5 796
Other	LEVH	505	540	449	481	599	960	67	40	91	26	304
Total America	LESN	16 628	18 574	19 428	22 173	24 269	27 420	33 351	30 707	39 462	41 679	37 046
Asia												
China	LEPK	71	68	105	132	174	217	206	258	309	546	348
Hong Kong	BFJU	2 507	2 458	2 695	3 034	3 265	2 596	2 080	1 738	1 690	1 420	1 773
India	BFNB	205	226	226	252	251	284	411	383	490	528	492
Indonesia	BFLP	110	82	115	138	181	303	238	157	149	225	193
Iran	ZWZG	132	106	79	113	118	64	36	37	50	42	38
Israel	BFMS	26	25	21	38	56	59	42	53	52	62	55
Japan	BFOP	9 100	8 102	7 425	8 869	7 516	7 171	6 872	7 288	9 521	8 119	5 610
Malaysia	BFPZ	302	337	369	366	418	481	356	420	497	423	542
Pakistan	BFRS	42	32	39	57	62	123	93	71	131	142	106
Philippines	BFRJ	95	110	110	115	133	103	136	98	179	157	131
Saudi Arabia	BFTC	86	115	136	154	127	144	195	221	296	261	196
Singapore	BFTU	1 877	2 024	2 111	2 602	2 689	2 668	1 810	1 536	2 863	2 600	2 600
South Korea	BFOY	137	127	159	267	407	564	363	301	427	491	523
Taiwan	BFUV	90	107	130	141	163	172	174	192	262	310	328
Thailand	BFUD	109	125	173	225	268	221	70	109	224	285	176
Residual Gulf Arabian Countries	JITQ	295	305	340	359	369	494	1 464	1 079	1 553	1 395	1 397
Other Near & Middle Eastern Countries	ZWZH	108	119	112	131	117	158	85	67	190	199	129
Other	LEWI	305	311	348	406	382	434	171	124	305	232	264
Total Asia	LETF	15 597	14 779	14 693	17 399	16 696	16 256	14 802	14 132	19 188	17 437	14 901
Australasia & Oceania												
Australia	CXAT	1 505	1 775	1 816	2 059	2 227	2 075	1 724	1 962	2 524	2 522	2 658
New Zealand	BFRA	378	416	433	472	493	390	276	387	328	423	430
Other	LEVQ	137	149	179	200	222	164	381	33	21	–	143
Total Australasia & Oceania	LETX	2 020	2 340	2 428	2 731	2 942	2 629	2 381	2 382	2 873	2 945	3 231
Africa												
Egypt	ZWZJ	65	64	41	57	69	79	–81	34	264	260	89
Morocco	ZWZK	43	40	30	36	55	23	15	24	29	30	22
South Africa	BFWX	531	540	554	661	703	761	748	983	1 206	1 379	1 147
Other North Africa	JIRR	172	141	118	106	83	87	98	57	97	142	99
Other	LEWR	545	574	620	648	666	553	547	602	771	732	710
Total Africa	LERV	1 356	1 359	1 363	1 508	1 576	1 503	1 327	1 700	2 367	2 543	2 067
International Organisations	CTFB	166	194	169	161	146	193	360	384	450	520	454
World total	HMBQ	66 704	72 928	74 383	88 019	92 532	96 344	104 507	100 689	135 468	142 525	123 075

9.6 Income
continued

£ million

United Kingdom Balance of Payments The Pink Book 2003 — Geographical breakdown of current account

		1992	1993	1994	1995	1996	1997	1998	1999	2000	2001	2002
Debits												
Europe												
European Union (EU)												
Austria	CUGZ	549	581	589	743	762	877	535	409	575	660	530
Belgium and Luxembourg	CTFL	3 443	3 802	4 087	4 873	4 373	3 798	4 418	4 265	5 060	5 551	5 280
Denmark	LEQV	514	722	582	692	987	1 028	920	796	1 062	918	869
Finland	LEUH	441	396	407	535	539	566	320	291	375	366	329
France	LEUQ	4 357	5 418	5 188	6 657	5 958	5 470	5 888	7 040	7 406	6 721	5 708
Germany	LEQM	6 505	7 849	7 711	9 904	8 966	8 420	7 735	7 758	11 637	9 557	7 967
Greece	LEUZ	279	246	271	471	758	860	692	649	805	631	393
Ireland	BFLZ	926	1 059	1 186	1 683	2 406	2 527	2 544	2 226	3 112	4 081	3 901
Italy	BFOH	1 962	2 127	2 221	2 755	3 259	3 686	3 448	2 813	2 847	2 984	2 144
Netherlands	BFQJ	3 959	4 201	4 204	5 051	5 691	4 335	4 120	6 356	12 284	12 333	10 215
Portugal	BFSL	429	456	316	437	435	396	260	212	236	286	204
Spain	LESX	727	1 301	1 271	1 816	2 124	1 744	1 926	1 320	1 233	1 504	1 180
Sweden	BFTM	1 175	1 167	1 009	1 230	1 522	1 223	1 170	1 388	1 328	1 320	1 092
European Central Bank	ZWZM	–	–	–	–	–	–	–	–	–	–	–
EU Institutions	CSFL	558	556	644	693	680	745	878	1 214	1 478	1 702	1 650
Total EU	LEQD	25 824	29 881	29 686	37 540	38 460	35 675	34 854	36 737	49 438	48 614	41 462
European Free Trade Association (EFTA)												
Iceland	BFNR	8	9	7	4	4	5	8	10	9	11	14
Liechtenstein	BFPI	113	114	113	129	126	125	106	75	109	299	326
Norway	BFQS	136	261	344	363	408	683	63	112	573	613	367
Switzerland	LEPC	6 255	6 623	6 453	6 934	6 897	6 897	6 074	7 473	11 061	9 705	6 187
Total EFTA	CTFU	6 512	7 007	6 917	7 430	7 435	7 710	6 251	7 670	11 752	10 628	6 894
Other Europe												
Albania	ZWZN	27	29	45	56	50	59	112	100	79	75	64
Belarus	ZWZO	27	27	43	53	46	56	70	55	41	23	15
Bulgaria	ZWZP	49	45	64	87	67	96	93	66	64	38	26
Croatia	ZWZQ	31	30	46	58	49	56	188	182	152	158	139
Czech Republic	LEPU	8	13	36	87	163	177	104	83	116	99	64
Estonia	ZWZR	32	32	46	57	49	59	59	41	31	9	3
Hungary	BFKS	94	60	62	92	89	101	90	81	69	35	30
Latvia	ZWZS	27	28	44	57	50	67	63	43	33	14	6
Lithuania	ZWZT	28	34	52	60	60	66	62	44	34	9	4
Poland	BFSC	76	100	108	158	163	266	190	137	168	154	92
Romania	ZWZU	47	52	71	78	91	124	78	48	47	35	27
Russia	BFSU	33	67	134	136	159	196	20	137	395	348	258
Slovakia	ZWZV	27	35	71	122	82	79	78	58	43	23	15
Slovenia	ZWZW	27	27	43	53	46	56	83	55	41	31	23
Turkey	BFUN	205	185	198	297	269	184	156	90	127	150	75
Ukraine	ZWZX	27	27	43	53	46	58	63	43	28	50	67
Yugoslavia	BFWG	77	57	108	127	161	165	58	40	29	44	45
Other	LEWA	3 334	2 708	2 388	3 218	3 935	4 935	5 909	5 640	6 849	7 253	5 561
Total Europe	LERE	**36 512**	**40 444**	**40 205**	**49 819**	**51 470**	**50 185**	**48 581**	**51 350**	**69 536**	**67 790**	**54 870**
America												
Argentina	ZWZZ	–63	–13	–21	–17	14	64	55	50	91	61	4
Brazil	LENS	86	104	78	274	402	290	244	154	176	138	56
Canada	LEOT	523	606	747	709	857	773	874	1 081	1 468	941	963
Chile	ZXAA	92	154	153	188	173	151	67	16	8	27	21
Colombia	ZXAB	161	118	79	83	137	81	38	20	35	39	17
Mexico	BFPR	180	158	109	114	122	119	152	147	219	242	75
United States of America	BFVF	10 460	13 010	12 740	15 133	18 489	19 886	20 327	23 135	25 668	28 795	26 378
Uruguay	ZXAC	38	30	35	20	24	30	–15	9	17	14	1
Venezuela	ZXAD	44	33	42	35	25	23	12	7	19	44	43
Other Central American Countries	JISQ	519	569	365	236	541	1 285	3 758	3 279	3 969	3 964	2 675
Other	LEVI	637	698	570	494	674	1 345	375	284	250	203	177
Total America	LESO	**12 677**	**15 467**	**14 897**	**17 269**	**21 458**	**24 047**	**25 887**	**28 182**	**31 920**	**34 468**	**30 410**
Asia												
China	LEPL	282	188	185	204	145	155	139	157	328	352	218
Hong Kong	BFJV	2 007	1 936	1 804	2 055	1 796	1 550	1 950	2 711	3 245	3 013	1 756
India	BFNC	162	180	303	347	305	370	343	298	338	507	415
Indonesia	BFLQ	117	108	87	113	119	96	39	47	74	99	55
Iran	ZXAE	163	148	149	179	213	133	91	87	206	259	96
Israel	BFMT	144	139	134	156	180	220	149	173	211	237	161
Japan	BFOQ	6 018	6 048	6 024	7 055	7 067	6 220	6 931	7 585	10 701	9 054	5 976
Malaysia	BFQA	135	162	247	311	412	430	192	231	312	241	114
Pakistan	BFRT	54	53	77	86	57	71	61	50	63	153	180
Philippines	BFRK	47	40	37	31	31	63	48	71	81	53	37
Saudi Arabia	BFTD	1 647	1 585	1 331	1 603	1 452	1 324	957	646	788	1 017	560
Singapore	BFTV	1 249	1 473	1 228	1 687	1 852	1 804	1 375	1 960	2 596	2 374	1 738
South Korea	BFOZ	103	106	85	155	157	202	189	84	136	186	32
Taiwan	BFUW	387	305	239	208	147	158	104	107	137	355	320
Thailand	BFUE	104	65	86	132	137	140	81	75	127	195	90
Residual Gulf Arabian Countries	JITR	709	641	486	533	493	558	945	863	1 302	1 777	1 350
Other Near & Middle Eastern Countries	ZXAF	433	388	285	303	262	318	214	189	244	287	231
Other	LEWJ	1 125	1 033	832	916	789	944	307	237	234	359	336
Total Asia	LETG	**14 886**	**14 598**	**13 619**	**16 074**	**15 614**	**14 756**	**14 115**	**15 571**	**21 123**	**20 518**	**13 665**
Australasia & Oceania												
Australia	CXCM	805	918	732	902	926	1 297	1 200	1 145	730	714	773
New Zealand	BFRB	30	53	98	105	163	181	178	47	99	131	110
Other	LEVR	15	7	8	2	5	13	–38	4	25	161	96
Total Australasia & Oceania	LETY	**850**	**978**	**838**	**1 009**	**1 094**	**1 491**	**1 340**	**1 196**	**854**	**1 006**	**979**
Africa												
Egypt	ZXAH	807	968	824	826	746	582	324	247	289	241	137
Morocco	ZXAI	41	45	56	40	58	54	34	31	28	42	37
South Africa	BFWY	13	67	28	58	112	216	421	770	681	724	551
Other North Africa	JIRS	191	106	107	159	136	254	115	95	157	185	128
Other	LEWS	327	199	243	336	292	510	539	496	582	720	578
Total Africa	LERW	**1 379**	**1 385**	**1 258**	**1 419**	**1 344**	**1 616**	**1 433**	**1 639**	**1 737**	**1 912**	**1 431**
International Organisations	CTFC	272	247	218	328	348	343	243	329	535	643	601
World total	HMBR	**66 576**	**73 119**	**71 035**	**85 918**	**91 328**	**92 439**	**91 601**	**98 267**	**125 705**	**126 337**	**101 956**

9.6 Income
continued

£ million

		1992	1993	1994	1995	1996	1997	1998	1999	2000	2001	2002
Balances												
Europe												
European Union (EU)												
Austria	CUHA	−132	−181	−165	−212	−232	−342	90	159	205	52	62
Belgium and Luxembourg	CTFM	−953	−1 167	−1 494	−1 760	−966	−281	−571	−709	1 215	1 457	216
Denmark	LEQW	130	−68	−75	−80	−362	−304	151	145	84	182	−14
Finland	LEUI	75	211	224	121	3	−47	147	114	222	269	304
France	LEUR	−447	−721	−328	−656	−53	−60	56	−1 027	242	2 098	1 600
Germany	LEQN	−2 757	−1 673	−1 119	−679	−18	−426	382	566	−1 080	2 228	1 702
Greece	LEVA	−57	−107	−73	−123	41	209	−37	175	205	192	385
Ireland	BFML	354	340	240	24	−490	−132	173	720	828	825	457
Italy	BFOI	2 495	2 489	2 245	2 432	1 826	1 466	3 530	2 332	3 692	3 417	2 749
Netherlands	BFQK	1 216	1 687	2 174	2 046	2 299	4 307	4 776	2 860	620	4 635	3 841
Portugal	BFSM	−176	−198	−29	−43	25	−4	209	252	440	526	641
Spain	LESY	319	58	140	−32	285	683	465	723	1 326	1 098	1 159
Sweden	BFTN	177	341	182	187	78	205	289	154	809	1 035	837
European Central Bank	ZXAK	−	−	−	−	−	−	−	−	−	−	−
EU Institutions	CSFM	−410	−343	−420	−482	−537	−582	−597	−991	−1 108	−1 211	−1 028
Total EU	LEQE	−166	668	1 502	743	1 899	4 692	9 063	5 473	7 700	16 803	12 911
European Free Trade Association (EFTA)												
Iceland	BFNU	52	46	29	28	21	15	24	19	26	24	12
Liechtenstein	BFPJ	−66	−73	−75	−78	−62	−73	−72	−37	−64	−260	−305
Norway	BFQT	397	292	181	168	180	−77	573	607	460	408	437
Switzerland	LEPD	−3 855	−3 834	−3 679	−3 645	−3 367	−3 319	−2 602	−3 122	−3 603	−4 084	−1 067
Total EFTA	CTFV	−3 472	−3 569	−3 544	−3 527	−3 228	−3 454	−2 077	−2 533	−3 181	−3 912	−923
Other Europe												
Albania	ZXAL	−27	−29	−45	−56	−50	−59	−112	−100	−79	−75	−64
Belarus	ZXAM	−27	−27	−43	−53	−46	−56	−70	−55	−41	−23	−15
Bulgaria	ZXAN	45	32	−49	−63	−51	−55	−72	−18	−26	48	29
Croatia	ZXAO	−27	−26	−42	−54	−45	−42	−179	−171	−137	−132	−121
Czech Republic	LEPV	−10	−14	−15	−38	−54	−47	9	40	9	102	63
Estonia	ZXAP	−31	−31	−45	−55	−46	−46	−46	−36	−29	−1	−1
Hungary	BFKT	27	44	24	14	91	117	85	167	379	296	303
Latvia	ZXAQ	−27	−28	−44	−55	−50	−66	−55	−43	−31	−14	−2
Lithuania	ZXAR	−28	−34	−52	−60	−55	−58	−58	−40	−25	−2	−
Poland	BFSD	−24	−51	−51	−44	−52	−147	−99	−32	−24	177	149
Romania	ZXAS	−42	−43	−61	−56	−49	−99	−56	−6	−27	43	26
Russia	BFSV	−28	−60	−52	−31	−29	38	249	52	−108	150	124
Slovakia	ZXAT	−25	−30	−69	−98	−31	−10	−41	−22	8	11	9
Slovenia	ZXAU	−27	−27	−43	−53	−46	−48	−61	−	7	70	34
Turkey	BFUO	−46	−15	−34	−161	−111	6	112	250	371	279	263
Ukraine	ZXAV	−17	−19	−33	−42	−38	−58	−47	−40	−28	−46	−66
Yugoslavia	BFWH	−10	−11	−80	−94	−104	−116	−58	−39	−28	−43	−44
Other	LEWB	−1 613	−1 492	−1 127	−1 989	−2 472	−2 334	−2 779	−2 814	−3 122	−4 122	−2 175
Total Europe	LERF	**−5 575**	**−4 762**	**−3 903**	**−5 772**	**−4 567**	**−1 842**	**3 708**	**33**	**1 588**	**9 609**	**10 500**
America												
Argentina	ZXAX	440	482	461	466	423	420	355	198	397	334	197
Brazil	LENT	510	612	824	779	677	500	532	179	369	319	485
Canada	LEOU	632	673	657	1 108	752	1 047	1 204	767	801	1 392	749
Chile	ZXAY	151	110	152	157	166	132	123	150	251	158	215
Colombia	ZXAZ	−105	−66	−24	−32	−69	11	3	78	286	189	214
Mexico	BFPS	791	742	609	516	333	416	252	390	239	40	386
United States of America	BFVG	1 448	484	1 736	1 506	156	1 239	4 721	293	4 125	3 310	1 126
Uruguay	ZXBA	−10	−11	−15	4	8	−1	38	−2	−1	−1	13
Venezuela	ZXBB	214	231	133	134	159	126	−60	−22	−107	134	3
Other Central American Countries	JISR	12	8	119	279	281	−132	604	738	1 341	1 513	3 121
Other	LEVJ	−132	−158	−121	−13	−75	−385	−308	−244	−159	−177	127
Total America	LESP	**3 951**	**3 107**	**4 531**	**4 904**	**2 811**	**3 373**	**7 464**	**2 525**	**7 542**	**7 211**	**6 636**
Asia												
China	LEPM	−211	−120	−80	−72	29	62	67	101	−19	194	130
Hong Kong	BFJW	500	522	891	979	1 469	1 046	130	−973	−1 555	−1 593	17
India	BFND	43	46	−77	−95	−54	−86	68	85	152	21	77
Indonesia	BFLR	−7	−26	28	25	62	207	199	110	75	126	138
Iran	ZXBC	−31	−42	−70	−66	−95	−69	−55	−50	−156	−217	−58
Israel	BFMU	−118	−114	−113	−118	−124	−161	−107	−120	−159	−175	−106
Japan	BFOR	3 082	2 054	1 401	1 814	449	951	−59	−297	−1 180	−935	−366
Malaysia	BFQB	167	175	122	55	6	51	164	189	185	182	428
Pakistan	BFRU	−12	−21	−38	−29	5	52	32	21	68	−11	−74
Philippines	BFRL	48	70	73	84	102	40	88	27	98	104	94
Saudi Arabia	BFTE	−1 561	−1 470	−1 195	−1 449	−1 325	−1 180	−762	−425	−492	−756	−364
Singapore	BFTW	628	551	883	915	837	864	435	−424	267	226	862
South Korea	BFPA	34	21	74	112	250	362	174	217	291	305	491
Taiwan	BFUX	−297	−198	−109	−67	16	14	70	85	125	−45	8
Thailand	BFUF	5	60	87	93	131	81	−11	34	97	90	86
Residual Gulf Arabian Countries	JITS	−414	−336	−146	−174	−124	−64	519	216	251	−382	47
Other Near & Middle Eastern Countries	ZXBD	−325	−269	−173	−172	−145	−160	−129	−122	−54	−88	−102
Other	LEWK	−820	−722	−484	−510	−407	−510	−136	−113	71	−127	−72
Total Asia	LETH	**711**	**181**	**1 074**	**1 325**	**1 082**	**1 500**	**687**	**−1 439**	**−1 935**	**−3 081**	**1 236**
Australasia & Oceania												
Australia	CYAA	700	857	1 084	1 157	1 301	778	524	817	1 794	1 808	1 885
New Zealand	BFRC	348	363	335	367	330	209	98	340	229	292	320
Other	LEVS	122	142	171	198	217	151	419	29	−4	−161	47
Total Australasia & Oceania	LETZ	**1 170**	**1 362**	**1 590**	**1 722**	**1 848**	**1 138**	**1 041**	**1 186**	**2 019**	**1 939**	**2 252**
Africa												
Egypt	ZXBF	−742	−904	−783	−769	−677	−503	−405	−213	−25	19	−48
Morocco	ZXBG	2	−5	−26	−4	−3	−31	−19	−7	1	−12	−15
South Africa	BFWZ	518	473	526	603	591	545	327	213	525	655	596
Other North Africa	JIRT	−19	35	11	−53	−53	−167	−17	−38	−60	−43	−29
Other	LEWT	218	375	377	312	374	43	8	106	189	12	132
Total Africa	LERX	**−23**	**−26**	**105**	**89**	**232**	**−113**	**−106**	**61**	**630**	**631**	**636**
International Organisations	CTFD	−106	−53	−49	−167	−202	−150	117	55	−85	−123	−147
World total	HMBP	**128**	**−191**	**3 348**	**2 101**	**1 204**	**3 905**	**12 906**	**2 422**	**9 763**	**16 188**	**21 119**

9.7 Current transfers

Geographical breakdown of current account — United Kingdom Balance of Payments The Pink Book 2003

£ million

		1992	1993	1994	1995	1996	1997	1998	1999	2000	2001	2002
Credits												
Europe												
European Union (EU)												
Austria	GXVQ	6	7	7	6	42	35	35	35	30	31	32
Belgium and Luxembourg	GXVR	59	109	129	120	267	221	252	245	224	218	239
Denmark	GXVS	6	36	21	57	92	52	47	42	28	30	35
Finland	GXVT	6	–	12	34	36	22	18	18	24	16	14
France	GXVU	389	365	258	432	524	340	360	326	278	332	295
Germany	GXVV	418	440	429	489	643	465	482	455	391	397	418
Greece	GXVW	38	58	73	59	110	59	60	53	40	42	42
Ireland	GXVX	197	215	209	239	281	167	166	152	114	165	134
Italy	GXVY	117	111	167	163	337	175	171	152	103	122	104
Netherlands	GXVZ	892	518	665	609	419	334	344	322	323	316	327
Portugal	GXWA	–	29	18	22	26	19	19	18	28	14	19
Spain	GXWB	79	93	77	90	160	116	120	110	91	98	95
Sweden	GXWC	–	54	70	79	171	113	109	103	89	94	90
European Central Bank	KNWK	–	–	–	–	–	–	–	–	–	–	–
EU Institutions	GXWD	4 138	5 336	4 362	4 419	7 188	5 422	5 103	6 541	5 574	7 423	6 302
Total EU	LGPH	6 345	7 371	6 497	6 818	10 296	7 540	7 286	8 572	7 337	9 298	8 146
European Free Trade Association (EFTA)												
Iceland	GXWF	4	3	3	5	41	36	36	36	33	34	34
Liechtenstein	GXWG	2	2	2	2	11	6	4	3	2	2	1
Norway	GXWH	40	52	47	51	149	86	83	77	61	62	71
Switzerland	GXWI	483	320	42	226	195	108	107	93	59	69	64
Total EFTA	GXWJ	529	377	94	284	396	236	230	209	155	167	170
Other Europe												
Albania	HZXP	–	–	–	–	–	1	–	–	–	–	–
Belarus	HZXQ	–	–	–	–	–	–	–	–	–	1	–
Bulgaria	KOLZ	–	–	–	–	–	–	–	–	2	–	8
Croatia	HZXR	12	25	24	29	12	6	4	3	2	2	2
Czech Republic	GXWK	4	4	3	4	14	7	5	4	6	2	2
Estonia	LWMG	1	2	2	2	1	3	–	–	–	–	–
Hungary	HZXT	–	–	–	–	–	–	1	–	1	1	8
Latvia	LWWC	11	23	22	27	11	4	4	3	2	2	5
Lithuania	LYTR	–	–	–	–	–	1	–	–	–	1	–
Poland	GXWL	9	9	9	9	16	29	7	5	3	2	12
Romania	HZXV	–	–	–	–	–	–	2	2	–	–	11
Russia	GXWM	28	21	21	23	62	29	32	23	10	13	13
Slovakia	HZXX	–	–	–	–	–	–	5	4	–	2	3
Slovenia	HZXY	–	–	–	–	–	–	–	–	–	–	5
Turkey	GXWN	24	22	22	24	60	36	36	35	28	31	31
Ukraine	HZYA	–	–	–	–	–	1	–	–	1	–	–
Yugoslavia	LTVE	–	–	–	–	–	–	–	3	2	2	2
Other	HKJF	53	102	98	123	50	25	25	19	12	32	15
Total Europe	GXWP	7 016	7 956	6 792	7 343	10 918	7 918	7 637	8 882	7 561	9 556	8 433
America												
Argentina	HZYJ	19	16	13	14	44	19	20	15	8	11	8
Brazil	GXWQ	17	12	11	15	56	25	25	21	10	15	12
Canada	GXWR	248	229	304	241	630	306	296	269	174	204	173
Chile	HZYL	14	12	10	10	33	15	15	12	7	11	7
Colombia	HZYM	29	25	21	22	70	29	27	24	14	26	13
Mexico	GXWS	28	23	20	24	75	37	35	30	18	21	21
United States of America	GXWT	3 014	2 261	2 586	2 753	4 394	2 206	2 101	1 866	1 208	2 384	1 264
Uruguay	HZYN	–	–	–	–	–	–	–	–	–	–	–
Venezuela	HZYO	20	17	15	15	48	22	27	19	8	11	9
Other Central American Countries	HZYG	254	217	186	186	604	261	253	227	144	157	135
Other	HZYI	19	16	13	14	44	19	19	16	8	11	10
Total America	GXWV	3 662	2 828	3 179	3 294	5 998	2 939	2 818	2 499	1 599	2 851	1 652
Asia												
China	GXWW	27	22	21	25	46	20	21	18	9	11	10
Hong Kong	GXWX	131	109	120	147	186	134	79	68	49	54	30
India	GXWY	61	56	54	58	36	17	18	20	15	23	20
Indonesia	GXWZ	26	20	17	21	85	37	38	30	17	21	18
Iran	HZYQ	7	6	6	7	11	6	4	3	3	2	2
Israel	GXXA	43	34	33	36	111	55	52	48	30	33	29
Japan	GXXB	162	147	181	234	364	175	173	149	99	116	104
Malaysia	GXXC	60	53	52	55	54	29	31	25	17	24	18
Pakistan	GXXD	2	2	2	2	13	8	7	6	3	4	3
Philippines	GXXE	16	11	9	12	45	22	20	15	8	10	8
Saudi Arabia	GXXF	33	28	30	33	472	487	492	505	484	494	484
Singapore	GXXG	38	31	30	32	47	21	23	17	8	16	10
South Korea	GXXH	19	16	15	17	44	19	19	20	9	13	14
Taiwan	GXXI	19	16	15	16	33	15	15	12	7	10	11
Thailand	GXXJ	13	11	11	11	23	9	9	8	4	5	6
Residual Gulf Arabian Countries	HZYS	135	108	104	121	202	177	176	177	161	166	165
Other Near & Middle Eastern Countries	HZYU	182	145	139	162	273	294	294	305	294	299	294
Other	HZVR	83	66	63	74	124	107	65	63	54	63	40
Total Asia	GXXL	1 057	881	902	1 063	2 169	1 632	1 536	1 489	1 271	1 364	1 266
Australasia & Oceania												
Australia	GXXM	386	346	342	380	362	224	206	196	156	171	177
New Zealand	GXXN	109	104	104	105	102	76	68	63	52	58	54
Other	GXXO	7	4	3	5	12	6	4	4	3	3	2
Total Australasia & Oceania	GXXP	502	454	449	490	476	306	278	263	211	232	233
Africa												
Egypt	LZDN	11	14	14	14	13	5	2	5	3	3	3
Morocco	HICY	9	12	12	12	11	6	4	3	2	2	2
South Africa	GXXQ	116	110	113	125	239	124	125	112	80	89	69
Other North Africa	HICX	20	27	26	28	25	13	15	12	10	10	11
Other	HZUI	82	109	105	112	100	53	55	45	33	37	34
Total Africa	GXXS	238	272	270	291	388	201	201	177	128	141	119
International Organisations	GXXT	–	–	–	–	–	–	–	–	–	–	–
World total	KTND	12 475	12 391	11 592	12 481	19 949	12 996	12 470	13 310	10 770	14 144	11 703

United Kingdom Balance of Payments The Pink Book 2003 — Geographical breakdown of current account

9.7 Current transfers
continued
£ million

		1992	1993	1994	1995	1996	1997	1998	1999	2000	2001	2002
Debits												
Europe												
European Union (EU)												
Austria	GXXV	33	25	27	31	20	23	16	18	23	23	24
Belgium and Luxembourg	GXXW	151	122	113	118	127	107	76	79	78	93	93
Denmark	GXXX	40	45	32	56	89	54	49	50	37	34	32
Finland	GXXY	16	13	13	15	27	13	12	12	22	16	13
France	GXXZ	317	220	290	332	457	256	245	336	267	295	308
Germany	GXYA	355	306	362	443	510	347	313	316	294	302	356
Greece	GXYB	68	57	21	40	100	48	49	44	50	48	41
Ireland	GXYC	493	448	417	486	741	726	773	411	470	487	502
Italy	GXYD	168	135	140	168	381	239	250	183	135	151	141
Netherlands	GXYE	237	426	452	534	222	147	135	172	187	148	168
Portugal	GXYF	39	28	42	49	28	27	25	31	48	37	40
Spain	GXYG	151	131	155	190	167	128	140	169	124	128	136
Sweden	GXYH	51	31	59	81	122	68	56	65	34	38	34
European Central Bank	KOEJ	–	–	–	–	–	–	–	–	–	–	–
EU Institutions	GXYI	6 970	8 260	7 431	9 192	9 277	8 268	10 265	10 524	10 719	9 557	10 097
Total EU	LGPL	9 089	10 247	9 554	11 735	12 268	10 451	12 404	12 410	12 488	11 357	11 985
European Free Trade Association (EFTA)												
Iceland	GXYK	8	6	6	8	11	6	4	3	4	2	5
Liechtenstein	GXYL	3	3	3	3	11	6	4	3	2	2	1
Norway	GXYM	105	60	74	78	139	84	74	95	57	61	53
Switzerland	GXYN	164	139	131	164	195	106	97	104	94	93	109
Total EFTA	GXYO	280	208	214	253	356	202	179	205	157	158	168
Other Europe												
Albania	HIDY	1	1	1	1	2	2	2	2	6	9	12
Belarus	HIDZ	1	1	1	1	2	2	2	4	–	6	11
Bulgaria	LTQA	–	–	–	–	–	–	–	8	12	8	14
Croatia	HIEA	1	1	1	1	12	13	8	5	8	7	6
Czech Republic	GXYP	16	14	15	16	20	15	14	21	9	9	10
Estonia	LWQY	–	–	–	–	–	4	–	–	–	–	–
Hungary	HIEC	10	8	8	9	13	17	18	17	16	12	19
Latvia	LYON	27	21	21	24	13	7	4	7	2	2	2
Lithuania	LYYJ	2	2	2	2	3	3	–	8	1	15	15
Poland	GXYQ	37	31	32	34	54	62	56	36	58	45	49
Romania	HIEE	22	17	18	20	13	13	14	10	14	11	20
Russia	GXYR	59	46	48	51	115	100	104	76	90	56	20
Slovakia	HIEG	4	3	3	3	5	8	10	7	5	3	6
Slovenia	HIEH	1	1	1	1	2	2	1	8	–	5	4
Turkey	GXYS	31	28	22	25	59	38	38	37	28	35	38
Ukraine	HIEJ	15	12	12	13	20	24	23	42	30	54	15
Yugoslavia	LWHC	2	2	2	2	3	1	–	9	67	39	31
Other	HZWJ	115	89	92	101	130	135	134	146	159	188	199
Total Europe	GXYU	**9 713**	**10 732**	**10 047**	**12 292**	**13 090**	**11 099**	**13 011**	**13 058**	**13 150**	**12 019**	**12 624**
America												
Argentina	HIES	24	18	19	23	46	21	21	17	16	19	16
Brazil	GXYV	28	20	21	24	68	39	41	43	36	47	55
Canada	GXYW	587	550	555	621	682	364	351	343	265	289	276
Chile	HIEU	28	21	23	26	38	21	19	17	12	13	11
Colombia	HIEV	29	22	24	28	76	37	33	33	23	32	19
Mexico	GXYX	36	27	27	29	81	42	40	38	25	24	24
United States of America	GXYY	2 043	1 539	1 550	1 985	4 519	2 332	2 113	2 098	1 447	2 543	1 522
Uruguay	HIEW	1	1	1	1	1	1	1	1	1	1	1
Venezuela	HIEX	22	16	17	20	44	19	19	16	9	12	10
Other Central American Countries	HIEP	477	364	384	450	875	568	616	526	433	462	435
Other	HIER	105	80	85	99	110	69	159	92	80	103	101
Total America	GXZA	**3 380**	**2 658**	**2 706**	**3 306**	**6 540**	**3 513**	**3 413**	**3 224**	**2 347**	**3 545**	**2 470**
Asia												
China	GXZB	61	46	47	51	119	92	109	103	82	86	125
Hong Kong	GXZC	138	116	105	121	151	99	92	133	117	120	121
India	GXZD	162	124	130	135	363	399	407	425	489	521	544
Indonesia	GXZE	80	62	60	67	179	104	102	85	54	47	45
Iran	HIEZ	22	20	21	17	23	23	20	20	20	23	24
Israel	GXZF	51	41	39	44	112	51	50	47	34	40	38
Japan	GXZG	203	156	149	170	359	171	160	160	97	111	106
Malaysia	GXZH	46	37	36	40	70	43	43	66	45	44	44
Pakistan	GXZI	80	61	67	67	149	182	158	152	144	156	229
Philippines	GXZJ	40	30	31	33	70	56	52	40	30	32	31
Saudi Arabia	GXZK	40	32	32	37	45	23	21	41	40	42	47
Singapore	GXZL	39	31	30	34	61	40	42	80	75	76	81
South Korea	GXZM	17	13	12	14	45	20	22	23	11	15	15
Taiwan	GXZN	14	11	9	11	33	16	15	17	7	11	11
Thailand	GXZO	15	12	12	13	30	20	18	25	28	31	37
Residual Gulf Arabian Countries	HIFB	144	134	139	112	119	95	87	97	73	89	86
Other Near & Middle Eastern Countries	HIFD	59	55	57	46	44	51	46	56	67	80	82
Other	HZWN	509	472	490	397	286	316	283	306	404	534	613
Total Asia	GXZQ	**1 720**	**1 453**	**1 466**	**1 409**	**2 258**	**1 801**	**1 727**	**1 876**	**1 817**	**2 058**	**2 279**
Australasia & Oceania												
Australia	GXZR	633	570	645	683	446	327	323	243	215	229	239
New Zealand	GXZS	111	114	121	134	110	83	80	58	65	67	67
Other	GXZT	82	72	69	77	32	32	25	32	11	9	21
Total Australasia & Oceania	GXZU	826	756	835	894	588	442	428	333	291	305	327
Africa												
Egypt	LZIF	22	19	17	18	11	5	–	29	24	24	26
Morocco	HIYZ	16	14	13	13	19	11	9	11	8	8	8
South Africa	GXZV	286	279	260	293	286	189	198	246	256	276	283
Other North Africa	HIYX	89	75	69	71	40	34	43	25	10	13	12
Other	HZUA	561	469	430	450	854	955	984	1 049	1 268	1 226	1 279
Total Africa	GXZX	**974**	**856**	**789**	**845**	**1 210**	**1 194**	**1 234**	**1 360**	**1 566**	**1 547**	**1 608**
International Organisations	GXZY	1 396	1 179	1 118	1 309	1 018	865	855	842	1 351	1 276	1 190
World total	KTNE	**18 009**	**17 634**	**16 961**	**20 055**	**24 704**	**18 914**	**20 668**	**20 693**	**20 522**	**20 750**	**20 498**

9.7 Current transfers
continued

£ million

		1992	1993	1994	1995	1996	1997	1998	1999	2000	2001	2002
Balances												
Europe												
European Union (EU)												
Austria	GZDU	−27	−18	−20	−25	22	12	19	17	7	8	8
Belgium and Luxembourg	GZDV	−92	−13	16	2	140	114	176	166	146	125	146
Denmark	GZDW	−34	−9	−11	1	3	−2	−2	−8	−9	−4	3
Finland	GZDX	−10	−13	−1	19	9	9	6	6	2	–	1
France	GZDY	72	145	−32	100	67	84	115	−10	11	37	−13
Germany	GZDZ	63	134	67	46	133	118	169	139	97	95	62
Greece	GZEA	−30	1	52	19	10	11	11	9	−10	−6	1
Ireland	GZEB	−296	−233	−208	−247	−460	−559	−607	−259	−356	−322	−368
Italy	GZEC	−51	−24	27	−5	−44	−64	−79	−31	−32	−29	−37
Netherlands	GZED	655	92	213	75	197	187	209	150	136	168	159
Portugal	GZEE	−39	1	−24	−27	−2	−8	−6	−13	−20	−23	−21
Spain	GZEF	−72	−38	−78	−100	−7	−12	−20	−59	−33	−30	−41
Sweden	GYRO	−51	23	11	−2	49	45	53	38	55	56	56
European Central Bank	ZWRB	–	–	–	–	–	–	–	–	–	–	–
EU Institutions	GYRP	−2 832	−2 924	−3 069	−4 773	−2 089	−2 846	−5 162	−3 983	−5 145	−2 134	−3 795
Total EU	LGPP	−2 744	−2 876	−3 057	−4 917	−1 972	−2 911	−5 118	−3 838	−5 151	−2 059	−3 839
European Free Trade Association (EFTA)												
Iceland	GXEL	−4	−3	−3	−3	30	30	32	33	29	32	29
Liechtenstein	GXEM	−1	−1	−1	−1	–	–	–	–	–	–	–
Norway	GXEN	−65	−8	−27	−27	10	2	9	−18	4	1	18
Switzerland	GZCH	319	181	−89	62	–	2	10	−11	−35	−24	−45
Total EFTA	GZCI	249	169	−120	31	40	34	51	4	−2	9	2
Other Europe												
Albania	ZWRF	−1	−1	−1	−1	−2	−1	−2	−2	−6	−9	−12
Belarus	ZWRI	−1	−1	−1	−1	−2	−2	−2	−4	–	−5	−11
Bulgaria	ZWRH	–	–	–	–	–	–	–	−8	−10	−8	−6
Croatia	ZWRS	11	24	23	28	–	−7	−4	−2	−6	−5	−4
Czech Republic	GZCJ	−12	−10	−12	−12	−6	−8	−9	−17	−3	−7	−8
Estonia	ZWRN	1	2	2	2	1	−1	–	–	–	–	–
Hungary	GYWH	−10	−8	−8	−9	−13	−17	−17	−17	−15	−11	−11
Latvia	ZWRV	−16	2	1	3	−2	−3	–	−4	–	–	3
Lithuania	ZWRU	−2	−2	−2	−2	−3	−2	–	−8	−1	−14	−15
Poland	GZCK	−28	−22	−23	−25	−38	−33	−49	−31	−55	−43	−37
Romania	ZWRX	−22	−17	−18	−20	−13	−13	−12	−8	−14	−11	−9
Russia	GZCL	−31	−25	−27	−28	−53	−71	−72	−53	−80	−43	−7
Slovakia	ZWRZ	−4	−3	−3	−3	−5	−8	−5	−3	−5	−1	−3
Slovenia	ZWRY	−1	−1	−1	−1	−2	−2	−1	−8	–	−5	1
Turkey	GZCM	−7	−6	–	−1	1	−2	−2	−2	–	−4	−7
Ukraine	ZWSA	−15	−12	−12	−13	−20	−23	−23	−42	−29	−54	−15
Yugoslavia	ZWSD	−2	−2	−2	−2	−3	−1	–	−6	−65	−37	−29
Other	ZWRC	−62	13	6	22	−80	−110	−109	−127	−147	−156	−184
Total Europe	GZCO	**−2 697**	**−2 776**	**−3 255**	**−4 949**	**−2 172**	**−3 181**	**−5 374**	**−4 176**	**−5 589**	**−2 463**	**−4 191**
America												
Argentina	ZWRG	−5	−2	−6	−9	−2	−2	−1	−2	−8	−8	−8
Brazil	GZCP	−11	−8	−10	−9	−12	−14	−16	−22	−26	−32	−43
Canada	GZCQ	−339	−321	−251	−380	−52	−58	−55	−74	−91	−85	−103
Chile	ZWRJ	−14	−9	−13	−16	−5	−6	−4	−5	−5	−2	−4
Colombia	ZWRK	–	3	−3	−6	−6	−8	−6	−9	−9	−6	−6
Mexico	GZCR	−8	−4	−7	−5	−6	−5	−5	−8	−7	−3	−3
United States of America	GZCS	971	722	1 036	768	−125	−126	−12	−232	−239	−159	−258
Uruguay	ZWSB	−1	−1	−1	−1	−1	−1	−1	−1	−1	−1	−1
Venezuela	ZWSC	−2	1	−2	−5	4	3	8	3	−1	−1	−1
Other Central American Countries	ZWRM	−223	−147	−198	−264	−271	−307	−363	−299	−289	−305	−300
Other	ZWRP	−86	−64	−72	−85	−66	−50	−140	−76	−72	−92	−91
Total America	GZCU	**282**	**170**	**473**	**−12**	**−542**	**−574**	**−595**	**−725**	**−748**	**−694**	**−818**
Asia												
China	GZCV	−34	−24	−26	−26	−73	−72	−88	−85	−73	−75	−115
Hong Kong	GZCW	−7	−7	15	26	35	35	−13	−65	−68	−66	−91
India	GZCX	−101	−68	−76	−77	−327	−382	−389	−405	−474	−498	−524
Indonesia	GZCY	−54	−42	−43	−46	−94	−67	−64	−55	−37	−26	−27
Iran	ZWRT	−15	−14	−15	−10	−12	−17	−16	−17	−17	−21	−22
Israel	GZCZ	−8	−7	−6	−8	−1	4	2	1	−4	−7	−9
Japan	GZDA	−41	−9	32	64	5	4	13	−11	2	5	−2
Malaysia	GZDB	14	16	16	15	−16	−14	−12	−41	−28	−20	−26
Pakistan	GZDC	−78	−59	−65	−65	−136	−174	−151	−146	−141	−152	−226
Philippines	GZDD	−24	−19	−22	−21	−25	−34	−32	−25	−22	−22	−23
Saudi Arabia	GZDE	−7	−4	−2	−4	427	464	471	464	444	452	437
Singapore	GZDF	−1	–	–	−2	−14	−19	−19	−63	−67	−60	−71
South Korea	GZDG	2	3	3	3	−1	−1	−3	−3	−2	−2	−1
Taiwan	GZDH	5	5	6	5	–	−1	–	−5	–	−1	–
Thailand	GZDI	−2	−1	−1	−2	−7	−11	−9	−17	−24	−26	−31
Residual Gulf Arabian Countries	ZWRQ	−9	−26	−35	9	83	82	89	80	88	77	79
Other Near & Middle Eastern Countries	ZWRR	123	90	82	116	229	243	248	249	227	219	212
Other	ZWRD	−426	−406	−427	−323	−162	−209	−218	−243	−350	−471	−573
Total Asia	GZDK	**−663**	**−572**	**−564**	**−346**	**−89**	**−169**	**−191**	**−387**	**−546**	**−694**	**−1 013**
Australasia & Oceania												
Australia	GZDL	−247	−224	−303	−303	−84	−103	−117	−47	−59	−58	−62
New Zealand	GZDM	−2	−10	−17	−29	−8	−7	−12	5	−13	−9	−13
Other	GZDN	−75	−68	−66	−72	−20	−26	−21	−28	−8	−6	−19
Total Australasia & Oceania	GZDO	**−324**	**−302**	**−386**	**−404**	**−112**	**−136**	**−150**	**−70**	**−80**	**−73**	**−94**
Africa												
Egypt	ZWRO	−11	−5	−3	−4	2	–	2	−24	−21	−21	−23
Morocco	ZWRW	−7	−2	−1	−1	−8	−5	−5	−8	−6	−6	−6
South Africa	GZDP	−170	−169	−147	−168	−47	−65	−73	−134	−176	−187	−214
Other North Africa	ZWRL	−69	−48	−43	−43	−15	−21	−28	−13	–	−3	−1
Other	ZWRE	−479	−360	−325	−338	−754	−902	−929	−1 004	−1 235	−1 189	−1 245
Total Africa	GZDR	**−736**	**−584**	**−519**	**−554**	**−822**	**−993**	**−1 033**	**−1 183**	**−1 438**	**−1 406**	**−1 489**
International Organisations	GZDS	−1 396	−1 179	−1 118	−1 309	−1 018	−865	−855	−842	−1 351	−1 276	−1 190
World total	KTNF	**−5 534**	**−5 243**	**−5 369**	**−7 574**	**−4 755**	**−5 918**	**−8 198**	**−7 383**	**−9 752**	**−6 606**	**−8 795**

Supplementary information

Balance of payments and the relationship to national accounts

This section is intended to help users of the Pink Book gain a better understanding of how the data fit within the broader economic accounts framework. It can be read as a stand-alone, although it makes several references to Blue Book tables and so readers are advised to have access to these if possible.

Introduction

Conceptually, the balance of payments, including the international investment position, form part of the broader system of the UK national accounts. The national accounts provide a comprehensive and systematic set of statistics for the UK economy, with information on economic transactions, other changes in the levels of assets and liabilities, and the levels of assets and liabilities themselves. The UK national accounts have generally been compiled according to the European System of Accounts *(ESA95)*. Linkages between the UK balance of payments and national accounts are reinforced by the fact that the UK balance of payments are compiled at the same time as the national accounts, as a component of the sector accounts and using many common data sources.

The national accounts are a closed system in which both ends of every transaction involving a resident economic entity are recorded. A set of accounts is introduced to capture transactions that involve economic relationships with non-resident entities. These accounts are known as the *rest of the world accounts* and are presented from the perspective of non-residents rather than residents. Consequently, entries in the balance of payments (which show transactions from the perspective of residents) are reversed in the presentation of the rest of the world accounts. The accounts for resident entities, which consist of the production, income and accumulation accounts, are described in more detail below.

Two important accounting differences occur when one compares the balance of payments and the national accounts. First, each transaction is recorded twice in the balance of payments (double entry) and four times in the national accounts (quadruple entry). This is because in the balance of payments the activity of only one transactor is recorded, that of the resident entity (with a non-resident entity), whereas in the national accounts the activity of both transactors is recorded (i.e. the activity of either two residents or a resident and a non-resident). Second, in the balance of payments, transactions are shown from the perspective of the resident entity; whereas in the national accounts, transactions are shown from the perspective of the resident in the production, income and accumulation accounts, and from the perspective of the non-resident in the rest of the world account.

Relations between national accounts and balance of payments concepts and classifications

Because the balance of payments, including the international investment position, forms an integral part of the national accounts, there is complete concordance between them in concept and classification, although the extent of cross-classifications may differ between the two systems.

The balance of payments and national accounts identify resident producers and consumers identically, and both invoke the same concepts of economic territory and centre of economic interest. Both use market prices as the primary concept of valuation of transactions and they adopt identical concepts of accrual accounting. The systems use identical conversion procedures to convert transactions which take place in foreign currency, to UK currency.

While for some purposes it would be convenient if classifications used in the rest of the world accounts and the balance of payments accounts were identical, differences between the two are justifiable because on occasion they serve different purposes. For example, in the balance of payments financial account, precedence is given to classification of transactions by type of investment (i.e. direct, portfolio, reserve assets, other), whereas in the rest of the world financial account the instrument of investment is the primary classification. More important is the fact that concepts, definitions and

149

classifications are consistent between the two systems.

The production, income and capital accounts of the national accounts

The national accounts tables reflect the basic aspects of economic life (production, income, consumption, accumulation and wealth). The tables which follow show summarised versions of the main accounts in the national accounts publications. The tables illustrate the main structure of the national accounts aggregates with particular reference to external transactions. An important element of the system is that a balance is derived in each table, which is then carried through to the next account.

For many analysts, *Gross Domestic Product (GDP)* is the key economic aggregate as it measures the total value added for the UK economy in any period. GDP may be measured as:

- the total value of output less the cost of goods and services used in the production process (intermediate consumption). This is referred to as the *output (or production) approach;*

- the value of income accruing from the production process to each of the factors of production (plus net taxes on production and imports). This is referred to as the *income approach;* or

- total final expenditure on goods and services during the period referred to as the *expenditure approach.*

Conceptually these measures are equal, but because different and imperfect data sources are used to measure each approach the measures may differ in practice. This difference is reflected in the statistical discrepancy item. The national accounts are regularly benchmarked to balanced annual supply and use (input-output) tables. This ensures that, except for the latest year, the three measures of GDP are equal on an annual basis, though there will still be a statistical discrepancy between the quarterly estimates based on the three approaches.

Blue Book table 1.2 presents the *Gross Domestic Product Account* for the whole economy, the derivation of GDP using the expenditure approach the income approach. Table 1.7.1, the *Production Account,* shows the derivation of GDP using the production approach.

- The expenditure based measure of GDP is derived as final consumption expenditure by government and households, plus investment in fixed capital formation and changes in inventories, plus exports minus imports of goods and services, plus (or minus) the statistical discrepancy. Exports and imports are the same as the balance of payments components, exports and imports of goods and services.

- The income based measure of GDP shows the components of factor income, namely compensation of employees, gross operating surplus and mixed incomes, plus taxes less subsidies on production and imports.

- The production based measure of GDP is shown as total gross output at purchasers' prices less intermediate consumption.

For the purpose of discussion here, all values are in current prices.

Blue Book table 1.7.3 presents the *National Income and Use of Income Account,* showing the derivation of gross national income, gross disposable income and use of gross disposable income. Gross national income is equivalent to GDP plus primary income receivable from non-residents, less primary income payable to non-residents. These primary income items are the same as the balance of payments income components which are used in the derivation of gross saving (gross disposable income less consumption) and net saving (gross saving less consumption of fixed capital). Table 1.7.3 illustrates how the various balance of payments income and current transfers components affect the nation's saving. To derive gross disposable income, net secondary income receivable from non-residents is added to gross national income; secondary income items are equivalent to the net current transfer components in the balance of payments. The segment of table 1.7.3 dealing with use of gross disposable income shows the derivation of gross saving (gross disposable income less consumption) and net saving (gross saving less consumption of fixed capital). Table 1.7.3 illustrates how the various balance of payments income and current transfers components affect the nation's saving.

Blue Book table 1.7.7, the *National Capital Account,* shows the link between gross saving and net lending/borrowing (to/from the rest of the world). The latter is derived as gross saving plus net capital transfers from non-residents less investment in fixed capital and inventories and the net acquisitions of non-produced, non-financial assets from non-residents. The items net capital transactions and net acquisitions of non-produced non-financial assets are both sourced from the balance of payments capital account. The capital account was introduced into the balance of payments to emphasise this clear relationship between the balance of payments and the national accounts.

The financial account and balance sheet of the national accounts

Net lending/borrowing is also the balance shown in *Blue Book* table 1.7.8, the *Financial Account.* The financial account shows how the net lending/borrowing is financed through a combination of transactions in financial assets and liabilities. As table 1.7.8 is a summary account for the economy, transactions between resident sectors are offset and eliminated. Therefore table 1.7.8 is also equivalent to the balance of payments financial account. However, there are some important differences in classification emphasis between table 1.7.8 and the balance of payments financial account. In table 1.7.8 the emphasis is on instrument of investment (currency and deposits, securities, loans, equity, etc.), while in the balance of payments financial account, the emphasis is on type of investment (direct investment, portfolio investment, and other investment). Both presentations give emphasis to the asset and liability classification.

It is worth noting that, if table 1.7.8 were expanded to include the financial transactions taking place between the various resident sectors, it would show the full financial account for the economy (which is published monthly in *Financial Statistics* and quarterly in *UK Economic Accounts*).

Blue Book table 1.7.9, the *National Balance Sheet*, shows the UK's non-financial assets (fixed assets, inventories, tangible and intangible non-produced assets such as land, copyright, etc.), financial assets, and liabilities and net worth at the end of the period. As table 1.7.9 is a summary account for the economy, financial assets and liabilities only measure financial claims by residents on non-residents and liabilities by residents to non-residents. In other words, in this table the financial assets and liabilities components are the international investment position statement for the UK. Claims and liabilities between resident sectors have been offset and eliminated. Again, there are some important classification differences between table 1.7.9 and the international investment position statement. In table 1.7.9 the emphasis is on instrument of investment, while in the international investment position statement the emphasis is on type of investment. Both presentations give emphasis to the asset and liability classification.

Rest of the world accounts of the national accounts

There are five accounts for the rest of the world in the national accounts shown in the *Blue Book*. These are:

(i) table 7.1.0, the *External account of goods and services;*

(ii) table 7.1.2, *the External account of primary incomes and current transfers;*

(iii) table 7.1.7, the *External capital account;*

(iv) table 7.1.8, the *External Financial Account;* and

(v) table 7.1.9, *the External Balance Sheet Accounts.*

The External Financial Account is published quarterly in *UK Economic Accounts*. As mentioned earlier, these accounts are required to close the system of national accounts and, while essentially the same as the balance of payments accounts and international investment position statement, they are compiled from the perspective of the non-resident transactor. Table 7.1.2 is essentially the current account of the balance of payments, table 7.1.7 the capital account, table 7.1.8 the financial account, and table 7.1.9 the international investment position. The reader should be able to readily identify the counterpart entries in all of these tables.

Methodological notes

Trade in goods (chapter 2)

Introduction

The IMF Balance of Payments Manual, 5th edition (BPM5) defines trade in goods as covering general merchandise, goods for processing, repairs on goods, goods procured in ports by carriers, and non-monetary gold.

General merchandise (with some exceptions) refers to moveable goods for which real or imputed changes of ownership occur between UK residents and the rest of the world.

Goods for processing: this covers goods that are exported or imported for processing and that comprise two transactions; the export of a good and the re-importation of the good on the basis of a contract and for a fee OR the import of a good and the re-exportation of the good on the basis of a contract and for a fee. The inclusion of these transactions on a gross basis is an exception to the change of ownership principle. The value of the good before and after processing is recorded. This is included in total trade in goods but cannot be separately identified.

Repairs on goods: this covers repairs that involve work performed by residents on movable goods owned by non-residents (or vice versa). Examples of such goods are ships, aircraft and other transport equipment. The value recorded is the value of the repairs (fee paid or received) rather than the value of the goods before and after repair.

Goods procured in ports: this covers goods such as fuels, provisions, stores and supplies procured by UK resident carriers abroad or by non-resident carriers in the UK.

Non-monetary gold: this is defined as all gold not held as reserve assets (monetary gold) by the authorities. Non-monetary gold can be subdivided into gold held as a store of value and other (industrial) gold – for further information see page 155.

Coverage and other adjustments

The balance of payments statistics of trade in goods compiled by the Office for National Statistics (ONS) are derived principally from data provided by HM Customs and Excise (HMCE) on the physical goods exported from and imported to the UK. However, this information is on a different basis to that required for Balance of Payments statistics. Accordingly in order to conform to the IMF definitions the ONS has to make various adjustments to include certain transactions which are not reported to HM Customs and Excise and to exclude certain transactions which are reported to them but where there is no change of ownership. In addition, since the value required for balance of payments purposes is the value of goods at the point of export (i.e. the Customs border of the exporting country) rather than the value of goods as they arrive in the UK. The freight and insurance costs of transporting the goods to the UK needs to be deducted from the values recorded by HMCE. Table 2.4 summarises this transition onto a Balance of Payments basis for each of the last 11 years.

Overseas trade statistics compiled by HM Customs & Excise

Statistics of the UK's overseas trade in goods have been collected for over 300 years by HM Customs & Excise. Since 1993 these data comprise statistics of UK imports from and exports to countries outside the EU. Data is compiled from declarations made to HM Customs & Excise by importers, exporters or their agents AND statistics of UK arrivals (imports) from and dispatches (exports) to other member states of the EU compiled from the Intrastat returns sent by traders or their agents to HM Customs & Excise.

Prior to 1993 statistics of UK imports from and exports to all countries in the world were compiled from declarations made to HM Customs & Excise by importers, exporters or their agents.

Information on trade with EU countries

The Intrastat system is linked to Value Added Tax (VAT) and has applied since 1993, with minor variations, in all EU member states. In the UK all VAT registered businesses are required to complete two additional boxes on their VAT returns, which are normally submitted quarterly. These show the total value of exports of goods to customers in other member states (dispatches) and the total value of imports of goods from suppliers in other member states (arrivals).

Traders whose annual value of arrivals or dispatches exceed given "assimilation" thresholds are required to provide a supplementary declaration each month, showing full details of their arrivals and dispatches during the month. These thresholds are reviewed annually. For the calendar year 2002 these thresholds were fixed at £233,000 both for arrivals and for dispatches. These detailed Intrastat declarations cover approximately 97 ½% of the value of trade.

Link with VAT

The information on the VAT returns serves three purposes; (i) to establish a register of traders and to determine which exceed the thresholds, (ii) to provide a cross-check with the supplementary declarations, (iii) to provide figures on the total value of trade carried out by traders below the thresholds.

Traders not registered for VAT and private individuals who move goods within the EU have no obligations under the Intrastat system and their trade is therefore not included in the statistics. Examples of commodities where this trade can be significant are works of art and racehorses.

Below threshold trade

The total values of arrivals and dispatches by traders below the Intrastat thresholds are available from their VAT returns. The figures are included in the month in which the VAT return is received by HM Customs & Excise, although the VAT return itself may relate to a period of more than one month. Detailed information on below threshold trade is not available. However it has been established that the pattern of that trade before the Intrastat system was introduced in 1 January 1993 was similar to that of traders just above the thresholds. Thus estimates enabling detailed allocations of below threshold trade can be made on this basis by the HMCE.

Non-response

Traders who have a legal responsibility to provide Intrastat declarations are required to do so by the end of the calendar month following the month to which the declaration relates. However, where traders have failed to provide returns to Intrastat, estimates of the total value of such trade are included. These are based on the trade reported by these traders in a previous period and the growth rate since that period experienced by traders who have provided returns for the current month.

Late response

Late declarations of trade with EU countries are subsequently incorporated into the month's figures to which they relate with a corresponding reassessment of the initial estimates for non-response.

Information on trade with non-EU countries

In general the figures for trade with non-EU countries show the trade as declared by importers and exporters or their agents and for which documentation has been received and processed by HMCE during the month.

Importers are usually required to present a Customs declaration before they can obtain Customs clearance and remove the goods. The great majority of imports are cleared immediately by a computerised system. Furthermore the import statistics include documents received by HMCE up to the third working day after the end of the month. Therefore the import figures correspond fairly closely to goods actually imported during the calendar month. Generally speaking about 75% by value and 85% by number of all entries relate to the calendar month with the bulk of the remainder relating to the immediately preceding month.

Under the procedures for the control of exports the principle is the same – namely that goods cannot be cleared for export until a Customs declaration has been made. Traders can, if they wish, submit a simplified declaration so that the goods can be exported which has to be followed within 14 days after date of shipment with a complete export declaration. Moreover the processing of these complete export documents begins three working days before the end of the calendar month (two working days for December). Thus the export statistics compiled for a month (which are based on the date of receipt of the complete export documents) do not correspond with goods actually shipped in the calendar month. Generally both in terms of the value and the number of documents, 65% relates to the calendar month with the bulk of the remaining 35% relating to the immediately preceding month.

Basis of valuation

For statistical purposes the UK adopts the valuation bases recommended in the 'International Trade Statistics Concepts & Definitions' published by the United Nations.

The valuation of exports (dispatches) is on a *free on board* (fob) basis, i.e. the cost of goods to the purchaser abroad, including:

- packaging;
- inland and coastal transport in the UK;
- dock dues;
- loading charges; and
- all other costs such as profits, charges and expenses (e.g. insurance) accruing up to the point where the goods are deposited on board the exporting vessel or aircraft or at the land boundary of Northern Ireland.

The valuation of imports (arrivals) is on a *cost, insurance and freight (cif)* basis including:

- the cost of the goods ;
- charges for freight & insurance; and
- all other related expenses in moving the goods to the point of entry into the UK (but excluding any duty or tax chargeable in the UK).

When goods are re-imported after process or repair abroad the value includes the cost of the process or repair as well as the value of the goods when exported.

Arrivals from and dispatches to EU countries

Because of its link with VAT the primary valuation for trade in goods with EU countries is that required for VAT accounting purposes, usually the invoice value. Regular sample surveys are conducted by HMCE to establish conversion factors to adjust the invoice values to produce the valuation basis required for statistical purposes. Separate factors are imputed for a range of different delivery terms and for trade with each member state.

The value recorded for arrivals and dispatches includes any duties or levies that have been applied to goods originating in non-EU countries but which have since cleared EU Customs procedures in one EU country prior to moving onto other EU countries.

Imports from non-EU countries

The statistical value of imports of goods subject to duty is the same as the value for Customs purposes. This value is arrived at by the use of specific methods of valuation in the following order of preference:

(i) the transaction value of the imported goods (i.e. the price paid or payable on the goods);

(ii) the transaction value of identical goods;

(iii) the 'deductive method' - value derived from the selling price in the country of importation;

(iv) computed value based on the built-up cost of the imported goods.

Imported goods are valued at the point where the goods are introduced into the Customs territory of the EU. This means that costs for delivery of the imported goods to that point have to be included in the Customs value.

For all other goods (i.e. goods free or exempted from duty and goods subject to a specific duty) the statistical value is determined in relation to the point at which the goods enter the UK.

An amount expressed in foreign currency is converted to sterling by the importer using a system of "period rates of exchange" published by HM Customs & Excise. These rates are normally operative for a four weekly period unless there is a significant movement in the exchange rate.

Treatment of Taxes

As described above, the value of all goods moving into and out of the UK is based on the transaction value recorded for Customs purposes or, in the case of trade in goods with EU countries, the invoice or contract value. In line with this principle the values recorded *exclude* VAT. For trade in goods with non-EU countries, all other taxes such as duties and levies applied to goods after arrival in the UK are *excluded*. For trade in goods with EU countries, the value recorded for imports and exports includes any duties or levies that have been applied to goods originating in non-EU countries but which have since cleared Customs procedures prior to moving onto other EU countries. However excise duties are *excluded* from the value recorded for trade.

Balance of payments statistics for trade compiled by ONS

Table 2.4 summarises the transition from trade in goods statistics on an Overseas Trade Statistics basis (compiled by HMCE) to those on a Balance of Payments basis (compiled by the ONS).

Valuation adjustments

Freight: The cost of freight services for the sea legs of dry cargo imports is estimated by applying freight rates (derived from the rates for a large sample of individual commodities imported from various countries) to tonnages of goods arriving by sea. For the land legs, estimates of freight rates per tonne-kilometre for different commodities and estimated distances are used. Estimates of rail freight through the Channel Tunnel are estimated from data provided by Le Shuttle and freight operators. The cost of freight on imports arriving by air is derived from information on the earnings of UK airlines on UK imports and the respective tonnages landed by UK and foreign airlines at UK airports. Pending investigations of an alternative methodology the cost of freight and insurance on oil and gas imports is projected from data formerly supplied by the Department of Trade and Industry.

Sources: Tonnages from HMCE; information on freight rates from Chamber of Shipping, Civil Aviation Authority and road hauliers; information from Le Shuttle.

Insurance: The cost of insurance premiums on non-oil imports is estimated as a fixed percentage of the value of imports.

Source – ONS estimate.

Coverage adjustments

Second-hand ships: to include purchases and sales of second-hand ships which are excluded from the Overseas Trade Statistics as the transactions are not notified to HMCE.

Source: Inquiries to UK shipowners conducted by the Department for Transport.

New ships delivered abroad: to include deliveries of new ships built abroad for UK owners while the vessel is still in a foreign port as the transactions are not notified to HMCE.

Source: Inquiries to UK shipowners conducted by the Department for Transport.

North Sea installations: to include goods (including drilling rigs) directly exported from and imported to the UK production sites in the North Sea. This adjustment is also used when there is a redistribution of the resources of fields which lie in both UK and non-UK territorial waters (e.g. the Frigg, Murchison and Statfjord). In these circumstances the contribution to (or reimbursement of) a proportion of the development costs has been treated as a purchase (or sale) of fixed assets at the date of the re-determination and appears as an adjustment to imports (exports) of goods.

Source: ONS inquiries to the petroleum and natural gas industry.

NAAFI: to exclude goods exported by the Navy, Army and Air Force Institute for the use of UK forces abroad since these are regarded as sales to UK residents.

Source: quarterly returns from NAAFI.

Goods not changing ownership: the Overseas Trade Statistics exclude temporary trade (i.e. goods that are to be returned to the original country within two years and there is no change of ownership). However goods may well have originally been recorded as 'genuine' trade but which are subsequently returned to the original country. Examples of these 'returned goods' are goods traded on a 'sale or return' basis; goods damaged in transit and returned for replacement or repair; and contractor's plant. The same amount is deducted from both imports and exports for the month in which the return movement is declared to Customs.

Source: HMCE (goods identified by reference to Customs Procedure codes (CPCs)).

Gold: trade in gold (i.e. gold bullion, gold coin, unwrought or semi-manufactured gold and scrap) is reported to HMCE but it is excluded from the statistics of total exports and imports published in the Overseas Trade Statistics. However, trade in ores and concentrates and finished manufactures of gold (e.g. jewellery) are included in total exports and imports.

For Balance of Payments purposes all trade in non-monetary gold should be included under trade in goods. Non-monetary gold is defined as all gold not held as reserve assets (monetary gold)

by the authorities. Non-monetary gold can be subdivided into gold held as a store of value and other (industrial) gold. The UK currently makes adjustments to include industrial gold. In exports the adjustment reflects the value added in refining gold and producing proof coins. In imports the adjustment reflects the value of gold used in finished manufactures (such as jewellery and dentistry).

Within the transactions of the London Bullion Market the UK cannot currently distinguish between monetary gold and non-monetary gold held as a store of value. Accordingly the UK has obtained an exemption from adopting IMF recommendations, as specified in the Balance of Payments Manual 5th edition, on treatment of gold until 2005. For the time being these transactions are included in the Financial Account.

Source: ONS estimate.

Letter post: to include exports by letter post which are not included in the Overseas Trade Statistics.

Sources: Books – ONS estimate based on historic information from publishers and booksellers; other items - ONS estimate based on historic sample inquiry made by the Post Office.

Additions and alterations to ships: to include work carried out abroad on UK owned ships and work carried out in UK yards on foreign owned ships.

Sources: Inquiries to UK shipowners conducted by the Department for Transport, (imports) and ONS estimates (exports).

Repairs to aircraft: to include the value of repairs carried out in the UK on foreign owned aircraft.

Source: ONS estimate.

Goods procured in ports: to include fuels, provisions, stores and supplies purchased for commercial use in ships, aircraft and vehicles.

Sources: Chamber of Shipping and Civil Aviation Authority for goods procured in foreign ports by UK transport companies (imports); UK oil companies, Civil Aviation Authority, BAA, municipal airports and port authorities for goods procured in UK ports by overseas transport companies (exports).

Smuggling of alcohol and tobacco: Customs provide volume figures for smuggled goods entering the UK based on published estimates of revenue loss and revenue evasion through smuggling. This information is supplemented by information on the average prices for alcohol and tobacco goods in France and Belgium from the published sources of the statistical and banking institutions in those countries in order to estimate the value of smuggled alcohol and tobacco entering the UK.

Sources: HMCE, INSEE & National Bank of Belgium

Territorial coverage adjustment: for the purposes of the Overseas Trade Statistics, "UK" is defined as Great Britain, Northern Ireland, the Isle of Man, the Channel Islands and the Continental Shelf (UK part). Therefore the Overseas Trade Statistics exclude trade between these different parts of the UK but include their trade with other countries.

For Balance of Payments purposes, the Channel Islands and the Isle of Man are not considered part of the UK economic territory. Adjustments are made to exports to *include* UK exports to those islands and to *exclude* their exports to other countries; and to imports to *include* UK imports from those islands and to *exclude* their imports from other countries.

Source: ONS estimate

Other adjustments

Diamonds: much of the World's trade in rough (uncut) diamonds is controlled from London by the Diamond Trading

Company, part of De Beers. Prior to 2001, in order not to distort the trade statistics, all imports into and exports from the UK of uncut diamonds which remain in the ownership of foreign principles are excluded from the Overseas Trade Statistics by HMCE. In addition the value of diamonds imported into the UK can be reassessed after the diamonds have been cleared by Customs. Prior to 2001 this adjustment reflects these changes in valuation. From 2001 the procedure for recording movements of diamonds was changed so that all trade was included in the Overseas Trade Statistics by HMCE. From 2001 this adjustment removes movements of diamonds where no change of ownership has taken place.

Source: Diamond Trading Company.

Adjustments to imports for the impact of VAT Missing Trader Intra-Community (MTIC) fraud: VAT intra-Community missing trader fraud is a systematic criminal; attack on the VAT system, which has been detected in many EU Member States. In essence, fraudsters obtain VAT registration to acquire goods VAT free from other Member States. They then sell on the goods at VAT inclusive prices and disappear without paying over the VAT paid by their customers to the tax authorities. The fraud is usually carried out very quickly, with the fraudsters disappearing by the time the tax authorities follow up the registration with their regular assurance activities.

Acquisition fraud is where the goods are imported from the EU into the UK by a trader who then goes missing without completing a VAT return or Intrastat declaration. The 'missing trader' therefore has a VAT free supply of goods, as they make no payment of the VAT monies due on the goods. He sells the goods to a buyer in the UK and the goods are available on the home market for consumption.

Carousel fraud is similar to acquisition fraud in the early stages, but the goods are not sold for consumption on the home market. Rather, they are sold through a series of companies in the UK and then re-exported to another Member State, hence the goods moving in a circular pattern or 'carousel'.

The VAT system (and therefore the Intrastat collection of trade statistics) picks up the exports of any 'carouselled' goods, but does not pick up the associated import at the time the carouselled goods entered the UK. As a consequence UK import statistics have been under reported.

ONS in partnership with HM Customs & Excise have developed a methodology to estimate these adjustments. The method used relies heavily on information uncovered during HM Customs & Excise's operational activity. As such it cannot be detailed for risk of prejudicing current activity, including criminal investigations and prosecutions and more generally undermining HM Customs & Excise's ability to tackle the fraud effectively. The method is applied only to some of the transactions involving mobile phones and computer components – the commodities of choice of the fraudsters. It specifically excludes other commodities and adjustments for the acquisition variant of the fraud which cannot be quantified at present.

Source: ONS estimate

Adjustment for under-recording and for currency and other valuation errors: these adjustments compensate for the following types of error:

- Failure on the part of traders or their agents to submit details of shipments;
- Incorrect valuations recorded;
- Declarations wrongly given in foreign currency instead of sterling.

Regular reviews show the adjustments for non-EU trade remaining broadly constant over time. Those for EU trade have reduced since the early days of the Intrastat system. The adjustments can be expressed as the following percentages of total trade excluding oil and erratics:

	Exports to: EU	Imports from: non-EU	EU	non-EU
Under recording	+½%	+1½%	+¼%	0
currency errors	0	-½%	0	0
other valuation errors	0	-½%	0	0

* (+1% for 1997 & +1 ½% 1993-1996)

Source – Sample surveys made by HMCE

Adjustments to estimates for non-response: a review of the introduction of the Intrastat system carried out in 1994 identified a number of difficulties in the initial monthly estimates of trade with EU countries provided by HMCE. The following describes the adjustments made by the ONS to cope with these difficulties.

The HMCE method of estimation for non-response relies on linking the values of trade reported by traders in the current period with previous periods. Problems can arise when traders change their VAT registration (perhaps as a result of an internal reorganisation, mergers or sales). Similarly problems can arise when a trader starts submitting returns for the first time. If the trader then becomes a non-responder there may be no history of previous trade upon which to base an estimate. To allow for this, the ONS makes an initial adjustment of +£30 million to both exports and imports (reducing to zero over the following two months).

Furthermore some traders may submit first declarations for a month that do not include all their trade in that month. Later declarations are then received for the rest of their trade. The pattern of receipt at HMCE of these partial returns is analysed to enable the ONS to make initial adjustments to both exports and imports to anticipate these later declarations. These initial adjustments are progressively reduced in subsequent months as late declarations are processed.

Currently the profile of these adjustments is as follows:

	Exports	£ million Imports
First published estimates	+400	+450
Second estimates	+150	+170
Third estimates	+80	+80
Fourth estimates	+40	+40
Fifth estimates	+10	+7
All subsequent estimates	0	0

Source - HMCE

Price and volume indices

When Intrastat was introduced it was envisaged that all declarations in respect of any particular month would be made within 6 months of the end of that month. As a consequence HMCE computer programs were designed to recalculate its initial estimates for non-response for six months after those estimates first appear in the Overseas Trade Statistics. However the reality is that some declarations are still being received and processed after that 6 month period. These are being included as additions to the value of reported trade with no corresponding reduction in the value of estimated trade. Accordingly, in order to eliminate this element of double counting the ONS makes a negative adjustment to the value of estimated trade equal to the value of these late amendments. Note where the value of late amendments exceeds the value of estimated trade the level of estimated trade is set to zero.

Source: ONS estimate.

Any difference between time periods in the total value of trade reflects changes in prices as well as changes in the levels of the underlying economic activity (e.g. the physical amounts of goods exported or imported). Separation of these changes greatly enhances the interpretation of the data and, for this reason, the ONS compiles separate data measuring changes in price and changes in volume. These data are presented in index number form.

References

Aggregate estimates of trade in goods, seasonally adjusted and on a balance of payments basis, are published monthly in a first release by National Statistics. More detailed figures are available from the Time Series Data Service and are also contained in the *Monthly Review of External Trade Statistics (Business Monitor MM24)* which is available, free of charge, in electronic format as a PDF on the National Statistics website.

Methodological notes

An article entitled 'UK visible trade statistics – the Intrastat system' was published in *Economic Trends*, August 1994.

A fuller version of these methodological notes appears in *Statistics on Trade in Goods (Government Statistical Service Methodological Series)*.

Trade in services (chapter 3)

Introduction

Trade in services covers the provision of services by UK residents to non-residents and vice versa. Trade in services are disaggregated into eleven broad categories of services, as follows:

(a) Transportation (Sea, Air and Other) – Passenger, freight and other

(b) Travel (Business and Personal)

(c) Communications services

(d) Construction services

(e) Insurance services

(f) Financial services

(g) Computer and information services

(h) Royalties and licence fees

(i) Other business services (Merchanting and other trade-related services; operational leasing services; miscellaneous business, professional and technical services)

(j) Personal, cultural and recreational services (Audio-visual and related services; other cultural and recreational services)

(k) Government services

Separate tables appear at Chapter 3 of this publication for each of the above categories except construction services, which are shown in the trade in services summary table 3.1.

The change from an industry to product based presentation on implementation of *BPM5* in 1998 meant that trade in services data at the individual product level could not always be constructed back in time. Preparation to collect trade in services by product commenced in 1996, with the introduction of the International Trade in Services (ITIS) survey. A full product based dataset is available from this date. Account totals, and some additional product estimates have been constructed back to 1991 or 1992, based on the relationship between the new ITIS data and the previous industry based data. It was not valid to project this relationship further back in time. For the transport, travel, royalties and government services accounts, there were only small changes from the industry based data, and it was possible to construct longer time series.

Construction services (Table 3.1)

Construction services cover work done on construction projects and installations by employees of an enterprise in locations outside their resident economic territory. The source of information is the International Trade in Services (ITIS) survey. For construction services, where a permanent base is established which is intended to operate for over a year, the enterprise becomes part of the host economy and its *transactions are excluded from the trade in services account*. Transactions where a permanent base is established are recorded under direct investment, within investment income.

Transportation services (Table 3.2)

The transportation account covers sea, air and other (i.e. rail, land, and pipeline) transport. It includes the movement of passengers and freight, and other related transport services, including chartering of ships or aircraft with crew, cargo handling, storage and warehousing, towing, pilotage and navigation, maintenance and cleaning, and commission and agents' fees associated with passenger/freight transportation.

Freight and the valuation of UK trade in goods

The trade in goods estimates included in the balance of payments *value imports* as they arrive in the UK valued f.o.b. (free on board) at the frontiers of the exporting country. This is net of the *cost of freight* to the UK border and any loss and damage incurred in transit to the UK. For UK importers who purchase goods f.o.b. and arrange transport themselves, their payment for the goods at the exporting countries' frontiers comprises:

(i) the value included in the trade in goods estimates (which is net of subsequent loss and damage);

(ii) the value of loss and damage incurred in transit.

In addition, such importers bear the costs of:

(iii) freight services outside the exporting countries;

(iv) insurance services (the excess of insurance premiums paid for the journeys over claims made).

Where importers purchase goods c.i.f. (cost, insurance and freight) on arrival in the UK - items (ii) to (iv) are paid by the foreign exporters in the first instance. The c.i.f. prices are set accordingly, however, and the UK importers are regarded as bearing the costs of items (i) to (iv).

Therefore, irrespective of the payment basis, items (ii) to (iv) represent costs to UK importers additional to the trade in goods entries (item i). Item (ii), the value of loss and damage, is part of the price paid to the foreign exporter and so always represents a debit entry in the balance of payments accounts. Items (iii) and (iv), freight and insurance services, also represent debit entries when provided by non-residents; where such services are provided by UK residents there is no balance of payments entry.

The estimates of trade in goods cover exports valued f.o.b. The valuation of exports at the UK frontier must, by definition, include any subsequent loss or damage en route to the importer. Therefore, unlike imports, there is no need to make an explicit adjustment for loss and damage to exports. However, foreign importers must additionally bear the costs of freight and insurance services for the journeys outside the UK and where such services are provided by UK residents this gives rise to credit entries in the services accounts.

The f.o.b. value for UK imports includes the cost of transport within the exporting country. Where this service is provided by a UK operator then the trade valuation of imports overstates the balance of payments effect and an offsetting credit entry is therefore included under "Road transport". Similarly, an offsetting debit entry is included for foreign operators' carriage of UK exports within the UK.

Sea transport

Exports by UK operators consist of freight services on UK exports (but not imports - see "Freight and the valuation of UK trade in goods", above) and on cross-trades, the carriage of non-resident passengers and the provision to them of services, and the chartering of ships to non-residents. Exports also include port charges and other services purchased in the UK by non-resident operators. Conversely, imports comprise services purchased abroad by UK operators, their chartering of ships from non-residents, and the carriage by non-resident operators of UK imports (but not exports) and goods on UK coastal routes and UK passengers.

Statistics relating to UK operators are provided by the Chamber of Shipping (CoS), which conducts inquiries into its members' participation in foreign trade. Until 1995, inquiries covering all CoS members were made every four years, with sample surveys for intervening years. Since 1995, the CoS has surveyed all its members annually. The services of offshore supply vessels and non-trading ships are not included in "Transportation" but in "Other business services" (Table 3.9).

Exports

Passenger revenue: the value of services provided to non-resident passengers comprises fares and passengers' expenditure on board. Since UK operators are not able to distinguish between fares received from UK residents and non-residents, fares collected abroad are assumed to represent fares received from non-residents (passenger revenue collected abroad from UK residents is thought to be small and is likely to be counter-balanced by that collected in the UK from foreign residents). An estimate of passengers' expenditure on board is added, taking the non-residents' proportionate share of the total to be the same as for fares.

Freight: earnings consist of freight services on UK exports and are based on data supplied to the Chamber of Shipping. Time charter receipts include receipts for charters with crew. Time charters without crew are included within the operational leasing component of Other Business Services (Table 3.9).

Disbursements: estimates of disbursements in the UK by foreign operators are formed from a variety of sources. UK income from port charges, towage, handling costs and other port related services was collected in 1996 from a survey of port authorities. Crews' expenditure is estimated from information on numbers of visiting seamen, supplied by the Immigration Service. Regular returns are received on light dues from Trinity House. Estimates of expenditure on ships stores and on bunkers are now included within the trade in goods data. Time charter payments made to UK residents are included under "Ships owned or chartered-in by UK residents".

Imports

Passenger revenue: estimates of passenger fares paid to non-resident operators are derived mainly from the results of the International Passenger Survey which is described in the notes below on "Travel". A further allowance is made for on board sales of goods and services. Passenger fares paid to non-resident operators for fly-cruises, however, together with other expenditure by UK passengers on board non-resident shipping, is included, but not separately identified, in "Travel" imports.

Freight: estimates of freight services on UK imports provided by non-resident operators are compiled as follows; the estimates of total freight services (provided by ALL operators) on the sea legs of UK imports of goods are taken as the starting point, as described in chapter 9. Chamber of Shipping estimates of the element provided by UK operated ships are then deducted to obtain the non-resident operators element which is then used in the transportation account. Charter payments cover payments for charters with crew.'

Disbursements: disbursements abroad include payments for canal dues, the maintenance of shore establishments, port charges, agency fees, handling charges, crews' expenditure, pilotage and towage, light dues and other miscellaneous port expenditure abroad. Payments for bunkers, ships stores and other goods purchased are now included within the trade in goods data.

Air transport

The exports of UK airlines comprise the carriage of non-resident passengers to, from or outside the UK, the carriage of UK exports of goods (but not imports - see "Freight and the valuation of UK trade in goods", above) and cross-trades and the chartering of aircraft to non-residents. Exports also include airport charges and services purchased in the UK by foreign airlines. Purchases of fuel and other goods are included within trade in goods.

Imports include expenditure abroad by UK airlines on airport charges, crews' expenses, charter payments, etc. They also include payments to foreign airlines for the carriage etc. of UK imports of goods (but not exports) and of UK mail;

Methodological notes

and for the carriage of UK passengers on flights covered by tickets for journeys to or from the UK (the carriage of UK passengers on other non-resident flights is included under "Travel").

The transactions of UK airlines are derived from returns supplied by the airlines to the Civil Aviation Authority.

Exports
Passenger revenue: this relates to all tickets sold outside the UK and used on UK aircraft, together with receipts from carrying passengers' excess baggage. An exercise by British Airways plc demonstrated that the value of tickets sold abroad to UK residents is roughly counter-balanced by sales in the UK to non-residents.

Freight: this consists of freight services on UK exports and the carriage of non-resident airmails, and is based on data supplied to the Civil Aviation Authority.

Disbursements and other revenue: These comprise expenditure in the UK by non-resident airlines on landing fees, other airport charges, handling charges, crews' expenses, office rentals and expenses, salaries and wages of staff at UK offices, commissions to agents and advertising. The estimates are based on returns from the Civil Aviation Authority, BAA plc and municipal airports on their receipts from non-resident airlines for air traffic control, landing fees and other airport charges; and survey information collected from large non-resident airlines operating in the UK on their other UK expenses. Purchases of fuel and other goods are now included within trade in goods.

Also included are receipts from the charter or hire of aircraft, and gross receipts of sums due from non-resident airlines under pooling arrangements and for services such as consultancy and engine overhaul.

Imports
Passenger: The information on fares paid by UK passengers to non-resident airlines is derived from the International Passenger Survey; see notes on "Travel" below.

Freight: Estimates of non-resident airlines' freight on UK imports are derived by subtracting from the estimates of total freight on imports of goods arriving by air (see chapter 9) the element provided by UK airlines, the residual being the freight services supplied by non-resident airlines. Other imports comprise payments to non-resident airlines for carrying UK airmails as reported by the Post Office to the Civil Aviation Authority.

Disbursements and other payments: disbursements abroad include airport landing fees, other airport charges, charter payments, crews' expenses, the operating costs of overseas offices, agents' commissions, advertising, settlements with non-resident airlines under pooling arrangements, and miscellaneous expenditure abroad. Purchases of fuel and other goods are now included within trade in goods.

Other Transport
This covers the movement of passengers and freight, and other related transport services, by rail, road and pipeline.

Rail: this consists primarily of expenditure on fares and rail freight through the Channel tunnel. Passenger revenue estimates are based on numbers of passengers through the tunnel and average fare information. Estimates of rail freight through the tunnel are based on data provided by Le Shuttle and freight operators.

As the tunnel operators are a joint UK/French enterprise, half of passenger and freight transactions are taken to accrue to the UK part of the business. That is, all tickets sold in France are assumed to be sold to non-UK residents (likewise, all tickets sold in the UK are assumed sold to UK residents). Of these, 50 per cent are assumed to accrue to the UK as they represent exports of rail transport services.

Road: exports comprise the earnings of UK road hauliers for the carriage outside the UK of UK exports of goods and the carriage within the exporting countries of UK imports (although excluding all such earnings from lorries leaving the UK via the Northern Ireland land boundary). Estimates of numbers of journeys to various countries are derived from the International Road Haulage Survey, and rates for each journey are estimated from trade and other sources.

Imports include payments to all non-resident land transport operators for the carriage of UK imports of goods between the frontiers of the exporting countries and the foreign sea ports. Estimates are made by subtracting from the estimate of total freight on imports for land legs (as described in chapter 9) an estimate of the element earned by UK operators (derived as for exports). Imports also include the earnings of non-resident road hauliers for carrying UK exports and imports (other than trade with the Republic of Ireland) within the UK. These are estimated from the statistics of ferry movements of foreign registered lorries, average loads, average lengths of haul within the UK and estimated freight rates. The disbursements abroad by UK road hauliers, and in the UK by non-resident road hauliers, are included within "Travel".

Pipeline: this covers the cost of transport of oil freight via undersea pipelines. Data are derived from a survey of North Sea Oil and Gas companies.

Travel (Table 3.3)

Travel covers goods and services provided to UK residents during trips of less than one year abroad (and provided to non-residents during similar trips in the UK), net of any purchases made with money earned or provided locally. Transport to and from the UK is excluded and shown as passenger services under transportation (see above). Internal transport within the country being visited is included within travel.

A traveller is defined as an individual staying, for less than one year, in an economy of which he/she is not a resident. The exceptions are those military and diplomatic personnel, whose expenditure is recorded under government services. The one year rule does not apply to students and medical patients, who remain residents of their country of origin, even if the length of stay in another economy is more than a year.

The estimates are based primarily on the International Passenger Survey, which seeks information on expenditure from samples of non-resident visitors leaving the UK and of UK residents returning from abroad. For package tourists, estimates of the transport elements are deducted from the reported total package costs. Estimates of the expenditure of UK residents visiting the Republic of Ireland and of Irish residents visiting the UK have been covered by the survey since the second quarter of 1999. Prior to this, data were derived from statistics published by the Irish Central Statistics Office.

Business travel
Business travel is divided into expenditure by seasonal and border workers (individuals who work some or all of the time in economic territories that differ from their resident households) and other business travel. Estimates are based on the International Passenger Survey.

Personal travel
Personal travel covers holidays, visits to friends and relatives, the expenditures of people visiting for education and health reasons and miscellaneous purposes. Visits for more than one purpose, where none is distinguished as the main purpose, are classified as other.

Education related travel exports covers the tuition fees and other expenditure of students who are funded from abroad and studying in the UK (imports covers the expenditure of UK students studying abroad). The figures also include the fees and other expenditure of pupils in UK private schools and students at other colleges and language schools. Income received direct from abroad by examining bodies and correspondence course colleges is included within personal, cultural and recreational services.

Fees and other expenditure paid by non-resident students for higher education is collected via a special International Passenger Survey (IPS) trailer which commenced in 1997. Expenditure of pupils in UK private schools is validated using data collected by the Independent Schools Information Service (ISIS), who run an annual survey of independent schools. For the 1996/97 academic year the survey included a new question for the balance of payments, which specifically identifies expenditure on school fees by persons classified as non-residents.

Health related travel covers the cost of medical and other expenses of those travelling abroad for medical treatment. Estimates are based on information supplied to the IPS.

Communication services (Table 3.4)

Communication services covers two main categories of international transactions: telecommunications (telephone, telex, fax, e-mail, satellite, cable and business network services) and postal and courier services. Information is obtained through the ONS International Trade in Services survey (ITIS) and direct from Parcel Force and the Post Office.

Insurance services (Table 3.5)

Insurance services cover the provision of various types of insurance to non-residents by resident insurance enterprises and vice versa. Insurance services include freight insurance on goods being imported or exported, direct insurance (life, accident, fire, marine, aviation etc.) and reinsurance. The amounts recorded in the accounts reflect the service charge earned on the provision of insurance services. This is equal to net premiums from abroad (premiums less claims), plus property income attributed to policy holders, less the change in the reserves for foreign business, less foreign expenses. The figures for insurance companies' and brokers' underwriting activities are derived from annual inquiries conducted by the ONS. Lloyds of London underwriting activity are based on data supplied by the Corporation of Lloyds; they also include receipts for management services provided to overseas members of Lloyds syndicates.

Life insurance and pension funds
Life insurance covers underwriting services associated with long term policies. Data are collected in the ONS inquiry into insurance companies. Pension fund services include service charges relating to occupational and other pension schemes, but not compulsory social security services.

Freight
Treatment of freight insurance is consistent with the f.o.b. valuation of trade in goods (see "freight and the valuation of trade in goods" above). That is, non-resident importers pay for freight and insurance on journeys outside the UK. Where such services are provided by UK residents, this gives rise to a credit entry.

Other direct insurance
Other direct insurance covers accident and health insurance; marine, aviation and other transport insurance; fire and property insurance; pecuniary loss insurance; general liability insurance, and other (such as travel insurance and insurance related to loans and credit cards).

Reinsurance
Reinsurance represents subcontracting parts of risks, often to specialised

operators, in return for a proportionate share of the premium income. Reinsurance may relate to packages which mix several types of risks. Exports of services are estimated as the balance of flows between resident reinsurers and non-resident insurers. Imports are estimated as the balance of flows between resident insurers and non-resident reinsurers.

Auxiliary insurance services

This covers insurance broking and agency services, insurance and pension consultancy services, evaluation and adjustment services, actuarial services, salvage administration services, regulatory and monitoring services on indemnities and recovery services. These are measured by net brokerage earnings on business written in foreign currencies, and sterling business known to relate to non-residents.

The main sources of information on insurance services are ONS inquiries to insurance companies and brokers, the ITIS survey and administrative data from Lloyd's of London.

Financial services (Table 3.6)

Financial services cover financial intermediary and auxiliary services other than those of insurance companies and pension funds. They include intermediary service fees associated with letters of credit, bankers' acceptances, lines of credit, financial leasing and foreign exchange transactions. Also included are commissions and other fees related to transactions in securities; e.g. brokerage, underwriting, arrangements of swaps, options and other hedging instruments etc.; commissions of commodity futures traders; and services related to asset management, financial market operational and regulatory services, security custody services etc. Estimates are based on returns from the Bank of England (for banks) ITIS , and directly from other sources including the Baltic Exchange.

From the 2001 edition of the *Pink Book*, the service earnings of financial institutions are presented on a gross exports and imports basis. This treatment is consistent with the BPM5 edition of the accounts. Trade in services transactions covered by type of financial institution are detailed below:

Monetary financial institutions (banks)

This covers UK banks' services giving rise to:

(i) commissions for credit and bill transactions such as advising, opening and confirming documentary credits, collection of bills, etc.;

(ii) spread earnings (dealing profits less holding gains) on foreign exchange transactions;

(iii) net receipts on foreign exchange dealing;

(iv) commission on new issues of securities, investment management and securities transactions;

(v) commission on derivatives transactions; and

(vi) banking charges, income arising from lending activities, fees and commissions in respect of current account operations, overdraft facilities, executor and trustee services, guarantees, securities transactions and similar services.

Estimates are based on inquiries carried out annually from 1986 to 1990 and for some earlier years. A quarterly survey was run in 1991. A new survey was introduced in 1992 to collect data on UK banks' current account transactions including services. The survey is completed quarterly by a selected sample of banks and annually by the full UK banking population.

Fund management companies

Service earnings from 1991, covering investment management fees and fees generated from advisory and other related functions, have been derived from a survey of companies whose main activity is fund management and from the ITIS survey since 2001. Earnings are net of any foreign expenses by the institutions concerned. They exclude earnings of insurance companies, which are covered by separate returns made to the Office for National Statistics (see above, under "Insurance Services").

Securities Dealers

The earnings of securities dealers are derived from a survey completed by members of the Securities and Futures Authority Ltd. (SFA). From the 1998 edition of the *Pink Book*, security dealers' spread earnings (dealing profits less holding gains) are included as part of securities dealers' overseas earnings. This treatment is consistent with the domestic accounts as described in the European System of Accounts (1995). Estimates of these spread earnings are based on information on acquisitions and realisations of various classes of securities derived from ONS inquiries, together with the bid and offer prices for certain international bonds.

Baltic Exchange

This covers the brokerage and other service earnings of members of the Exchange for chartering, sales and purchases of ships and aircraft and other associated activities. Estimates are based on a survey of Exchange members.

Other

This includes commissions etc. received from abroad by UK residents (other than monetary financial institutions and oil companies, whose earnings are included elsewhere) for dealings in physical goods and in futures and options contracts. From 1990 the Office for National Statistics has carried out an annual survey of dealers in physical commodities. The foreign earnings of financial futures and options dealers are assumed to have moved in line with the corresponding total earnings of such dealers reported in statutory returns to supervisory bodies.

This component also includes those financial services not included elsewhere, including financial service transactions (exports and imports) picked up from the ITIS survey, and service charges on purchases of International Monetary Fund resources.

Computer and information services (Table 3.7)

Computer and information services cover computer data and news related service transactions including databases, such as development, storage and on-line time series; data processing; hardware consultancy; software implementation; maintenance and repair of computers and peripheral equipment; news agency services; and direct, non-bulk subscriptions to newspapers and periodicals. Information is obtained from the ITIS survey.

Royalties and license fees (Table 3.8)

Royalties and licence fees cover the exchange of payments and receipts for the authorised use of intangible, non-produced, non-financial assets and proprietary rights (such as patents, copyrights, trademarks, industrial processes, franchises etc.) and with the use, through licensing agreements, of produced originals or prototypes (such as manuscripts and films).

The heading includes royalties, licenses to use patents, trade marks, designs, copyrights, etc.; manufacturing rights and the use of technical "know-how"; amounts payable or receivable in respect of mineral royalties; and royalties on printed matter, sound recordings and performing rights. Data are obtained through the ITIS survey. Film royalties from the ONS Films and TV inquiry are also included. Royalties incorporated in the contract prices of UK exports and imports of goods are recorded under "Trade in Goods". The outright sale of a copyright is treated as a sale of a non-produced, non-financial asset and is recorded within the Capital Account (Table 6.1).

Other business services (Table 3.9)

Other business services cover a range of services including merchanting and other trade-related services, operational leasing (rental) without operators and miscellaneous business, professional and technical services.

Merchanting and other trade related services

Merchanting is defined as the purchase of a good by a resident from a non-resident and the subsequent resale of the good to another non-resident, without the good entering the compiling economy. The difference between the purchase and sale price is recorded as the value of merchanting services provided.

Estimates of the net profits of UK firms from third country trade in goods are derived from an annual survey. Since 1990 the ONS has carried out a sample survey of export houses. This information is supplemented by merchanting and trade related services reported to the ITIS survey. This component also covers fees charged for ship classifications and other related services, including information supplied by Lloyds Register of Shipping.

Operational leasing
Operational leasing covers leasing (other than financial leasing) and charters of ships, aircraft and other transportation equipment without crews. Operational leasing data are derived from the ITIS survey and from the Chamber of Shipping.

Miscellaneous business, professional and technical services
Miscellaneous services include legal, accounting, management consulting and public relations; advertising and market research and development; architectural, engineering and other technical services; agricultural, mining and on-site processing services associated with agricultural crops (protection against disease or insects), forestry, mining (analysis of ores) etc.; and other services such as placement of personnel, security and investigative services, translation, photographic etc. This item includes data from a number of different data sources - the most important of which is the ITIS survey.

Estimates of the earnings of solicitors are based on surveys held in respect of 1980 and annually since 1986 by the Law Society (in which amounts forwarded to barristers are included). From the 2000 edition of Pink Book, earnings of solicitors are collected as part of the ITIS survey. Other legal services also included estimates of the overseas earnings of UK barristers as supplied by the Commercial Bar Association.

From Pink Book 2001, estimates of banks' and securities dealers' management services appear in the other business services account. Previously, these management services were implicitly included in the financial services account.

The North Sea oil and gas exports data mainly consists of work done abroad by UK owned drilling rigs and offshore supply boats and by UK seismic survey contractors, services provided by UK residents to the owners of foreign drilling rigs, the treatment of Norwegian oil and gas at the Seal Sands and St.Fergus terminals and the transporting of Norwegian gas to the latter terminal and receipts of the UK company operating the Murchison field from the Norwegian partners in respect of their share of the operating costs of the field. The imports item comprises services such as the hire of drilling rigs and marine support vessels, consultancy, diving and insurance (premiums less claims). The estimates are based on returns to the ITIS survey by companies classified to the industry (Class 11.20 of the Standard Industrial Classification, 1992).

Methodological notes

Personal, cultural and recreational services (Table 3.10)

Personal, cultural and recreational services are divided into audio-visual and related services and other. The first category covers services and associated fees relating to the production of motion pictures (on film or video tape), radio and television programmes (live or on tape), and musical recordings. It includes rentals, fees received by actors, directors, producers etc. The second category covers all other personal, cultural and recreational services including those associated with museums, libraries, archives, provision of correspondence courses by teachers or doctors etc. Income received direct from abroad by examining bodies and correspondence course colleges is also included. Most of the information is obtained from the ITIS survey but there is a special ONS inquiry for the film and television industry.

Government services (Table 3.11)

Government services include all transactions by embassies, consulates, military units and defence agencies with residents of staff, military personnel etc. in the economies in which they are located. Other services included are transactions by other official entities such as aid missions and services, government tourist information and promotion offices, and the provision of joint military arrangements and peacekeeping forces (e.g. United Nations). Information comes directly from government departments (including the Ministry of Defence and the Foreign and Commonwealth Office), foreign embassies and United States Air Force bases in the UK.

Exports
Expenditure by foreign embassies/ consulates in the UK: this comprises the cost of operating and maintaining Commonwealth High Commission offices, foreign embassies and consulates in the UK, including the personal expenditure of diplomatic staff, but excluding the salaries of locally engaged staff which are included within income; and similar expenditure by the UK offices of non-territorial organisations. In 1993 the Office for National Statistics conducted an inquiry to all high commission offices, embassies, consulates and international organisations in the UK. This figure has been updated for subsequent years using information obtained from several key high commissions and embassies.

Military units and agencies: this includes expenditure by the United States Air Force (USAF) in the UK (excluding the pay of locally engaged staff which is included within compensation of employees), together with receipts for services provided in the UK and elsewhere to non-residents, such as military training schemes.

European Union institutions exports: these are services of the UK government in collecting the UK contributions to the EU Budget, and services provided at the site of the EU's Joint European Torus project in Oxfordshire.

Other: this comprises goods and services which the government provides to non-residents under its economic aid programmes (these are offset under "Bilateral aid" transfer debits) and miscellaneous goods and services supplied by the UK government to foreign countries, including the reimbursement from other member states of the EU for treatment given by the National Health Service to their nationals.

Imports
Expenditure abroad by UK embassies and consulates: goods and services provided by local residents to UK embassies, High Commission offices, Consulates and the British Council account for most of this heading. It also includes the goods and services provided by local residents to UK diplomatic and other non-military personnel stationed abroad, excluding the salaries of locally engaged staff.

Expenditure abroad by UK military units and agencies: this includes expenditure on food, equipment, fuel and services purchased locally. These items are recorded partly on a net basis - that is, after deducting receipts arising locally.

Other: this includes goods and services provided by local residents to the UK Government, excluding military and diplomatic expenditure. It covers expenditure abroad of the British Council and the reimbursement to other member states of the EU for medical treatment given to UK nationals.

References

United Kingdom Trade in Services UKA1 contains service sector information highlighting the UK's major trading partners, the services which are common to a number of industries, and the geographical breakdown on services and industries.

Sea transport: an annual analysis describing the international activities of the UK shipping industry is published by the Department for Transport, in Transport Statistics Great Britain (The Stationery Office).

Air transport: Information relating to passenger expenditure is published by the Civil Aviation Authority in CAA Monthly and Annual Statistics.

Travel: details are published regularly in National Statistics monthly *First Releases* and quarterly *Business Monitors (MQ6),* both titled "Overseas Travel and Tourism", and in the annual publication *Travel Trends.*

Income (chapter 4)

Introduction

The income account covers compensation of employees and investment income. For compensation of employees, estimates for total credits, debits and the balance appear at Table 4.1 but no detailed breakdown of the account is available. Investment income is broken down into four main categories; direct investment, portfolio investment, other investment and reserve assets.

Compensation of employees

Compensation of employees comprises wages, salaries, and other benefits, in cash or in kind, earned by individuals in economies other than those in which they are residents, for work paid for by residents of those economies. Employees in this context, include seasonal or other short term workers (less than one year), and border workers who have centres of economic interest in their own economies. Compensation of employees also includes pay received by local (host country) staff of embassies, consulates and military bases as such entities are considered non-resident of the host economy.

Personal expenditure made by non-resident seasonal and border workers in the economies in which they are employed are recorded under travel within trade in services. Wages and salaries are recorded gross, with taxes paid, recorded under current transfers.

Credits
(i) wages, salaries and other benefits earned by UK seasonal and border workers, together with employers' contributions. The International Passenger Survey has been amended to collect this information alongside expenditure of non-resident seasonal and border workers from 1998. Estimates for earlier years are based on the growth of travel and average earnings data.

(ii) wages and salaries earned by UK employees in US military bases in the UK. Information is supplied to the ONS by US military bases.

(iii) wages and salaries earned by UK employees of foreign embassies in the UK. In 1993, the ONS conducted an inquiry to all high commission offices, embassies, consulates and international organisations in the UK, asking for information on expenditure - including that of locally employed staff. This figure has been updated for subsequent years using information from a small sample of key embassies.

Debits
(i) wages, salaries and other benefits earned by non-resident workers employed in the UK for less than one year. The International Passenger Survey has been amended to collect this information alongside expenditure of non-resident seasonal and border workers from 1998. Estimates for earlier years are based on the growth of travel and average earnings data.

(ii) wages, salaries and other benefits earned by foreign workers working in UK embassies and military bases abroad. Information on *pay of locally engaged staff* in UK embassies and military bases abroad is obtained from the Government Expenditure Monitoring System (GEMS) and the Ministry of Defence (MOD).

Investment income
(Table 4.1 and 4.2)

The investment income account covers earnings (e.g., profits, dividends and interest payments and receipts) arising from foreign investment in financial assets and liabilities. Credits are the earnings of UK residents from their investments abroad and other foreign assets. Debits are the earnings of foreign residents from their investments and funds held in the UK and other UK liabilities. The flow of investment is recorded separately from the earnings in the *Financial account,* although reinvested earnings of companies with foreign affiliates are a component of both – see *Earnings on direct investment* below. The total value of UK assets and liabilities held at any time is also recorded separately under the *International Investment Position.* The presentation of these three sections is almost identical, although there are small differences in coverage in some cases, mainly because full information is not available for all items.

Earnings on the credit side of the account cover such items as interest on UK residents' deposits with banks abroad, profits earned by UK companies from their foreign affiliates, and dividends and interest received by UK investors on their portfolio investments in foreign companies' securities, etc. Similarly, debits cover earnings by foreign investors on deposits held with UK banks, profits of foreign companies from their investments in their affiliates in the UK, and dividends and interest paid to foreign investors on their holdings of UK bonds and shares, including British government stocks, etc.

Earnings on assets and liabilities are defined to include all profits earned and interest and dividends paid to UK residents from non-residents or to non-residents by UK residents. They are, where possible, measured net of income or corporation taxes payable without penalty during the recording period by the enterprise to the economy in which that enterprise operates and, in the case of profits, after allowing for depreciation. Dividends are recorded when they become payable, whereas interest is recorded on an accruals basis.

Profits and dividends include the (credit) earnings from foreign affiliates of UK registered companies and the (debit) earnings of profits and dividends by UK based affiliates of foreign based companies. Conceptually, stock appreciation and other unrealised capital gains and losses should be excluded from the flows entered in the balance of payments accounts, because they represent only valuation changes. Profits retained abroad by foreign affiliates or retained in the UK by affiliates of foreign companies are included in the flows of earnings and offset in the financial account. All interest flows between UK residents and non-residents are in principle included.

Earnings on direct investment (Table 4.3 and 4.4)

A direct investment relationship exists if the investor has an equity interest in an enterprise, resident in another country, of 10 per cent or more of the ordinary shares or voting stock. The direct investment relationship extends to branches, subsidiaries and to other businesses where the enterprise has significant shareholding.

Credits

Direct investment earnings include interest on inter-company debt, profits from branches or other unincorporated enterprises abroad and the direct investor's share of the profits of subsidiary and associate companies. It includes the direct investor's portion of reinvested earnings, which is also treated as a new investment flow out of the parent's country into the affiliate's and appears in the financial account (Table 7.3) as an offsetting entry to the earnings one.

Estimates of profits are made after providing for depreciation, the companies' own estimates of depreciation being used. Although depreciation is estimated at replacement cost in the national accounts, there is little doubt that the estimates in the balance of payments are, in the main, measured at historic cost (different treatments of depreciation result in different entries in the current and financial accounts, but the sum of the two entries will always be the same). Refunds of tax made retrospectively under double-taxation agreements are included in the period when they were made rather than the earlier periods in which they could be deemed to have accrued. Dividend receipts and payments include subsidiaries payments of withholding tax. Estimates for reinvested earnings are not collected separately but are derived by deducting dividends paid from total subsidiaries' profits.

Monetary financial institutions (banks): information on the direct investment earnings of UK registered banks, from their foreign branches, subsidiaries and associates are collected by the Bank of England from a selection of banks quarterly and from all banks annually, which are, or have, a direct investment enterprise.

Insurance companies and other financial intermediaries: a comprehensive annual inquiry forms the basis for estimates of direct investment earnings by UK insurance companies and other financial intermediaries; these results are supplemented by a quarterly survey. Prior to 1991, the insurance part of the inquiry was conducted by the Association of British Insurers (ABI) on behalf of the ONS. Earnings from foreign property by financial companies are also included here. They are estimated from the levels of such assets held by financial companies and information on their total income from abroad.

Private non-financial and public corporations: earnings, both credits and debits, of all private and public non-financial corporations are estimated from the results of the ONS' annual direct investment inquiry. This inquiry covers a sample of UK companies that either have foreign affiliates or are affiliated to a foreign parent. Returns are imputed for concerns which are not approached in the inquiry but which are known to have direct investment links. Results of the annual inquiry are available about twelve months after the end of the year and are published in a *National Statistics First Release* and in *Business Monitor MA4*. The estimates for the latest year are based on a quarterly inquiry.

Earnings on foreign assets by the household sector: this comprises *household sector* investment in property abroad. Estimates for household sector investment in property abroad are purely notional as no data exists for such earnings.

Debits

Estimates for income earned from direct investment in the UK are based on the same inquiries to banks, financial institutions and private non-financial corporations as credits. Foreign earnings on property investment in the UK comprises estimates of interest due to foreign owners of residential and certain commercial property in the UK. Holdings of property by foreign parent companies through affiliates in the UK are classified as part of companies' direct investment and are covered in the appropriate category above, not under this heading. Only properties owned directly by foreign residents are covered in this heading. Estimates of earnings on the commercial component are based on estimated liability levels (derived from cumulating and revaluing capital flows) and use implied rates of return.

Earnings on portfolio investment (Table 4.5 and 4.6)

Credits

Earnings of UK residents on portfolio investment abroad are sub-divided into earnings on equity securities and earnings on debt securities; debt securities are further sub-divided into earnings on bonds and notes and money market instruments.

Earnings on equity securities: earnings on equity securities consist of dividends received by UK residents on their holdings of shares of foreign registered companies.

Earnings on bonds and notes: earnings on bonds and notes, within debt securities, consist of interest received by UK residents on their holdings of foreign government and municipal loan stock and bonds of foreign registered companies. A large part of the total earnings of UK residents on equity securities and bonds and notes are earned on their investments that are not considered to have led to the acquisition of a foreign affiliate, and so classified as portfolio rather than direct investment.

Estimates of earnings by monetary financial institutions (banks and building societies), are derived from statutory inquiries conducted by the Bank of England. Insurance companies and pensions funds and other financial intermediaries, including securities dealers, are derived from ONS inquiries.

Estimates of earnings by private non-financial corporations on equity securities and bonds and notes are derived from survey-based asset levels to which rates of return on comparable assets shown by financial institutions are applied.

Estimates of the household sector largely consist of earnings by members of Lloyd's of London which are supplied annually by Lloyd's. They include portfolio investment income on funds which are held abroad to support business underwritten in those countries. This income, which is generally reinvested in these foreign funds (see *Portfolio investment*) is net of earnings distributed to Lloyd's foreign members. In early years information from the Inland Revenue on UK residents' portfolio earnings from abroad was also used.

Earnings on money market instruments: earnings on money market instruments, within debt securities, consist of earnings of UK residents on holdings of foreign commercial paper, certificates of deposit etc. Data are derived from statistical surveys undertaken by the ONS and the Bank of England.

Debits
Foreign earnings on portfolio investment in the UK are sub-divided into earnings on equity securities and earnings on debt securities while debt securities are further sub-divided into earnings on bonds and notes and money market instruments.

Earnings on equity securities: estimates of foreign earnings from UK equity securities consist of dividends paid to foreign holders of UK company ordinary shares. These estimates are calculated from Stock Exchange data on dividend payments, which are applied pro-rata to levels of non-resident holdings of UK shares derived from the ONS' share ownership surveys.

Earnings on bonds and notes: interest on UK foreign currency bonds and notes, within debt securities, relates to bonds issued to foreign official holders of sterling in 1977 and HM Government's 1978 US $350 million New York bond issue. Also included is interest on foreign currency securities originally issued by public corporations under the exchange cover scheme and subsequently assigned to HM Government. This series also covers interest paid to foreign residents on their holdings of HM Government's floating rate notes (part of the US $2.5 billion issued in 1985 and redeemed in 1988, the US $4 billion issued in 1986 and redeemed in 1996 and a further US $2 billion issued in 1996). There was a further US $2 billion fixed rate bond issue in 1996. These data are estimated from the liability level and known interest rates. Also included is interest on HM Government's 10 year ECU 2.5 billion bond (issued in 1991), interest on the 3 year ECU/Euro Treasury Note programme (first issued in January 1992) and interest on the Dm 5 billion and US $3 billion bonds issued in 1992. The Dm 5 billion bond issue was redeemed in 1997.

Foreign earnings on British government stocks (gilts), within debt securities, is estimated from information on the levels outstanding and appropriate rates of interest. These earnings are calculated gross of UK income tax. Most gilts are issued by the UK government at a discount to the redemption value. This is recorded as interest accruing over the lifetime of the gilt.

Foreign earnings on bonds issued by local authorities and public corporations, within debt securities, have been zero in recent years; for earlier years estimates were made by the Bank of England.

From 1992, total interest paid on all bonds and notes issued by UK monetary financial institutions and other sectors (other than domestic debentures and loan stock) has been estimated from records of capital issues held by the London Stock Exchange and the Bank of England. These sources also provide estimates of the total value of bonds on issue, and foreign receipts have been allocated pro rata to their holdings.

Earnings on money market instruments: foreign earnings on UK money market instruments, within debt securities, consist of earnings on foreign holdings of UK treasury bills, certificates of deposit and commercial paper. Estimates of interest paid to foreign holders of sterling and, between 1988 and 1999, ECU/Euro denominated treasury bills are calculated on the basis of levels outstanding and appropriate interest rates. Estimates of foreign earnings on holdings of UK certificates of deposit and commercial paper are derived from statistical inquiries conducted by the ONS and the Bank of England, and from information supplied by the UK's Debt Management Office.

Earnings on other investment (Table 4.7 and 4.8)

Credits
Earnings of UK residents on other investment abroad are sub-divided into earnings on trade credit, loans, deposits and other assets.

Trade credit: Only a minimal amount of data is available within trade credit. See Financial account notes for detail.

Earnings on loans: earnings on loans are sub-divided into earnings on long-term loans and earnings on short-term loans; short-term loans are those which are repaid in full within one year. It is not possible to separate out UK monetary financial institutions' earnings on lending abroad from their earnings on deposits abroad and estimates for earnings on such loans are therefore included indistinguishably within earnings on deposits (see below).

Long-term loans consist of loans by UK banks guaranteed by the Export Credit Guarantee Department (ECGD), loans by the ECGD themselves, as well as loans by the Commonwealth Development Corporation. These data are derived from information supplied by the Bank of England, the ECGD and by the Commonwealth Development Corporation. Short-term loans mainly consist of loans by non-governmental sectors other than monetary financial institutions. Earnings on such loans are derived from banking statistics.

Earnings on deposits: estimates of earnings on deposits relate to private sector earnings.

Estimates of monetary financial institutions' earnings are sub-divided into earnings on sterling and foreign currency deposits abroad. This heading includes earnings on foreign lending as it is not possible to separate out UK banks' earnings on their lending abroad from earnings on their deposits abroad. These earnings consist of the interest received by UK banks from non-residents on overdrafts and loans made to them in sterling and foreign currencies. UK banks cover all banks in the UK, including (with effect from 1 April 1998) the Banking Department of the Bank of England. The figures are based on returns made by banks to the Bank of England. In 1992, a new reporting form for UK banks was introduced to improve the cohesiveness of banks' current account transactions (services, interest on non-securitised borrowing and lending and direct investment earnings).

Estimates of securities dealers' earnings on deposits abroad are derived from an ONS statistical inquiry. Estimates of the UK private sector (excluding monetary financial institutions and securities dealers) earnings on deposits abroad are largely estimated from levels of such assets (mainly those reported in banking statistics of countries in the BIS reporting area) and appropriate rates of interest. Adjustments are made to remove as far as possible the effects of incomplete coverage and breaks in the reported assets series. Estimates of the appropriate earnings of miscellaneous financial institutions are included. These are derived from information on asset levels and appropriate interest rates.

Earnings on other assets: until 2001 earnings from trusts and annuities were estimated from Inland Revenue data on all reported interest and dividend receipts from abroad. From 2001 Inland Revenue have ceased to collect this data, and from this point the data should be regarded as being of lower quality. Interest earned from currency exchanges undertaken prior to the abolition of exchange control was estimated from debt levels and appropriate interest rates. There have been no such earnings since 1986. Imputed income to UK households from net equity in life assurance reserves and in pension funds is recorded in the balance of payments because households are regarded as owning the net equity of pension funds and life assurance reserves; i.e. the funds set aside for the purpose of satisfying the claims and benefits foreseen. The estimates are derived from data collected on ONS statistical inquiries.

Debits

Foreign earnings on other investment in the UK are subdivided into earnings on trade credit, loans, deposits and other liabilities.

Trade credit: Only a minimal amount of data is available within trade credit. See Financial account notes for detail.

Earnings on loans: this covers interest on loans raised from commercial banks abroad, the European Investment Bank (EIB) and interest on public corporations borrowing from abroad. It is not possible to separate out earnings on foreign loans to UK banks from earnings on foreign deposits with UK banks. The estimates for foreign earnings on UK banks' loans from abroad are therefore included indistinguishably within earnings on deposits.

Interest paid on central government long-term fixed-interest loans such as Lend-Lease and the Lines of Credit is reported by HM Treasury. Interest on the Very Short-term Financing Facility (VSTFF) taken out during 1992 and repaid in 1993 is also included here. Estimates of interest on local authorities' borrowing from abroad are made by the Bank of England on the basis of levels outstanding and appropriate discount rates. Estimates of interest on public corporations' borrowing from abroad are made by the Bank of England.

Estimates of foreign earnings on securities dealers' loans from abroad are derived from an ONS statistical inquiry. For estimates of foreign earnings on loans to the UK private sector (excluding monetary financial institutions and securities dealers) most interest payments are estimated from levels of liabilities to banks abroad (as published in the BIS international banking statistics) and appropriate interest rates. Information on interest paid by the UK non-bank private sector to the EIB is supplied by the EIB.

Earnings on deposits: foreign earnings on deposits with UK monetary financial institutions are sub-divided into earnings on deposits with banks and earnings on deposits with building societies. It is not possible to separate out foreign earnings on deposits with UK banks from foreign earnings on loans to UK banks. The estimates for foreign earnings on loans to UK banks are therefore included indistinguishably within earnings on deposits.

Foreign earnings on deposits with UK banks consist of interest on foreign residents' deposits in sterling and foreign currencies. They include the interest paid on deposits which are the counterpart to foreign currency loans made to HM Government and, under the public sector exchange cover scheme, to local authorities and other public bodies. Estimates are made from banking statistics. Estimates of interest paid abroad on deposits with UK building societies are estimated by applying appropriate interest rates to levels outstanding.

Earnings on other liabilities: imputed income to foreign households from UK insurance companies' technical reserves is recorded in the balance of payments because households are regarded as owning the net equity of pension funds and life assurance reserves; i.e., the funds set aside for the purpose of satisfying the claims and benefits foreseen. The estimates are derived from data collected on ONS statistical inquiries.

Earnings on reserve assets (Table 4.1)

Interest received on the official foreign exchange reserves and on the UK's holdings of Special Drawing Rights with the IMF and other remuneration received from the IMF (related to its holdings of sterling), is recorded within the Exchange Equalisation Account by the Bank of England.

Current transfers (chapter 5)

Introduction

Most entries in the balance of payments accounts represent resources provided (goods and services exported or imported or the use of investments) or changes in financial assets and liabilities. Most transactions between UK residents and non-residents give rise to two such entries, which are theoretically recorded in the accounts with opposite signs. For some transactions however, only one such entry appears. Examples are a gift of goods sent abroad (which appears as a positive entry under "Trade in Goods") and a transfer to abroad of financial assets (which appears as a positive entry in the financial account). The entries in this section represent the counterpart to such entries (the value of the gift of goods or of the assets transferred, with a negative sign in both the examples).

Transfers are separately identified as either current or capital. Capital transfers relate to the transfer of ownership of a fixed asset, or the forgiveness of a liability by a creditor, when no counterpart is received in return. Counterparts to the capital account entries resulting from money being brought to, or taken from, the UK by migrants are included within the *Capital account*.

Current transfers are sub-divided into those of central government and other sectors. UK's contributions to and receipts from the European Union budget are recorded on a gross basis.

Central government current transfers

Central government transfers include receipts, contributions and subscriptions from or to European Union (EU) institutions and other international bodies, bilateral aid and military grants. Information comes from government departments (HM Treasury, Foreign & Commonwealth Office and Department for International Development).

Credits
These comprise receipts to the UK central government from EU institutions (VAT Abatement and other smaller, miscellaneous EU receipts), taxes on income (compensation of employees and subsidiaries withholding tax) and social contributions paid by non-resident workers and inward direct investors, and payments to the UK in respect of the UK's costs incurred in the Gulf conflict in the early 1990s. From the 1998 edition of the Pink Book, VAT Abatement has been treated as a credit entry to the UK balance of payments, rather than simply netted off VAT based contributions.

Debits
These comprise payments by the UK central government to international organisations and other non-residents.

European Union institutions: payments are part of the UK contribution to the EU budget.

Other international organisations: this includes contributions to the military budget of NATO, contributions to the European Development Fund and agencies of the United Nations to provide economic assistance to developing countries, and subscriptions to cover the administrative expenses of various other international bodies.

Bilateral Aid: this covers technical co-operation and non-project grants (project grants are included within capital transfers as they fund capital projects). Technical co-operation covers the provision of technical "know-how" to developing and transitional countries either as qualified manpower or as facilities for the training of nationals of these countries. Non-project grants are cash grants to developing countries for use in financing imports and budgetary support, together with the value of goods and services provided by the UK government as food aid or disaster relief.

Military Grants: these consist of cash grants for military purposes and the value of goods and services of a military nature provided without charge to foreign countries and international organisations by the UK government.

Social Security benefits: these consist of national insurance retirement and war pensions paid abroad.

Collaborative projects: these include the UK contribution towards the JET programme.

Other sectors' transfers

Other sectors' transfers cover current taxes paid, receipts and payments to EU institutions, net non-life insurance premiums and claims, and other payments and receipts of households, including workers remittances. Compensation received from the EU to assist with the foot and mouth outbreak in 2002 are also included here.

Credits

Receipts from EU institutions: comprise receipts in respect of the EU's Agricultural Guarantee Fund (including subsidies relating to foot and mouth) and Social Fund. They are treated as non-government transfers within the national accounts and balance of payments, as the UK government acts as an agent for the ultimate beneficiary of the transfer.

Net non-life insurance premiums: comprise the actual premiums received from non-residents plus the imputed premium supplement (see chapter 10), less the insurance service charge. The source for these data are the ONS surveys of insurance corporations, which collect premiums by type of insurance product, and Lloyd's of London.

Net non-life insurance claims: these are based on information supplied to the International Trade in Services survey on insurance claims received from non-resident insurance companies.

Other receipts of households: consists of three main components:

(i) Workers remittances, estimated as the savings from work of UK nationals temporarily resident in Middle East oil exporting countries, estimated from the number of UK passport holders resident in these countries, and assumed average savings per worker. These data are supplemented by information in the global transfer debits of the countries concerned.

(ii) Pension payments and other transfers (excluding immigrants assets) from OECD countries, estimated mainly from information supplied by these countries on their payments to the UK.

(iii) Similar transfers from other countries. These are estimated from published current transfer debits figures, supplemented by bilateral information on payments to the UK, supplied directly to the ONS. Also included are UK receipts from voluntary aid agencies or non-profit institutions serving households (NPISH's).

Debits

Current transfers on income: these are taxes on the incomes of UK seasonal and border workers (recorded as Compensation of employees) and withholding taxes paid abroad by UK direct investment corporations. These estimates are based on estimates of tax based on seasonal and border income information and the ONS inquiries into foreign direct investment.

Payments to EU institutions: these comprise agricultural and sugar levies, customs duties and VAT based contributions.

Net non-life insurance premiums: this covers premiums paid by UK companies to non-resident insurance companies collected via the International Trade in Services survey.

Net non-life insurance claims: this covers settlement of claims by UK insurance companies to non-resident claimants which are regarded as a transfer debit. The total of claims equals the total of net premiums (service charges having been deducted), as the essential function of non-life insurance is to redistribute resources. The source for these data are the ONS surveys of insurance corporations and Lloyd's of London.

Other payments of households: these include a number of separate components:

(i) Cash gifts from UK households to dependants etc. abroad. Data were obtained from exchange control records until 1979. Estimates for later years are based on information supplied by a number of countries on their receipts from the UK. These data are used in conjunction with historical information on gifts collected in the Family Expenditure Survey and, for recent years, the trend in UK personal disposable income.

(ii) Payments abroad by voluntary aid agencies or non-profit institutions serving households (NPISHs). Data are supplied by the Institutions.

(iii) The estimated value of gifts sent abroad by parcel post.

Capital account (chapter 6)

The capital account comprises two components: capital transfers and the acquisition/disposal of non-produced, non-financial assets.

Capital Transfers

Capital transfers are those involving transfers of ownership of fixed assets, transfers of funds associated with the acquisition or disposal of fixed assets, and cancellation of liabilities by creditors without any counterparts being received in return. As with current transfers, they can be sub-divided into central government transfers and other sectors transfers. The main sources of information are government departments (Department for International Development and HM Treasury) and the Bank of England.

Central government capital transfers: these consist of debt forgiveness and project grants (there are no receipts in recent years). Debt forgiveness is defined as the voluntary cancellation of debt between a creditor, in this case the UK government, and a debtor in another country. Data are supplied by the Department for International Development. Project grants are cash grants to developing countries for the establishment of production and infrastructure facilities. Such transfers are distinguished from current transfers as they are conditional on the acquisition of fixed assets. Data are supplied by the Department for International Development.

Other sectors capital transfers: these include migrant transfers, debt forgiveness and capital transfers from European Union Institutions.

Credits

Migrants' Transfers: these are recorded as being equal to the net worth of the migrants, as they arrive in the UK. Estimates are based on information on number of migrants and average assets being transferred as supplied to the International Passenger Survey. These data are supplemented by information on migrants to and from Ireland and asylum seekers, which are not covered by the IPS.

EU Institutions: regional development fund and agricultural guidance fund receipts from the EU are considered to be capital rather than current transfers as they relate to infrastructure projects. Data are supplied by HM Treasury.

Debits

Migrants' transfers: these represent the net worth of emigrants as they leave the UK. Estimates are based on information on the number of migrants and average assets being transferred as supplied to the International Passenger Survey. These data are supplemented by information on migrants to and from Ireland and asylum seekers, which are not covered by the IPS.

Debt forgiveness: this consists of non-government debt forgiveness by monetary financial institutions and public corporations. Data on monetary financial institutions is supplied by the Bank of England and data on public corporations is supplied by the Export Credit Guarantee Department.

Acquisition/disposal of non-produced, non-financial assets

This heading covers intangibles such as patents, copyrights, franchises, leases and other transferable contracts, goodwill etc. and transactions involving tangible assets that may be used or needed for the production of goods and services but have not themselves been produced, such as land and sub-soil assets. The use of such assets are recorded under trade in services as royalties and license fees; only the outright purchase or sale of such assets are recorded in the capital account.

The International Trade in Services (ITIS) survey has collected information on the sale and purchase of copyrights, patents and transferable contracts from 1996. Such transactions are indistinguishable from other areas of the current account for years before 1996.

Financial account (chapter 7)

Introduction

The financial account covers transactions which result in a change of ownership of financial assets and liabilities between UK residents and non-residents. The financial account is broken down into five main categories; direct investment, portfolio investment, financial derivatives, other investment and reserve assets.

In the balance of payments accounts, the term "investment" has a wide coverage. It does not refer only to the creation of physical assets but also, for example, to the purchase (or sale) of paper assets, such as shares, bonds and other securities. Investment also covers the financing of trade movements and other financial transactions between related companies in the UK and abroad. These "other financial transactions" consist mainly of borrowing and lending by banks, both transactions by UK banks with non-residents and transactions of banks abroad with UK residents. Such borrowing and lending may be associated with UK trade in goods. For example, a non-resident may borrow from a UK bank to pay a UK exporter; alternatively he may use money already on deposit with the bank. Such borrowing or use of deposits will be included in the appropriate item in the financial account offsetting the entry under trade in goods.

Banking transactions may also arise from the financing of other financial transactions. For example, a UK company may borrow from a foreign bank in order to finance investment ("direct investment") in one of its subsidiary companies abroad. In this case, both the bank borrowing and the investment would be recorded in this section of the accounts and the two entries would offset each other; the investment would increase UK assets abroad while the borrowing would increase UK liabilities to foreign residents.

The total value of assets and liabilities held at the end of each year is recorded separately under the International Investment Position (see Chapter 8) and the income earned from them is recorded under investment income within the income account (see Chapter 4). The presentation of these sections are almost identical although there are small differences in coverage in some cases, mainly because full information is not available for all items. The financial account tables appearing at Chapter 7 show net debits (UK assets) above net credits (UK liabilities), in order to allow easier read across with the investment income and international investment position tables which appear at chapters 4 and 8.

Direct investment (Table 7.3 and 7.4)

The term "direct investment" defines a group of transactions between enterprises, usually companies, that are financially and organisationally related and are situated in different countries. Such related enterprises – "affiliates" – comprise subsidiaries, associates and branches. Further details are given in the Glossary. Direct investment refers to investment that is made to add to, deduct from, or acquire, a lasting interest in an enterprise operating in an economy other than that of the investor and which gives the investor an effective voice in the management of the enterprise. Other investments in which the investor does not have an

Methodological notes

effective voice in the management of the enterprise (i.e., the investor has less than 10 per cent of the voting shares) are regarded as portfolio investments. The estimates of direct investment include the investor's share of the reinvested earnings of the subsidiary or associated company, the net acquisition of equity capital, changes in inter-company accounts and changes in branch/head office indebtedness.

Outward investment abroad

Direct investment abroad by UK residents comprises net investment by UK companies in their foreign branches, subsidiaries or associated companies. The figures of outward investment also cover the transactions of a number of concerns which were previously classified as public corporations. Transactions of central government are excluded from direct investment. Outward direct investment includes property transactions and other financial intermediaries' loans and mortgages to foreign residents.

Inward investment in the UK

Direct investment in the UK by foreign residents comprises net investment by foreign companies in branches, subsidiaries or associated companies in the UK. Miscellaneous property investments in the UK by foreign residents are those made by individuals or by companies which do not trade in the UK.

Estimates of direct investment are mainly derived from quarterly and annual inquiries by the ONS and the Bank of England, the combined results of which are published periodically in National Statistics First Releases and *Business Monitor MA4;* the latter provides geographical analyses.

Information on property transactions is obtained by the Inland Revenue, the Office for National Statistics and the Bank of England. Some of this is published in Financial Statistics, and that relating to transactions by insurance companies and pension funds, in *Business Monitor MQ5*.

Portfolio investment
(Table 7.5 and 7.6)

Portfolio investment is sub-divided into investment in equity securities and investment in debt securities while debt securities are further sub-divided into investment in bonds and notes and money market instruments.

Outward investment abroad

Transactions in equity securities and bonds and notes: these represent net transactions by UK residents in shares of foreign registered companies while transactions in bonds and notes, within debt securities, consists of net transactions in foreign government and municipal loan stock and bonds of foreign registered companies. Investment abroad by Lloyd's of London, representing mainly net dollar investment, trust funds held in North America and elsewhere and statutory deposits held abroad, is also covered here, under household sector transactions in bonds and notes.

Until mid-1980 the figures were based partly on exchange control returns (and returns submitted on a voluntary basis after the lifting of controls in October 1979) and partly on a Bank of England inquiry into foreign portfolio investment. From mid-1980 to 1991 a statistical inquiry undertaken by the Bank of England to UK dealers in securities and banks on their customers' transactions was used. Information is now obtained from inquiries to UK monetary financial institutions (banks and building societies), insurance companies and pension funds and other financial intermediaries. From 1989, estimates for securities dealers' foreign investment, within other financial intermediaries, are based on integrated financial returns, with transactions aligned with changes in balance sheets. With effect from 1991 data, the annual inquiries to insurance companies and pension funds have changed from voluntary to statutory (and similarly for the quarterly inquiries with effect from the first quarter of 1992). Adjustments are made to the reported data for insurance companies to remove the commission charges and other local costs included in the gross acquisitions and sales figures which are not appropriate to the financial account.

Estimates of portfolio investment transactions of private non-financial corporations are derived from asset levels at end-1990 and at each end year from then, measured in the Financial Assets and Liabilities inquiry, linked back to earlier levels of holdings; from 1991, estimates are also based on a smaller quarterly inquiry. Estimates for household sector foreign investments other than Lloyd's of London (see above) are largely based on Inland Revenue data.

Transactions in money market instruments: these consist of transactions in foreign commercial paper and certificates of deposit. Estimates are derived from statistical surveys undertaken by the ONS and the Bank of England.

Inward investment in the UK

Transactions in equity securities: the main source for the estimates of transactions in ordinary shares is the portfolio investment inquiry which was introduced in mid-1980. However, the data from the beginning of 1985 have been adjusted to take account of total levels of foreign investment in shares indicated by the results of the ONS' share register surveys held annually from 1989 to 1994 and annually from 1997.

Transactions in bonds and notes: this includes foreign net acquisitions of bonds denominated in US dollars, Deutschmarks, Swiss Francs, and Yen and sold to official holders of sterling in April 1977; an issue in New York in 1978 of US $350 million of HM Government 7 and 15 year bonds; an issue in 1991 of ECU 2.5 billion HM Government 10 year bonds; issues in 1992 of Dm 5 billion (redeemed in 1997) and US $3 billion HM Government 5 and 10 year bonds respectively; issues commencing January 1992 of 3 year HM Government ECU/Euro Treasury Notes and an issue in

1996 of a US $2 billion HM Government 5 year bond. The estimates for foreign currency notes comprise foreign residents' purchases of HM Government's October 1985 US $2.5 billion floating rate note issue (redeemed in 1988), the September 1986 US $4 billion issue (partially redeemed in 1991 and fully redeemed in 1996) and a further US $2 billion floating rate note issue in 1996, and subsequent net transactions by foreign residents.

Foreign transactions in British government stocks, within debt securities, consists of net transactions by central banks and international organisations and private foreign residents in government and government guaranteed stocks. It is measured from banking statistics and other Bank of England sources. Most gilts are issued by the UK government at a discount to the redemption value.

Foreign transactions in bonds issued by local authorities and public corporations, within debt securities, have been zero in recent years. Public corporations' securities include issues under the public sector exchange cover scheme. Any such issues subsequently assigned to HM Government are not included as transactions in the balance of payments accounts; their redemptions will be included in due course as redemptions of British government foreign currency bonds and notes (see above). They are measured from official records.

Foreign transactions in bonds and notes issued by UK monetary financial institutions and other sectors up to the end of 1986 are estimated from the Bank of England's database of all UK bonds and notes known or estimated to have been issued to foreign residents together with information obtained from the portfolio investment inquiry. The latter covers secondary market trading and some new issues but not redemptions. From 1987 onwards estimates of total foreign transactions in bonds have been obtained by assuming that any net transactions in UK securities not attributable to the domestic sectors of the UK (using all available data sources) are attributable to foreign residents. For 1987 to 1991, estimates of capital issues have been obtained from balance sheet returns for banks and building societies; and from the Bank of England's records of capital issues for other UK companies. From 1992, estimates of net capital issues by UK companies come from the London Stock Exchange's records of securities with a listing in London; and from the Bank of England's records for securities listed elsewhere or without a listing. Building society issues are taken from balance sheet returns. Transactions under the exchange cover scheme relate to redemptions by British Airways plc and British Telecom plc after privatisation. The original issues and redemptions before privatisation are included within public corporations' transactions. The estimates are based on information obtained by the Bank of England.

Transactions in money market instruments: these consist of net acquisitions of UK treasury bills, certificates of deposit and commercial paper. Foreign residents' net transactions in sterling and, between October 1988 and September 1999, ECU/Euro denominated Treasury bills exclude any bills held by the Bank of England as the sterling counterpart of foreign currency deposits arising from central bank assistance. Estimates of foreign transactions in UK certificates of deposit and commercial paper are derived from statistical inquiries conducted by the ONS and the Bank of England, and from information supplied by the UK's Debt Management Office.

Financial derivatives (7.1)

Financial derivatives include options (on currencies, interest rates, commodities, indices, etc.), traded financial futures, warrants and currency and interest swaps. Estimates for financial derivatives are currently unavailable except for settlement receipts/payments on UK banks' interest rate swaps which are supplied by the Bank of England. From Pink Book 2001 the UK moved to new international standards that now treat settlement payments and receipts on interest rate swaps as financial flows (rather than investment income).

Other investment (Table 7.7 and 7.8)

Other investment is sub-divided into trade credit, loans, currency and deposits and transactions in other assets.

Outward investment abroad

Trade credit: represents the extent to which the flows of payments for imports and exports follow or precede the flow of goods or services in the current account. Lending activity to facilitate trade, including those loans underwritten by the Export Credit Guarantee Department, is treated as loans and not trade credit within the accounts *(see loans)*. Trade credit within related firms (i.e. credit received or extended between a UK business and a foreign affiliate or parent company) is treated as an investment in the affiliate or parent company, and is therefore recorded under direct investment.

At present only a minimal amount of data is recorded within trade credit. Some data previously recorded in this area has been reclassified as bank lending (see above), and is now within the loans data in other investment abroad. Other data are no longer suitable for inclusion and have been removed from the accounts, generally back to 1999. Work is underway to produce alternative estimates of UK trade credit assets and liabilities.

Loans: these are sub-divided into long-term and short-term loans; short term loans are those which are repaid in full within one year. Long-term loans consist of inter-government loans by the UK central government, loans by the Commonwealth Development Corporation (a public corporation), loans by UK banks guaranteed by the ECGD and loans by the ECGD themselves. Inter-government loans covers drawings on and repayments of loans between the UK government and foreign governments. Estimates for loans by the Commonwealth Development Corporation are obtained directly from the Corporation, UK banks' loans data are supplied by the Bank of England, whilst information on loans by the ECGD are supplied direct by the Department.

Estimates for short-term loans mainly consist of loans by UK banks and miscellaneous financial institutions (within "other sectors") and are derived from banking statistics.

Currency and deposits: estimates of UK residents' deposits abroad relate to private sector deposits.

Deposits abroad by UK monetary financial institutions are sub-divided into sterling and foreign currency deposits by UK banks. Some transactions in banks' foreign assets and liabilities taking place between two UK residents are also included, sometimes indistinguishably. However, these are matched by offsetting entries elsewhere in the accounts.

Estimates of monetary financial institutions' sterling deposits abroad are derived from banking statistics. Estimates for foreign currency deposits abroad have been calculated from the end-quarter balance sheets as reported by all UK banks and similar institutions to the Bank of England. Adjustments have been made to the reported changes in balance sheets to exclude revaluations resulting from changes in exchange rates.

Estimates of securities dealers' deposits abroad since the second quarter of 1989 have been derived from their asset levels reported to the Office for National Statistics from the third quarter of 1992. Estimates for earlier years, back to 1986, are based on information from published annual accounts and data reported to the Bank of England.

Estimates of the UK private sector (excluding monetary financial institutions and securities dealers) are based on counterpart information obtained from the Bank for International Settlements (BIS). Due to limitations in the coverage of the BIS data, statistical adjustments have been applied from 1994 to improve the overall coherence of the sector financial accounts. The financial flows are estimated from changes in levels adjusted for exchange rate movements. They omit as far as possible, the effects of any discontinuities in the levels series.

Estimates for transactions in foreign notes and coin by the UK private sector other than monetary financial institutions are based on tourists' expenditure. Transactions in non-monetary gold covers net transactions in gold, which is held as a financial asset by listed institutions in the London Bullion Market (LBM). Estimates are derived from data collected from banking statistics.

Other assets: this includes central government subscriptions to international organisations and covers capital subscriptions to international lending bodies other than the IMF, i.e. regional development banks, the International Finance Corporation and the International Fund for Agricultural Development. Some transactions are in the form of non interest-bearing promissory notes and are included in the accounts as the subscriptions fall due, irrespective of the time of encashment of the notes. The information is obtained from official records.

The entry for UK banks' and ECGD's debt forgiveness offsets the corresponding entry in the capital account. Other sectors' short-term assets largely relate to assets of UK insurance companies and pension funds and other financial intermediaries other than those classified under portfolio investment, estimates for which are obtained from ONS statistical inquiries.

Inward investment in the UK

Trade credit: only a minimal amount of data is available within trade credit. See outward investment notes for detail.

Loans: these are sub-divided into long-term and short-term loans, and the former are further sub-divided into drawings and repayments. It is not possible to separate out loans from abroad to UK banks from foreign deposits with UK banks; all such transactions are therefore assumed to be deposits.

Long-term loans consist of drawings and repayments by central government, local authorities and public corporations. Public corporations' borrowing directly from foreign residents under the exchange cover scheme is included. Repayments under the scheme by former public corporations that have since been privatised are included under repayments from central government, to whom their foreign debt was transferred following privatisation; such debt is known as novated debt. In recent years only local authorities have engaged in long-term borrowing from abroad; estimates are obtained from the Department for Transport, Local Government and the Regions. Estimates for other long-term loans are largely obtained from the Bank of England.

Estimates for central government short-term loans from abroad covers the Very Short-term Financing Facility (VSTFF) which was taken out during 1992 and repaid in 1993. Estimates for securities dealers' short-term loans from abroad from 1989 are estimated from levels of liabilities reported in a statistical inquiry. Since 1995 statistical adjustments have been applied to the data for securities dealers' short-term loans in order to improve the overall coherence of the sector financial accounts

Estimates of borrowing by UK residents other than banks are based on data reported to the Bank for International Settlements (BIS), and are generally confined to borrowing from commercial banks based within the BIS reporting area (see glossary). The data relate to levels of liabilities; flows have been estimated from changes in levels, adjusted to remove the effects of exchange rate movements and discontinuities in coverage. Due to limitations in coverage of the BIS data, statistical adjustments have been applied to the estimates since 1994 in order to improve the overall coherence of the sector financial accounts. Additional information on borrowing from the European Investment Bank (EIB) is obtained from the EIB.

Currency and deposits: these are sub-divided into transactions in sterling notes and coins, and deposits from abroad with UK monetary financial institutions including deposit liabilities of the UK central government.

Estimates of transactions in sterling notes and coin by private foreign residents (other than monetary financial institutions) are based on ONS statistics of tourists' expenditure. While sterling bank notes are issued by the Bank of England, which is classified to monetary financial institutions, coins are issued by the Royal Mint, which is classified to the central government sector. In the absence of any separate data for notes and coin, it is assumed that notes make up 90 per cent of total notes and coin.

Foreign deposits with UK monetary financial institutions are sub-divided into deposits with banks and deposits with building societies. It is not possible to separate out foreign deposits with UK banks from foreign loans to UK banks. The estimates for foreign loans to UK banks are therefore included indistinguishably within deposits.

Within deposits with UK monetary financial institutions, estimates for sterling deposits are derived from banking statistics and include both current and deposit accounts. Foreign currency deposits comprise all external borrowing denominated in foreign currencies by UK banks (sometimes described as Euro currency transactions). They consist of changes in deposits with, and other lending to, UK banks from abroad. These transactions may be a reflection of (i.e. the counterpart to) a variety of other foreign or domestic transactions by UK banks. These other transactions could be: foreign currency lending to UK residents (which are not balance of payments transactions); net purchases of foreign securities by the banks (which are included in direct or portfolio investment abroad as appropriate); any switching of banks' liabilities between foreign currencies (including gold) and sterling; or any change in the amount of foreign currency capital raised by banks.

Estimates for foreign currency deposits with UK monetary financial institutions have been calculated from the end-quarter balance sheets as reported by all UK banks and building societies to the Bank of England. Adjustments have been made to the reported changes in balance sheets to exclude revaluations resulting from changes in exchange rates.

Deposit liabilities of UK central government include short-term inter-government loans and transactions with non-residents under minor government accounts in the form of changes in balances not attributable elsewhere in the accounts. In recent years this has consisted entirely of balances held by the Paymaster General on the European Union (EU) account.

Other liabilities: these are sub-divided into long-term and short-term liabilities.

Long-term liabilities consist of net equity of foreign households in life assurance reserves and in pension funds and prepayments of premiums and reserves against outstanding claims which are recorded in the balance of payments because households are regarded as owning the net equity of pension funds and life assurance reserves; i.e., the funds set aside for the purpose of satisfying the claims and benefits foreseen. The estimates are derived from data collected on ONS statistical inquiries.

Short-term liabilities largely consists of additions to insurance companies' technical reserves, estimates for which are derived from ONS statistical inquiries, and non-interest bearing notes, estimates for which are obtained from the Bank of England. Non-interest-bearing notes are issued by HM government and are held by international organisations.

Reserve assets (Table 7.9)

This item consists of the sterling equivalent, at current rates of exchange, of drawings on, and additions to the gold, convertible currencies and Special Drawing Rights (SDRs) held in the Exchange Equalisation Account; and of changes in the UK reserve position in the IMF. From July 1979 convertible currencies also include European Currency Units acquired from swaps with the European Monetary Co-operation Fund (until December 1993), the European Monetary Institute (until December 1997) and the European Central Bank (from 1998). The swap arrangement was terminated in December 1998.

International investment position (chapter 8)

Introduction

The international investment position brings together the available estimates of the levels of identified UK external assets (foreign assets owned by UK residents) and identified UK external liabilities (UK assets owned by foreign residents) at the end of each calendar year.

The presentation of the international investment position is almost identical to the presentation of investment income, within the income account (see Chapter 4) and the financial account (see Chapter 7) although there are small differences in coverage in some cases, mainly because full information is not available for all items.

Changes in balance sheet levels will reflect not only transactions in the corresponding assets and liabilities but also changes in valuation and certain other changes. Changes in valuation will occur in the following circumstances:

(i) where assets and liabilities are denominated in foreign currencies, their sterling value may change because of changes in foreign exchange rates;

(ii) where assets and liabilities are regularly bought and sold (e.g. British government stocks, UK and foreign company securities), the current market value may be different from the value at which they were acquired;

(iii) where the holders of assets and liabilities change their values in preparing their accounts to reflect what is thought to represent the current position (e.g. bad debts may be written off and direct investment assets may be written up or down in the books of the investing company).

In addition to changes in the valuation of identical underlying assets and liabilities, changes in recorded levels of external assets and liabilities will also reflect some changes in coverage which introduce discontinuities in the series: e.g. the introduction of new series on certain assets and liabilities of securities dealers from 1989 onwards.

Assessment of the international investment position

Because of the very varied data sources used to derive the estimates for the international investment position, there are some inconsistencies between the different figures in the tables, resulting particularly from different methods of valuation. Wherever possible, figures are at market values. However, for significant items such as direct investment, the figures are at book values and are subject to all the limitations of data taken from accounting balance sheets as a reflection of current market values. To the extent that the conventional valuation basis for direct investment is book values, an up-to-date valuation closer to market values is likely to be higher.

In addition, some assets and liabilities are measured very imperfectly (e.g. for a number of items levels of assets and liabilities are not directly reported but derived from cumulating recent identified transactions and allowing for estimated valuation changes). The balance between the estimates of identified external assets and liabilities has always been an imperfect measure of the UK's debtor/creditor position with the rest of the world.

To the extent that net errors and omissions reflect unrecorded or misrecorded financial transactions, the external balance sheet will tend to fail to capture the corresponding levels of assets and liabilities, although much will depend on the categories of assets and liabilities concerned.

(a) Where both levels and transactions are reported (e.g. portfolio investment by most financial intermediaries), there may be similar deficiencies to estimates of both levels and transactions, although levels may tend to be more accurate to the extent they are derived from annual accounting data.

(b) Where only levels are reported and transactions are derived from changes in levels, allowing as far as possible for valuation changes, (e.g. non-portfolio transactions of UK and foreign banks), there may be errors in the estimates of transactions (e.g. in allowing for valuation changes) with no corresponding error in levels.

(c) Where only transactions are reported and levels are calculated by cumulating transactions and allowing for valuation changes, e.g. inward portfolio investment in UK company bonds, errors in recording transactions will lead to corresponding errors in levels. Thus if part of the net errors and omissions represents such missing portfolio investment inflows, the identified net assets figures will be overstated.

Allocation of Special Drawing Rights

These are issued to the UK by the IMF but are not regarded by them as a liability of the UK and do not form part of total external liabilities in this table.

Direct investment levels (Table 8.3 and 8.4)

Outward investment abroad

Direct investment abroad by UK residents: this represents the stock of investment in foreign branches, subsidiaries and associates and in real estate abroad. Figures for insurance companies, other financial intermediaries and private non-financial corporations are based on ONS survey data. Since 1988, the annual Foreign Direct Investment Inquiry has collected balance sheet information to produce estimates of the net book value of direct investment for the end of each year. The figures for 1992 to 2001 are based on the annual inquiry data and the 2002 figures are a projection taking into account flows of direct investment, exchange rate changes and other projected revaluations.

The surveys relate to total net asset values attributable to investing companies, i.e. book values of fixed assets less accumulated depreciation provisions plus current assets less current liabilities. The book values of direct investments are likely to be less than the values at written down replacement cost and less than the market values. There are no official estimates of the market value of UK direct investment assets and liabilities. However, research by Cliff Pratten (Department of Applied Economics, University of Cambridge) indicated that, on certain assumptions, the market value of UK direct investments abroad at end-1989 might be about double their book value, while the market value of foreign direct investment in the UK might be just under double their book values at the same point of time. However there are considerable uncertainties in making such estimates.

The comparison between transactions in the balance of payments account and changes in total assets and liabilities is not affected by allowances for depreciation of fixed assets as charged to the profit and loss account; such allowances are deducted before arriving at the earnings included in the current account, and the provision for depreciation is regarded as maintaining the total book value of the existing assets. Similarly, the comparison is unaffected by the treatment of reinvested earnings from direct investments, since these appear both in the current account as earnings and in the financial account as a flow of capital adding to the stock of assets. However, the values are affected by the treatment applied in their consolidated accounts by UK companies to value newly acquired foreign companies. Under both merger and acquisition accounting the increase in the net book value can be less than the net investment to complete the acquisition. The difference represents goodwill and the other costs associated with the transaction which are written off directly against reserves.

Direct investment by insurance companies and the household sector include estimates of all property investments together with related foreign loans of non-bank financial institutions.

The figures for UK monetary financial institutions have been based on periodic censuses of foreign assets and liabilities carried out by the Bank of England, the latest being for end-2002; values for other years are estimated by similar methods to those used for other companies. From December 1998 a new annual report form was introduced for banks. The level of investment is defined as the sum of reporting institutions' investment in ordinary and preference shares, loan and working capital and other capital funds and reserves of their foreign affiliates; less certain funds raised by foreign affiliates through the issue of loan stocks and subsequently redeposited with their UK parents.

Inward investment in the UK

Direct investment in the UK by foreign residents: this represents the stock of investment by companies incorporated abroad in their UK branches, subsidiaries and associates. The estimates relate to book values and are measured in the same way as those for direct investment abroad. The latest year estimates are based on accumulated flows. Foreign direct investment in private non-financial corporations includes foreign residents' holdings of UK real estate not held through companies trading in the UK. It is estimated from the financial flows and appropriate indicators of market prices.

Portfolio investment levels (Table 8.5 and 8.6)

Portfolio investment abroad is sub-divided into equity securities and debt securities while debt securities are further sub-divided into bonds and notes and money market instruments.

Outward investment abroad

Equity securities and bonds and notes: equity securities consists of UK residents' holdings of shares of foreign registered companies while investment in bonds and notes, within debt securities, consists of holdings by UK residents of foreign government and municipal loan stock and bonds of foreign registered companies.

Since the abolition of exchange control in 1979, the total is calculated using a combination of banking statistics, the results of the portfolio investment inquiry to banks and dealers in securities on their customers' transactions (from mid-1980 to 1991 undertaken by the Bank of England) and information, from inquiries to insurance companies and pension funds and other financial intermediaries. Estimates for securities dealers, within other financial intermediaries, are derived from a statistical inquiry, initiated by the Bank of England in 1989 and undertaken by the Office for National Statistics from the third quarter of 1992.

Estimates for Lloyd's of London fall within household sector investment in bonds and notes; estimates are derived from data supplied by Lloyd's. Estimates of assets held by the household sector other than Lloyd's of London are largely based on Inland Revenue data.

Estimates of assets held by private non-financial corporations are derived from quarterly inquiries from end 1990 (the Financial Assets and Liabilities Survey). Adjustments were made to previous estimates to make them consistent with the new data.

Money market instruments: this consists of holdings of foreign commercial paper and certificates of deposit. Estimates are derived from statistical surveys undertaken by the ONS and the Bank of England.

Inward investment in the UK

Equity securities: the market value of inward portfolio investment in listed ordinary shares from 1989 onwards is based on the results of share ownership surveys, carried out annually from 1989 to 1994 and annually from 1997. Adjustments are made to exclude holdings of a direct investment nature and to establish the beneficial ownership of nominee share holdings (the latest Share Ownership Survey, covering end-2002, was published by the ONS in July 2003).

Bonds and notes: Investment in UK foreign currency bonds and notes consists of bonds denominated in US dollars, Deutschmarks, Swiss Francs, and Yen and sold to official holders of sterling in April 1977; an issue in New York in 1978 of US $350 million of HM Government 7 and 15 year bonds; an issue in 1991 of ECU 2.5 billion HM Government 10 year bonds; issues in 1992 of Dm 5 billion (redeemed in 1997) and US $3 billion HM Government 5 and 10 year bonds respectively; issues commencing January 1992 of 3 year HM Government ECU/Euro Treasury Notes and an issue in 1996 of a US $2 billion HM Government 5 year bond. As well as securities issued by HM Government, this item also includes some securities originally issued by public corporations under the exchange cover scheme and subsequently assigned to HM Government. There are no corresponding transactions in the financial account as the assignments are UK domestic transactions. Values have been translated to sterling at end-year middle-market rates. The estimates for foreign currency notes comprise foreign residents holdings of HM Government's October 1985 US $2.5 billion floating rate note issue (redeemed in 1988), the September 1986 US $4 billion issue (partially redeemed in 1991 and fully redeemed in 1996) and a further US $2 billion floating rate note issue in 1996.

Levels of British government stocks held by foreign central banks, international organisations and private foreign residents are measured from banking statistics and other Bank of England sources including the Central Gilts Office; the most recent Gilts survey recorded non-resident holdings as at end-2002. Foreign holdings of local authorities and public corporations bonds have been zero in recent years. Public corporations' securities issued under the exchange cover scheme and later assigned to HM Government are covered here until the date of assignment and thereafter under UK foreign currency bonds and notes, above.

Inward investment in bonds and notes issued by UK monetary financial institutions and other sectors is estimated from information derived from Bank of England and London Stock Exchange records of UK company bond issues, accumulated financial transactions and price and exchange rate movements.

Money market instruments: this consists of foreign holdings of UK treasury bills, commercial paper and certificates of deposit. Estimates are derived from statistical surveys undertaken by the ONS and the Bank of England, and from information supplied by the UK's Debt Management Office.

Other investment levels (Table 8.7 and 8.8)

Other investment abroad is sub-divided into trade credit, loans, currency and deposits and other assets. For trade credit and loans see notes under "Other Investment abroad" under *Financial account*.

Outward investment abroad

Currency and deposits: Estimates of UK residents' deposits abroad relate to private sector deposits. Deposits abroad by UK monetary financial institutions are sub-divided into sterling and foreign currency deposits by UK banks and are derived from banking data.

Estimates of securities dealers deposits abroad since the second quarter of 1989 have been derived from a statistical inquiry, taken over from the Bank of England by the Office for National Statistics from the third quarter of 1992.

Estimates of the UK private sector (excluding monetary financial institutions and securities dealers) assets with banks abroad are derived from the banking statistics of countries in the BIS reporting area (as defined in the Glossary) obtained from the Bank for International Settlements. They include the working balances of various UK companies. Due to the limitations in the coverage of the BIS data, statistical adjustments have been applied to the financial flows data since 1994 to improve the overall coherence of the sector financial accounts. In order to maintain consistency between financial flows and balance sheet levels corresponding coherence adjustments have been applied to the International Investment Position.

Estimates of foreign notes and coin covers the estimated holdings (excluding gold coin) by UK residents except banks and financial intermediaries. The estimates are derived from the transactions with an allowance for exchange rate movements.

Other assets: For central government subscriptions to international organisations see notes on "Other investment abroad" in the Financial account. Other sectors' long-term and short-term assets largely relate to assets of UK insurance companies and pension funds and other financial intermediaries other than bonds and shares etc., estimates for which are obtained from ONS statistical inquiries.

Inward investment in the UK

Other investment in the UK is sub-divided into trade credit, loans, currency and deposits and other liabilities. For trade credit, long-term loans and short-loan loans to central government, local authorities, public corporations and securities dealers see notes on "Other Investment in the UK" under Financial account.

Short-term loans to the UK private sector other than monetary financial institutions and securities dealers: estimates for such loans are derived mainly from the banking statistics of countries in the BIS reporting area. Adjustments have been made to eliminate overlap with other items. The limitations in the BIS data has resulted in statistical adjustments being applied to the financial flows data from 1994 to improve the overall coherence of the sector financial accounts. In order to maintain consistency between financial flows and balance sheet levels corresponding coherence adjustments have been applied to the International Investment Position. Borrowing from the European Investment Bank is also included. The liabilities of miscellaneous financial institutions to banks abroad are also included here.

Currency and deposits: levels of sterling notes and coin held by private foreign residents (other than monetary financial institutions) are estimated from the financial flows.

Foreign deposits with UK monetary financial institutions are sub-divided into deposits with banks and deposits with building societies. It is not possible to separate out foreign deposits with UK banks from foreign loans to UK banks. The estimates for foreign loans to UK banks are therefore included indistinguishably within deposits.

Within deposits with UK monetary financial institutions, foreign currency deposits include deposits and advances received from foreign residents . It includes foreign liabilities arising from UK banks' participation in the US $2.5 billion and US $1.5 billion facilities arranged for HM Government and other borrowing to finance UK bank lending to the public sector. Estimates for both sterling and foreign currency deposits with UK monetary financial institutions are derived from banking statistics.

Deposit liabilities of UK central government include short-term inter-government loans and transactions with non-residents under minor government accounts in the form of balances not attributable elsewhere in the accounts. In recent years this has consisted entirely of balances held by the Paymaster General on the European Union (EU) account.

Other liabilities: Long-term liabilities consist of net equity of foreign households in life assurance reserves and in pension funds and prepayments of premiums and reserves against outstanding claims which are recorded in the balance of payments because households are regarded as owning the net equity of pension funds and life assurance reserves; i.e., the funds set aside for the purpose of satisfying the claims and benefits foreseen. The estimates are derived from data collected on ONS statistical inquiries.

Short-term liabilities largely consist of non-interest bearing notes, estimates for which are obtained from the Bank of England. Non-interest-bearing notes are issued by HM government and are held by international organisations.

Reserve asset levels (Table 8.9)

These comprise gold, convertible foreign currencies, IMF Special Drawing Rights (SDRs) and the UK's reserve position in the IMF. Currencies may be held in the form of financial instruments. Until 1999 securities are valued at historic cost but translated to sterling as set out below. From July 1979 convertible currencies also include European Currency Units acquired when 20 per cent of the gold and dollar holdings in the reserve assets were deposited on a swap basis with the European Monetary Co-operation Fund, the swap arrangement being renewed quarterly. As from January 1994 the swap was with the European Monetary Institute and as from January 1998 was with the European Central Bank. The swap arrangement was terminated in December 1998.

Gold is valued at the ruling official price of 35 SDRs per fine ounce until end-1977 and at end-year market rates from end-1978 to end 1999. SDRs and convertible currencies (including ECUs) are valued throughout at closing middle market rates of exchange. Since 2000 all reserve assets are valued at end-period market prices and exchange rates.

Financial derivatives (Table FD)

Financial derivatives are defined as financial instruments that are linked to the price performance of an underlying asset and which involve the trading of financial risk. Examples of the underlying asset might include a financial instrument, commodity, bilateral foreign exchange rate, movement in stock index, or interest rate. Financial derivatives include options, futures/forwards, swaps, FRAs, warrants and certain credit derivatives. The rationale for separate recording of derivatives contracts in the financial account is to keep the distinction between them and other transactions (e.g. securities) to which they may be linked for hedging purposes. Derivatives are valued at current market prices.

Data on UK Banks' gross asset and liability positions in derivatives are collected quarterly by the Bank of England; no data are available prior to 1998. Data on securities dealers' assets and liabilities are collected by the ONS; similarly there are no data available prior to 1998.

Data published in table FD form supplementary information as estimates for financial derivatives have yet to be fully implemented in either the UK international investment position or in the UK's national accounts balance sheets. Work is continuing to validate and improve the estimates and obtain more information on the types of derivatives traded.

Geographical breakdown on the current account (chapter 9)

Introduction

The geographical data, is consistent with level 3 of Eurostat's Vade Mecum (64 individual countries, 9 geographical regions and 5 continents). The figures for the European Union (EU) relate to the current membership. EU Institutions are also included in the EU aggregate and are excluded from the International Organisations total. For the purposes of this publication Belgium and

Luxembourg, which already have an economic union, are treated as one entity - data are not available separately. Data for China exclude Hong Kong, which is shown as an individual item.

Reliability of estimates

The United Kingdom's (UK) balance of payments accounts are primarily compiled on a global basis. Not all of the data sources used in preparing the accounts attempt to distinguish transactions on a full country basis, although the majority do. Where individual country information is not reported, estimates are made by using the geographical detail for a related category; for example, the geographical breakdown of financial assets and liabilities is used to allocate some components of investment income.

In addition to the imputation of geographical detail for some categories where the data are incomplete, there remains a margin of uncertainty regarding the accuracy of reported data by country. The finer the level of geographical detail sought the greater the likelihood of misallocation. Enterprises are encouraged to make their best estimates, when asked to report geographical data, but as country allocation may not be a crucial aspect of the information from which details are extracted, a significant degree of estimation may occur.

Given these conceptual and practical limitations, these estimates should be seen as a broad indication of the economic relationships between the UK and the rest of the world economies. They will be more reliable and meaningful in terms of broad geographical areas and major partner countries than for smaller partners. Estimates for recent years, are currently more reliable than those for earlier years, since some data sources do not extend back over the whole published period.

Approach for country allocation

The following notes summarise the main criteria of country allocation adopted for the various categories of the current account. In general the figures are not likely to be consistent with those recorded by countries which allocate regional balance of payments estimates on a cash settlements basis.

Trade in goods
Exports of goods are allocated to the country of last known destination. Imports of goods are allocated according to the country of consignment. The principal data source for trade in goods is HM Customs and Excise (see methodological chapter on Trade in Goods for more details).

Trade in services
The geographical breakdown of exports and imports of services are largely based on the existing sources of information for the global estimates, although there is some use of proxy information for some components. The change from an industry to a product based presentation with the introduction of the fifth edition of the IMF Balance of Payments Manual in 1998, and the consequent change to data collection, means that data from 1996 onwards is largely based on reported geographical breakdowns of the new products. Earlier geographical estimates are based on the industry based geographical breakdowns in the fourth edition of the IMF Balance of Payments Manual, adjusted to take the changes to the trade in services classification into account.

Sea transport: estimates relating to ships owned or chartered by UK operators are taken from inquiries carried out by the Chamber of Shipping.

Geographical breakdowns of freight services on exports and cross trades are allocated using the ports at which the goods are unloaded. For non-resident operators freight on UK imports, the nationality of the exporting country is used as a proxy to allocate the freight payments. The resulting proportions are used to calculate the shares of non-resident operators' disbursements in the UK. Disbursements abroad by UK operators are supplied annually by the Chamber of Shipping.

Passenger revenue export estimates are derived from information supplied annually by the Chamber of Shipping. Passenger revenue import estimates are based on assumptions about the likely markets for cruises and on other information relating to the movements of UK shipping.

Air transport: passenger revenue exports are based on information supplied to us by the Civil Aviation Authority, which gives the required country analysis of fares paid. Other transactions with foreign airlines are allocated by nationality of airline. Receipts by UK airlines from foreign passengers are allocated to the countries in which the ticket is purchased. Freight services on UK imports earned by foreign airlines are allocated to the countries of consignment of the imports.

Other transport: rail passenger exports are based on assumptions of the likely nationality of channel tunnel users. Rail imports are allocated entirely to France. Estimates for road freight exports and imports are based on information supplied by the Road Haulage Association. Pipeline transport is based on those countries that are assumed to import / export North Sea oil and gas.

Travel: a detailed geographical split of travel expenditure, both exports and imports are supplied to us by the International Passenger Survey. Allocation of expenditure of overseas visitors to the UK is by country of residence. UK residents' expenditures abroad are allocated to the country in which most time was spent, or, if this cannot be determined, the furthest country visited. As a result, expenditure in countries with appreciable numbers of transit tourists may be understated.

Other services: data for communication, construction, computer and information, royalties and other business services is largely based on information supplied to the ITIS survey, supplemented with information from the Royal Mail.

Insurance services: estimates are based on detailed geographical data provided by Lloyds of London, as well as the ITIS survey for insurance imports provided to non-insurance institutions. The geographical split of trade in goods' imports are used as a proxy for freight insurance imports. Other insurance services, geographical splits are based on fixed weights.

Financial services: geographical information on exports and imports of banking services are obtained from the Bank of England. Estimates for all other financial services are based on limited geographical breakdowns collected in the ITIS inquiry and the use of proxies.

Government services: for the major components, detailed geographical information on the location of those receiving or making payments is available from returns provided by the Ministry of Defence, Department of Social Security and the Foreign and Commonwealth Office. The United States Air Force also provide data on expenditure of US Forces in the UK. Expenditure by foreign embassies and consulates in the UK is based on information supplied by some overseas embassies and statistical institutions, supplemented by information on numbers of accredited diplomats by country.

More detailed information on the geographical breakdown of trade in services estimates, including definitions of geographical regions, are outlined in the notes of the publication UK trade in services - UKA1 (available in electronic format from the ONS website).

Income
Compensation of employees: estimates of the geographical breakdown of seasonal and border workers earnings are based on information supplied to the International Passenger Survey. Figures for the earnings of locally engaged staff are based on information supplied by government departments.

Direct investment income: figures are based on the annual foreign investment inquiries and include reinvested profits. Geographical information is based on the country of registration of the immediate foreign parent company and the location of the foreign affiliate, except for banks where the information relates to the country of residence of the ultimate owner (for inward investment) or the country of residence in which the direct investment enterprise is located.

Portfolio investment income: credits are the earnings accruing to UK residents from their investment in equities and debt securities, in the form of bonds and notes and money market instruments, issued by foreign institutions. Estimates are derived from surveys of UK end investors (banks, securities dealers, unit and investment trusts, insurance companies, pension funds and some industrial companies).

Deriving a geographical breakdown of portfolio investment income flows is one of the most problematic areas of Balance of Payments compilation. Portfolio investment income is particularly difficult to allocate correctly to the actual country owning or issuing the security, as the transactions are often made through financial intermediaries in a third country. With the launch and subsequent expansion of the IMF's Co-ordinated Portfolio Investment Survey, an important new data source is now available. Participants in the CPIS survey collect a geographical breakdown of their portfolio investment assets, which are coordinated and disseminated by the IMF. Results for 2001 are now available. An article was published in the May 2003 edition of *Economic Trends*, detailing the results of the 2001 survey. The results for 2002 will be available in the autumn and will be used to refine the 2002 estimates.

Information on the geographical breakdown of portfolio investment credits are derived from the geographical breakdown of portfolio investment assets collected as the UK's contribution to the IMF's CPIS exercise. Bank of England information on the geographical breakdown of levels is applied to the estimates of global earnings also obtained by surveys of UK banks. Similarly for non-banks, a geographical breakdown of portfolio investment income is derived from the geographical breakdown of portfolio investment assets.

Information on the geographical breakdown of UK portfolio investment debits (dividends and interest payments made to overseas residents by issuers of UK securities), are based on other countries' participation in the CPIS exercise. The IMF act as a central clearing house for the compilation of aggregate data from countries that have participated in the CPIS and disseminate the information to BoP compilers. These data can provide us with information on participating countries' holdings of UK issued equity and debt securities. For earlier years, surveys of share ownership are used to allocate portfolio holdings of UK equity securities and associated dividends by country of holder. For interest on holdings of debt securities, data derived from the 2001 CPIS exercise has been projected back in time.

Other investment income: gross interest flows between UK banks and the rest of the world are estimated, by the Bank of England, by allocating the global interest receipts and payments in proportion to the corresponding levels of assets and liabilities of UK banks. Interest flows for UK non-bank deposits with and borrowing from banks in the BIS reporting area are allocated in proportion to the levels supplied by the BIS. The interest on reserve assets is estimated from official records. Figures for UK banks are used as proxies to estimate a country breakdown for the remaining components of earnings on other investment.

Adjustments, applied to the global earnings on other investment to exclude the Channel Islands and the Isle of Man, have been used to estimate other investment income between the UK and the offshore islands. These data have been allocated to 'Other Europe'.

Current transfers

The geographical allocation of withholding taxes are based on the geographical allocation of inward and outward direct investment as published in *Business Monitor MA4*. The geographical allocation of insurance premiums are based on information supplied by Lloyds of London. Data on EU transfers are provided by the Treasury, and the geographical allocation of social security and aid payments are supplied by the Department for Work and Pensions and the Department for International Development, respectively. Other geographical breakdowns are based on proxy data and global transfer estimates.

Glossary

Acceptances
See Bills and acceptances.

Accrued interest
A method of recording transactions to relate them to the period when the exchange of ownership of the goods, services or financial asset applies. For example, value added tax accrues when the expenditure to which it relates takes place, but Customs and Excise receive the cash some time later. The difference between accruals and cash results in the creation of an asset and liability in the financial accounts, shown as amounts receivable or payable.

Advance and progress payments
Payments made for goods in advance of completion and delivery of the goods.

Affiliates
Branches, subsidiaries or associate companies.

Allocation of SDRs
See Special Drawing Rights.

Arbitrage
Buying in a market in one centre and selling in a similar market in another centre, in order to exploit a temporary misalignment of prices at little or no risk.

Assets
This term commonly refers to financial assets that are claims on non-residents, from whose point of view the same item is a liability to a UK resident. Among reserve assets, however, gold and SDRs have a value which exists independently of any corresponding liabilities. Real assets such as merchandise, although they may be entered in company accounts as assets, are seldom described as assets in balance of payments analysis.

Associated companies
Companies in which the investing company has a substantial equity interest (usually this means that it holds between 10 per cent and 50 per cent of the equity share capital) and is in a position to exercise a significant influence on the company. (See Subsidiary.)

Balancing item
See Net Errors and Omissions.

Bank of England - Issue Department
This part of the Bank of England deals with the issue of bank notes on behalf of central government. It was formerly classified to central government though it is now part of the central bank/ monetary authorities sector. Its activities include, inter alia, market purchases of commercial bills from UK banks.

Bank for International Settlements (BIS)
An international institution based in Basle, Switzerland, established in 1930. Its main functions today are to promote international monetary co-operation; to observe the work of the IMF, Finance Ministers and Central Bank Governors of the group of ten countries; and to provide monetary research. The BIS data used within the UK balance of payments accounts cover non-bank borrowing from banks in the following countries: Australia, Austria, the Bahamas, Bahrain, Belgium/ Luxembourg, Canada, Cayman Islands, Denmark, Finland, France, Germany, Guernsey, Hong Kong, India, Ireland, Isle of Man, Italy, Japan, Jersey, Netherlands, Netherlands Antilles, Norway, Portugal, Singapore, Spain, Sweden, Switzerland, Taiwan, Turkey, United States of America and branches of US banks in Panama.

Banking statistics
A term used in this publication to denote an integrated set of returns, covering all UK banks, and collected by the Bank of England. The returns were first introduced in late 1974 and during 1975. Since then, various reviews of the requirements of data from banks have been conducted and forms amended, introduced or dropped as necessary. The data collected covers all listed banks up to the end of 1981 and the revised group of institutions classified as UK banks from 1982 onwards. It collects on a regular basis extensive information relating to the levels of, and changes in, assets and liabilities. Revised banking returns were introduced from the end of 1997 to reflect the requirements of the IMF Balance of Payments manual 5th edition and to remove the Channel Islands and the Isle of Man from the definition of the economic territory of the United Kingdom.

Banks (UK)
Banks are defined as all financial institutions recognised by the Bank of England as UK banks. For statistical purposes this includes:

- institutions which have a permission under Part 4 of the Financial Services and Markets Act 2000 (FSMA) to accept deposits other than (I) credit unions (ii) firms which have a permission to accepts deposits only in the course of carrying out contracts of insurance in accordance with that permission (iii) friendly societies and (iv) building societies;

- European Economic Area credit institutions with a permission under Schedule 3 to FSMA to accept deposits through a UK branch; and

- the Banking and Issue Departments of the Bank of England (the latter from April 1998).

Prior to December 2001, banks were defined as all financial institutions recognised by the Bank of England as UK banks for statistical purposes, including the UK offices of institutions authorised under the Banking Act 1987, the Banking and Issue Departments of the Bank of England (the latter from April 1988), and deposit-taking UK branches of 'European Authorised Institutions'. This includes UK branches of foreign banks, but not the offices abroad of these or of any British owned banks.

An updated list of banks appears regularly in the Bank of England's 'Monetary and Financial Statistics publication' and can also be found on the Financial Services Authority website at: www.fsa.gov.uk/list_banks

Bills and acceptances
A bill is an unconditional order in writing addressed by the drawer to the drawee to pay to the drawer a fixed sum on a specified date. A UK resident may draw a bill in Sterling on a foreign resident representing credit extended by the UK resident to the foreign resident. If the UK resident sells the bill to a UK bank, generally at a price less than the nominal value of the bill, the bank is said to discount the bill, and the claim on the foreign resident is transferred to the UK bank.

A bill is known as an acceptance when the drawee accepts the bill. A UK bank may accept a bill on behalf of a foreign resident in which case the UK resident draws the bill on the UK bank and not on the foreign resident. The accepting bank has a claim on the foreign resident and expects to be paid by him before the bill matures.

Bond
A financial instrument that usually pays interest to the holder, issued by governments as well as companies and other institutions, e.g. local authorities. Most bonds have a fixed date on which the borrower will repay the holder. Bonds are attractive to investors since they can be bought and sold easily in a secondary market. Special forms of bonds include deep discount bonds, equity warrant bonds, Eurobonds, and zero coupon bonds.

Branch indebtedness
Net amounts owed by a branch to its head office (or vice versa).

British government stocks
Securities issued or guaranteed by the UK government. Also known as gilts.

Building societies
Building societies are mutual institutions specialising in accepting deposits from members of the public and in long-term lending to members of the public, mainly to finance purchase of dwellings; such lending being secured on dwellings. Their operations are governed by special legislation which places restrictions on their recourse to other sources of funding and other avenues of investment.

Capital account
The capital account consists of capital transfers (see Transfers) and acquisition/disposal of non-produced, non-financial assets (see separate entry in glossary).

Capital transfers
See Transfers.

Certificate of deposit
A short term interest-paying instrument issued by deposit-taking institutions in return for money deposited for a fixed period. Interest is earned at a given rate. The instrument can be used as security for a loan if the depositor requires money before the repayment date.

c.i.f. (cost, insurance and freight)
The basis of valuation of imports for Customs purposes, it includes the cost of insurance premiums and freight services. These need to be deducted to obtain the *free on board* valuation consistent with the valuation of exports which is used in the economic accounts.

Commercial paper
This is an unsecured promissory note for a specific amount and maturing on a specific date. The commercial paper market allows companies to issue short term debt direct to financial institutions who then market this paper to investors or use it for their own investment purposes.

Commodity gold
See Gold.

Commonwealth Development Corporation
A public corporation which finances development projects abroad.

Compensation of employees
Total remuneration payable to employees in cash or in kind. Includes the value of social contributions payable by the employer.

Counterpart items
Certain items in the balance of payments exist only as counterpart items, introduced to balance the inclusion of other items that do not fall naturally into the double-entry system. The allocation of SDRs is an example of an artificial counterpart item introduced into the balance of payments to offset the corresponding increase in SDR holdings within official reserves (as SDRs are no one sector's liabilities). (See Special Drawing Rights.)

Cross-trades
See Third country trade.

Current account
The account of transactions in respect of trade in goods and services, income and current transfers.

Current balance
The balance of current account transactions.

Current transfers
See transfers

Debt forgiveness
The voluntary cancellation of all or part of a debt within a contractual arrangement between a creditor in one country and a debtor in another country.

Debt securities
Debt securities cover bonds, debentures, notes etc., and money market instrument. These are split into long and short (less than 1 year) term, based on original maturity.

Derivatives
See financial derivatives.

Direct investment
Net investment by UK/foreign companies in their foreign/UK branches, subsidiaries or associated companies. A direct investment in a company means that the investor has a significant influence on the operations of the company. (See Branch indebtedness, Subsidiary and Associated companies.) Investment covers not only acquisition of fixed assets, stock building and stock appreciation, but also all other financial transactions, such as: additions to or payments of working capital; other loans and trade credit; and acquisitions of securities. Estimates of investment flows allow for depreciation in any undistributed profits. Funds raised by the subsidiary or associate company in the economy in which it operates are excluded as they are locally raised and not sourced from the parent company.

Disbursements
Operating expenses e.g., by operators of ships or aircraft.

Dividend
A payment made to company shareholders from current or previously retained profits. Dividends are recorded when they become payable.

Equity
Equity is ownership or potential ownership of a company. They differ from other financial instruments in that they confer ownership of something more than a financial claim. Shareholders are owners of the company whereas bond holders are outside creditors.

Equity securities
Equity securities are shares issued by companies to shareholders. Purchases of equity securities in which the purchaser does not have any significant degree of control over the company (i.e., less than 10 per cent of the equity capital) fall within portfolio investment; otherwise it falls within direct investment. Equity securities include mutual fund shares.

Eurocurrency market
All borrowing and lending by banks in currencies other than that of the country in which the banks are situated.

Euro/European Currency Unit (ECU)
The ECU was officially introduced in 1979 in connection with the start of the European Monetary System (EMS). In the EMS, the ECU served as the basis for determining exchange rate parities and as a reserve asset and means of settlement. It was a composite currency which contained specified amounts of the currencies of the member states of the European Union. The currencies making up the ECU were weighted according to their economic importance and use in short-term finance. As from September 1989 the weightings of the ECU were revised to include both the Spanish peseta and Portuguese escudo. The ECU was converted into the Euro at the start of European Monetary Union on 1 January 1999, with Greece joining on 1 January 2001.

European Central Bank (ECB)
The Monetary Authority for the Euro currency, based in Frankfurt. The ECB, together with the national central banks of the member states, manages monetary policy and the banking system across the European Monetary Union area.

European Investment Bank (EIB)
This was set up to assist economic development within the European Union. Its members are the member states of the EU.

European Monetary System (EMS)
This was established in March 1979. Its most important element is the mechanism (the ERM – Exchange Rate Mechanism) whereby the exchange rates between the currencies of the participating member states are kept within set ranges. The UK joined the ERM on 8 October 1990. On 16 September 1992 the UK's membership of the ERM and the EMS was suspended. The EMS was superceded by the single currency when eleven of the participating member states joined European Monetary Union on 1 January 1999, with Greece joining on 1 January 2001.

Exchange control
A legal control imposed by Governments on the ability of persons, businesses and others to hold, receive and transfer foreign currency. The extent of the Exchange Control Act of 1947 was considerably reduced in June and July 1979 and the act was repealed in 1987.

Exchange cover scheme (ECS)
A scheme first introduced in 1969 whereby UK public bodies raise foreign currency from abroad, either directly or through UK banks, and generally surrender it to the EEA (see below) in exchange for sterling for use to finance expenditure in the United Kingdom. HM Treasury sells the borrower foreign currency to service and repay the loan at the exchange rate that applied when the loan was taken out. The transactions relate to net borrowing by British Nuclear Fuels plc and repayment by HM Government following the privatisation of other former public corporations (see Novations).

Exchange Equalisation Account (EEA)
The government account with the Bank of England in which transactions in reserve assets are recorded. These

transactions are classified to the central government sector. It is the means by which the government, through the Bank of England, influences exchange rates.

Export credit
Credit extended abroad by UK institutions, primarily in connection with UK exports but also including some credit in respect of third–country trade.

Export credit; identified long-term
Credit extended by UK banks under the ECGD's buyer credit and specific bank guarantees schemes.

Export Credits Guarantee Department (ECGD)
A government department whose main function is to provide insurance cover for export credit transactions.

Financial account
The financial account records transactions in external assets and liabilities of the UK, e.g., the acquisitions and disposals of foreign shares by UK residents. The financial account consists of direct investment, portfolio investment, other investment, financial derivatives and reserve assets.

Financial auxiliaries
Auxiliary financial activities are ones closely related to financial intermediation but which are not financial intermediation themselves, such as the repackaging of funds, insurance broking and fund management. Financial auxiliaries include insurance brokers and fund managers.

Financial corporations
All bodies recognised as independent legal entities whose principal activity is financial intermediation and/or the production of auxiliary financial services. However, the United Kingdom currently treats financial auxiliaries as non-financial corporations.

Financial derivatives
Any financial instrument the price of which is based upon the value of an underlying asset (typically another financial asset). Financial derivatives include options (on currencies, interest rates, commodities, indices, etc.), traded financial futures, warrants, and currency and interest swaps. Under *BPM5*, transactions in derivatives are treated as separate transactions, rather than being included as integral parts of underlying transactions to which they may be linked as hedges. Only estimates for settlement receipts/payments on UK banks' interest rate swaps and forward rate agreements are currently included.

Financial gold
See Gold.

Financial Leasing
See Leasing.

Financial surplus or deficit (FSD)
The former term for Net lending(+)/Net borrowing(-), the balance of all current and capital account transactions for an institutional sector or the economy as a whole.

f.o.b. (free on board)
A f.o.b. price excludes the cost of insurance and freight from the country of consignment but includes all charges up to the point where the goods are deposited on board the exporting/importing vessel or aircraft. Trade in goods exports are valued on a f.o.b. basis in the balance of payments accounts.

Foreign
In this publication "foreign" denotes residence outside the United Kingdom rather than nationality. In some contexts "external", "abroad" or "non-resident" are used with the same meaning. See entry for 'residency'.

Futures
Instruments which give the holder the right to purchase a commodity or a financial asset at a future date.

Gilts
Bonds issued or guaranteed by the UK government. Also known as gilt-edged securities or British government securities.

Gold
In the accounts a distinction is drawn between gold held as a financial asset (financial gold) and gold held like any other commodity (commodity gold). Transactions in commodity gold are recorded in the trade in goods account and include foreign trade in finished manufactures together with net domestic and foreign transactions in gold moving into or out of finished manufactured form (i.e. for jewellery, dentistry, electronic goods, medals and proof – but not bullion – coins).

All other transactions in gold (i.e. those involving semi-manufactures such as rods, wire, etc., or bullion, bullion coins or banking-type assets and liabilities denominated in gold, including reserve assets) are treated as financial gold transactions and included in the financial account. The distinction between commodity and financial gold differs from that drawn by the IMF, in its *Balance of Payments Manual (5th edition, 1993)*, between non-monetary and monetary gold. The United Kingdom has obtained an exemption from adopting the *BPM5* recommendations on treatment of gold until the year 2005 in order to avoid distortion of its trade in goods account by the substantial transactions of the London Bullion Market.

Gross
The separate identification of both credit/debit, export/import for any particular transaction.

Hedging
Hedging is accomplished by the temporary purchase or sale of futures/swaps contracts to offset the position or anticipated position in the cash markets. This may benefit banks, financial institutions, pension funds and corporate treasuries who hold interest rate, exchange rate or stock price sensitive assets or liabilities.

Households
Individuals or small groups of individuals as consumers and in some cases as entrepreneurs producing goods and market services.

Import credit: long-term agreements
Credit received on imported ships, commercial aircraft and certain North Sea installations.

Income
The income account forms part of the current account and consists of compensation of employees and investment income, both of which have separate entries in this glossary.

Inter-company accounts
Accounts recording transactions between parent and subsidiary or associated companies, and balances owed by one to the other.

Interest rate swaps
An obligation between two parties to exchange interest-related payments in the same currency from fixed rate into floating rate, or vice versa, or from one type of floating rate to another. A swap can be used to reshape the coupon payments of either new or existing debt. The only movement of funds is a net transfer of interest payments between the two parties. The interest payments are calculated on an agreed principal amount, which is not exchanged. The settlement receipts/payments on UK banks' interest rate swaps appear in the financial account under financial derivatives.

International Investment Position (IIP)
The international investment position records end of period balance sheet levels of UK external assets and liabilities. The IIP consists of direct investment, portfolio investment, other investment and reserve assets. Financial derivatives are not currently included in the IIP, but presented separately in table FD.

International Monetary Fund (IMF)
A Fund set up as a result of the Bretton Woods Conference of 1944 which began operations in 1947. It includes most of the major countries of the world. The Fund was set up to supervise the fixed exchange rate system agreed at Bretton Woods and to make available to its members a pool of foreign exchange resources to assist them when they have balance of payments difficulties. Further definitions relating to the IMF are given in the IMF section in the 1981 and earlier editions of this publication. See also "Special Drawing Rights".

Intervention Board for Agricultural Produce
The UK agency which operates the support arrangements of the EU Common Agricultural Policy within the United Kingdom.

Investment
In a balance of payments context this is categorised as either direct, portfolio or other investment. See appropriate headings for definitions.

Investment income
All investment income accruing to UK residents from non-residents or payable abroad by UK residents after allowing for depreciation. The balance on credits and debits equals "net property income from abroad" as shown in the National Accounts.

Investment trust
An institution that invests its capital in a wide range of other companies' shares. Investment trusts issue shares which are listed on the London Stock Exchange and use this capital to invest in the shares of other companies. See also Unit trusts.

Leasing
In the balance of payments accounts all financial leases and some long-term operating leases (e.g. for aircraft) are regarded as loans to finance the purchase of goods. The lessor thus makes a loan to the lessee who subsequently repays this with interest. The lessee is regarded as the purchaser of the goods.

Liabilities
In balance of payments terminology, liabilities are the financial claims of non-residents on the UK.

LIBOR
London Interbank Offered Rate. The rate of interest at which banks borrow funds from other banks, in marketable size, in the London Interbank market.

Local authorities
Elected councils responsible for the administration of certain services in particular areas within the United Kingdom.

Merchanting
Trade between two countries other than the United Kingdom, in which the United Kingdom may participate as an intermediary or by providing transport, insurance services or credit facilities.

Miscellaneous financial institutions
These include certain institutions not classified as UK banks whose main function is to extend credit abroad, and certain listed institutions in the London Bullion Market which are not UK banks.

Monetary Authorities
Institutions (usually central banks) which control the centralised monetary reserves and the supply of currency in accordance with government policies, and which act as their governments' bankers and agents. In the United Kingdom this is equivalent to the Bank of England and part of the Treasury (the Exchange Equalisation Account). Data is not separately available in the UK accounts for monetary authorities.

Monetary financial institutions
Banks and building societies.

Monetary gold
See Gold.

Money market
The market in which short-term loans are made and short-term securities traded. 'Short term' usually applies to periods under one year but can be longer in some instances.

Money market instruments
Money market instruments, within portfolio investment, generally give the holder the unconditional right to receive a stated, fixed sum of money on

a specified date. These are short term instruments usually traded at a discount, the discount being dependent upon the interest rate and the time remaining to maturity. Included are such instruments as acceptances, treasury bills, commercial paper and certificates of deposit.

Navy, Army and Air Force Institute (NAAFI)
A body which provides goods and services for use by the UK armed forces abroad.

Net
In this presentation of the balance of payments accounts, the term "net" is generally applied only to transactions in financial assets or liabilities. Purchases of assets are recorded net of sales; similarly with liabilities. In the current and capital accounts, where the operations of UK and foreign residents are taken together in particular transactions areas, the term "balance" is used.

Net Errors and Omissions
The item included to bring the sum of all balance of payments entries to zero. Also known as the balancing item.

Non-monetary gold
See Gold.

Non-produced, non-financial assets
Non-produced, non-financial assets, within the capital account, include land purchased or sold by a foreign embassy, patents, copyrights, trade marks, franchises and leases and other transferable contracts, but not finance leasing. Only the purchase and sale of such assets are proper to the capital account; earnings from them are recorded under trade in services.

Novations
This term defines the reassignment of debt (for balance of payments, usually foreign debt) of public corporations to central government following the privatisation of the public corporation. This does not normally change the overall balance of payments situation as the debt is still regarded as a UK liability.

NPISH
Non-profit institutions serving households.

Official reserves
See Reserve assets.

Operating leasing
Operational leasing (rental) covers resident/non-resident leasing (other than financial leasing), charter of ships, aircraft and transportation equipment without crew. Leasing of ships, aircraft and transportation equipment with crew are included in the transportation account.

Ordinary share
The most common type of share in the ownership of a corporation. Holders of ordinary shares receive dividends. See also Equity.

Other Investment
Investment other than direct and portfolio investment. Includes trade credit, loans, currency and deposits and other assets and liabilities.

Parent
In a balance of payments context this means a company with direct investments in other countries.

Pension funds
The institutions that administer pension schemes. Pension schemes are significant investors in securities. Self-administered funds are classified in the financial accounts as pension funds. Those managed by insurance companies are treated as long-term business of insurance companies. They are part of S.125, the Insurance corporations and pension funds sub-sector.

Portfolio investment
Investment in equity and debt securities issued by foreign registered companies, other than that classed as direct investment, and in equity and debt securities issued by foreign governments. A portfolio investment, unlike a direct investment, does not entitle the investor to any significant influence over the operations of the company or institution and represent less than 10 per cent of the equity capital.

Preference share
This type of share guarantees its holder a prior claim on dividends. The dividend paid to preference share holders is normally more than that paid to holders of ordinary shares. Preference shares may give the holder a right to a share in the ownership of the company (participating preference shares). However in the UK they usually do not, and are therefore classified as bonds.

Private sector
Private non-financial corporations, financial corporations other than the Bank of England (and Girobank when it was publicly owned), households and the NPISH sector.

Promissory note
A security which entitles the bearer to receive cash. These may be issued by companies or other institutions. (See Commercial paper).

Public corporations
These are public trading bodies which have a substantial degree of financial independence from the public authority which created them. A public corporation is publicly controlled to the extent that the public authority, i.e. central or local government, appoints the whole or a majority of the board of management. Since the 1980s many public corporations, such as British Telecom, have been privatised and reclassified within the accounts as private non-financial corporations.

Public sector
Central government, local authorities and public corporations.

Refinanced export credit
Identified long-term credit extended for UK exports initially by banks and refinanced with the ECGD, the Trustee Savings Banks and the Central Trustee Savings Bank.

Reinvested earnings
The direct investor's share of earnings not distributed as dividends (by subsidiaries) or branch profits. As this income remains with the foreign subsidiary or branch (it is reinvested by the parent) an amount will appear in the financial account equal to (and with opposite sign) the corresponding entry within direct investment income.

Related companies
Branches, subsidiaries, associates or parents.

Related import or export credit
Trade credit between related companies included in direct investment.

Repo
This is short for "sale and repurchase agreement". One party agrees to sell bonds or other financial instruments to other parties under a formal legal agreement to repurchase them at some point in the future - usually up to six months - at a fixed price. Repo transactions are treated as borrowing/lending within other investment, rather than as transactions in the underlying securities.

Reserve assets
Short term assets which can be very quickly converted into cash. They comprise the UK's official holdings of gold, convertible currencies, Special Drawing Rights, and changes in the UK reserve position in the IMF. Also included between July 1979 and December 1998 are European Currency Units acquired from swaps with the European Cooperation Fund, EMI and the ECB. Reserve assets were referred to as "official reserves" in editions of the *Pink Book* prior to 1998.

Reserve position in the Fund
The United Kingdom's position in the IMF's General Resources Account. This position is the sum of the United Kingdom's reserve tranche purchases, and any indebtedness of the Fund (under a loan agreement) that is readily payable to the United Kingdom.

Residency
UK residents are those with a centre of economic interest within the UK of at least one year's duration - nationality does not play a part in determining residency status. There are a number of exceptions to the standard residency classification: UK embassies and military bases abroad are deemed to be residents of the UK (conversely other nations' embassies and military bases in the UK are classed as non-residents), as are students studying abroad who are normally resident in the UK.

Royalties
These form part of trade in services. They represent payments for services by, or to, UK residents in respect of the right to use processes and other information, e.g. licences to use patents, trade marks, designs, copyrights, etc. Sales and purchases of patents are included within the capital account.

Security
Security against loans involves the depositing of a document or asset which is retained by the bank as a charge for an advance. This form of security may include stocks and share certificates, debentures, and insurance policies.

Smuggling
Smuggling is the importation of goods acquired duty free or duty paid in another country for re-sale in the UK without payment of UK duty and (where appropriate) VAT.

Special Drawing Rights (SDRs)
These are reserve assets created and distributed by decision of the members of the IMF. Participants accept an obligation to provide convertible currency, when designated by the IMF to do so, to another participant, in exchange for SDRs equivalent to three times their own allocation. Only countries with a sufficiently strong balance of payments are so designated by the IMF. SDRs may also be used in certain direct payments between participants in the scheme and for payments of various kinds to the IMF.

Subsidiary
A registered company in which another registered company has ownership of the majority of the voting share capital; i.e. greater than 50 per cent.

Subsidies
Current unrequited payments made by general government or the European Union to enterprises. Those made on the basis of a quantity or value of goods or services are classified as 'subsidies on products'. Other subsidies based on levels of productive activity (e.g. numbers employed) are designated 'Other subsidies on production'.

Suppliers' credit
Export credit extended abroad directly by UK firms other than to related concerns (see Export credit).

Third country trade or cross-trade
See 'merchanting'.

Trade credit
See Export credit and Import credit.

Trade in goods
Trade in goods covers general merchandise, goods for processing, repairs on goods, goods procured in ports by carriers and commodity gold (see Gold). General merchandise is defined for BOP purposes as covering, with a few exceptions, all movable goods for which actual or imputed changes of ownership occur between residents and non-residents.

Trade in services
Provision of services between UK residents and non-residents, and transactions in goods which are not freighted out of the country in which they take place, for example purchases for local use by foreign forces in the United Kingdom and by UK forces abroad, and purchases by tourists. Transactions in goods which are freighted into/out of the United Kingdom are included under trade in goods.

Transfers
Transfers are payments or receipts where there is no corresponding exchange of an actual good or service. These transfers are split between current transfers, which form part of the current account, and capital transfers which form part of the capital account. Most transfer payments are central government transfers, i.e., receipts from and payments to institutions of the European Union.

Travel
The travel account gives the earnings from and expenditure on international tourism and business and other travel, but excludes transport between the UK and other countries (included within the transportation account). An international tourist is defined as a resident of one country who visits another country and stays there for a period of less than 12 months. This definition excludes travellers who visit another country to take up pre-arranged employment or education there, military and diplomatic personnel, merchant seamen and airline crews on duty.

Treasury bills
Short-term securities or promissory notes which are issued by government in return for funding from the money market. In the United Kingdom, every week, the Bank of England invites tenders for sterling Treasury bills from the financial institutions operating in the market. ECU/Euro-denominated bills were issued by tender each month but this programme has now wound down; the last bill was redeemed in September 1999. Treasury bills are an important form of short-term borrowing for the government, generally being issued for periods of 3 or 6 months.

Unit trusts
Institutions through which investors pool their funds to invest in a diversified portfolio of securities. Individual investors purchase units in the fund representing an ownership interest in the large pool of underlying assets, i.e. they have an equity stake. The selection of assets is made by professional fund managers. Unit trusts therefore give individual investors the opportunity to invest in a diversified and professionally-managed portfolio of securities without the need for detailed knowledge of the individual companies issuing the stocks and bonds.

Very short term financing facility (VSTFF)
This is a facility available within the EMS where a central bank makes short term credit facilities in its own currency available to another central bank.

Index

Bold indicates name of chapter. *Figures* indicate table numbers. *P* indicates Page number.
G indicates the item appears in the Glossary.

A

Accrued interest, G
Acquisition/disposal of Non-produced, non-financial assets, p171
Administrative and diplomatic expenditure, 3.11
Advertising, 3.9
Air transport, p159, 3.2
Arbitrage, G
Assets, G
  summary of UK external assets, 1.3, 8.1
Associated companies, G

B

Balance of Payments, p1
Balancing item, G – see "Net Errors and Omissions"
Baltic Exchange, p162, 3.6
Bank of England, G
Bills and acceptances, G
Bonds, G – see also "Debt securities"
Bonds and notes:
  earnings, 4.5
  transactions in, 7.5
  stock outstanding, 8.5
Borrowing – see "Loans"
Branch, p8
Branch indebtedness, G
British government foreign currency bonds and notes:
  earnings, 4.5
  transactions in, 7.5
  stock outstanding, 8.5
British government stocks, G
  earnings, 4.5
  transactions in, 7.5
  stock outstanding, 8.5
Building societies, G

C

Capital account, G, p11, p170, 6.1
Capital transfers, G, p170, 6.1
Cargo – dry and wet, 3.2

Certificates of Deposit, G
  earnings, 4.5
  transactions in, 7.5
  stock outstanding, 8.5
Chartering of ships, 3.2
c.i.f., G
Commercial paper, G
  earnings, 4.5
  transactions in, 7.5
  stock outstanding, 8.5
Commonwealth Development Corporation, G
  earnings, 4.7
  transactions in, 7.7
  stock outstanding, 8.7
Communication services, p161, 3.4
Companies securities, G – see "Debt securities" and "Equity securities"
Compensation of employees, G, p11, p165, 4.1
Consultancy firms, 3.9
Counterpart items, G
Coverage adjustments – trade in goods, 2.4
Currency and deposits, 4.7, 7.7, 8.7
Current account, G, 1.2
Current balance, G, 1.1, 1.2
Current transfers, G, p11, p169, 5.1

D

Debt forgiveness, G, p171, 6.1
Debt securities, G
  earnings, 4.5
  transactions in, 7.5
  stock outstanding, 8.5
Deposits abroad – see "Currency and deposits"
Deposits, earnings on, 4.7
Derivatives, G – see "Financial derivatives"
Direct investment, G
  earnings, 4.3, 4.4
  transactions, 7.3, 7.4

  stock of investment, 8.3, 8.4
Disbursements, G, 3.2
Double entry accounting principle, p4

E

Equity, G
Equity capital, G – see "Direct investment"
  earnings, 4.3
  transactions, 7.3
  stock of investment, 8.3
Equity securities, G
  earnings, 4.5
  transactions, 7.5
  stock of investment, 8.5
Euro/European Currency Unit, G
European Union, p174, 3.11, 5.1, 6.1, 9.1 - 9.7
European Monetary System, G
Exchange control, G
Exchange cover scheme, G
Exchange Equalisation Account, G
Export credit, G
Exports
  goods; commodity analysis, 2.1
  services; summary, 3.1
External borrowing and lending – see "Loans"

F

Films and television, p164, 3.8
Financial account, G, p11, p171, 7.1 - 7.9
Financial derivatives, G, p12
Financial leases, p8
Financial leasing – see "Leasing by specialist finance leasing companies"
Financial services, p162, 3.6
Financial gold, G
f.o.b., G
Foreign – definition of, G
Foreign military forces expenditure, 3.11
Freight and insurance - trade in goods, 2.4

Freight on cross-trades, 3.2
Freight on UK trade, 3.2
Fund management companies, p162

G

Goods and services, G – see "Trade in goods" and "Trade in services"
Goods for processing, p8
Gross recording, G, p9

I

Import credit, G
Imports
  goods; commodity analysis, 2.1
  services; summary, 3.1
Income, G, p11, p164, 4.1-4.8
Instruments of investment, p12
Insurance services, p161, 3.5
Inter-company accounts, G, 7.3, 8.3
Inter-government loans – see "Loans"
International Investment Position, G, p2, 8.1 - 8.9
International Development Association, 7.7, 8.7
International Monetary Fund (IMF), G
Intervention Board for Agricultural Produce, G
Investment, G – see "Direct investment", "Portfolio investment" and "Other investment"
Investment income, G, p165, 4.1 - 4.8

L

Land transport, 3.2
Leasing by specialist finance leasing companies, G
  earnings, 4.7
  transactions, 7.7
  stock of investment, 8.7
Liabilities, G
License fees – see "Royalties and license fees"
Local authorities, G
  earnings, 4.2
  transactions, 7.2
  stock of investment, 8.2
Loans
  earnings, 4.7
  transactions, 7.7
  stock of investment, 8.7

M

Management and economic consultants, 3.9
Migrants transfers, p7
Military expenditure and receipts, 3.11

Miscellaneous financial institutions, G
Monetary authorities, G
Monetary financial institutions, G
  earnings, 4.2
  transactions, 7.2
  stock of investment, 8.2
Money market brokers, 3.6
Money market instruments, G
  earnings, 4.5
  transactions, 7.5
  stock of investment, 8.5

N

Navy, Army and Air Force Institute – "NAAFI", G
Net, G
Net errors and omissions, G, p5, 1.1
Non-produced, non-financial assets, G
North Sea oil and natural gas companies, 3.9
Notes and coin – see "Currency and deposits"

O

Oil – exports and imports, p27, 2.1 - 2.3
Other business services, p163, 3.9
Other investment, G, p12
  earnings, 4.7, 4.8
  transactions, 7.7, 7.8
  stock of investment, 8.7, 8.8
Overseas Trade Statistics - see "Trade in goods"

P

Portfolio investment, G, p12
  earnings, 4.5, 4.6
  transactions, 7.5, 7.6
  stock of investment, 8.5, 8.6
Private sector, G
Public corporations, G
  earnings, 4.2
  transactions, 7.2
  stock of investment, 8.2
Public sector, G

R

Refinanced export credit, G
Reimbursement by EU for NHS treatment, p164
Reinvested earnings, p7, p165, 4.3, 7.3
Reserve assets, G, p12
  earnings, 4.1
  transactions, 7.9
  stock of investment, 8.9
Reserve position in the Fund, G, 7.9, 8.9
Residency, G

Revaluation of assets and liabilities, p9
Royalties and license fees, G, p163, 3.8

S

Sea transport, p159, 3.2
Sectorisation, p13, p149
Securities dealers, 3.6, 7.5, 8.5
Shares – see "Equity securities"
Sign convention, p5
Solicitors and barristers, 3.9
Special Drawing Rights, G
  in reserve assets, 7.9, 8.9
Subscriptions to international organisations, 7.7, 8.7
Subsidiary, G

T

Telecommunications and postal services – see "Communication services"
Territorial coverage, p2
Timing of transactions, p6
Trade credit, p173
  earnings, 4.7
  transactions, 7.7
  stock of investment, 8.7
Trade in goods, G, p11, p152, 2.1 - 2.4
Trade in services, G, p11, p158, 3.1 - 3.11
Trade in ships – trade in goods, 2.4
Transfers, G – see "Current transfers" and "Capital transfers", p11
Travel, G, 3.3
Treasury bills, G
  earnings, 4.5
  transactions, 7.5
  stock of investment, 8.5

U

United Kingdom, p2
UK banks, G – see "Monetary Financial Institutions"
UK companies' securities, G – see "Debt Securities" and "Equity Securities"
Unremitted profits – see "Reinvested earnings"

V

Valuation, p5
Very short term financing facility, G